MW00826763

"These NEA Indian Department presentations, which Larry Skogen does a masterful job of editing, provide an important window into how many people in the United States thought about American Indians and American Indian education in the beginning of the twentieth century. Skogen has done a remarkable job providing the reader with background information, both in his introduction to each document and in the extensive notes and references he provides."

—JON A. REYHNER, author of *American Indian Education: A History*

"Where historians have used the tools of social history to examine the lives of employees in the Indian schools, Skogen's work uses an intellectual lens to demonstrate how these workers drove important changes in curriculum and policy. This detailed and nuanced work helps to untangle the genocidal roots of boarding school systems and to see more clearly the challenges that Native people faced in moving their communities and cultures through the difficult years of the early twentieth century."

—KEVIN WHALEN, author of *Native Students at Work: American Indian Labor and Sherman Institute's Outing Program 1900–1945*

"As our nation struggles with the realities of the Indian boarding school experience, it is important that we understand the motives and educational philosophies of those who administered and worked at those schools. In this groundbreaking work, Larry Skogen provides us with the story of the Indian service educators when they were part of the National Education Association. Through these selected papers, we get a firsthand account of their efforts to assimilate Native students forcibly into white society. One cannot read these papers without feeling a sense of shame at the educators' attitudes toward their own Native students. But it is important history that we need to acknowledge."

—BYRON L. DORGAN, former U.S. senator and chairman of the U.S. Senate Committee on Indian Affairs, author of *The Girl in the Photograph*

"The National Education Association is a voice for education professionals and dedicated to preparing students for success in a diverse and interdependent world. That doesn't mean, however, that the NEA hasn't made mistakes and missteps along the way. With this important work, Larry Skogen provides a window into a time when the federal government forced a curriculum upon Native American students that subjugated them into a marginalized role in our country. The papers of the NEA Department of Indian Education (1900–1904) reveal the association's role in advancing this harm. This critical study is a reality check for all Americans to learn our true history so that we better understand the mistakes of our past, can be a part of repairing harm, and can be agents of change to make a better future for all of our students and communities."

—BECKY PRINGLE, president of the National Education Association

# To Educate American Indians

Indigenous Education

SERIES EDITORS

Margaret Connell Szasz
*University of New Mexico*

Brenda J. Child
*University of Minnesota*

Karen Gayton Comeau
*Haskell Indian Nations
University, emeritus*

John W. Tippeconnic III
*Pennsylvania State University*

Matthew Sakiestewa Gilbert
*University of Illinois
at Urbana-Champaign*

# To Educate American Indians

Selected Writings from the National Educational Association's Department of Indian Education, 1900–1904

*Edited and with an introduction by* LARRY C. SKOGEN

FOREWORD BY *David Wallace Adams*

University of Nebraska Press | Lincoln

© 2024 by the Board of Regents of the University of Nebraska. All rights reserved.

The University of Nebraska Press is part of a land-grant institution with campuses and programs on the past, present, and future homelands of the Pawnee, Ponca, Otoe-Missouria, Omaha, Dakota, Lakota, Kaw, Cheyenne, and Arapaho Peoples, as well as those of the relocated Ho-Chunk, Sac and Fox, and Iowa Peoples.

*Library of Congress Cataloging-in-Publication Data*
Names: Skogen, Larry C. (Larry Clifford), 1952–, editor. Adams, David Wallace, writer of foreword. | National Educational Association (U.S.) Department of Indian Education.
Title: To educate American Indians: selected writings from the National Educational Association's Department of Indian Education / edited and with an introduction by Larry C. Skogen; foreword by David Wallace Adams. Other titles: Selected writings from the National Educational Association's Department of Indian Education
Description: Lincoln: University of Nebraska Press, [2023] | Series: Indigenous education | Includes bibliographical references and index. | Contents: [Volume 1.] 1900–1904 — [volume 2.] 1905–1909
Summary: "To Educate American Indians presents the most complete versions of papers presented at the National Educational Association's Department of Indian Education meetings during a time when the debate about how best to 'civilize' Indigenous populations dominated discussions. During this time two philosophies drove the conversation. The first, an Enlightenment era-influenced universalism, held that through an educational alchemy American Indians would become productive, Christianized Americans, distinguishable from their white neighbors only by the color of their skin. Directly confronting the assimilationists' universalism were the progressive educators who, strongly influenced by the era's scientific racism, held the notion that American Indians could never become fully assimilated. Despite these differing views, a frightening ethnocentrism and an honor-bound dedication to 'gifting' civilization to Native students dominated the writings of educators from the NEA's Department of Indian Education." Provided by publisher.
Identifiers: LCCN 2023012605
ISBN 9781496236760 (v. 1: hardback)
ISBN 9781496237415 (v. 1: epub)
ISBN 9781496237422 (v. 1: pdf)
ISBN 9781496240453 (v. 2: hardback)
Subjects: LCSH: Indians of North America—United States—Education—History—20th century. | Indian youth—Education—United States. | Off-reservation boarding schools—United States. | Indians of North America—Cultural assimilation—United States. | Indians of North America—Vocational education—United States. | Education and state—United States. | National Educational Association (U.S.) Department of Indian Education. | BISAC: SOCIAL SCIENCE / Ethnic Studies / American / Native American Studies | EDUCATION / History
Classification: LCC E97.5 .T64 2023 | DDC 371.829/97—dc23/eng/20230908
LC record available at https://lccn.loc.gov/2023012605

Set in Miller Text by A. Shahan.

For Charlotte (Schmaltz) Olson

In memoriam
Robert A. Trennert Jr.
(1937–2019)

# Contents

List of Illustrations     xii

Foreword by David Wallace Adams     xiii

Acknowledgments     xv

Introduction     xxi

Note on Editorial Style, Citations, and Names     xli

List of Abbreviations     xlii

---

Part 1  |  Charleston, South Carolina, July 7–13, 1900     1

1. What Is the Relation of the Indian of the
   Present Decade to the Indian of the Future?     7
   H. B. FRISSELL, *Principal, Hampton Normal
   and Agricultural Institute, Hampton, Virginia*

2. The Indian Problem     12
   H. B. FRISSELL, *Principal, Hampton Normal and
   Agricultural Institute, Hampton, Virginia*

3. The Proper Relation between Literary and
   Industrial Education in Indian Schools     25
   A. J. STANDING, *Assistant Superintendent, Carlisle
   Indian Industrial School, Carlisle, Pennsylvania*

4. The Training of Teachers for Indian Schools     31
   CHARLES BARTLETT DYKE, *Director of
   the Normal Department, Hampton Normal and
   Agricultural Institute, Hampton, Virginia*

5. Teaching Trades to Indians     35
   FRANK K. ROGERS, *Director, Armstrong-Slater
   Memorial Trade School, Hampton Normal and
   Agricultural Institute, Hampton, Virginia*

6. The Training of the Indian Girl as the
   Uplifter of the Home                                      39
   JOSEPHINE E. RICHARDS, *Head of the Indian
   Department, Hampton Normal and Agricultural
   Institute, Hampton, Virginia*

7. Practical Methods of Indian Education                     45
   JOHN SEGER, *Superintendent, Seger Colony School,
   Colony, Oklahoma*

---

PART 2 | Detroit, Michigan, July 8–12, 1901                  51

8. President's Address: Learning by Doing                    61
   H. B. FRISSELL, *Principal, Hampton Normal and
   Agricultural Institute, Hampton, Virginia*

9. Civilization and Higher Education                         75
   WILLIAM T. HARRIS, *U.S. Commissioner of Education,
   Washington DC*

10. The Reservation Day School Should Be the
    Prime Factor in Indian Education                         81
    C. C. COVEY, *Teacher, Pine Ridge Indian
    School, Pine Ridge, South Dakota*

11. The Unification of Industrial and Academic
    Features of the Indian School                            85
    O. H. BAKELESS, *Carlisle Indian Industrial School,
    Carlisle, Pennsylvania*

12. What Shall Be Taught in an Indian School?                96
    CALVIN M. WOODWARD, *Director, Manual Training
    School of Washington University, St. Louis, Missouri*

13. An All-Around Mechanical Training for Indians            105
    FRANK K. ROGERS, *Director, Armstrong-Slater Memorial
    Trade School, Hampton Normal and Agricultural
    Institute, Hampton, Virginia*

14. Practical Methods in Indian Education                                        109
    JOSEPH W. EVANS, *Teacher, Chilocco Indian School,*
    *Chilocco, Oklahoma*

15. Character Building among Indian Children                            116
    CORA M. FOLSOM, *Teacher and Indian Corresponding*
    *Secretary, Hampton Normal and Agricultural Institute,*
    *Hampton, Virginia*

16. The Day School: The Gradual Uplifter of the Tribe            125
    MACARIA MURPHY, *Teacher, Odanah Day School,*
    *Odanah, Wisconsin*

17. The Necessity for a Large Agricultural School
    in the Indian Service                                                            128
    C. W. GOODMAN, *Superintendent, Chilocco*
    *Indian School, Chilocco, Oklahoma*

---

PART 3 | Minneapolis, Minnesota, July 7–11, 1902            133

18. President's Address                                                              141
    S. M. MCCOWAN, *Superintendent, Chilocco*
    *Indian School, Chilocco, Oklahoma*

19. The Value of an Agricultural School in the Indian Service   151
    S. M. MCCOWAN, *Superintendent, Chilocco*
    *Indian School, Chilocco, Oklahoma*

20. The Value of the Outing System for Girls                        154
    LAURA JACKSON, *Girls' Manager, Carlisle Indian*
    *Industrial School, Carlisle, Pennsylvania*

21. What Is Our Aim?                                                              161
    E. A. ALLEN, *Assistant Superintendent, Carlisle*
    *Indian Industrial School, Carlisle, Pennsylvania*

22. Needed Changes in Indian Schools                               169
    A. O. WRIGHT, *Supervisor of Indian Schools,*
    *Washington DC*

23. The Value of Day Schools     178
JAMES J. DUNCAN, *Day School Inspector, Pine Ridge,
South Dakota*

24. Newspapers in Indian Schools     183
WILLIAM T. HARRIS, *U.S. Commissioner of Education,
Washington* DC

---

PART 4  |  Boston, Massachusetts, July 6–10, 1903     187

25. President's Address: Our Work, Its Progress and Needs     195
H. B. PEAIRS, *Superintendent, Haskell Institute,
Lawrence, Kansas*

26. To What Degree Has the Present System of Indian
Schools Been Successful in Qualifying for Citizenship?     208
H. B. FRISSELL, *Principal, Hampton Normal and
Agricultural Institute, Hampton, Virginia*

27. An Alaskan Start toward Citizenship     212
SHELDON JACKSON, *General Agent of Education
in Alaska, Washington* DC

28. The White Man's Burden versus Indigenous
Development for the Lower Races     223
G. STANLEY HALL, *President, Clark University,
Worcester, Massachusetts*

29. Heart Culture in Indian Education     229
CHARLES F. MESERVE, *President, Shaw University,
Raleigh, North Carolina*

30. Tenure in the Civil Service     237
JOHN T. DOYLE, *Secretary of the U.S. Civil
Service Commission, Washington* DC

PART 5 | St. Louis, Missouri, June 27–July 1, 1904     247

31. Efficiency in the Indian Service     255
    JOHN T. DOYLE, *Secretary of the U.S. Civil*
    *Service Commission, Washington* DC

32. Indian Music and Indian Education     260
    NATALIE CURTIS, *New York, New York*

33. What's in a Name?     265
    EMILY S. COOK, *Office of Indian Affairs, Washington* DC

34. Indian Names     269
    ALICE C. FLETCHER, *Ex-President of the*
    *Anthropological Society, Washington* DC


Conclusion     275

Notes     285

Bibliography     343

Index     361

# Illustrations

PHOTOGRAPHS  (*after page 132*)

1. Estelle Reel, superintendent of Indian schools, 1898–1910
2. Irwin Shepard, secretary of the National Educational Association, 1893–1912
3. Freundschaftsbund Hall, Charleston, South Carolina
4. Cadillac Hotel, Detroit, Michigan
5. West Hotel, Minneapolis, Minnesota
6. Rogers Building, Massachusetts Institute of Technology, Boston, Massachusetts
7. Department of Indian Education meeting at St. Louis, Missouri

TABLE

1. Number of Indian schools and average attendance from 1877 to 1902                198

# Foreword

DAVID WALLACE ADAMS

IN THE LAST DECADES OF the nineteenth century, few issues captured the attention of policy makers in Washington DC, more than the question of how to solve the so-called Indian Problem. Convinced that the alternatives facing Native Americans were either racial extinction or long-term assimilation into mainstream society, most policy makers favored the latter. But how to accomplish it? Generally, those responsible for formulating Indian policy believed that the focus of this assimilation movement should be on Native American children—that is, those least wedded to the "savage" lifeways of their ancestors. What Native children needed, toward that end, was a heavy dose of white schooling, which, in turn, required constructing a full-blown federal Indian school system. It followed that in the coming years Indian children would attend reservation day and boarding schools, and even off-reservation boarding schools, the latter seen as a means of wielding a much more intense assimilationist environment, since it removed children from their parents and communities for longer periods of time.

In the past thirty years, scholars have made great strides in describing this too often tragic chapter in Native American education. What they have not succeeded in doing is documenting how leading educators of the day viewed the proper ends and means of Indian schooling. With the publication of *To Educate American Indians*, this gap in the historical record is now closed. As Larry C. Skogen points out, the origins of these documents can be traced back to 1899 with the National Educational Association's decision to establish a Department of Indian Education. In the coming years, the association's annual meetings invited leading educators—both in and out of the federal Indian service—to present formal papers on Indian schooling, which were subsequently published in the organization's proceedings.

While the general ends of Native American education were well established, policy makers still had a range of questions about the directions of Native schooling. For instance, was Native children's mental capacity equivalent to their white counterparts? Was special training needed by teachers of Native American children? Which of the three institutional settings—day school, reservation boarding schools, or off-reservation boarding schools—were best suited to accomplish federal aims? What curriculum optimized the goal of preparing Indian girls for their future roles as homemakers and domestic workers? Should there be greater emphasis on placing Native girls in "outing" programs, which offered the opportunity to live in middle-class, white, patricentered families and earn a small wage by working as domestic workers? Must every scintilla of Indian identity be eradicated to accomplish the broader goal of assimilation? For example, was there a place for the Native arts in the school curriculum? These and related issues are frequent topics in the papers in this collection.

Skillfully edited and contextualized by Larry Skogen, this compilation constitutes a monumental contribution to the documentary record of the complex and troubled history of Native American education. Henceforth, scholars will have at their fingertips a wealth of information hitherto denied them on the major considerations impacting policy makers as they attempted to formulate the most effective educational means for integrating Native American children into modern American life.

# Acknowledgments

MY FIRST INTRODUCTION TO THE National Educational Association's (NEA) *Journal of Proceedings and Addresses* that contains papers from its annual meetings was when I was a graduate student at the University of Central Missouri, Warrensburg, in the early 1980s. In my readings I had encountered ubiquitous references to nineteenth- and early twentieth-century white Americans engaged in "civilizing" Native Americans. In a project directed by Guy P. Griggs Jr., I wrestled with the question of what "civilizing" American Indians meant. During that quest I discovered that the NEA had for a short time a Department of Indian Education (1900–1909), and that the papers from those educators were published in the NEA *Proceedings*. I used those documents in my research along with other contemporary publications and drew my conclusions from them. Lingering in the back of my mind, however, were several questions about those NEA-published papers—for instance, who were these educators? Were the papers in the NEA *Proceedings* the actual papers delivered at the conferences (many were labeled "An Abstract")? And what were the circumstances and social and political currents under which these papers were delivered? In the end I was confident that the papers in the published NEA *Proceedings* did not tell the whole story about these educators and their "civilizing" efforts.

Many years later I broached this topic and posed those questions to Robert "Bob" A. Trennert Jr., my dissertation advisor at Arizona State University. I suggested to him that I would eventually like to gather selected papers from those journals with the goal of finding complete papers instead of the edited versions in the NEA publications; tell the story of the NEA Department of Indian Education; identify the educators who presented the papers; and provide the social, political, and educational setting for each year papers were delivered. Bob thought it a wonderful project that would make a significant contribution to our understanding of "Indian education." As he had established himself as a scholar of Indian education with his *The Phoenix Indian School* (1988) and numerous article publications, I asked him if he would write a foreword to this work, if I completed it. He graciously and enthusiastically said he would. Regrettably, my career paths, first in the U.S. Air Force, then in higher education, prevented me from diligently pursuing this project. Ultimately, this project would not be completed until after I retired from the presidency of Bismarck State College (BSC) in 2020. Before then I had managed to work on it piecemeal, and by the time of my retirement I had accumulated boxes of documents. This long delay in getting the project done, however, prevented Bob from writing the foreword. In my last communications with him, he told me that, due to health issues, he was no longer able to write it and suggested that I reach out to David Wallace Adams, whose *Education for Extinction* ([1995] 2020) had become a standard work in Indian education. Bob then passed away in 2019. For his scholarly contributions to history and his mentorship and friendship, it is an honor to publish this volume in memory of him.

Following Bob's advice I contacted David Adams, who kindly agreed to review a rough draft of a couple of chapters. Dave concurred with Bob about the value of this project and agreed to pen the foreword. I am honored that my and Dave's names appear together on the cover of this book. I thank him for picking up the baton that Bob could no longer carry and for running it over the finish line. I also thank him for the wonderful friendship that blossomed from this endeavor.

I appreciate the scholars who responded to my inquiries, read portions of the manuscript, or simply offered valuable insights and encouragement as I traveled along this journey. William E. Foley, Professor Emeritus at the University of Central Missouri, and Herman J. Viola, Curator Emeritus at the Smithsonian's National Museum of Natural History, are both mentors and friends. I am grateful for their supportive comments on early drafts. Michelle Patterson, Jean Keller, and Michel Gobat responded to cold-call email requests for assistance and provided warm and valuable responses. Jon Reyhner read the entire manuscript and made wonderful comments. An unnamed peer reviewer provided incredibly valuable feedback for which I am very thankful. I am deeply in debt to all who read and provided feedback. To them goes much credit; any mistakes or deficiencies are mine alone.

A project that spans decades from inception to completion has also indebted me to many individuals and institutions without whom I could never have completed this task. Add to this the fact that I retired during the early stages of the COVID-19 pandemic, and one can imagine the problems affecting my research while libraries and archives were shut down. I have the deepest gratitude to numerous librarians, archivists, and other staff members who moved mountains to get me the documents and the support that I needed. Without them I would have been a sailing ship on a windless sea. Among those to whom I offer my sincere appreciation for their help both before and during the pandemic are Debbie Van Berkom and Janell Campbell, my executive assistants at BSC; the BSC library staff of Marlene Anderson, Sandi Bates, Tina Stockdill, and Laura Kalvoda; Vakil Smallen at Gelman Library, George Washington University; Mary Frances Ronan, Jake Ersland, Wade Popp, Rose Buchanan, Sarah Waitz, Valerie Szwaya, George Fuller, Jennifer Albin, and Richard Fusick at National Archives and Records Administration; Joan Popek and Olivia Gattis at the National Education Association; Barbara Landis and Linda F. Witmer at the Cumberland County Historical Society; Alex Fergus at Joel E. Ferris Research Archives of the Northwest Museum of Arts and Culture; Emily Pursley at Pike County Historical Society; Jessica Cosgrove and Ann Nelson at the Wyoming State Archives; Sarah Horowitz at the Quaker & Special Collections of Haverford College Libraries; Beth Mariotti at the Godfrey Memorial Library; Lara Szypszak in the Manuscript Division at the Library of Congress; Tracy Rebstock at Washington State Archives; Patricia Nunes, Sarah Biller, and Mallory Covington at the Oklahoma Historical Society; Jessica Suarez at Harvard Divinity School; Kate Johnson at the Michener Library of the University of Northern Colorado; Christopher J. Anderson at the Divinity Library of Yale University; June Can at Beinecke Library of Yale University; Lina Rosenberg Foley at Lawrence University Archives; Jacalyn Pearce at McFarlin Library at the University of Tulsa; Larry Treadwell at Shaw University Library Archives; Dan Hinchen, L. J. Woolcock, and Heather Wilson at the Massachusetts Historical Society; Sunshine Thomas-Bear at the Angel De Cora Museum of Little Priest Tribal College; Steve Henrikson at the Alaska State Museum; Freya Anderson at Alaska State Libraries, Archives & Museum; Paul Pelletier at the Robert H. Goddard Library of Clark University; Martin Leuthauser at the Denver Public Library; Rick Bernstein at the Dane County Historical Society; Charlene Peacock at the Presbyterian Historical Society; Melissa Watterworth Batt at the

University of Connecticut; A. Warren Dockter at the East Tennessee Historical Society; Eric Head at the Knox County Archives; Brian Shetler at Princeton Theological Seminary; Halley Hair at the South Dakota State Archives; Jackie Reese at the University of Oklahoma Libraries; Taylor Henning and Katherine Majewski at the University of Illinois Archives; Marieke Van Damme at the Cambridge Historical Society; Janet Bunde and Jasmine Sykes-Kunk at NYU Special Collections; Donzella Maupin at Hampton University Archives; Bethany Williams at the Stephen H. Hart Research Center at History Colorado; Sonya Rooney at the Julian Edison Department of Special Collections of Washington University in St. Louis; Amy Cary at Raynor Memorial Libraries of Marquette University; Harry Whitlock at the University of Wyoming Libraries; Natalie Kelsey at the Division of Rare and Manuscript Collections of Cornell University; Daniel DiLandro at Buffalo State College; Marianne Arnold at the Bibliotheque nationale de France; Lewis Zimmerman and Jane Dugger at the Westminster Law Library of the University of Denver; Karen Muchow at the Alden Historical Society; Jill Sturgeon at the William A. Wise Law Library of the University of Colorado Law School; Daniel Benedetti at Boston University Libraries; Jennifer Greif Green, the editor of the *Journal of Education*; Al Bredenberg and Brad Whitman at the Natalie Curtis Burlin Archives; Jennifer Schmidt at the Milwaukee County Federated Library System; Anthony Frausto at the Milwaukee Public Library; Kevin Abing at the Milwaukee History; Cali Vance and Allee Monheim at the University of Washington Libraries; Jeremy Dimick at the Detroit Historical Society; Molly Silliman at the South Carolina Historical Society; Clayton Lewis at the William L. Clements Library of the University of Michigan; Sarah McLusky and Herb Dittersdorf at the Bentley Historical Library; Carla Reczek at the Detroit Public Library; Steve Yaeger and John Wareham at Star Tribune Media Company; Jennifer Huebscher at the Minnesota Historical Society; Carmen Redding at the North Dakota State Library; Bailey Diers at the Hennepin County Library; Sarah Ferguson at the Historic Charleston Foundation; Alex McGee at the Massachusetts Institute of Technology Libraries; Amanda Claunch at the Missouri Historical Society Library and Research Center; Susanne Caro at North Dakota State University Library; John Hallberg at North Dakota State University Archives; Bryan Whitledge at the Clarke Historical Library of Central Michigan University; Liza Katz at the Center for Brooklyn History; Katlynn Friedman at the Autry Museum of the American West; Janice Loo, at the National Library, Singapore; Aloha Pa'akaula-Lozier at Kamehameha Schools Archives; and the Franciscan Sisters of Perpetual Adoration in La Crosse, Wisconsin. I hold these professionals, and the many more not named, in the highest esteem for what they do. We historians would not have much to do in a world without them.

In addition to the many individuals at libraries and archives who made the research for this work possible, many behind-the-scenes individuals made online resources available. Through their technical and dedicated expertise they provide a wealth of information that is accessible from the comfort of our own offices. To name just a few of the sites I visited most frequently: the excellent resources available at Carlisle Indian School Digital Resource Center (carlisleindian.dickinson.edu); FamilySearch (https://www.familysearch.org/en/); HeinOnline (HeinOnline.org, bismarckstate .edu); Hathi Trust Digital Library (https://www.hathitrust.org/); Internet Archive (https://archive.org/); Newspapers.com by Ancestry (https://www.newspapers.com/); Ancestry (ancestry.com); Findmypast (findmypast .com); JSTOR (https://www.jstor.org/); and University of Wisconsin–Madison Libraries (wisc.edu). Those who labor to provide such websites are the unsung heroes for today's researchers.

Thank you to staff at the University of Nebraska Press: Clark Whitehorn, who saw fit to pass my proposal to the right acquisition editor; Heather Stauffer, acquisitions editor, for believing in this project, providing incredibly valuable and insightful advice that has vastly improved the product, and marshaling this project through to completion; Ann Baker, manager of the Editorial, Design, and Production Department, who, to this former Air Force guy, seems like the air traffic controller that gets everything off the ground and landed again; Emily Shelton, copyeditor, who ensured we crossed every "t"; Bridget Barry, editor in chief, at whose desk final decisions about publication are made; the faculty advisory board, whose members not only approved this publication but also offered valuable counsel to make it a better book; Judy Staigmiller, InOrder Freelance Indexing, because the use of a good book depends upon the quality of its index; and many others who made countless contributions along the way.

Finally, I thank Charlotte, life partner and extraordinary "research assistant." From mastering the digital camera setup at archives to proofreading every page of the manuscript countless times to participating in years' worth of conversations about the nuances of educational philosophies, she made this a far better book. That she spent her professional career as a classroom mathematics teacher caring so deeply about her students sharpened my understanding of the lack of compassion early twentieth-century Indian school educators had for their own Native students. I thank her for her heartfelt support for my work and, with deep appreciation, dedicate this book to her.

# Introduction

TODAY'S NATIONAL EDUCATION ASSOCIATION (NEA) has a history that begins in Antebellum America. For one small slice of that history, from 1900 to 1909, the NEA included a Department of Indian Education whose members worked for the U.S. Indian School Service. Papers delivered at the annual NEA meetings were published in the *Journal of Proceedings and Addresses of the National Educational Association*.[1] This volume covers selected writings from that department's meetings for the years 1900 to 1904. During that time the two schools of thought regarding how best to educate American Indians clashed most openly. When the Indian Office's *Course of Study* promoted Native arts, for example, old assimilationists such as Richard H. Pratt, the Carlisle Indian Industrial School superintendent, unapologetically defied official policy.[2] Open praise for the large boarding schools still existed, and presenters at annual NEA meetings often represented those schools. The papers contained in this volume also demonstrate a time when tensions existed between those who believed Native Americans eminently capable of achieving full citizenship in the United States, such as Pratt (even if for fundraising purposes),[3] and those who, like Estelle Reel, the superintendent of Indian schools, believed that American Indians, as a "child race," lacked the innate intellectual capacity to be any more than a laboring class.[4]

In this regard Superintendent Reel was a "progressive" educator of her time. As one newspaper headline from July 14, 1899, heralded, "Cooking Taught the Girls and They Are in Great Demand as Servants." The attending story noted, "Miss Reel says that Indian children, while they have little or no inventive or creative powers, are wonderful imitators." Furthermore, "she says the Indians cannot master mathematics or the higher branches of education, but are apt pupils in domestic and manual labor."[5] The papers of the NEA Department of Indian Education mark the ascendency during this period of such progressive "low expectations" for Native students.[6]

This volume also encompasses most of the years of the administration of William A. Jones (1897–1904), commissioner of Indian affairs and himself an avowed assimilationist. Jones saw his role as commissioner to implement policies to end the "reservations and tribal organization that had so perpetuated barbarism and retarded civilization" with the goal of enabling an American Indian to emerge as "a man indistinguishable from his white counterpart save for the color of his skin."[7]

The second volume of this set covers the years 1905 to 1909, nearly the complete administration of Commissioner Francis E. Leupp prior to his resignation in June 1909, just weeks before the final meeting of the NEA Department of Indian Education.[8] The second volume contains praise for the preservation of Native arts and music, along with the promotion of day schools, as well as growing criticism of the boarding schools. In 1907, for example, Leupp told the Department of Indian Education, "In time we shall put one reservation boarding-school after another out of commission," while an anxious Haskell Institute employee said to him, "I have read several things that you have said in regard to abolishing all the non-reservation schools."[9] Collectively, the papers of these educators presented a decidedly different tone with respect to Indian education between 1900 to 1904 than that which dominated the years 1905 to 1909.[10] Unfortunately, this different tone did not include a contrasting view regarding the educators' belief in Anglo-Saxon superiority, and both volumes demonstrate the ascendency of educators' full acceptance of scientific racism.

The vast majority of these selected writings are by educators who had a direct influence on the tragic boarding school experience of America's Native populations.[11] As of this writing, Canada is dealing with the discovery of undocumented graves at its boarding schools,[12] while Deb Haaland, the United States' first Native secretary of the interior, announced a federal Indian boarding school initiative that "will serve as an investigation about the loss of human life and the lasting consequences of residential Indian boarding schools."[13] About these schools scholar Jean A. Keller notes that crowded dormitories, with multiple children sleeping in a single bed, along with "inadequate nutrition, poor sanitary conditions, and the tremendous stress of living in an unfamiliar environment," threatened the lives of the schoolchildren.[14] The Indian school workers who wrote these papers well knew these facts and the inherent tragedy of these schools. As a superintendent of a large boarding school matter-of-factly told his colleagues in

1903, "During the early years of Indian education buildings were carelessly erected. No thought was given to furnishing proper systems of ventilation, lighting, and heating. As a result, children in many schools broke down in health, sickened and died."[15] Six years later an Indian service medical doctor speaking to the educators about tuberculosis admonished them: "Have we not been guilty of criminal negligence if we have not prevented spitting around our schools and in them? Have we not been guilty if we have failed to disinfect the rooms, bedding, and clothing of tubercular children sent from our schools? Have we not been guilty of the spread of tuberculosis and other contagious diseases when we put two or more children in one bed?" He concluded: "Personal attention to the health of the individual child is frequently neglected."[16]

Such rebukes had little effect. In 1913 a school inspector—the same man as the superintendent quoted earlier—reported: "An inspection of the boys' dormitory building revealed the fact that there were 46 boys rooming in 1 room where the capacity was only 23; 52 were in another room of the same size; 27 were in a room with capacity for 14. In the girls' building there were 40 girls in a room which had capacity for 24."[17] Thus, the tragedy of the Indian boarding schools is not a new realization. The following selected papers make plain that early twentieth-century contemporaries well understood this tragedy. Yet the cruelhearted system, perpetuated by these workers and supported financially and politically by the U.S. government, continued, with the consequence that, as the 1928 Meriam Report found, "Indian children were six times as likely to die in childhood while at boarding schools than the rest of the children in America."[18] Furthermore, they demonstrate for all time that the authoritative assuredness of opinion as expressed in these papers does not constitute righteousness or faultlessness.

While researching boarding schools and Indian education in general, the papers in these volumes are frequently used by researchers and are available at libraries and online. However, there are four inherent problems in using those resources. First, the papers published in the NEA journals may be edited versions of the original papers delivered at the annual meetings. Irwin Shepard, the NEA secretary, established strict guidelines for the papers that would eventually see their way into the NEA *Proceedings*.[19] In addition to requiring prior to the meeting "five typewritten copies of a synopsis of about 300 words . . . for the local press and the various Press

Associations of the United States," Secretary Shepard notified presenters that they were "respectfully requested to prepare one copy of your paper especially for publication in the annual volume." He limited each paper to three thousand words and required it to be delivered to the department secretary "at the close of your reading." Furthermore, "each department shall be limited to thirty-five pages of space in the volume."[20]

As a result of Shepard's requirements, department secretaries edited papers for publication, sometimes shortening them, and identified such papers as "Abstracts" in the *NEA Proceedings*. In the 1902 *NEA Proceedings*, for example, the only footnote to the Department of Indian Education section stated, "The following papers have necessarily been abbreviated by the department secretary [who was Estelle Reel], for want of room for publication in full."[21] The year before, when she was not the department secretary, a similar footnote recorded that "the following papers and discussions have been selected for publication by Miss Estelle Reel. . . . Most of the papers are necessarily published in abstract because of the limits of available space."[22] Reel's edits, which frequently reduced the length of the presented papers, caused the NEA editors in 1903 to lament, "It is a matter of regret that only abstracts of most of the following addresses were furnished for publication by the secretary of the department."[23] Consequently, NEA Department of Indian Education papers in the *NEA Proceedings* are often not the papers as delivered at the annual meetings. Rather, they are the papers as Reel edited them.[24] Therefore, these volumes contain many complete—or, at least more complete—papers than the *NEA Proceedings*.[25]

The footnotes in the *NEA Proceedings* also indicate Reel's control over the NEA Department of Indian Education. In 1900, the year the department first met, Reel's chief clerk served as "acting secretary," although Edgar A. Allen, superintendent of the Albuquerque Indian School, New Mexico, was listed officially as department secretary. The second year she was not the department secretary, but, as a footnote indicated, she performed that function by selecting and editing the published papers. Then, the next year, 1902, until the termination of the department in 1909, she was the department secretary. In the department's ten-year history, no one else selected or edited the papers of the NEA Department of Indian Education.[26] What readers see in the *NEA Proceedings* today is what Reel wanted them to see.

Each original paper went through a two-part editing process.[27] Reel received the original papers from presenters. In many cases she edited papers for length, while, in some cases, she edited for content—for instance, changing a sentence's meaning or deleting what could be considered controversial or objectionable material—and, at other times, sent papers to NEA editors as originally written. The NEA editors then corrected ill-placed punctuation, fixed tortured language to convey ideas more clearly, and, generally, made the papers more standard and readable. However, the most distinctive feature of NEA editing was the adoption of Simplified Spelling.

The NEA was a strong proponent of the Simplified Spelling movement at the turn of the century.[28] This movement, in the words of President Theodore Roosevelt, was "to make our spelling a little less foolish and fantastic." In 1898 the NEA approved a list of twelve words "used most frequently in common writing and printing which can be spelled more simply than previous custom allows. All contain a number of silent letters. In the reform the words are spelled according to their sounds and contain no useless letters." When a presenter used the word "thorough," NEA editors changed it to "thoro." Editors simplified the word "although" to "altho." In this manner NEA editors "simplified" the published papers.[29] Thus, through the entire editing process, papers were frequently shortened, sometimes changed in meaning, and often underwent cosmetic changes. When possible the following papers reflect more closely the presenters' original addresses.

The second problem with the papers published in the NEA *Proceedings* is that allusions over a century old are stale or outmoded. Early twentieth-century listeners readily understood names of individuals, political events, social currents, and the nuances that accompany them as each paper was presented. It is equally important that modern readers understand these allusions to appreciate fully the ideas each writer was communicating. Appropriate introductions and detailed annotating of the papers provide this information.

Moreover, the papers must be put into their proper historical context for a deeper understanding of them.[30] Each of the documents is placed in its proper context by understanding the flow of relevant events of the year the paper was presented, the setting for that presentation, and the political landscape that unfolded with the coming of each annual meeting as it related to the men and women involved in Indian education. Contextualization provides evidence of the thinking of educators of that era.

Finally, who were the individuals who wrote and presented the following papers? In some cases, such as Estelle Reel or Alice Fletcher, they are well known in the field of Indian education. To acquaint readers with the array of presenters, introductions are added to provide a window into the lives of the Indian school workers who participated in the annual NEA meetings.

Through this window readers will see the eclipse of a Prattian view of Indian education and the advocacy of off-reservation schooling, the promotion of reservation day schools, and the ascendency of industrial, agricultural, and domestic training with an equal deemphasis of academic education for Native students. Readers will also see marching through the years a growing sense of urgency to preserve Native arts and music—the very "Indianness" the "old assimilationists" had hoped to eradicate. Evident as well is a rise in musings that, probably, the educators of American Indian students had figured out an educational model suited to the rest of the country,[31] and observations by national figures who told Indian school workers that their efforts were like those of other educators "uplifting" colonized people around the world.[32] Readers will clearly see, as Reel had planned by establishing a department within the NEA, Indian school educators were brought into the fold of the nation's mainstream education—at least for a while.

The view that educating American Indians was like the work of others lifting up colonized people around the globe was predicated on racism, and racist over- and undertones dominate the NEA addresses. Whether discussing Native Americans as a "child race" or a "lower order" race, or simply their "lack" of innate abilities, these educators often demonstrated a disingenuous respect for Native culture, on the one hand, and, on the other, intoned a bigoted philosophical dismissal of American Indians' ability to assimilate fully into American society. In the end their comments about educating Natives reflected the scientific racism that dominated the educational environment that Reel superintended for the decade of the existence of the NEA Department of Indian Education. The NEA papers, however, do not reflect the experiences of the Natives who were subjected to these Eurocentric philosophies, the racism embodied in them, or the consequences of those experiences. There are many excellent works that shine a light on how the policies, attitudes, and pedagogical designs of the educators ultimately affected the students subjected to the Indian school system within which these government workers operated.[33] That American Indian people and nations are "still here" nevertheless reflect the resilience of the continent's indigenous peoples against the best efforts of the Indian school educators. Those best efforts and the nation's desire to mold Native Americans into white-defined roles within society are demonstrated in the papers of the NEA Department of Indian Education.

## The NEA Department of Indian Education

British writer Gilbert K. Chesterton wrote in 1924, "Education is simply the soul of a society as it passes from one generation to another. . . . The culture, the colour and sentiment, the special knowledge and aptitudes of a civilisation must not be lost, but must be left as a legacy."[34] This simple passing of the "soul of a society" to future generations is the direct antithesis of what in the United States was called "Indian education." As Ojibwe writer David Treuer has insightfully stated, "Indian kids went to school to be not-Indian." Carlisle Indian Industrial School founder Richard Henry Pratt more coldheartedly said that the purpose of Indian education was to "kill the Indian in him, and save the man."[35]

Consistent with these ideas, the U.S. government developed an Indian education policy in the late decades of the nineteenth century that the Native American Rights Fund found "was, at its core, a policy of cultural genocide."[36] Rather than passing souls to subsequent generations, this policy sought to eradicate "Indianness" among the Native populations and strove for the "civilization" of American Indians so they would assimilate into the dominant white society. The only way this could be accomplished, write scholars K. Tsianina Lomawaima and Teresa L. McCarty, was to "replace heritage languages with English, replace 'paganism' with Christianity, [and] replace economic, political, social, legal, and aesthetic institutions." The "logical choice" for this "Native American cultural genocide," they note, was the nation's educational system.[37]

Two schools of thought dominated discussions by the late 1800s and early 1900s regarding "Indian education" and how best to "civilize" the nation's Indigenous population.[38] The first philosophy, an Enlightenment-era influenced universalism, had its American roots among the Founders, including Thomas Jefferson, who believed "the Indian . . . to be in body and mind equal to the whiteman [*sic*]."[39] Convinced that the continent's aboriginal people must eventually accept white civilization or perish, he included intermarriage between Natives and whites to his assimilationist quiver.[40] In 1808 he told a visiting Native delegation, "When once you have property, you will want laws and magistrates to protect your property and persons, and to punish those among you who commit crimes. You will find that our laws are good for this purpose; you will wish to live under them, you will unite yourselves with us, join in our Great Councils and form one people with us, and we shall all be Americans; you will mix with us by marriage, your blood will run in our veins, and will spread with us over this great island."[41] In the post–Civil War era, this enlightened universalism motivated much of the country's reform movement to solve the "Indian problem."

Commissioner Thomas Jefferson Morgan articulated this universalism when he presented his educational plan in 1889 in which he defined Indian education as "that comprehensive system of training and instruction which will convert [Natives] into American citizens."[42] He and like reformers held that through an educational alchemy American Indians would become productive Christianized Americans.[43] The "secret sauce" of this alchemy was forced total assimilation, or, as noted previously, "cultural genocide," whereby any vestiges of Native lifestyles, religions, languages, and so forth would be totally eliminated from the American landscape. These assimilationists believed that they would be providing American Indians with the profound gift of civilization by eliminating the "tedious evolution," in Commissioner Morgan's words, through which whites had traveled.[44]

The progressive educators, strongly influenced by the era's scientific racism, represented the second school of thought that directly confronted the universalism of the old assimilationists. The new theory held, education historian Thomas Fallace writes, that societies and individuals "passed through the same linear stages" of "savagery, barbarism, and civilization," and "non-White individuals and societies were stuck in an earlier sociological-psychological stage . . . that had been abandoned by the civilized."[45] Progressive educators believed that American Indians could never become "white."[46] In other words, there was no way to avoid "tedious evolution." "Many white Americans," historian Jacqueline Fear-Segal notes, "were never able to concede full equality to Indians and progressively situated them within the developing discourse of scientific racism."[47] Therefore, scientific racism provided a rational for believing in the superiority of whites. According to Pawnee lawyer Walter R. Echo-Hawk, it "clothed simple prejudice and base racism with the imprimatur of science."[48]

Francis E. Leupp evidenced this racist viewpoint shortly after he became commissioner of Indian affairs in 1905, when he dismissed what he believed to be the wrong-headedness of the concept of universalism. "The commonest mistake made by his well-wishers in dealing with the Indian," he wrote, "is the assumption that he is simply a white man with a red skin."[49] Leupp and like-minded reformers believed that no amount of transformation would elevate American Indians to the status of white American citizens, who, they believed, were farther along the path of evolutionary advancement. Despite having this low opinion of the intellectual abilities of Natives, Leupp and his ilk *liked* them and their Indianness. As early as 1900, he wrote, "I like the Indian for what is Indian in him. . . . Let us not make the mistake, in the process of absorbing them, of washing out of them whatever is distinctly Indian."[50] This was a decidedly opposing view from Pratt's "Kill the Indian."

Differing rhetoric and philosophies notwithstanding, the overall objective in civilizing Native Americans through education was to assimilate them into the religious, economic, linguistic, political, and legal fabric of American society. That is not to say that other—probably larger—motives did not contribute to the drive for Indian education. Historian and Ojibwe writer Brenda J. Child, for example, has argued that, if assimilation were the objective, why establish *segregated* Indian schools? She maintains that Indian education was more about a "land grab" than assimilation. Her point is well taken when considering how much of federal Indian policy was to facilitate transferring Indian lands to non-Indian hands. In sarcastically summarizing the entire "commodification" process of Native lands from colonial to modern times, Canadian historian Allen Greer writes, "All will be well as indigenous land is absorbed into the Euro-American 'mainstream' and indigenous people disappear into oblivion."[51] Thus, Indian education for assimilation as it evolved in the late nineteenth and early twentieth centuries and the "land grab" are intricately woven together, and Child certainly identified this larger national policy of Indian affairs.[52]

Nevertheless, civilizing for assimilation—to varying degrees—remained *an* objective among Indian school educators and reformers of the day. All of these approaches required conversion to Christianity, communications in English, and practical skills training to labor in white society. Educators and reformers, however, aggressively debated the degree to which Indian education should amputate students from tribal, including familial, ties in the process of assimilation.[53]

The evolution of this Indian education during the nineteenth century resulted in the establishment of "three institutions—the reservation day school, the reservation boarding school, and the off-reservation boarding school."[54] Each institution represented in its own way the philosophical discussions of the late nineteenth and early twentieth centuries. The type of institution Native students attended defined the degree of interaction those students would have with their Native communities and families, and how much Indianness would be "killed" or educated out of them. Students enrolled in a reservation day school continued to live within their communities and became instruments by which the rest of the community members were to be *uplifted* into the dominate white society. Reservation boarding schools offered the same advantage, only in more limited doses, such as during school holidays.

Conversely, the off-reservation boarding school removed students from their communities, often from the geographic region, to be schooled for years at a time in isolation from families and communities. The masthead of the Carlisle Indian Industrial School newspaper best defined the reformers' view in this approach: "To Civilize the Indian; Get Him into Civilization. To Keep Him Civilized; Let Him Stay."[55] These advocates believed that only through total and unbroken immersion into white society, without any opportunity to "return to the blanket"—as "backsliding" into Native culture was derisively called—could American Indian students successfully make the transformation to white society.[56] Dr. Carlos Montezuma, Yavapai from Arizona, went so far as to say, "Away with the reservation schools." He continued, "You can never civilize the Indian until you place him while yet young (and the younger the better) in direct relations with good civilization."[57] Such advocates believed that total immersion into white society (the sooner the better) would metamorphose Natives into good American citizens.

Despite the quibbling over the philosophies represented by each of the three Indian educational institutions, there was no disagreement about the ends to be achieved: civilization of the Native American population and its assimilation, to varying degrees, into the dominant white society. Commissioner Morgan wrote in 1889, "This civilization may not be the best possible, but it is the best the Indians can get. They can not escape it, and must either conform to it or be crushed by it." In 1899 another reformer stated, "[American Indians] must either accept the white man's civilization or disappear from the earth."[58] The men and women who worked in Indian education, possessing what Francis Paul Prucha calls "an ethnocentrism of frightening intensity," used the educational environment to steamroll Native American cultures to ensure conformity to this "gift of civilization." Robert A. Trennert Jr. writes that "although this promise [of civilization] meant little to Native Americans, the reformers of the late nineteenth century felt honor-bound to carry it out."[59]

One display of the frightening ethnocentrism and the honor-bound dedication to "gifting" civilization to Native students is in the writings of educators from the NEA Department of Indian Education and, as mentioned, published in the *Journal of Proceedings and Addresses of the National Educational Association*, 1900–1909. During this ten-year period, Indian school educators gathered with other educators from across the country at the NEA annual meetings. By 1900 such meetings attracted thousands of educators of every stripe who came together to discuss the educational currents of their respective disciplines and to hear addresses from national speakers. That had not always been the case. Moreover, these educators and the Department of Indian Education to which they belonged were a late, albeit short-lived, addition to the NEA organizational structure and its annual meeting agenda.

By 1857 many of the Northern states had formed statewide teachers' associations, as well as a variety of literary and professional organizations, all involved in education. These organizations fought for the recognition of the teaching profession, ran institutes to provide professional development for educators, and published a dizzying array of journals dedicated to scholarship. Forty-three leaders of these various organizations came together in Philadelphia in that year to form the National Teachers' Association (NTA).[60] Predictions for the success of this effort could not have been good. The nation was hurtling toward a civil war, as disunion and sectionalism militated against the success of any national organization. Regardless, the NTA held its third annual convention in 1859 in Washington DC, where President James Buchanan became the first chief executive to acknowledge its attendees, all whom he invited to the White House. By 1870, despite an intervening civil war, the NTA had held eleven annual meetings, changed its constitution to allow women into its membership, and renamed itself the National Educational Association.[61]

Despite these apparent advances, anemic membership numbers continued to plague the organization and hindered its ability to become "one great Educational Brotherhood [and now, Sisterhood]."[62] From its founding in 1857 to 1883, active annual membership never reached 400 members. Under an aggressive new leader during the latter year, membership skyrocketed in 1884 to over 2,700 members, with over 5,000 attendees at that year's annual meeting in Madison, Wisconsin. Financial insecurities and struggles to publish its annual *NEA Proceedings* evaporated.[63] The *NEA Proceedings*, which included papers delivered at each of the annual meetings, captured the educational currents that represented the academic interests of the members.

Initially, members at the annual meetings met as one group in general sessions but, beginning in 1870, members also met in departments "for the presentation and discussion of papers on specific and technical subjects related to the various divisions of educational work." The first four departments of the NEA were the Departments of School Superintendence, Normal Schools, Higher Education, and Elementary Education, all established in 1870.[64] Over the ensuing years, the NEA board of directors approved departments based on "the written application of twenty active members of the association for permission to establish a new department," naming the departments to reflect the function or expertise to be represented by the departments' members.[65] This process reflects the creation of the NEA Department of Indian Education in 1899.

NEA interest in Indian education began much earlier than the creation of this department. Samuel Chapman Armstrong, founder of Virginia's Hampton Institute, presented papers in 1883 and 1884 on his school's experience in mechanical and agricultural arts for American Indian students.[66] In 1884 and 1895, Pratt spotlighted his school's work with Native students.[67] William Hailmann, the superintendent of Indian schools, addressed an 1895 NEA general session with his paper "The Next Step in the Education of the Indian."[68] The NEA was also keen on passing resolutions supporting the nation's American Indian education initiatives:

1885: We heartily commend the efforts made to solve the so-called Indian problem by educating the young Indians out of the savagery of their parents into the industries and attainments of civilization, in which families shall be set apart by themselves in well-ordered houses with individual possession of land and other property, and enter as proposed upon the duties and accept the obligations of citizenship.[69]

1887: We express our profound interest in the education of the Indians; heartily commend the spirit of liberality shown by Congress in the matter, and call special attention to the important and encouraging results already achieved.[70]

In 1890 a resolution commended Commissioner Morgan and his "plans . . . for establishing national schools" for Native youth. Moreover, "we hail it as a sign of progress in American civilization, that the United States Government is making this effort to educate all of the Indian race for future citizenship, and that we pledge our cordial support as educators."[71] Five years later the NEA members resolved that they "cordially sympathize with Superintendent Hailman's [*sic*] appeal to the teachers of the land for active interest on their part in the civilization of the Indians and for a concerted effort to bring the Indian under the same law with the white man in the several states."[72]

Through papers presented and resolutions passed at its annual meetings, the NEA had demonstrated an interest in American Indian education prior to 1899. The establishment of the Department of Indian Education, however, brought Indian school educators into the fold of national educators, recognizing their unique category just as the Departments of Elementary Education, Natural Science Instruction, Secondary Education, and the rest of the eighteen departments listed in the NEA Constitution recognized those specialties. After 1899 these educators saw their work endorsed with the Department of Indian Education also listed in the NEA Constitution.[73]

The establishment of this department also emphasizes the *segregated* nature of the education of Native students, as Brenda Child points out.[74] As will be seen, through the years when they had their own department, Indian school educators met in joint sessions with other NEA departments, such as the Departments of Manual Training and Elementary Education.[75] These joint meetings indicated the commonality in the work of specialized educators in Indian schools and the nation's public schools. In other words, manual training and elementary education had similarities for both Native and white students. However, the fact that there was a Department of Indian Education provides resounding evidence that educators believed that there were also chasms too wide to span between the education of America's Native students and the rest of the population.[76]

Estelle Reel, the superintendent of Indian schools from 1898 to 1910, was the alpha and the omega of that department. An incredibly active member of the NEA after joining in 1894, she was the driving force in creating the Department of Indian Education. Without her it is likely there would not have been one, or, if there were, it would look very different from what existed. The NEA Department of Indian Education was *her* department. She organized its meetings and established its agendas, invited its speakers, and served as its secretary for all but two years of its existence ensuring that the educators' papers, edited by her, were published in the NEA *Proceedings*, and oversaw the last meeting of the department after its single-decade journey with the parent organization.[77]

Born in 1862 and raised in Illinois, Reel signaled early on that she would not follow the societal expectations for her gender. During her high school graduation speech, she argued for women's equality, including self-sufficiency and the right to vote. She received her university education in St. Louis, Chicago, and Boston, then began her career in education teaching in her hometown of Pittsfield and nearby Griggsville. In what is assuredly the most momentous decision of her life, "seeking a more healthful climate" she relocated in 1887 to Cheyenne, Wyoming, where her older half-brother, Alexander Hector "Heck" Reel, had moved in 1867 and now served as mayor. Living in a state that allowed women to participate in the political process, coupled with her drive toward self-sufficiency, it is not surprising that Reel quickly became involved in first local, then state, then national governance. After a short-lived teaching career in Cheyenne, she entered the political world in 1890 when she ran successfully as a Republican for Laramie County superintendent of schools—an accomplishment she repeated in 1892. Two years later she became one of the first women in the United States to hold a statewide office when she won the election to become Wyoming's state superintendent of public instruction.[78]

Just as her relocation to Wyoming allowed her to enter the political arena, Reel's decision to align herself with the Republican Party ensured her continued political ascendancy. She actively supported Republican presidential candidate William McKinley in his 1896 bid for the Oval Office, including visiting him in July at his home in Canton, Ohio, where he ran his "front-porch" campaign. She then distributed campaign literature and stumped Wyoming and other western states with women's suffrage to get out the female vote for him. Although McKinley did not win those states, he was undoubtedly impressed with Reel's political acumen and, more importantly, wished to compensate her for her efforts on his behalf.[79] Reel was not shy about pursuing that reward.

As state superintendent of public instruction, she also held the offices of secretary of the State Board of Charities and registrar of the State Land Board. These two official, statewide positions vastly expanded her political and professional network far beyond educational circles and occasionally brought her to Washington DC, where she cultivated more political connections.[80] One newspaper noted that she had "been able to form a very wide acquaintance among prominent men of the nation."[81] In 1897 she sought information on the Department of Interior's employees' terms of office and salaries, and in 1898 no doubt watched with interest "the efforts of [Superintendent of Indian Schools] Dr. Hailmann's enemies to procure his removal" that had "been renewed recently with fresh vigor."[82]

Swiss-born William N. Hailmann immigrated to the United States in 1852 and, along with his wife, Eudora, quickly became an advocate for education in America, particularly kindergarten. He had joined the nascent National Teachers' Association by 1863, delivered his first paper to that organization in 1872, and served as president for the Departments of Kindergarten Education and Elementary Education.[83] His national reputation in education resulted in his appointment as superintendent of Indian schools in 1894.[84]

While a newspaper in his adopted state of Indiana declared him "the most valuable man who ever filled" that office, political currents, a feud with Pratt, complaints about Hailmann's reluctance to conduct fieldwork by visiting Indian schools, and elements of the Indian reform movement that "ran out of steam," all pointed to a change in that office with the inauguration of the McKinley Administration in March 1897. Despite strong opposition to the removal of Hailmann, he lost the support of his superiors by 1898, and it was just a matter of time when he would be replaced.[85]

In the meantime, with a letter-writing campaign, Reel energized her political supporters and the educational network she developed in her work for Wyoming and through the NEA. Although she was not accused of pushing Hailmann out of his position, she certainly took advantage of his tenuousness in that office to ensure she would be considered the right person to succeed him. She also benefited, no doubt, from the late nineteenth-century trend that saw women being promoted into prominent positions in the Indian service. Her work and this trend resulted in President McKinley appointing her as superintendent of Indian schools in June 1898, making her the first female outside of the postal service requiring Senate confirmation to a federal executive office.[86] The same Indiana newspaper that lauded Hailmann reported about her appointment: "To Miss Reel's credit, it should be said that she has steadily declared her admiration of Dr. Hailmann and his work, and her unwillingness to be considered a candidate as long as he remained at this post. It was only in view of the fact that a change was to be made anyway that she was willing to apply for the appointment. Personally she has made an excellent impression wherever she has appeared, and her record as Superintendent of Public Instruction in Wyoming is said to be very good."[87]

Not everyone so graciously accepted Reel's appointment. Herbert Welsh counted among the detractors. He had been the primary organizer of the Indian Rights Association in 1882 and worked passionately in lobbying efforts "on civilizing, christianizing, and americanizing the American Indian."[88] Following the removal of Hailmann and the appointment of Reel to that position, he addressed the National Civil-Service Reform League in December: "Dr. Hailmann was removed upon no charges or objections, certainly upon none which can stand the light, and thus the ablest and best equipped man who has ever held that position was lost to the Indian service. His successor was a young woman [thirty-five years old],[89] unequipped, as I believe on excellent authority, for a place so responsible and difficult. Undoubtedly it was the pressure of the strong political backing which won for her the prize."[90]

Regardless, win the prize she did, and assumed the superintendent's office on June 21, 1898. Within a month she traveled to Colorado Springs, Colorado, where a three-week summer institute for Indian school educators convened on July 18. Former superintendent Hailmann, who had organized the event, agreed to participate, and concluded his remarks to the gathered two hundred participants by "prettily introducing" his successor to them. In her 1898 annual report, Reel noted that at the institute "agents, superintendents, principal teachers, disciplinarians, industrial teachers, cooks, field matrons, nurses, and physicians discussed and practically illustrated the methods in use and suggested for use in the [Indian] schools."[91]

Such summer institutes for the professional development of educators became an American standard by the 1840s. Small and large political subdivisions sponsored these educational gatherings, which lasted for a couple of days or for as long as two months. The organizations that came together to form the NTA sponsored a variety of these institutes.[92] However, the Indian service had been slow to adopt the practice, undoubtedly because it had been slow to organize as a national education organization. Not until the 1880s did Congress authorize a "school inspector" to oversee the growing number of Indian educational institutions. This position quickly morphed into the superintendent of Indian schools.[93]

Consistent with these organizational developments, Indian school educators participated in summer institutes to enhance their skills beginning in 1884. The first of these was held in Puyallup, Washington. A small affair with representatives from only six Indian schools attending, it would take time for these summer institutes to develop into substantial professional development opportunities for these educators.[94] The Puyallup Agency held three more teacher institutes by 1890, but they again only included six schools. Institutes were also held in 1890 in Marietta, California, and Pine Ridge, South Dakota. Each of these institutes counted roughly a dozen attendees representing a few schools. After recounting this history in his annual report, Daniel Dorchester, superintendent of Indian schools, plaintively acknowledged that while there was "much desire" to have such gatherings, there remained many obstacles to holding them, such as the "magnificent distances" that required expensive railway travel, as well as the Indian Office agents who could not see their "way clear to encourage such gatherings." He suggested that "if the Department could take some action to open the way for these institutes and to aid them, agents might be freer to act." He concluded that teachers attending such institutes "would be stimulated by new ideas, aided by new suggestions, and refreshed by contact with other workers."[95]

These early convocations never did materialize into true teacher institutes until Hailmann assumed the superintendency in 1894. He held five

such institutes the first summer of his administration in Chilocco, Oklahoma; Santa Fe, New Mexico; Chemawa, Oregon; Fort Shaw, Montana;
and St. Paul, Minnesota. He estimated the number of attendees at these
institutes from 50 to 250.[96] The agenda for the Santa Fe institute held July
9–14 demonstrates how ambitious these institutes had become. Presenters
included Hailmann; Pratt; New Mexico's governor; a variety of Indian
school employees, from matrons to superintendents; an archbishop; and
an infantry band. Hailmann did complain, however, that a railroad strike
prevented the Santa Fe institute from being larger.[97]

He then organized very elaborate Indian service institutes from 1895
through 1898. Gone were the days of a dozen or so workers representing a
few schools getting together in the summertime. Hailmann claimed that
for the three 1895 institutes "nearly 500, or fully one-third of the entire
force of school employees" attended the sessions.[98] He believed that these
institutes inculcated a sense of camaraderie among Indian school workers
by "the removal from the service of a narrow factional spirit" detrimental
to the service's overall work. He also credited the institutes with "lifting
the workers out of the depth of narrow local empiricism upon the plateau
of broad, scientific principles."[99] He concluded in 1897 that "the summer
institutes have continued to exercise their favorable influence upon the
organization and character of work in Indian schools."[100] By the time
Reel assumed the reins of office in 1898 and met with her educators in
Colorado Springs in July, these institutes were well-organized and well-
attended events.

When exactly the new superintendent decided to combine her educators
and a summer institute with the NEA is not known. The seed for that idea
probably germinated quickly during her time in Colorado Springs, where
she may have had conversations with other Indian school educators interested in the NEA.[101] By then she had been an NEA member for about four
years and had become highly active in that organization. She was elected
vice president at the Denver, Colorado, meeting in 1895; reelected to that
position at the Buffalo, New York, meeting in 1896; delivered a paper on
American public education at the Milwaukee, Wisconsin, 1897 meeting;
and, just prior to traveling to Colorado Springs, attended the July 1898
annual meeting in Washington DC, where she was elected a director of
NEA's Western Division.[102] Moreover, she was well acquainted with educational summer institutes and oversaw a number of them during her

time in Wyoming.[103] Based on this background, she probably envisioned an NEA Department of Indian Education while attending the summer institute at Colorado Springs.

Reel quickly acted on that vision preparing to make it a reality at the NEA's next annual meeting scheduled for July 1899. By March of that year, she had notified educators through the commissioner of Indian affairs that the Indian school service institute would be held "in connection with the National Educational Association, from July 10th to 25th" in Los Angeles.[104] The timing of Reel's summer institute provided the educators the opportunity to attend the NEA annual meeting from July 11 through 14, and immediately following it, still hold a thorough summer institute, for which she solicited topics.[105] Secretary Shepard, "as per the request of Miss Estelle Reel," sent notices in April of the upcoming meeting "to the Superintendent of each Indian School in the United States." He wrote: "It will be a pleasure to the officers of the NEA to cooperate with the officers of the Indian Bureau in their plans for the Los Angeles meeting."[106] On the morning of July 10, the day before the NEA annual meeting began, Shepard punctuated this cooperation by addressing the gathered Indian service educators "on behalf of the teachers of the nation, and bade them a hearty welcome to the National Educational Association convention."[107]

By that time Reel had already begun laying the groundwork for the creation of a Department of Indian Education. On July 10, the same day of Shepard's address to her educators, under the headline "A New NEA Department May Soon Be Organized," the *Los Angeles Times* reported: "A department of Indian education will probably be the next outgrowth of the National Educational Association. Miss Estelle Reel, United States Superintendent of Indian Schools, is in attendance upon the NEA Convention. Under her direction a conference will be held of those interested in work among the Indians."[108]

In a report from Los Angeles datelined the same day, the *San Francisco Call* used Reel's own words to explain her logic in wanting to join forces with the NEA: "We believe that every teacher can learn, and I think that when the teachers who come from every section of the United States meet in session it will be possible for the teachers employed in the Indian service to be able to study method, by hearing eminent scholars discuss pedagogic questions. The influence is for the better, and our teachers will be made stronger and become imbued with a higher conception of their calling."[109]

Reel wasted no time in making this happen. On the first day of the annual meeting, the NEA board of directors, one of whom was Reel, met in the Directors' Room of the Los Angeles Chamber of Commerce. After the more mundane business of dealing with a resignation, the finances, and a thank-you to the Central Woman's Christian Temperance Union of Los Angeles for giving the NEA a national flag, Reel presented her "petition, signed by twenty-five active members [the NEA Constitution required only twenty], for the formation of a department of Indian education." Not every director liked the idea. One wanted more time to consider the petition; another worried about the cost; another questioned the advantage for Indian service educators when they could be members of the NEA "under the present conditions." Supportive directors, however, parried all concerns, and Reel explained "that there would be a great advantage to the Indian school workers in the fact of being members . . . and in being assured of the fellow-feeling and sympathy of other teachers." The chair ruled "out of order" one final effort to make it an "affiliated department" rather than a full department. The petition then passed. Reel now had her NEA Department of Indian Education, a development supported by the commissioner of Indian affairs.[110] Thus, beginning with the next annual meeting held at Charleston, South Carolina, and for the nine years following it, Indian school educators had a formal department within the NEA.

## Note on Editorial Style, Citations, and Names

I HAVE ENDEAVORED TO REPRODUCE the papers as readers would have seen them over a century ago. The archived manuscripts and reprints of the presentations from a variety of newspapers and journals contain many irregularities in punctuation, capitalization, hyphenation, paragraphing, representation of numbers, and other stylistic deviations from modern convention. I use brackets and changes to the original papers only when it is required to make the message of the paper clearer. Otherwise, the reprints look like the original papers, warts and all.

I have added to the original presentations a number of citations. I encourage readers to turn to the endnotes if they are interested in digging deeper into concepts, or to learn about individuals referenced by the presenters, or to learn where edits were made from an original paper to the NEA-published version. In a very few cases, I have preceded the superscript reference number with an asterisk. In those cases, I strongly encourage readers to read those citations. They identify areas where presenters made factual errors or fabricated information, where Estelle Reel significantly edited papers, probably for political reasons, or other nuanced information that is vital to understanding the paper.

Finally, Indian school names were and are frequently used inconsistently. For example, Carlisle Indian Industrial School is often called Carlisle Indian School or simply Carlisle. The same is true about Indian schools such as, for example, Haskell or Chilocco. Presenters in the Department of Indian Education did the same in their papers. Those inconsistencies are present in the narrative and in the reprints of these papers.

# *Abbreviations*

| | |
|---|---|
| ARCIA | Annual Report of the Commissioner of Indian Affairs |
| CISDRC | Carlisle Indian School Digital Resource Center |
| CIA | Commissioner of Indian Affairs |
| COS | *Course of Study for the Indian Schools of the United States* |
| DOI | Department of the Interior |
| ERM-JEFRA | Estelle Reel Meyer Collection, Joel E. Ferris Research Archives of the Northwest Museum of Arts and Culture |
| ERM-WSA | Estelle Reel Meyer Collection, Wyoming State Archives |
| HCQSP | Haverford College, Quaker & Special Collections |
| KSA | Kamehameha Schools Archives |
| NARA | National Archives and Records Administration |
| NEA | National Educational Association and National Education Association |
| NEA-Gelman | Records of the NEA, Gelman Library, George Washington University |
| OIA | Office of Indian Affairs |
| OSIS | Office of the Superintendent of Indian Schools |
| PHS | Presbyterian Historical Society |
| RCE | Report of the Commissioner of Education |
| RSIS | Report of the Superintendent of Indian Schools |
| SIS | Superintendent of Indian Schools |

# To Educate American Indians

"WE STAND TONIGHT ON HISTORIC grounds," the famous Black educator Booker T. Washington told the educators gathered to hear him on Wednesday evening, July 11, 1900. "Charleston and South Carolina have made history—history that will always occupy a prominent place in the annals of our country. But South Carolina was never greater or prouder than tonight, when, with open arms and generous hospitality, she extends a welcome to the educators of America, regardless of race or color. The world is moving forward, not backward."[1] With these words the president of the Normal and Industrial Institute in Tuskegee, Alabama, captured the upbeat tone of the 1900 NEA meeting.[2]

NEA leadership had been exuberant about holding the meeting at Charleston. The executive committee sent a memorandum to its membership in February of that year promising a large attendance from the region, along with "commodious" meeting spaces and adequate housing for attendees that met all the committee's expectations. The committee left no doubt about its prospects for a great meeting.[3]

Estelle Reel, superintendent of Indian schools, was also enthusiastic about the Charleston meeting. Her work at the 1899 meeting in Los Angeles, seeking the NEA board of directors' approval for an Indian education department, had paid off. Now 1900 became the first year in the NEA's forty-three-year history that a Department of Indian Education was listed in the official program's Directory of Department Meetings. She and her fellow Indian school educators planned to meet at Freundschaftsbund Hall, located at the intersection of Meeting and George Streets. According to the official program, Carlisle's superintendent, Richard Pratt, was set to preside as the department's first president; however, he never attended. Instead, Professor Oscar H. Bakeless participated as the "Carlisle School representative."[4]

However, exuberance for the meeting could not overcome the fact that it was being held in Charleston, once "the largest port of entry for slaves arriving in North America," and where federal troops at Fort Sumter heard the first cannonade of a long, sanguinary civil war to end slavery.[5] The NEA executive committee obliquely referenced these historic facts when telling its membership that "the new National spirit which has arisen from cooperation in the recent Spanish-American war [of 1898]" could result in "a closer and more helpful fellowship in solving the peaceful and important problems of national life and education." Moreover, the committee believed that holding the meeting in Charleston "can do a great national service," as teachers from the North and the West would "gain a personal acquaintance with the South and its peculiar social and educational conditions."[6]

One of those "peculiar . . . conditions" was, of course, race relations in the South and the Jim Crow laws that forced segregation on African Americans. Cognizant of this reality, the NEA leadership secured from the Charleston local planning committee assurances "that colored members of the Association wearing the membership badge should share alike with white members all the privileges of the floor of the convention in both general and department sessions."[7] Despite such assurances one newspaper reported that, prior to Washington's address, Blacks had been forced from the main floor of the church where the general session was being held. "The colored people who came to listen," New York's the *Independent* affirmed, "were required to take separate seats, and policemen drove them out when they took their seats elsewhere." "Drove them out" was literal: "A policeman's club compelled them to leave." The *Independent*'s editors were not surprised at the discrimination, because, as they opined, it "is so much a matter of course [in the South] and to be expected." However, in a direct affront to the NEA, the editors asserted that "this is a very different case from a purely Southern police regulation, such as separates the races in cars, for it makes a national association responsible for insults to its members, not to speak of the question of veracity involved, said to be always a tender one in the South."[8]

Irwin Shepard, the NEA secretary, railed at the notion that the local committee had not lived up to its word, or that the NEA had not protected its membership in a Jim Crow environment. He agreed that "local custom was naturally followed in seating the large audience of colored non-members" on the evening Washington spoke, but, as far as he and the other NEA officers knew, no member, regardless of color, "was barred from the full membership privileges agreed upon." Shepard charged that the paper's reporting had been "inconsiderate and unjust" and offered that the paper would surely want to print a correction.[9]

The *Independent* printed a subsequent editorial that presented the NEA's interpretation of events surrounding Washington's speech. However, the editors still maintained "that the statements made by us were correct." They continued tactfully, "We do not doubt that it was the desire of the local committee that no discrimination should be shown." Perhaps, the editorial concluded, "the distinguished colored educators who were driven from their seats by the police before Booker T. Washington's address wore no badges."[10]

As the cudgeling of African Americans demonstrated, antebellum slavery and its hangover racism lay heavy in the Charleston air. Even Washington endorsed the value of the institution of slavery—undoubtedly a diplomatic sanction.[11] Moreover, the Indian service educators in Washington's audience had already heard a defense of slavery. The Friday before Washington's Wednesday evening address, Reverend Hollis B. Frissell, the principal of Hampton Institute, told Indian school educators that slavery had provided enslaved Africans the "habits of work," as well as "the white man's language and religion." He opined, "Never has a great mass of barbarous people advanced so rapidly" than did Africans under American slavery.[12] It is not surprising that, in an environment where speakers could morph slavery into a positive experience to enlighten and lift a "barbarous people," a policeman's cudgel enforced "local custom" by driving Black educators from their seats.

There is no evidence that the group of Indian service employees knew about this police enforcement of "local custom," or, if they did, how they reacted to it. However, George H. Benjamin, Reel's chief clerk and the acting secretary for the NEA Department of Indian Education, was African American. As we will see in part 3, in 1902 the civil service commission called Reel to account for her support of Benjamin when she asked unauthorized questions during the hiring process. Specifically, she asked whether white employees would take directions from him. However, at the Charleston meeting, one may only surmise her reaction to the imposition of Jim Crowism upon Black attendees. Regardless, for her educators, this incident did not dampen the first meeting of their NEA Department of Indian Education.

Reel approached the organization of this first meeting with great alacrity. Upon receiving Shepard's notice that the annual meeting would be held in Charleston, she began laying plans for her educators. She intended to include more at the meeting than routine roundtable discussions and the presentation of papers, which she judged were important in helping Indian school educators "keep abreast of the most advanced educational methods, and thus raise the standard of our schools."[13] She also planned "a small display of school work [*sic*]" designed "to impress the visitors with a due appreciation of what is being accomplished at our institutions."[14] In Los Angeles the year before, she also incorporated into the meeting "a small display of school work"; however, at that time, it was "not desirable to undertake a large collection of samples of the work, but simply a few pieces from each school."[15] She had bigger and more exacting plans for an exhibit at Charleston. She wrote to Indian service educators asking for "excellent colored maps," "artistic drawings," and the "best industrial drawing, a sheet of penmanship, and a sample of industrial work and fancy work." She asked that all work be identified with "the pupil's name, age, and school printed at the bottom of the work" and sent to her office "not later than June 1st." Finally, she directed that it all be sent "unmounted, as this work can be uniformly done in this office."[16]

Her plan "to impress the visitors" worked. The exhibit was held in the Charleston Hotel, where, one newspaper noted, "the parlors of the hotel are crowded from morning till night with an interested and admiring throng of people who are anxious to note the progress that is being made by the Indians."[17] Another writer proclaimed, "This is the finest exhibit the Indian schools has ever had, and an inspection of it will well repay those who see it, and impress the visitors with the work that is being done by the schools under Miss Reel's supervision."[18]

Reel had chosen well. The items on display demonstrated to visitors that the Indian schools taught "the ornamental . . . [and] useful." The news report continued: "The colored maps of the different countries, drawn by the pupils, are so true that they seem to have been cut from the geographies. The other drawings and paintings, some being original concepts and some being from copies, are excellent." While the "ornamental" items on display certainly impressed the visitors, so, too, did the demonstration of "useful" skills:

> In the exhibit are to be seen neatly made calico and gingham dresses, tucked, ruffled and lace-trimmed white dresses, well-made woollen [*sic*] garments, trimmed with braid, aprons and girls' uniforms. A fine suit

of clothes cut out, fitted, sewed and pressed by a youth of 15, shows that this part of the education of the hand has not been neglected. Beautiful rugs, upon which one may step with comfort on cold winter mornings, are also on exhibition.

Then there is a variety of sloyd work.[19] Hammers, anvils, rakes, pitchforks, knives, saws, window cases and many other useful articles show the practical trend of the teaching that is being carried on in these schools. Shoes made in the latest style, of leather tanned to kid-like softness by Indian boys, were sent by several schools, while the neat patching of garments shows what deft fingers these children of the forest possess.[20]

The demonstration of "useful" skills was paramount, Reel believed, to the work of the Indian schools. "Industrial training," she told fellow educators,

will make the Indian boy a useful, practical, self-supporting citizen. It will make the Indian girl more motherly. This is the kind of a girl we want—the one who will exercise the greatest influence in moulding [*sic*] the character of the nation. Vigorous efforts are now being made to prepare the rising generation of Indians for self-support by providing schools in which they can not only receive careful Christian training and instruction in the branches usually taught in the common schools, but, as well, how to make a living by manual labor. Thus will they become useful members of this great Republic, and if compulsory education is extended to all the tribes there is little reason to doubt that the ultimate civilization of the race will result.[21]

With these sentiments Reel reflected the movement of Indian service educators from earlier optimism about educating American Indians in academic pursuits to pessimism about their innate abilities. Reel codified this change of attitude in her *Course of Study* published in 1901, about which historian Frederick E. Hoxie concludes, "Hers was a curriculum of low expectations and practical lessons."[22] The following addresses from the 1900 annual meeting of Indian service educators demonstrate that these "low expectations" were already well entrenched before the publication of Reel's *Course of Study*; moreover, they were also reflected in the racial makeup of the educators in attendance. Carlisle's newspaper, the *Red Man and Helper*, editorialized that "the Indian was made conspicuous by his absence at the Charleston Indian Institute. We heard of but seven in attendance including baby Lincoln Levering."[23] Considering that Native Americans comprised 45 percent of Indian school service employees in 1899, and that only seven Natives, including the infant Lincoln, attended the Charleston NEA meeting, shows just how peripheral they were within the Indian schools.[24] In his groundbreaking work on assimilation, Wilbert Ahern argues that the large number of Native employees in the Indian school service "suggests an official commitment at some point to place American Indians in positions of responsibility for bringing about change in the orientation of their peoples."[25] The number of those who attended the Charleston meeting, however, demonstrates that, consciously or coincidentally, Reel's commitment to professional development opportunities for her Indian school employees through membership in the NEA does not appear to have included many of her Native employees.[26]

# What Is the Relation of the Indian of the Present Decade to the Indian of the Future?

H. B. FRISSELL, *Principal, Hampton Normal and Agricultural Institute, Hampton, Virginia*

**Source:** News clipping from *News and Courier* (Charleston, South Carolina), July 7, 1900, "Indian Affairs and Institutes," H60–110, Scrapbooks, 63, box 2, ERM-WSA.

Hollis Burke Frissell (1851–1917), born and raised in New York, began his service at Hampton Normal and Agricultural Institute, Virginia, in 1880 when he became that institution's chaplain. Samuel Chapman Armstrong started Hampton Institute, as it was normally called, in 1868 as a private, nondenominational school to instruct formerly enslaved Blacks in vocational, practical skills. Armstrong served as Hampton's first principal: a position assumed by Frissell upon the former's death in 1893. Frissell held that position until his own death in 1917. Christian teachings and hard work formed the nucleus of Hampton's curriculum. At the urging of Richard H. Pratt, Hampton began enrolling American Indian students in 1878, the first seventeen being former prisoners of war held at Fort Marion, Florida. There was a direct connection between those students and the Charleston meeting. Booker T. Washington, whose general session speech is noted earlier and once an employee at Hampton, had served in 1879 as "'a sort of house father to the Indian young men,' in charge of their discipline, clothing, and rooms."[27] Moreover, there was in the minds of contemporaries a belief in the similarities in "uplifting" formerly enslaved people and Natives. Both had suffered wrongs at the hands of whites, and their "citizenship status was uncertain," but both could be prepared for full citizenship through educational programs, "making them self-sufficient."[28]

Pratt's subsequent association with Hampton, however, was short lived, as he chaffed at being Armstrong's subordinate and founded his own school at Carlisle Barracks in Pennsylvania. Nevertheless, Hampton continuously enrolled Natives from 1878 until 1923. During this time 1,388 Indians attended Hampton, but only 160 ever graduated from its program. Part of the demise of Indian education at Hampton was Frissell's lack of interest. Cora Folsom, who worked at Hampton from 1880 to 1922, noted, "Frissell did not like Indians and they did not like him."[29]

Frissell gave three papers at the Charleston meeting. He delivered "The Training of Negro Teachers" to the Department of Normal Schools. Even at that department meeting, he had Native Americans on his mind, with what was a clear indictment of Pratt's assimilationist views:

> We have heard men say that "the only good Indian is a dead Indian," and working on this principle, they have endeavored to eliminate all Indian traits in their education of the red man. Some of our colleges were started with the thought of making white men of the Indians. They have never succeeded. Many years ago a long-headed Indian chief refused the offer of the commissioner of education in Virginia to give his son a collegiate education on the ground that it would not fit him to endure hunger, to kill a deer, or to build a tepee; and the Indian was right. The white man's collegiate education was utterly unfitted for the red man's son.[30]

That philosophy is evident in the two papers he delivered to the Department of Indian Education. Also evident are his views toward people of color—views consistent with contemporary progressive education and scientific racism of the time, and views that will be seen repeatedly in this volume. What he said will make modern readers uncomfortable, but it is important to remember, as Stephen Jay Gould reminded readers about these "progressive" thinkers of the early twentieth century, that they were not "crackpots," but well-respected thinkers and leaders.[31]

Reel listed the first of his papers that follows in the secretary's minutes in the *NEA Proceedings* but did not publish it. It was, however, printed in the local Charleston newspaper, which she clipped for her scrapbook. His second address, an evening lecture, Reel published in full in the *NEA Proceedings*, although she did not list it in her secretary's minutes.[32]

THERE ARE SOME ADVANTAGES IN being at a distance from the Indian question. Sometimes one sees things in a different light when at a distance. In order to discuss the question, What is the relation of the Indian of the present decade to the Indian of the future? it is very important that we should know something of the Indian of the present, in order that we may have slight knowledge of what the Indian of the future will be. The Indian of the present is very different in different places. Thus we have with us this morning representatives of Indians who are still in the blanket, who are leading uncivilized lives, and who have very little idea of what it means to be a civilized being. There are others who come from reservations where the Indian lives upon his own land and has comfortable homes. There are certain things which might be said of all Indians so far as I have seen them. I have had at Hampton representatives of almost every race. As a race the Indians are people of the child races. They have the characteristics of childhood, and in looking forward to their future I believe we should teach them to labor in order that they may be brought to manhood. So in a general way I should say that the Indian of the present is in his childhood, and what we, as Indian educators, are endeavoring to do is to bring him to his manhood.

What are the characteristics of child races? One of the first characteristics of childhood is that children do not know very much about work. This is true of the Indian, that he has not learned very much about the necessity and the dignity of labor. The Indian, being the first settler of the soil, seems to think that he has certain privileges, and one of these is his exemption from labor. Now I need not say that no race can amount to anything until there is created in it some respect for labor, for the work of the hand. Whether it is the white, black [*sic*] or the red race, it seems to me that we have to deal with this problem, and we should impress upon them the moral value of work. My illustrious predecessor, Major Armstrong, who lived in the Sandwich Islands, learned in his childhood some lessons along that line which have been of the greatest value to the people of this country. He saw those people gathering in God's houses for worship and yet going home, where the father, mother and children were huddled together in one-room houses, where they lived in perfect idleness. He realized then that no race could amount to anything that lived in that way, and the thought with which he came to this country, and which he gave to the whole work among the races of this country, was as to the absolute necessity of labor; in other words, in order that a race might be elevated it must labor. With all of the Anglo-Saxon races labor is known to be a necessity, but the truth of the matter is that neither the Indian nor the negro [*sic*] race has come to look upon labor as a necessity. We are coming as a country to deal very largely with this great problem, and it seems to me of vital importance that it should be impressed upon all races that no progress can be made until they learn to work with their hands and learn to have a regard for the dignity of labor. The Hampton School has sent down some pictures here, which it is sending to Paris, and I would be very glad if some of you would call at the Charleston Hotel and examine these pictures, as they illustrate what can be done in the way of teaching these people how to love labor.[33]

**Good Common Sense**

In our kindergarten it is just as easy to to [sic] commence with the children and interest and teach them to wash in the wash tub [sic] and to iron on the ironing board as it is to teach them games. We take the young people out to the farm and give them a little hoe and rake, and they enjoy working in the soil. We commence with children of four or five or six years of age, and train them in the dignity and necessity of labor. This is what we ought to do. We should create in them the working habit. This is very necessary and important. A man who does not learn to work and love work is not one who is going to accomplish anything and no race that does not learn that lesson will make any progress in this world, for the Good Book says we must work out our own salvation.

I find at Hampton that these young people take to books and we have to teach them that books are only tools and are only important as they teach the Indian to work. We put them in the laboratory, where they can learn things about things before they learn anything in regard to the words about things. Still, words are important and I do not wish to underrate the value of language in its relation to education, but vitally more important and above everything is a knowledge of things. And so I believe that in education of these young people we should emphasize the point of doing, and we should teach them to learn by doing from the kindergarten to the post-graduate [sic].

Another characteristic of the Indian race which belongs to the children is the lack of responsibility. This is especially true of the Indian race. I need not explain to you what the effect of the ration system has been upon the Indian. It has taken away from him the necessity of labor, the necessity of caring for himself. The Indian is in his childhood because of the irresponsible life he has lived. In school each child should be held responsible. In our white schools if, instead of the teacher taking all of the responsibility upon himself, the child could be made to feel that he would be held responsible for work faithfully performed, including not only school work [*sic*], but saw mill [*sic*], laundry work, work of the various shops, etc., and would get the idea of responsibility and love it, he would feel a certain manhood and strength that only comes when a man is responsible for something. We fe[e]l that we are something and do something because of the responsibilities that are placed upon us in life. And in training the Indian we should give special prominence to those duties which create this feeling in him.

### Home Life of the Indians

There is one more point upon which I wish to speak. These people have very little idea of home life. Of course the Indian, under the tribal system which has existed in the past, could have very little idea of a home. Some fathers have trained their children carefully, but under this system it was impossible for the Indian to have a right Christian influence. Great stress, therefore, should be laid on the teaching of the things having relation to the home life. Teach the child to take up those duties which belong to the home. I consider at Hampton that the dining room and the domestic part of our work is the most vital department, and I am trying all the time to make the academic work merely help that part which has to do with the home. The progress in the way of living is the way by which we are to judge of the progress of his work, not the knowledge of arithmetic or history. We should judge our progress by the success we attain in teaching how to live decent Christian lives. This, it seems to me, is of vital importance and by that we are to judge our progress.

The Indian for many years to come should be a farmer and tiller of the soil. I think we are coming to learn that these people will have to live on the soil if they are going to live at all. They cannot live in the city. They should have a knowledge of the things about them. They should see God in the plants, the animals and all things about them. He has been taught by his parents to love these things, and to draw them away from the love of these so that they do not care for them is little less than criminal. The Indian of the future is to live in the country and he should find his comfort and happiness in the things of nature.

# 2 | The Indian Problem

H. B. FRISSELL, *Principal, Hampton Normal and Agricultural Institute, Hampton, Virginia*

Source: NEA *Proceedings*, 1900, 682–92, noted as a "stenographic report."

I REALIZE THAT IN SPEAKING to the audience gathered here I am addressing many who know much more of the Indian problem than I do—men and women who have devoted their lives to its solution, whose daily contact with the red man in his own home has given them opportunities of understanding him and his needs such as are not possible to us who live at a distance and gain much of our knowledge at second hand or from occasional visits to the Indian's home. And yet there are some advantages in viewing objects at a distance. Those of us who have to do with eastern schools are watching with sympathetic interest the work which the great body of western Indian workers are accomplishing, realizing to some extent the great difficulties under which you labor, rejoicing in your successes, and modestly forming opinions as to the things that need still to be done before our brethren in red shall attain to the full stature of American citizenship. Allow me to thank you and our superintendent of Indian schools for the opportunity of saying a few words to you on the problem to the solution of which many of you have given your lives.

I am grateful, too, for the privilege of speaking of this subject before an audience composed largely of southern men and women, who are struggling with the greatest race problem which this or any other country has had to meet; for, while the Indian and negro problems are very unlike, yet they have many things in common. The western reservation resembles to some extent the southern plantation, and I believe that those of us who have to do with the education and civilization of Indians can learn many things from the dealings of our southern friends with the plantation negro. While we all rejoice in the fact that slavery is a thing of the past, yet I firmly believe that under the most favorable conditions it was a much more successful school for the training of a barbarous race than is the reservation. Slavery brought the colored man into close contact with his white brother, training him in habits of work, giving him a knowledge of the white man's language and religion. Never, I believe, in the history of our civilization has a great mass of barbarous people advanced so rapidly as have the blacks on this continent in the last three hundred years. On almost all the southern plantations, and in the cities also, negro mechanics were bred, as well as excellent blacksmiths, good carpenters, and house-builders capable of executing plans of high architectural merit. The negro was taught to work, to be an agriculturist, a mechanic, a material producer of something useful. We can hardly claim such results from our reservation system. It separates the Indian from the white man, it pauperizes him by giving him rations, and while of late years instruction in agriculture and industrial pursuits has been given, yet we have been slow to realize that the opportunity and disposition to labor make the basis of all our civilization.

The Indian's point of view.—In order to understand the difficulties that we, as Indian workers, have had to meet, it will be necessary to consider the attitude in which the Indian and the white man have stood to one another. The Indian in his wild state was a natural aristocrat. He looked with contempt upon the white man, considering him as belonging to an altogether lower order of creation. Like the men who came to England with the Conqueror, whose names were written in the *Doomsday Book* entitling them to land and to lives of luxury while others labored, so, I believe, the Indian considered himself a superior being whose ownership of land gave him the right to live without labor, which, however, it was quite proper and fit that we poor white people should perform. He also despised the white man as a soldier. He did not believe in his courage or in his ability to contend with him. One who has had long years of dealing with the Indian told me of the remarks that were made by the Sioux at the time of the Custer massacre. They spoke of the whites as children unfit to bear arms. They also had a contempt for white morality, and not without reason. Their treaties had been broken; the white men they were accustomed to see about the reservations twenty years ago were not of such a character as to command respect for themselves or the civilization which they represented. Not only did they despise the white man, but they hated him as well. The race prejudice which is so strong in the white race is vastly stronger, I believe, in the Indian race. The children from their earliest infancy are taught to hate the white man. He represents to them all that is bad. It is not strange, then, that progress in the education of Indian children by white people was slow, nor that those who have gone back from our Indian schools to the West have had a hard fight. They have had to struggle against a race prejudice which had behind it the sanction of religion and was bound up with all the tribal customs of the people. It is a cause for thankfulness that they have done as well as they have. Many a brave fight has been fought by those students who have gone out from our schools, and the progress of the last thirty years is largely due to the influence they have exerted. Many of them have failed, as was to be expected. They have been exposed to the sneers of the whites, who are not always glad to have intelligence and business ability increase too rapidly among the Indians. Little has been said of their struggles to do right, or of their successes, but their failures have been made known to the whole country.

Annihilation of the Indian is still much more popular with a large portion of the people of this country than is assimilation. When you talk with a white man on the borders of a reservation about the education and uplift of the Indian, you are quite likely to meet with the sort of sympathy which General Whittlesey met with in one of his visits to the Crows of Montana.[34] The rough westerner who drove the stage-coach [*sic*] said to him: "Are you one of them that is trying to tame these Indians? Well, I'll tell you how I tame 'em. There's a well in my backyard; there ain't no water in it, but there's seven tame Indians in it."

It is because the Indian problem is so much the problem of educating the white man and lifting him out of his barbarism that it is so discouraging. Some years since a company of legislators visited an Indian school on the sabbath. In his address to the school one of these lawmakers said: "The Bible tells us that it is right to lift an ox or an ass out of a ditch on the sabbath day, and I reckon that is what the principal of this school is trying to do for us."

What long years of struggle it has taken to make the average American citizen believe that there are any possibilities in his red brother! There are few things more significant as to the attitude of the ordinary well-dressed American citizen than to hear his remarks in visiting a class of Indian boys and girls; he speaks of them as tho [*sic*] they were "dumb driven cattle."

"Are you civilized?" was the question put by a visitor to an intelligent Sioux boy. "No," said he; "are you?"

When we are asked, then, why it is that it takes so long to civilize 250,000 Indians, one answer certainly is that we have had to wait to civilize white men about them. The education of the white and red races has had to go on together, and I for one believe that God has left this red race with us that he might teach us some lessons in righteousness, in truth, in love, and in self-sacrifice.

Many of the men in Washington look upon those who come there to plead the cause of the Indian as wild fanatics, who take time which ought to be devoted to the discussion of the currency, the tariff, or the river and harbor bill. And yet year after year they have been obliged to take the time to discuss questions concerning the homes and lands and schools of native [*sic*] Americans. I believe that no part of the education of our lawmakers at Washington has been more wholesome and helpful to them or to the country than those discussions. If there is to come to us as a nation any good out of what seems to many a public calamity in the expansion of our rule over the islands of the sea, I believe it will be not so much because of our added commerce and increased wealth as because we shall be obliged to consider more and more what the relation of the wise ought to be toward the ignorant—what duties the civilized owe to the uncivilized. We shall be obliged to learn that we, who are strong, ought to bear the infirmities of the weak.

What has been gained.—What, then, has been gained by these years of struggle? A lifelong friend of the Indian took me aside in Boston the other day and said to me: "You know how some of us here in Boston have been exposed to the gibes and sneers of those who think that it is vain to try to uplift the Indian, and that there is no profit in all this work. Tell me, are you losing heart? How does it seem to you? Is it really worth while [*sic*]?" I am sure that all of you who are before me tonight feel that this work which you are doing is really worth while. You do not need to be told of the improved sentiment at Washington, or of the advance of appropriations for Indian schools from $20,000 in 1876 to $2,936,080 in 1899. Nor need I dwell upon the vast improvement there has been in honest dealing on the part of the government. Dr. Edward Everett Hale[35] once told at Mohonk[36] of an interview with Charles Sumner in Washington,[37] in the year 1865, when he said to him: "Look here, Sumner, you have got these colored people free, and there seems to be a chance that you will get an amendment to the constitution thru. Why don't you take care of the Indians now?" Dr. Hale said that he paused for a whole minute before replying, adding that it was the only time that he ever saw him look thoroly [*sic*] dejected. Then he said: "Hale, I don't think you know what you ask." I said I guessed I knew what I asked. "I don't think you do," he answered; "Hale, the whole Indian system in this country is so rotten that anybody who takes hold of it has to tear it all up from the roots and turn it all bottom-side up. There isn't a thing in it which is right, and everything has got to be torn up and planted over again before it will live." But, as Dr. Hale went on to say, it has been torn up by the roots, and things have been turned over and over again. What Charles Sumner said of the Indian service in 1865 could not be said with truth today. Altho [*sic*] there still remains much land to be possessed, altho our senators and representatives are not yet all saints, still there is an earnest endeavor on the part of the majority of them to give the Indian his rights. We have had at the head of the Indian Office for years men who have labored diligently and honestly for the uplifting of the Indian. The whole tone of the Indian service at Washington has undergone a change within the last thirty years for which we have reason to be thankful.

My opportunities for observation in the field have been limited compared with yours, but I have seen great improvement there also in the twenty years since I have had to do with Indian affairs. Tho it is still true that the agent is sometimes much more the agent of cattlemen, land-grabbers, and lumber trusts than of the Indian, and while it must be confessed that the rights of the Indian have been sacrificed to the supposed necessity of pushing war measures and expanding our territory, there is yet no reason to doubt that there has been, and still is, a great movement forward. There are many good agents in the field; our Indian inspectors are, for the most part, intelligent men, who have thoro knowledge of their work, and the superintendents and teachers of the Indian schools are a fine body of men and women. Here civil-service reform has had fair play, and most of these people have been chosen, not to pay political debts, nor thru the influence of senators or representatives, but because of their ability to teach and their interest in their work.

Progress has been made.—I believe it is fair to say that what we call the state has made progress in its Indian work. I wish that I could say as much for the church. It is not worth while to discuss here the oft-argued question of government aid for mission schools; I think there has been a distinct loss in power since such men as Bishop Whipple,[38] Dr. Strieby, and others went to Washington to advocate just measures of legislation.[39] They were an education to the church as well as to the state. I feel that the Indian cause needs the help of every possible influence for good, whether it comes thru Catholic priest or Protestant layman. I do not believe in the infallibility of the pope or of the General Assembly. The work of both needs inspection and supervision by the people; but I wish both might have every possible chance to work for the poor and ignorant of every race. It may have been wise to withdraw government aid from sectarian schools. It certainly was not wise for the churches to withdraw their help from the Indians, nor to feel that the government could do the work of the church. I am much more in sympathy with a Catholic who fights for appropriations and keeps up his own contributions than with a Protestant who gives up appropriations and withdraws his support. When, in response to the cry of separation of church and state, the Protestant churches gave up their government appropriations, there was a distinct promise on their part that private beneficence should take the place of government help; that the Indian should in no wise be neglected. The promise has not been kept. Just at the time when the Indian needed most the help of faithful Christian missionaries in the passage from barbarism to civilization, church aid was largely withdrawn.[40] The work of men such as Bishop Hare[41] and Bishop Whipple, the Riggses[42] and the Williamsons,[43] was much curtailed. The Unitarians gave up the work among the Crows; the Friends relinquished White Institute, where excellent work was done.[44] The failure on some reservations of the land-in-severalty bill was distinctly traceable to this cause.[45]

The wonderful progress of the last twenty years among the Indians is largely due to the work which the early missionaries performed. The Minnesota massacre of 1862, where 500 whites, with women and children, were slaughtered in retaliation for real or fancied wrongs, resulted in the defeat of 2,000 warriors, of whom thirty-nine were hanged and over three hundred held for three years in jail.[46] It was the beginning of the advance of the great Sioux nation. From the work of a few missionaries among those imprisoned men, who for the first time listened to the gospel, grew seven churches and an impulse which created among the Sioux universal respect for the representatives of Christianity and a confidence in their teaching which has gone far toward making possible their progress in later years. These Indians and their friends were all finally assigned to Devil's Lake, Sisseton, Santee, and Flandreau agencies, in Dakota, with plenty of land, but no food except what they could earn by their own labor. Fortunately, they were long kept under good and permanent agents, who saw that they were provided with seeds, implements, etc., and who wisely assisted them in cultivating and, in some cases, selling their land. The result is that they, 3,500 in number, are today self-supporting and the most progressive of all the Sioux. The eight hundred Santees, descendants of those who thirty-two years ago were condemned to death, and who were so hated by the whites of Minnesota that they threatened to hang the missionaries who taught them while in prison, are now homesteaded, Christianized American citizens and voters.

Give the Indian in general such treatment as this handful of desperate Sioux warriors received, and the trouble is over. The past century has been one of blundering rather than of dishonor, and from the first it has been a question of men rather than of measures.[47] Personal contact has been the mainspring of all Indian progress in this country. It is the secret of the wonderful success of Major Pratt, Rev. Dr. Williamson and his sons, and the Riggses of Dakota, of Archdeacon Kirby in British America,[48] of Mr. Duncan's great work in Alaska; and it is the vital point in all uplifting work.[49] The touch of the noble lives which are being spent in the service of the red man is better than any spoken word. The first step with the Indian is to gain his confidence; and no man, saint or sinner, who ever [sic] trusted an Indian has found his confidence misplaced. More than a hundred thousand Indians are today challenging American Christianity to do its best for them, and I am glad to say here that not a few of their own people have come to the front and are now holding the remoter outposts as teachers and catechists, setting such examples of decent living as make them leaders in progress and types of what all Indians with a fair chance may become. The Christian church should take no backward step.

Tribal system weakened.—Let me speak briefly of the improvement among the Indians in the matter of land, homes, and schools. Altho the land-in-severalty bill has not effected in some cases what was hoped for it, there is no doubt of the valuable results that have been brought about thru the allotment of land to individual Indians. The hold of the tribal system has been gradually weakened, and the rude shacks with their stacks of hay and grain make it clear, even to the superficial observer, that the Indian's roving days are over. Altho it is undoubtedly true that some of the reservations have been opened to the whites before the Indians were ready for it, and altho the onset of the lower element of whites upon the Indian lands has resulted, in many instances, in the demoralization of the Indian, yet it is only thru this hard process that he is to come to stronger manhood. There is no question that the giving up of the agent, the letting in of whiskey, the leasing of the Indians' land to the white man, have usually resulted in a temporary backward movement; yet even in the worst of these cases, among such tribes as the Omahas and the Winnebagoes, where drunkenness and licentiousness have held alarming sway, there is evidence of a consciousness on their part of their degraded condition and a reaching out toward better things. In the case of the Sioux Indians, where the agents have been retained while the allotment was going on, and where there was more help from missionaries, the change has come without such dreadful demoralization.

Occasionally visits to the agencies along the Missouri river have made clear the vast improvement that is going on. Twenty years ago citizens' clothing was the exception; now it is the rule. The coat has replaced the blanket, leggings are giving way to trousers, and the curious bond that comes from wearing the same style of garments is felt. It is like speaking the same language, and results at once in increased friendliness. Citizens of Pierre, Chamberlain, and other towns near the reservations, who are certainly not likely to be prejudiced in favor of their Indian neighbors, spoke to me of the changes for the better among the Indians in the last few years, especially of their civilized appearance, and of their straightforward business dealings. The vices of civilization, as represented by whiskey and gambling, stand always between the Indian and progress, but in spite of this the contact at Crow Creek, Lower Brule, and elsewhere with white settlers has been invaluable. The universal testimony is: "The more of it the better." There has been marked improvement in the quality of white frontiersmen. The "scum" of twenty years ago is giving place to a class of good citizens. The Indian can learn much from them, and they will, I believe, do him substantial good as they gradually surround him. Rough and careless at first they certainly are, but the better element soon takes hold. Courts are established, and there is a fair show all around.

Reservation life dying.—These changing conditions, however, have their dangers. Agents and thoughtful men are anxious. Reservation life is dead or dying. It must go. The time is ripe, not for destruction, however, but for development, and the old life, the old system, must be used only as a foundation for the new, and to this end ought to be carefully studied. Among the 15,000 Sioux the encampments are, for the most part, broken up, and the people settled chiefly on the river bottoms, where they can get wood and water. In certain parts of Dakota the Indians have covered the land as far as the eye can reach with farms of from one to thirty acres, all protected by wire fences, each with its log hut, and beside it one or two summer tepees, as graceful as the other is ugly and crude. Many of the farmers are shareholders in reaping machines, and I was much impressed by seeing a returned Hampton student driving a self-binder around his own wheat fields. Generally the men are in the fields, the women either with them or at work about the house. The old relation of brave and squaw is passing away before the influence of homestead life, just as the tepee must vanish before the mud-roofed log hut, which represents the first forward (if well-nigh fatal) step in civilization. Untidy and ill-ventilated as it is, it fixes its owner, putting an end to his nomadic life, making possible the use of chairs, tables, and dishes, and the development of a home attachment. The fact that these houses have but one room is not so dangerous to morality as one would suppose, but only because the Indian is not grossly sensuous. Christian teaching is, of course, on the side of soap and water, and it is curious to notice how largely the use of these articles is affected by the proximity of church and schoolhouse. A missionary visitor demands and is acknowledged to have a right to a chair, a bed, clean dishes, and soap and towels.

What remains to be done.—What are the things that remain to be accomplished? In the first place, it is important to remember that in dealing with these Indians we are dealing with people of very various degrees of development, and methods of work which are applicable to one tribe are not at all applicable to others. This has been especially true of the land-in-severalty bill. While no one can doubt the value of this bill, it is very doubtful whether all tribes are equally ready to take their own part in life's struggle. Instead of making them independent, it has, in some cases, really made them paupers. Not only ought regard to be had to the progress of the Indian, but to the condition of the country in which he lives.

As Mr. Grinnell says in his recent book, *The Indians of Today*: "To force allotments on a tribe living in a region where the average yearly rainfall is only a foot or fifteen inches may be a real hardship, even though on the pretense that the acres given them are grazing lands. Each receives twice as much as if it were farming land. In a very large number of cases these so-called grazing lands produce nothing, not even enough vegetation to keep a single cow. Sometimes they are without water, even without access to water."[50] To insist that the Indians become self-supporting on such land is to ask what is impossible. Mr. Grinnell instances the Oneida Indians as showing how the Allotment Act, when applied to a race that has had contact with whites for three hundred years, is most helpful, while in the case of the Apaches, who speak only their own tongue and inhabit a desert, it is disastrous. How harmful the allotment bill has been in certain cases as regards the introduction of liquor, the failure of the parents to send their children to school, and in the matter of idleness, resulting from the leasing of land, we all know. We are obliged to remember that the Indians are, for the most part, children; that they have the weaknesses of children; and that, while we are to help them toward manhood as rapidly as possible, they will not attain to it in a day, nor in a single generation. While wisdom must be shown in the passage from barbarism to civilization, it is important that both agents and Indians understand that the reservation is a temporary expedient; that, while it may be necessary for those who are unable to care for themselves, the government and all who have to do with its schools are striving to fit the young Indians for the fuller, freer life of citizenship. In order to do this, discontent with the reservation system must be produced. It is sometimes said of the schools off the reservation that when their students return they are not willing to live as their parents did. It is much to be hoped that their school life will bring about just this result. If school life, either in the East or in the West, makes students unwilling to meet the difficulties of the situation, it is opened to criticism, but a wholesome discontent is a most hopeful sign.

A good sign.—The petition of the Lower Brule Sioux, asking that their annuity of rations and clothing be stopped, and that they be allowed to sell a portion of their land and purchase cattle with the proceeds, is a move in the right direction.[51] The sooner the ration system can be stopped the better. No student goes back from school who does not feel the degradation of it. While the beef-killing, with its brutalizing influence, has been discontinued on some of the reservations, on others it still remains, and the biweekly pilgrimage from the distant parts of the reservation to the agency still continues. By this means regular work on the farm and the raising of crops and of animals is prevented, while the old roving habit, which is so opposed to all progress in civilization, is cultivated.

In spite of all that has been done toward the education of the Indian, it is estimated that only about one-half of the Indian youths of school age are receiving instruction. This is a poor showing. There ought to be school accommodation for every Indian child. The sooner we come to compulsory education for every child in this country the better. To give citizenship to people without requiring their education is the greatest unwisdom. The system of day schools so successfully started and carried on by Major Wright on the Pine Ridge reservation and by others in the Indian country, which makes the school the center for improvement in home life and agriculture, and gives the agent a hold on Indian families in remote parts of the reservation, is of the greatest value.*[52] More use ought to be made of the common day school in the uplifting of the community. The introduction of cooking and sewing, as well as some simple lessons in harvesting and the use of garden tools, together with instruction in the common English branches, would make these schools a great power for good on the reservation.

The reservation boarding schools, with their gardens and farms, are most useful. Just as far as possible there ought to be built up about these schools mills for the grinding of wheat and small manufactories for the construction of articles used on the reservations, where the Indians may become familiar with the usages of civilized life. It is a shame that so large a part of the Indians' supplies should be bought elsewhere, when the Indians need so much the training and the work which might be used in their production. The non-reservation schools, both eastern and western, ought to have close relations with one another and with the reservation schools. They ought to develop certain special lines of work and instruction that the Indians need. If one devote [*sic*] itself to agriculture especially, then another could make a specialty of business methods, others of certain trades, and still others of normal training. Instead of struggling with one another for pupils, as has sometimes happened, they should be thoroly [*sic*] in harmony with one another. Each of these schools ought to be a sort of experiment station in Indian education, demonstrating what can be done along special lines. We are all indebted to Major Pratt for the success which has attended the pushing of the outing system.[53] Each Indian institution, in addition to the regular work which it has to do, should try to develop some specialty, which should be of value to all. As a rule, it seems to me that we in the East ought to do advanced work, admitting only those who have passed thru the western schools, and not competing for a lower grade of pupils. Coming east ought to be considered a reward of merit for good work in western institutions.

Many difficulties.—I have been impressed with the difficulties under which the heads of government Indian schools have labored because of their inability to control the appointment of their subordinates. As long as teachers are appointed in Washington and the head of the school has little or no voice in the matter, so long will the schools lack harmony. No superintendent can really be held responsible for the management of his school until he has a controlling influence. We all believe in the reform brought about by the civil service in the taking out from the hands of politicians the appointments of superintendents and teachers. But if civil-service reform rules stand in the way of the appointment of teachers by the head of a school, they should be modified to correct this abuse.[54]

The main object of the education of the Indian should be to make him self-supporting, and, as Mr. Grinnell says: "An aim quite as important as this, indeed included in it, is to make the Indians less unlike us than they are. They exist as an element of our population; they are Americans, and they should be put in a position to develop into a constituent part of our new race, just as the immigrants from a dozen foreign lands have developed into good, useful citizens of these United States." These two problems—as to how the Indian can be made self-supporting and thus gain the self-respect and independence which are impossible without it, and how he can be made one with the white race of the land—should be continually before the mind of every Indian worker. We ought to rejoice in the coming of the railroad, of trade, of every influence that helps to make the Indian one of us. While each race has its own peculiarities, and while, as Mr. Leupp, in a recent article in the *Southern Workman*, declares, it is "improvement, not transformation," of the Indian that is needed; while we are to realize that the Indian can never be an Anglo-Saxon; while we are to develop the noble qualities which the Indian possesses, we must also realize that it is not good for any individual or race to be alone.[55]

In closing I wish to extend my congratulations to those who are laboring for the advancement of the Indian because of the success that has attended their efforts. I believe with Bishop Whipple that Indian workers are the best-paid workers in the world, and that no missionary work promises swifter or more satisfactory returns than that among the red men of this land.

# 3

# The Proper Relation between Literary and Industrial Education in Indian Schools

A. J. STANDING, *Assistant Superintendent, Carlisle Indian Industrial School, Carlisle, Pennsylvania*

**Source:** *NEA Proceedings*, 1900, 692–95, contains an abstract of Standing's paper; Carlisle's school paper, the *Red Man and Helper* 16, no. 5 (July 20, 1900): 1, 4, published it "almost in full." The latter version is included here.

Alfred John Standing (1847–1908), an English immigrant, helped establish the Carlisle Indian Industrial School at the invitation of Richard Pratt. The two became acquainted during their contemporaneous service at Fort Sill, Oklahoma, in the early 1870s. By the late 1870s, when Pratt began his educational work with the Native prisoners at Fort Marion, Florida, Standing ran an agency school at Fort Sill. Standing then left the Indian service and began farming in Kansas, but shortly returned to Indian education as Carlisle's assistant superintendent, a position he held for twenty years. In that position he supervised all the "industrial work at the school." Standing resigned from his position with the Indian school about the time this paper was presented. He later became superintendent of grounds and buildings at Dickinson College, also at Carlisle. Professor Oscar H. Bakeless, a Carlisle colleague, read his paper to the gathered Indian school educators at Charleston.[56]

In his paper Standing highlights the major issue about which there was agreement between the old guard assimilationists and the new progressive movement represented by Reel—that is, industrial and agricultural education offered the only hope for American Indians to become "self-supporting." Educators believed, as Standing stated, that there would be far more manual workers coming from Indian schools than professional folk. Therefore, the focus for Indian education for both these camps was making laborers of their students. Recent scholarship has demonstrated, however, that, rather than becoming a force for assimilation, students and their communities used such labor for "American Indian adaptability and perseverance."[57]

THE OBJECT OF A SCHOOL is to educate. The purpose of education is primarily to qualify for self-support, and the general work and business of life in all ways. To accomplish this in the quickest and best manner possible, special schools are organized, as the Business School, Law School, Medical School, Trade School, etc., etc.

Where special classes are to be educated, as the blind, the deaf, the feeble minded or the criminally inclined, we have schools so organized and conducted as to meet the special and direct needs of of [sic] the class concerned.

Therefore, while the Indians cannot be considered as coming under any of the heads previously mentioned, they yet present unusual conditions and the schools for them need to be organized so as to meet the special conditions they present.

The Indians of to-day [sic] being for the most part only about one generation removed from the nomadic state, and having had to undergo within this brief period a complete change in mode of life, have no accumulated knowledge of the requirements of civilized life, or how to obtain a living in any of the great variety of avenues that present themselves to the white boy or girl, whose parents for generations perhaps have followed some special avocation with which the children of the family from their earliest years become familiar and when old enough engage in for the purpose of self-support, are at a peculiar disadvantage in the struggle for bread and home, except in so far as they have been and now are cared for by the Government. This special care, however, is intended, and properly so, to be but temporary, and the Government has for many years been following various plans, intending to lead the Indian to self-support and independence, so ending the need for the special care and guardianship that is now assumed to be necessary.

**Made Slow Progress at First**

Wonderfully handicapped by a multiplicity of tongues and a life generally beyond the limit of settlement and consequent teaching by observation, the Indian made but slow progress in the way the Government desired he should go, until the day of Indian Schools was inaugurated. The early results obtained in these schools seemed so full of promise for the future, that education in schools has become the main policy and hope of the nation for Indian Civilization.

The conditions presented by the In[d]ians of to-day which call for a special class of schools for them, are that nearly all of those who attend will, in the battle of life have to support themselves by manual labor of some kind. A very large proportion also have had nothing in the shape of home training, while all must be instructed in the English language to such an extent that it shall be their language for the future; so learned as never to be forgotten.

**Great Educator, but More Needed**

The American District School with the American home is a great educator; but without the supplementary teaching of the civilized Christian home its work becomes necessarily very imperfect. It is easy to see, therefore, that the needs of the Indian are not met by the ordinary district school; nor by the ordinary Boarding School or Academy; that to civilize, educate and train the Indian industrially something more than either of these is needed. The effort to meet this need has evolved the system of Indian schools as they now exist comprising all grades from the reservation Day School to the most complete of the system as represented by the manifold interests and pursuits of Carlisle.

The experience so far gained has shown that self-support, the prime object of Indian Schools, has been attained, in the proportion in which they properly combine industrial training with literary education. The latter [,] while desirable for all, will furnish bread to the few only, but the competent laborer, male or female, is in a position of comparative independence on the question of subsistence.

**The Aim**

The aim then, of Indian education should be that during the receptive and formative period of life every young Indian should receive such industrial training as will place him clearly beyond the ranks of the incapable; among the competent working and producing class.

To do this, rational Industrial Education is a necessity, and so much of the school period of life as may be needed, should be devoted to its attainment. Any Indian school of whatever class that fails to give this, or makes it a secondary consideration is failing of its chief end and object.

Industrial Education does not mean and should not involve mere drudgery; to make it do so will beget an antipathy to the very thing we desire to foster and encourage. Care should be taken everywhere and at all times to honor the worker of whatever degree, and by no means allow the idea to enter that a farmer or mechanic is not as worthy of respect as a teacher or clerk.

My experience with the administration of Indian Schools has been, that vastly more thought and attention has been bestowed on the literary course of study to be pursued—which publishers' text books [*sic*] shall be used; and what particular method of writing shall be taught—than upon the industrial education that can and should be given to every Indian child of suitable physique.

### Industrial Departments Should be Well Organized

I would like to see the force and equipment for teaching the various industrial occupations in Indian Schools, as well organized and as complete as now is the case with the department of the school-room [*sic*] proper.

This should embrace all the household occupations of the school, which should be so conducted as not at all to convey the idea that the time so spent was not just as profitably spent as in the school-room.

The same general idea should be carried to all the out-door [*sic*] interests and occupations of the school, the farm, the stock, the trades. Give them an equal place with the school-room, not a secondary one, and how much more popular such interest would become! It is the nature *of the young to enjoy physical effort*, so that it does not become drudgery.

Were these ideas to be adopted and officially promulgated as the basis on which the Indian Schools were to be conducted there would appear at once a number of reasons why the plan was not applicable to this or that school. I will admit that in practice education in industries is not applicable to all schools alike; but the principle is, and that of itself is vastly important. There are, however, but few schools where some really good practical work cannot be done along some productive line, selected as the specialty of the school by reason of its location or condition, as gardening, fruit culture, and farming, on such a moderate scale that it shall be thoroughly instructive, as well as productive of corn and potatoes. Take the time for it. In season dismiss the school if necessary. The first need of our nature is life, the second to make a living, and other things in their order.

I do not wish to be understood as recommending an attempt to carry on a multiplicity of industries such as Carlisle and some other large schools have in operation, into places where they would be out of place, but in every school large or small, to plant the idea that those who have ability to produce with their hands the necessaries of life are as worthy, as honorable, and as successful, as those who do the same thing by their ability to teach, or knowledge in other directions.

### The Prime Need

The prime need in industrial education is intelligent agriculture, which includes also gardening and fruit culture, dairying, care of stock, etc. We have the promise of the One who changes not, "That so long as the world endures, seed time and harvest shall not fail."[58] Here then is supplied the prime necessity of life, the means to live.

It is not my purpose to particularize as to methods by which industrial education should be pursued in Indian Schools, but to urge that it be given its rightful place and consideration, that as much care, thought, and talent, be expended on the proper industrial equipment and methods as is now the case on the school-room work and appliance.

But few amongst the Indians now in school will be able to live by their literary attainments exclusively; the many will depend on their hands, therefore let the main effort be in the direction that is going to be the greatest good to the greatest number, not by any means to the exclusion of culture in other ways, but giving equal opportunity in both directions so that individual capacity may develop in whatever direction it is best qualified for, finding equal opportunities in either.

I also make the assertion that the competent manual worker will be more likely to develop into an independent self-supporting person, than the one who is teaching or clerking for a living, depending on the pleasure or needs of others for the salary on which he or she lives.

A bushel of wheat or corn has its cash value, so has fat stock, the shoeing of a horse, the building of a house, or skilled labor in any direction and the Indian who has grain or stock to sell, or skill in the occupations mentioned will not be apt to want for bread.

### An Incident

I offer just one incident in illustration of my position. It is an axiom of Carlisle school that every pupil must have some practice in agricultural pursuits. This is obtained in part on the school farms but mainly under the Outing System.

A boy who had been several years at school returned to his home. His father and neighbors had bought a self-binding reaper. The agent was to come on a certain day and set the machine up and show the Indians how to work it.

He did not come.

The boy having used a similar machine during his school life at Carlisle put this one together and cut the crop.

The agent came, asked who had done the work. The Indian told him his son had set up the reaper and started it.

"Well," said the agent, "I am paying men $4.00 a day for just that work, and would as soon pay your son as any body [*sic*]."

**Soon Will be Able to Cope**

Let us therefore give the chief place in our Indian Schools to those pursuits, which will give to the many the manual skill and ability needed for self-support; which will be in about the proportion of 99 manual workers to one lawyer or doctor.

It requires no gift of prophecy to foretell that if such a policy in Indian education be adopted and continued, combined with the Carlisle Outing System, the day is not far distant when the Government could justly say to the Indian:

You are no longer incompetents; you are able; you are skilled; you have the opportunity, henceforth make your own living, take care of yourselves! The duties of national guardianship have been performed; such care is no longer necessary for you. You are citizens of the Republic. Enjoy your liberty, your homes, your property! Vote, hold office, do your best, and Uncle Sam will be proud of his Red children.

# 4

The Training of Teachers for Indian Schools

CHARLES BARTLETT DYKE, *Director of the Normal Department, Hampton Normal and Agricultural Institute, Hampton, Virginia*

Source: *NEA Proceedings*, 1900, 696–98, contains an abstract of Dyke's paper; RSIS, 1900, 43–45, contains his paper. The latter version is reprinted here.

Charles Bartlett Dyke (1870–1945) from Ohio, demonstrated wanderlust early in his educational life when he received degrees from Stanford University (1897) and Columbia University (1899). In between the two, he spent a year on the faculty at the State Normal School, Mankato, Minnesota. After Columbia he spent one year at Hampton Institute, when he delivered the following paper.[59] The next four years found him as the first principal of the consolidated Kamehameha Schools, Hawai'i, which served, and continues to serve, students of Hawai'ian ancestry.[60] Dyke left Hawai'i in 1904 due to health issues, then in 1905 moved to Boulder, Colorado, where he held positions in the local school district and the University of Colorado.[61] In 1911 he resigned over a disagreement with the school board and moved to Youngstown, Ohio, becoming principal of South High School.[62] A local woman's club there pushed for an investigation into his conduct "after many unwholesome stories concerning [him] were circulated."[63] The superintendent exonerated Dyke and moved to fire the women teachers who had "induced the students to take issue with the high school head" over allegations of "his alleged ill treatment of women teachers."[64] In 1915 Dyke alighted at Millburn, New Jersey, where he served as superintendent of schools until 1937—a remarkable twenty-two years, given his employment history prior to Millburn.[65]

Dyke gave two papers to the NEA Department of Indian Education: the one that follows, given at the department's inaugural meeting in 1900, and another in 1909, its last meeting. His papers and accounts of his work demonstrate his conviction in the lack of intellectual capacity of students of color—any color. When he became principal at Kamehameha Schools, for example, he deemphasized academic training and established industrial and agricultural training for the Native Hawai'ian students. In his first annual report he noted, "The aim of our [new] course of study is to give high ideals in morals, in social relations and in religion, to encourage a wholesome yet simple standard of living, and to equip students with sufficient technical skill to enable them by industry to supply all things necessary to happy homes." In his second annual report, Dyke lauded the success of his course of study because "this advanced manual work testifies to the natural ability of Hawaiian boys in manual pursuits."[66] Dyke clearly reflected the larger movement in Indian education that relegated colonized students to "practical" studies. As will be seen in his paper, he also, quite matter-of-factly, epitomized the uberscientific racism of his time.

THE TEACHER IS THE MAKER and protector of our American civilization, and with him rests the future of the American Indian, and in common with all other teachers, he must possess the spirit of service. All else falls into insignificance compared with this first essential. This spirit of service can not be a general diffused, vague sort of thing. It must be a definite, concrete devotion to the uplifting of a race.

It is through wise religious training, through constant suggestion, through the inspiration of the ideals already attained by returned students that these natural impulses are to be converted into a sustained spirit of service.

Fellowship with the world.—Not until a white man has seen something of the inner life of other races does he realize the vastness of his birthright, his manners, his personal habits, his food and clothing, his intellectual and spiritual attitudes, his likes and dislikes, his hopes and ideals, all his inheritance from civilization, all necessary to the maintenance of civilization. What he is born into, the Indian child must acquire if he is to survive on the face of the earth. The teachers of Indian children must, then, feel their fellowship with all humanity.

We constantly hear of the folly of attempting to make an Indian into a white man, and there is truth in the assertion. The Indian must live in and become a part of the white man's civilization. The general atmosphere of civilization breathed into the life of the Indian for generations must conduce to this fellowship with the world, but more important is the conscious training given through certain subjects of study. Especially is this true of every kind of trade work. The ability to supply to the public what the public needs establishes a bond of sympathy, and the Indian wheelwright or mason or electrician becomes an integral part of humanity with the satisfaction of humanity's wants, while the Indian girl rises into a new sphere of life with her successful production of the food and clothing of civilization.

The Hon. William T. Harris emphasizes the necessity of language as that instrument which makes possible human social organization.[67] "The most practical knowledge of all, it will be admitted, is a knowledge of human nature—a knowledge that enables one to combine with his fellow men and to share with them the physical and spiritual wealth of the race."[68]

Again, the Indian teacher should go into his work with some absorbing interest of his own—some hobby, some fad, if you will—for the inspiration of a teacher is his own interest. It may be the fossils of the plains, the flowers or birds of the mountains. It may be Sunday schools, or raising horses, or making roads. But no school life should come to a close before some intense personal interest is aroused.

The lack of professional training I regard as the greatest weakness among Indian teachers. If the teacher of white children needs to know the principles and aims of education, how much more does the Indian teacher need to know them, he who is to enter upon a much more difficult work.

But the professional training of the Indian teacher should include more than a knowledge of the principles and aims of education. You and I are born with an economic sense. That sense of money making, of getting on in the world has found deep root in all Americans. The Indian is without this economic sense. He must be taught to seize upon existing conditions and to use them to his own advantage. The Indian teacher must be the center of economic and social progress.

Practice teaching.—Under careful supervision with a maximum of responsibility. I wish to place the emphasis on these two words: Careful supervision and responsibility.

In the judgment of the committee on normal schools at the Los Angeles meeting last year, practice teaching under careful supervision ranks as the most valuable course in the professional training of teachers. While actual teaching contributes much to the theory of education, it also gives training in the application of knowledge. It is usually more difficult to apply knowledge than it is to acquire it; but, since practice in teaching does both, it is an especially valuable line of work. To assume the responsibility of a schoolroom is a powerful force in the development of a teacher. Familiarity with programmes [*sic*], with good text-books [*sic*], and with all the minor details of the schoolroom, are no slight aid; but responsibility transforms the careless, impertinent, sullen, impatient student into the careful, self-controlled teacher.

One of our Indian girls last year, who was notorious for her sulkiness, met her Waterloo in the practice room, where she was obliged to deal with her exact facsimile. What should she do with Susie? If Susie made a mistake she would just stand still and look as if she did not hear or see anybody in the world. The foresight and quick encouragement, the determined will necessary in dealing with Susie, the delight of success, actually changed this girl's entire demeanor, and the responsibility thrown upon her developed an undreamed-of strength, which will make her a most valuable teacher of her race.

But let us not think for a moment that practice teaching alone is sufficient. Practice teaching establishes right habits of the teaching art, but any plan of training which is founded on habit alone partakes of the merits and of the defects of the apprentice system. The apprentice becomes skilled in his art, but is apt to lose the power of personal initiative. Leaders in education as in any other sphere of human activity must have right habits of work, but they must also be masters of themselves and capable of directing their own powers at will. This is to be attained only through a knowledge of the principles of society and education.

In my opinion the function of the teacher of Indian schools is one on which the very lives of his pupils depend. It is the substitution of civilization for barbarism. That teacher alone can effect this work who goes into it with a spirit of service, with a conscious substitution of the ideals of civilizations for those of barbarism. This demands wisely chosen subject-matter [*sic*], a knowledge of society, and of the laws of mind. It demands enthusiasm guided by the principles of psychology and sociology, and it involves the application of these principles under supervision. Teachers with this training will bring their people into a fellowship with the civilized world, and the Indian will thus become a valuable American citizen.

# 5 | Teaching Trades to Indians

FRANK K. ROGERS, *Director, Armstrong-Slater Memorial Trade School, Hampton Normal and Agricultural Institute, Hampton, Virginia*

SOURCE: NEA *Proceedings*, 1900, 698–701, contains an abstract of Rogers's paper; RSIS, 1900, 41–42, contains his paper. The latter version is reprinted here.

Frank Knight Rogers (1864?–1938) came to Hampton in 1897 at the invitation of Frissell, Hampton's principal, to organize the trade school of that institution and become its first director. The organization of the trade school and Rogers's appointment to it reflected Frissell's shift beginning in 1893 from Hampton founder Armstrong's emphasis, in priority order, "on education of the head (academic), hand (industrial training), and the heart (Christian training and character building)" to a new priority of "the hand (industrial trades and manual training), head (academic), and heart (Christian training and character building)."[69] Rogers's appointment and his new school at Hampton confirmed the ascendency of the idea of practical studies for Blacks and Natives over academic training, a tenet that Reel wholeheartedly embraced.

While in his position as director of Hampton's trade school, Rogers delivered two papers to the NEA Department of Indian Education: this paper during that department's inaugural meeting, and a second presentation the next year. In 1905 he became assistant treasurer for the school and in 1908 assumed the position as Hampton's treasurer, an office he held until his retirement in 1932. He then moved to Essex, Connecticut, where he died in July 1938.[70]

MY FIRST EXPERIENCE WITH INDIANS was in the late summer of 1897, when I met a score or more who had just arrived at Hampton Institute. These were almost the first Indians I had ever seen outside the Wild West shows and the Kickapoo medicine troop.[71] When these Indians arrived at Hampton and passed the porch where I was standing with my little girl, she exclaimed, "Why, where are their feathers, papa?"

This remark set me to thinking that my work was soon to begin with these boys and that there were grave problems before me to grapple with. Here were boys, some of whom were not more than once removed from barbarism, who had been transported from 1,500 to 2,000 miles so that they might complete and supplement their earlier school work by industrial training at Hampton.

The question, Has the Indian the mental capacity for the complicated problems associated with the trades? has been solved to my entire satisfaction in the affirmative. I have reached the point, too, where I feel that genius should be recognized in Indian or white, and that diverting an Indian from his natural bent is not to be done without serious consideration and especially good reasons.[72]

An interesting instance connected with this thought comes to my mind. A young Papago arrived at Hampton a year ago, and when questioned as to what he wanted to do there surprised us by saying he wished to learn the machinist's trade. This for a Papago seemed so incongruous that we questioned him pretty thoroughly, thinking his desire might be only a passing one, which had been aroused, perhaps, by visiting the machine shop before being questioned by us. However, he stood persistently by his first choice, saying that in some parts of his country there were silver mines and he had seen some of the mining machinery and he knew they sometimes needed men to set up such and run it. He thought he could find good employment at least as a helper. He was allowed to spend two days a week in the machine shop, and has shown that he has the necessary qualification for a very good machinist and is anxious to keep on. The machinist's trade is one which can be grasped only by one of considerable mental ability, and he must have much good judgment in tracing out cause and effect. It seems to me that what this particular boy must have in order to be most useful is not so much to be able to do the delicate hand work necessary to building machinery as to be able to size up the general assemblage of parts, to know how things go together, and how to repair broken pieces.

Except in a few cases, Hampton does not believe in the machinist's trade for Indians, but rather emphasizes those industries which may be of use in smaller communities and that relate more directly to their own home life—as, for instance, housebuilding, wheelwrighting, blacksmithing, shoe and harness making. We feel, more and more, too, that in many cases a part of several trades is more beneficial. Thus housebuilding should have as a foundation carpentry, but allied with it should be some knowledge of painting, plastering, bricklaying, and enough tinsmithing to be able to do flashing, gutter and spout work.

Wheelwrighting, blacksmithing, and a little painting would go well together, and shoe and harness making are also closely connected. With all of these trades there should be incorporated as much of agriculture as it is possible to give. Blacksmithing seems to be as popular a trade as any, and one in which the Indian seems to excel. It is considerable of a revelation to see one toiling away, blowing his own fire and striking the red-hot iron, with the perspiration rolling from his head in streams.

The Indian boy does very well in mechanical drawing, which should be taught in connection with all trades when the expression of one's work can be planned on paper. For instance, such trades as machinist, carpentry, wheelwrighting, and bricklaying should have mechanical drawing, but printing would not especially need it. Painters, tailors, shoe and harness makers should have free-hand drawing.

The one thing more than all others to be considered in teaching a trade to Indians is power of adaptability. Teaching a full trade for the sake of its industrial value alone does not appeal to many people who know the Indian's home life and the difficulty he will have among his own people of making a livelihood. In most cases, it seems to me, the trade, after all, is only of secondary importance, and the real thing to be gained is the feeling of power which comes with the accomplishment of any difficult task. Let us look for a minute at the blacksmith's trade for the Indian. (I have mentioned before in this paper that it is as popular as any we teach.)

I do not feel that the utilitarian accomplishments of bending, upsetting, and welding, while they are of inestimable value, are the only good things the boy has gotten out of the practice at the forge, but that along with all these processes in the thousand and one modifications and applications comes a mental stimulus, a power of concentration and adaptability, which leads to healthier activities and growth. The same thing is true of any trade or occupation, but as the boy's own inclination and love for a particular kind of skill must be acknowledged to a certain extent in the selection of a handicraft for him, it follows that there will be a general diversity of trades among the boys from any reservation.

Character building is, after all, the keynote in any kind of education. It may seem to be entirely submerged at times, but be it classical or industrial, the outcome is not a mere bunch of facts gleaned from the fields of literature and labor, but along with such a whole world of power and possibility. Many times to all of us has come the now stereotyped expression that the Indian's education is all a mistake and that it simply upsets him and in the end makes less of a man of him than he would have been had he grown up in the old way. This may be true in some instances and it may seem true in many more, taking the present time into consideration, but the thing to be considered is that this is after all only the seed time; the harvest is not yet, though I think a few at least begin to see signs of its approach.

If I thought we were making carpenters, blacksmiths, and wheelwrights of the Indians, and that they got out of the trades only the cold, hard facts which provided a means of a livelihood, I should feel that we were doing a progressive work. What I do believe is that the power that comes with reading and writing, welding and planing, cooking and sewing, is upbuilding to any race, causing it to grow until its influence is felt as a factor in the common good of mankind. In these days the lack of such power will surely send a race to the wall.

# 6 The Training of the Indian Girl as the Uplifter of the Home

JOSEPHINE E. RICHARDS, *Head of the Indian Department,*
*Hampton Normal and Agricultural Institute, Hampton, Virginia*

**Source:** NEA *Proceedings*, 1900, 701–5; another version of this paper is found in
the *Southern Workman* 29 (September 1900): 507–10. Included here is the NEA
version but it has sentences and phrases from the *Southern Workman* version that
were not included in the NEA *Proceedings*. Additions from the *Southern Workman*
are underscored.

Born in Massachusetts but raised in Connecticut, Josephine Ellis Richards
(1847–1918), daughter of a Congregational minister, planned early in her life
"to go as a missionary to some foreign land."[73] Instead her missionary zeal
brought her in 1881 to Hampton Institute, where she began her career as a
teacher of Native students and the eventual head of the Indian Department.[74]
This change in her humanitarian crusade may have been brought about by
Helen Hunt Jackson's *Century of Dishonor*, published that same year. *The
Indian's Friend* editor, in eulogizing her, noted that "Miss Richards was
among the chosen few who were moved to service" by Jackson's work.[75] She
left Hampton circa 1900, and thereafter with her sister Anna made "usual
winter visit[s]" to the institute.[76] On December 1, 1918, during one of those
annual visits, Richards died at Hampton.[77] Her necrologist reported, "She
lost no opportunity to enlist sympathy and friends for the Indians, and in
her death they have lost a most faithful friend and advocate."[78] Upon her
death relatives and friends established the Josephine E. Richards Memorial
Book Fund "to be spent by the Library for books and pictures relating to
the American Indians."[79]

Richards's promotion of the female gender role in "uplifting" her students'
home communities was consistent with the contemporary prevailing idea
of the women's role in the social evolutionary process, although it certainly
flies in the face of the traditional role of most of those students.[80] While

any generalizations about the role of women across hundreds of tribal communities would be fraught with errors, Richards's goal, as will be seen through the papers of many Indian school educators, was to inculcate young women with white gender roles of Eastern seaboard haute bourgeois communities. The domestic educational goals of such educators would have likewise seemed alien to white women living in sod houses on America's frontiers.

MISS ALICE FLETCHER ONCE TOLD of a visit she paid to Sitting Bull, and the plea he made, in view of the changed conditions, for the women of his race.

"Take pity on my women," said he, "for they have no future. The young men can be like the white men—till the soil, supply the food and clothing; they will take the work out of the hands of the women, and the women, to whom we have owed everything in the past, will be stripped of all which gave them power and position among the people. Give a future to my women."

We are surely working along the line of the old chief's appeal when we consider how the Indian woman, as she ceases to set up the tepee, can become the true uplifter of the home.

Let us consider some of the crying needs of the Indian home of the present day, and also the training which will best fit the Indian girls in our schools to meet those needs.

Let us note first the lack of system in the domestic arrangement of the household, the need of promptness and orderliness, not only of "a place for everything and everything in its place" but of a time for everything and everything done on time. I think those of us who have firm faith in many native virtues of the Indian would yet hesitate to claim punctuality and dispatch as among them. The reason may not be far to seek; for, after all, one does not have to go back a very long way in his history to get quite beyond clocks and bells, and all the civilized appliances for keeping the Anglo-Saxon "up to the minute," and enabling a great community of busy workers to act in unison. But what a transformation it would effect in the hogan of the Southwest and the shack of the Northwest, not to mention certain framed houses of some of the more well-to-do, if there were regular hours, and those early ones, for rising and retiring; if meals were prepared and cleared away at set times; if beds were put in order the first thing in the morning; if Monday were washing day, Tuesday ironing day, and so on thru the weekly calendar of a thrifty household! Illustrative of the axiom that "order is heaven's first law," I recall an address of Bishop Hare's to a company of Indian students, in which he drew a most practical lesson from the command to the disciples to make the multitude sit down by hundreds and fifties, as he carried the principle even into the cabin cupboards and charged the girls to see that the dishes there were arranged in orderly fashion—plates in one pile, saucers in another.

Most closely linked to orderliness is cleanliness. We remember reading a graphic and appalling description of the minutiæ of house-cleaning operations by a young Indian field matron and her assistant in a neighboring cabin, where the cellar for keeping supplies was a hole under one of the beds, and where other things were on a similar plane of untidiness. A recent letter from the teacher of a camp school speaks of her little pupils as "so bright, quick, ambitious to learn, but oh! so dirty." A running stream furnishes a bath-tub [*sic*] in summer, but in winter a bath is an unheard-of luxury, and a change of clothes once a week or once a month is <u>usually</u> not to be thought of. It is quite true that on many reservations a crusade against dirt must be waged against great odds, even by the most willinghearted. The scarcity of water, the clouds of prairie dust, the stream of unkempt visitors, the constant presence of four-footed hangers-on—these are anything but helpful to the young housekeeper. In some favored sections these difficulties do not exist; in not a few instances they are bravely overcome; but the question is an intensely practical one: What sort of training will best prepare our girls to fight these obstacles in their own homes, or in the homes of Indians among whom they may be working?

It is not enough to teach these girls how to sweep and scrub and wash and iron; we must strive so to get them in the habit of being neat in person and surroundings that they really cannot be comfortable otherwise. Perhaps nothing does this more effectually than the "outing system," when the home to which the pupil is sent is of the right sort. The living week after week in a quiet, refined, well-ordered household is of inestimable value in fostering a "noble discontent" with dirt and disorder.

In addition to this we have found a housekeeping cottage to be a very helpful adjunct to the training in dormitories, cooking classes, laundry, etc., during the school year. A member of the faculty was accompanied on a trip to the West one summer by a friend. The latter, struck with the dearth of cooking utensils in the log cabins they visited, remarked: "Why don't you build a cottage at Hampton, put into it a stove, kettle, frying-pan, one or two spoons, and a very few dishes, and teach the girls to keep house with only such appliances?" The suggestion was acted upon. A tiny, three-roomed cottage (built when we brought on married couples) was fitted up for classes in housekeeping.[81] Its equipment was somewhat more ample than the above, but there was no patent egg-beater [*sic*], there was not even a rolling-pin until an Indian boy made one in the shop. The screen in the little parlor was the handiwork of a girl who had learned to use tools, and the lounge was a small iron bedstead, with mattress and cushions covered with blue denim. Four days in the week a squad of three girls went out to the cottage with the lady in charge, after school, and prepared their evening meal. Milk and flour were furnished them; also fifty cents a week, afterwards increased to sixty, with which other supplies were purchased. Careful forethought and economy were thus cultivated. The menus were written down in a blank book, and accounts were strictly kept. The girls learned to make bread and biscuit, and to prepare many simple dishes, sometimes even to make their own butter. They were taught to utilize odds and ends, also how to scrimp a little here if they wished to launch out there. The table was neatly spread with a white table-cloth [*sic*] and napkins, and sometimes decorated with flowers. Once a week the custom was to invite another teacher to take tea with them, and then one girl must act as hostess and another do the necessary waiting. The whole spirit of the thing was wonderfully suggestive of a little bit of home set down in the midst of the great school. When Mrs. Dorchester, wife of the then superintendent of Indian schools, visited Hampton, she gave her cordial approval of the scheme.[82] It seemed that she had felt the need of something similar in the western schools, and had pleaded for a small house adjoining the main buildings, where the girls could be so trained. Now, she said, she felt she could urge it the more strongly, since she had actually seen her "model cottage." This work has now been merged in that of the Abby May Home, where the girls in the advanced course have lived together as a small family, and where pupils from the middle class have gone to prepare meals; and in that of the domestic-science building, with its courses in sewing, cooking, sloyd, and dairying, and also its model dining-room [*sic*] and bedroom, the latter with all its furniture, except the bed and the mirror, made by the girls.[83]

The hygienic value of cleanliness cannot be too strongly impressed upon future home-makers [*sic*], and this naturally broadens out into ideas of ventilation, drainage, and the prevention of tuberculosis by care and sanitary precautions. Where girls leave school before they have taken up a text-book [*sic*] on physiology and hygiene, it seems most desirable that simple oral lessons be given them along these lines. Wholesome food also, as has been often said, is a subject in which they need instruction, especially in regard to the addition of milk, cereals, and vegetables to their bill of fare.

A love for house decorations has to be cultivated rather than implanted in the Indian. One evening the past winter, a company of Indian boys and girls met with some of their teachers to discuss the question, "How can we improve our homes?" Besides taking up more important matters, the raising of flowers was touched upon and the choice of pictures. One of the girls showed how pretty and effective the Perry pictures are (though some of them cost but a penny) when mounted on cardboard, and one of the boys contrasted these with illustrations he had seen the Indians cut from newspapers and slap on the walls with paste.[84] Just here comes in the desirability of some means of earning a little money when at home, a need which seems admirably met by the lace-making introduced by Miss Carter, since two or three dollars even will provide a few yards of scrim for the windows, pretty denim for a table-cover, and seeds for the garden or window box.[85] If a taste for reading has been duly fostered at school—and this surely is far truer education than the mere recitation of allotted lessons in history and geography—then with the proceeds of her toil in odd moments she can subscribe for some magazine, which will be a welcome guest every month. All possible encouragement, we believe, should also be given to the beautiful native industries, in order that the beadwork, pottery, and basket-weaving of her grandmother may not be lost arts to the Indian girl of the period. Here, too, is a means, not only for cultivating a taste for what is really artistic in itself, but, thru its commercial value, of helping to make the home comfortable and attractive. But "home is not merely four square walls." Back of "the outward and visible signs" of order and purity we want the "inward, spiritual grace," the atmosphere of uprightness and goodness, which the children of the household will drink in as plants the sunshine. Of course, the very corner-stone [*sic*] of such a happy family life must be the mutual love and respect of its united head.

And just here, it seems to me, not a few young educated Indians make shipwreck, tho the mistake is not confined surely to our brothers and sisters in red. I have wondered whether, as teachers, we did as much as we might to inspire them with high and sacred ideals of all that pertains to home, and with the need of earnest thought in the choice of a life-companion. We have to be constantly on our guard against any infringement of the necessary rules regulating the intercourse of our young men and women while in school, frowning even upon things which under other circumstances would be quite proper, and deprecating any interest which diverts their minds from study.

Is there not sometimes danger that, while thus striving to steer clear of the Scylla, we fall upon Charybdis, and send our girls out into life's battle without due training how to meet one of its most fateful issues? May not even a few quiet talks during their last year from someone in the school, or from some sweet, wise woman who has a home of her own outside, which the girls themselves would recognize as ideal, do much to fortify them in this direction?

There is another point which may need to be guarded. We are proud and happy when we hear that one of our girls has received an appointment as employé [*sic*] or teacher in a government school, and is useful and self-supporting. Perhaps, when the young teacher goes home for her vacation with fresh, pretty clothes, and money in her purse, and talks of her pupils, her methods, her hopes of promotion, some former schoolmate, now tied hand and foot by her duties to her husband and children, looks wistfully at her friend's career, and feels as if she alone were realizing the visions of uplifting their race, which they used to share while their hearts were thrilled by earnest commencement speakers. Perhaps her own life seems to her rather a failure. But if her humble home is an object-lesson to all who enter it, if gentleness and kindliness reign there, if the boys and girls after they grow up are trained in Christian citizenship and taught by example to "lend a hand" to all around them who need help, who shall say that her mission is not even more heaven-sent than her friend's?

# 7 | Practical Methods of Indian Education

JOHN SEGER, *Superintendent, Seger Colony School,*
*Colony, Oklahoma*

**Source:** NEA *Proceedings*, 1900, 707–11.

John Homer Seger (1846–1928) was born in Ohio, but his family soon moved to Illinois, where he spent his childhood and early adult life.[86] Formal education eluded him. As he admitted he "had scarcely a common school education."[87] Thus, unlike many Indian service educators who, through formal education or economic advantage, were missionaries, schoolteachers, philanthropists, or clergy, Seger began his long career with the U.S. Indian Service as a mason, first posted to the Darlington Cheyenne-Arapaho Indian Agency in 1872. Violence at the agency in 1874 frightened away the Arapaho School superintendent, and the Indian service agent turned to Seger to fill that position. "It is not because I was prepared for the work by any former training," Seger told Reel in 1900. Rather, "the only question that confronted a superintendent when I took charge was how to civilize the Indians and retain his own scalp. . . . and as I wore very short hair, I was considered eligible."[88]

During the mid-1880s increasing pressure to open Indian Territory to white settlement began a movement to lease Native lands to white cattlemen and to "colonize" both American Indians and whites preparatory to the allotment of lands to the Natives and the homesteading by whites. Seger, described by historian Jack Rairdon as "one of the leading colonizers" of Indian Territory, thus established Seger Colony and its school along the Washita River fifty miles southwest of the Cheyenne-Arapaho Agency.[89] At the school, Seger informed Reel, "we teach the children industries, politeness, and the proper use of the English language, and as far as possible to forget that they are Indians. . . . The more I write," he began the closing of his letter to her, "the more I think there is nothing that I can say that would be worth talking about at an institute."[90] Regardless, he submitted a paper for the Charleston meeting. Levi Levering, an Omaha; a Carlisle graduate; an employee of the Fort Hall Indian School, Idaho; and father of the infant Lincoln, read the paper to the gathered educators.[91]

Seger emphasized private land ownership and labor on those lands for Native individuals to attain civilization and citizenship. As such, in his educational endeavors, he promoted the breaking up of tribal lands, the commodification of those lands and the labor, and the conversion to Christianity.

IN MY OPINION, THE ONLY way to teach the Indian self-support and the value of property is to devise some plan whereby, without special urging, he may be induced to support himself by his own efforts.

I give you, herewith, a short history of my experiences with Indians, and a brief outline of the plan we are at present following.

My first experiment originated thru my proposing to three Indian boys at our school that, if they would each milk a cow thru the summer, I would give them the calf which the cow had. Altho [*sic*] they had never milked a cow in their lives, they agreed to do their best, and were duly rewarded. This placed them in a conspicuous position among the other children, as being owners of property, and it enabled me the next spring to get ten boys to volunteer to raise corn. The agent thought the idea so unpromising that he said the boys might have all the corn they could raise.

The Indians then regarded all work as degrading, and these boys knew they would be taunted and ridiculed as squaws all thru the season. Nevertheless they persevered and had great success with their crop. I marketed the corn for them, and with the proceeds purchased thirty-five head of cattle, which I divided among them, branding each boy's cattle with a distinct brand, thus giving him an individual ownership.

The success of the boys naturally had its effect on the other children, and the next spring I had volunteers enough to undertake to raise 100 acres of corn, giving half of the crop to the government for the use of the land. From this land we raised about 3,000 bushels of corn, and with the proceeds of the boys' share I bought 100 head of heifers. We were obliged to bring these cattle from a distance of 140 miles, and altho the country for the whole distance was entirely wild, and inhabited only by Indians, yet with three of these Indian boys we drove up the cattle, swimming them across rivers and watching them at night, occupying ten days in the journey.

When we arrived at the school, the children manifested the most intense interest in the herd, and all who were receiving wages wanted to use it in the purchase of cattle for themselves. Even the girls caught the enthusiasm to become property-owners. This spirit I encouraged, and allowed those who were earning wages to use a part of it each month in creating a fund with which to buy cattle. We worked along this line until our school herd numbered about 400 head.

It was not long before our success in this venture attracted the attention of the inspectors, and eventually the Indian Office. The government officials reasoned that, if the school could raise cattle profitably, why not the Indians, and thus make them self-supporting? Following this up, they secured an appropriation to buy 400 head of cattle, to be issued to the adult Indians of the reservation. The agent on learning of this advised the Indian Office that it was impracticable for the Indians to engage at that time in the raising of cattle, as they were continually moving about, sometimes being absent on a buffalo hunt three months at a time. He therefore recommended that these 400 head of cattle be given to my school, which was done.

While I had control of the herd no white man had anything to do with their care, they being looked after altogether by Indian boys under my supervision. This I considered the very best education I could give them. The plan I had in view was eventually, thru this herd of cattle, to make the schools of the agency self-supporting.

I also had in mind the establishing of a large pasture, which I proposed inclosing [sic] with a wire fence. Around this pasture I would locate young Indians as they married and settled down in life. They would be obliged to care for the fence and keep their cattle inside the pasture. As the care of their cattle would occupy but a portion of their time, I also included in my plan the allotting to each individual settling around the pasture land enough to make a small farm. As their ponies were not adapted to plowing the prairie sod, cattle might be taken from the herd and broken in as oxen. In preparation for this I had some oxen at the school which I trained the Indian boys to drive and handle.

At the time of my resignation from the school superintendency our herd consisted of 1,000 head.[92] By careful breeding we had improved their grade to a degree far above the native Texan stock with which we began.

Almost from the very first the parents of the children manifested a deep interest in the success of the project, and encouraged and aided it in every possible way. A number of Indian chiefs made donations toward it, and a single Indian woman gave fifty head of cattle to the school to be the property of her daughter, and her husband also gave a large number of ponies to the boys for use in caring for the herd. These and many other instances are evidence of what may be expected from the Indians if their ambition and spirit of emulation are aroused.

At our present institution in Oklahoma, the Seger Colony School, we are pursuing the same object of making it self-supporting and have adopted the plan of stock-raising and farming in conjunction, of which I shall speak later.

This school was started seven years ago, at which time 100 head of cattle were given us by the government. These cattle cost $1,300, and for the last five years this small herd has supplied the school with over $1,000 worth of beef each year, besides proving a practical education for our boys. Our herd now numbers 141, of an excellent grade.

The main features of the plan I am at present endeavoring to carry out are as follows:

The land is divided into sections of perhaps one hundred acres each, and upon each section four families are located, giving each about twenty-five acres. These four families thus form a group and are of mutual assistance to each other in their farm-work [sic]. Upon locating they are required to sign a contract by which they agree to remain on their farms at least three years; to haul the lumber and build a suitable house on the farm; to keep at least one cow, a hog, and a small amount of poultry; to give half of their crops toward the support of the school; and that not more than one of the four shall be absent from home at a time, so that the others may look after his premises. Other restrictions tending to prevent the Indian from wasting his capital, in the prodigal fashion so characteristic of him, may be incorporated.

The Indians must earn the horses they need, but all implements necessary for conducting their farms are furnished by the school.

The first year the land is planted in cotton and the second year in wheat. When the cotton is well up, cattle may be allowed to run in it without damage. The interval between the planting of the cotton and picking time is about three months, and during this period work is provided for them in some shop, so that they can make a living. When the cotton is ready to pick, the whole school assists. When the crop is sold, half goes to the family raising it and half to the school. The profits are invested in cattle, which is considered the very best investment, bringing on the average a return of 25 per cent. [*sic*] on the capital invested. This is repeated at the end of each season, and in three years I estimate that each family will be worth $1,000 and be able to support itself. If they will allow me to write the agreement as to what they shall do, I am positive this result can be attained in every case. The cattle belonging to each family are held as security for the observance of their contract.

In our colony at present we have over 70 per cent. of the Indians in houses. It is a rare sight to see an Indian wearing a blanket. I wanted to take an Indian boy's picture as he looked a few years ago and as he looks now, but he would not think of having his picture taken with his legs bare.

In this connection, also, it may not be amiss to say a word regarding their religious and social development. There is a splendid field here for missionary work, and religious teaching is an element that is very much needed.

Some young men of the tribe, having been elected to leadership, came to me and asked my advice as to their course, saying they wanted to do what was best for their people. I told them that as long as I had been among them I had known of nothing that had kept them back so much as their religion. I said: "You have your sun dance and other dances, and you are apt to change again to some other kind of religion. The white people's religion has remained unchanged for thousands of years, and my advice to you would be to throw aside your heathen worship and become Christians." They replied: "We know nothing about the Christian religion." To this I said: "A man has come here to explain it to you. He will tell you everything about the Christian religion, the existence of God, the birth of Christ, his crucifixion, and that he died for us. All of you who would learn about this religion and become Christians come over and give him your hands." The whole camp immediately came over and shook hands with him. Soon after they built a church, and have since built a parsonage. Already they have expended over $6,000 in this work.

An Indian club-house [*sic*] has also been built. The funds for this were raised at the Lake Mohonk conference by the friends of Indian education, and turned over to Mr. Walter Roe,[93] a nephew of E. P. Roe, the novelist.[94]

It is known as "The Lodge," and, in addition to tables with magazines, games, etc., it is fitted up with all the appliances for housekeeping. When a family comes to visit, it must bring its own provisions and live and eat in a civilized manner. Other rooms are provided with cots, and the visiting Indians bring their bedding with them and put it down on these cots, thus doing away with camp life entirely. The Lodge also has bath-rooms [*sic*] and everything necessary for cleanliness. When an Indian or an Indian family comes to stay at the Lodge, they must keep it neat while there and leave it in good condition. Mr. Roe receives a great deal of clothing, which he gives to the old and young, but not to the middle-aged. To these he gives cloth and lets them make their own clothes.

Here also there is a sewing machine, and the Indians learn to use it in making their clothes. The result is that all the Indians dress in citizens' clothes, and they take great pride in imitating white people in dress.

Mr. Roe and his friends have undertaken to hire a matron for the Lodge, and have asked Mr. Andrew Carnegie for a donation. The Lodge plan is excellently adapted for relieving the Indians of the evils of camp life.

At every Indian school there should be a good hospital, and every girl who leaves school should know how to take care of the sick. Often they are twenty-five miles from a physician, and the girls ought to know how to give medicine and use hygienic means in caring for the sick. The boys will learn it by being treated in a hygienic way, and the whole family will also profit by the knowledge of the girls.

ESTELLE REEL HAD POSITED TO the NEA board of directors in 1899 that bringing Indian service educators into the fold of the NEA would reap benefits.[1] She could leave the Detroit meeting in 1901 confident that that had happened. "Miss Reel," the *Southern Workman* lauded, "deserves great credit for bringing the gathering of Indian teachers into close relation with the meeting of the National Educational Association, and so giving them an opportunity to hear the leading educators of the country. The success of the [1901] conference was largely due to her enterprise and hard work."[2] The *Detroit Free Press* added to these acknowledgments when it reported, "Though the department of Indian education has belonged to the association but two years, it bids fair to rival its elder sisters."[3] The Department of Indian Education had presented Indian school educators with professional development opportunities unavailable to them in previous years. More importantly, it also brought the business of Indian education into the consciousness of fellow educators who began to wonder if the emphasis on practical, vocational, and industrial education had not provided the rest of the country with a model to follow. At the 1901 meeting as well, Reel unleashed her unabashed support for the revitalization of Native arts—a direct contravention of the old guard assimilationist's tenet to "kill the Indian." As will be seen, she basked in the glow of the accolades for her role in all of these things.

Estelle Reel had a very busy year in 1901. She reported that between October 1900 and October 1901 she "traveled 24,493 miles by rail and 269 miles by team," visiting nineteen states and territories and nearly four dozen schools.[4] She calculated that, since assuming her office in 1898, she "traveled more than sixty-thousand miles, much of the distance being covered by stage-coach, in the saddle, and often even by burro and on foot."[5] During that same time, she continued to "study the peculiar needs of the Indian school work" and "prepared a comprehensive Course of Study, which includes not only the ordinary literary subjects, but a large number of industrial branches as well, such as agriculture, gardening, dairying, sewing, cooking, housekeeping, carpentry, etc."[6] Her *Course of*

*Study* replaced the Indian service's first standardized curriculum propagated by Commissioner Thomas Jefferson Morgan in 1890.[7]

Reel's new *Course of Study* included twenty-six discipline areas; two sections instructing faculty on their responsibilities to read literature supportive of those areas and how to conduct evening activities for their students; a section called "Physiology and Hygiene," with instructions for maintaining the health and welfare of the children; and the "Carlisle Outing System," which she wholeheartedly endorsed because "its value as a means of educating and elevating the Indian can not easily be overestimated."[8] She came to this conclusion despite Pratt's own conviction that "frontier 'outing' [i.e., in western schools] is and must be a flat failure."[9] The reality was that different motives drove these two outing systems. "Pratt created the outing system," writes historian Kevin Whelan, "as a vehicle to propel Indians onto equal footing with white Americans." The Reel or western version was an outing system designed "as a means to prepare students for a second-class existence."[10] While Reel included the "Carlisle Outing System" as an integral part of her *Course of Study*, the motives were hers, not Pratt's.

As the very term "Carlisle Outing System" indicates, previous institutional work in Indian education informed Reel's curriculum. She incorporated aspects of industrial training from Indian schools and a variety of other educational experts and institutions, as well as her own work in Wyoming. The curriculum of the Hampton Institute, however, was the greatest influence. "I shall appreciate your opinion more than I can say," she wrote to Hampton's principal Frissell, "as most of the ideas embodied in the *Course* were obtained from Hampton."[11]

Reel left no doubt about the objective of this compendium of instructional directives: "The chief end in view should be the attainment of practical knowledge by the pupil." By "practical knowledge" she meant not wasting time with superfluous details. "As far as possible," she admonished her educators, "teach the children that the cultivation of good habits, self-control, application, and responsiveness are recognized as being on a higher educational plane than a knowledge of definitions and unimportant dates."[12] This was not a new view for Reel; in 1897 she enjoined the teachers of Wyoming's white students in nearly the same language.[13]

Reel complained in later years about Indian service teachers who wasted time on such "unimportant" information. As she lamented to the Indian commissioner about Carlisle teachers, "Too much time is still being devoted to the study of subjects that will be of little assistance to pupils in their efforts to earn a living—for example, ancient history, foreign geography, etc."[14] She deplored in other schools the time wasted by girls "practicing on the piano."[15] Conversely, Reel applauded the work of Hampton Institute instructors who eliminated "unnecessary material from the textbooks [sic] and only endeavor to interest the pupils in practical work." She approvingly explained that "the keynote to Hampton's method is best exemplified in the fact that it discards the theory that it is necessary to study useless things in order to get the discipline necessary for doing useful things."[16] Practical studies and practical studies alone, she believed, would "lift" American Indians into civilization.

Reel's use of the Carlisle Outing System in her *Course of Study* indicated her agreement with that signature program of Pratt's, albeit differently motivated, but her curriculum and her plans for the 1901 meeting in Detroit punctuated a break from his "Kill the Indian" philosophy. Pratt had seen this coming. He stopped going to the annual institutes of Indian service educators by 1899 prompting Commissioner Jones to ask him why. Pratt responded, "I am tired of contending with my brother superintendents of the agency and the other non-reservation schools near the Indians. They have opposing views and purposes in part begotten of their environment and which I think are encouraged from your office, and they are largely banded against Carlisle. There are so many of them and so few of me that they carry the day."[17]

The commissioner pressed him to go to the 1899 Los Angeles meeting to express his "views and endeavor to make our people accept them" (at least according to Pratt).[18] So he went. Much to his surprise, probably, and satisfaction, undoubtedly, he proposed a resolution, first tabled, then passed that read:

> Whereas, local prejudice on the part of the whites against the Indians, in the vicinity of every tribe and reservation, is such as to make attendance of the Indian youth in the public schools there impracticable, and whereas, the ignorant prejudice and whimsical nature of the parents also militate against such attendance; and, whereas, there is no prejudice preventing attendance of Indian youth, in such public schools as are remote from the tribe and reservation; therefore, be it

> Resolved, that it is the duty of the government to establish Indian
> schools, in our well populated and suitable districts, as remote from
> the tribe as possible.

His resolution further proposed that "ten such schools be tentatively
established at once."*[19] That it passed delighted Pratt. He wrote, "That I
held up my head and walked with steadier pace for some time thereafter
was not to be wondered at, for it had been a long fight."[20]

His euphoria was short lived. Within weeks of his success in Los Angeles, the *Annual Report of the Commissioner of Indian Affairs* concluded,
"The present number of nonreservation schools is sufficient to meet all
the requirements of the service."[21] His persuasiveness at the 1899 Los
Angeles meeting turned out to be a hollow victory. Clearly Pratt's total
assimilationist philosophy of Indian education was waning.

One aspect of Reel's *Course of Study* singularly signaled the demise
of his brand of pedagogy and his influence. In a section titled "Basketry
and Caning," Reel emphasized the revival and preservation of Indian arts
to include baskets, rugs, bead work, and pottery. She launched a direct
assault on Pratt's ideas when she wrote that basket makers should weave
"into their baskets the designs which symbolize the history and traditions
of their tribe, making them distinctively Indian." Reel was not, however,
simply a Native art aficionado; she possessed practical, economic motives
for the preservation of such art. "If the tribe is one of the blanket weavers," she wrote, "it is advised that the services of the best weavers of the
tribe be engaged [as teachers] and instruction given regularly in the art,
that the pupils may become skillful in doing the work and thus be able to
place upon the markets the beautiful blankets that have made their tribe
famous and which are always in demand."[22] Reel would also be the one
deciding what Native art was worth preserving for the marketplace. Art
educator Kevin Slivka has succinctly stated that Reel was "embracing
rhetoric that claimed to save the Natives' traditional art and craft culture
while diminishing any preconceived cultural importance in order to supply the demands of the American market."[23] Moreover, by incorporating
Native arts into the Indian school curriculum, to be taught whenever
administrators or teachers decided it should be taught, she disassociated
the cultural value inherent in "seasonal cycles" that resulted in the production of these useful works of art, such as blankets and baskets. Instead,

the Indian school's curriculum "focused only on" production, "providing students with materials ready for assembly."[24]

Reel's inclusion of Native arts in her *Course of Study* received positive reviews from her contemporaries—excluding, of course, the Prattian old assimilationists. George Bird Grinnell wrote to her, "I am especially interested in your recommendation that the native arts and handicrafts should be encouraged and made the most of." Because self-support was the goal of "efforts to civilize the Indians," he proposed that it could "most easily and most speedily" be done "by encouraging the Indians to practice the arts with which they have long been familiar, or kindred arts and handicrafts to which they are adapted and can easily learn."[25]

Her *Course of Study* would not be released until August 1901, one month after the Detroit gathering, but it was certainly on her mind when she invited the educators to the meeting. She scheduled three department sessions to discuss it and planned to use the meeting to launch her revival of Native arts embedded in the new document.[26] Reel also prepared to accentuate this revival by incorporating such art into an exhibit for Detroit, showing the pupils' work. Unlike in the previous year, when Reel asked only for a display of "school work [*sic*]," for the Detroit meeting she wanted "a display of school work and the native arts." Writing to her educators about plans for this exhibit, she asked for drawings of fruits and vegetables and compositions on housekeeping and preparing a garden. She also asked for a student essay responding to the statement "What I am going to do when I leave school." Highlighting her expectations for students, she provided two options for the latter essay: "(1) Handling stock; (2) Dry weather farming." She chose her requests to demonstrate the practical nature of the work being done at the schools. Finally, she also desired "some of the native work done by the Indians of each tribe under your care. . . . All work sent to this Office," she wrote, "will be returned to the schools after the meeting at Detroit, unless it is to be sold, in which case, please have the price marked distinctly on each article."[27] Reel ensured that her 1901 display of American Indian students' work—a very popular attraction at the 1900 meeting—would promote Native art and its sale and demonstrate the "practical" skills focus of Indian education, as in her new curriculum.

Reel's agenda for the 1901 department sessions also diverged significantly from the agenda in Charleston. Although he did not attend, Pratt nominally held the position as department president for the 1900 meeting. As noted, he had successfully persuaded fellow educators in 1899 to pass a resolution to educate American Indian students "as remote from the tribe as possible." Nothing in the agenda of 1900 contradicted that sentiment.[28] Reel had different plans for 1901. Not only did she schedule papers addressing the value of education on the reservation but she also planned an entire session around the statement: "*Resolved*, That the reservation day school should be made the prime factor in Indian education." Then she published papers in the 1901 NEA *Proceedings* praising the value of reservation day schools to the mission of the Indian school service. Her agenda has the appearance of a planned repudiation of Pratt and his old assimilationist philosophy. Regardless, Reel did schedule him to give three addresses at the meeting, but, again, he did not attend.[29]

Pratt held no more enthusiasm for Reel's pedagogy than she had for his. He had no plans to adopt Reel's support for Native arts or adhere to her instructions in the *Course of Study* that such arts would be taught at government Indian schools. He wrote to her in January 1903,

> We have not undertaken any of the native industries and arts at this school, and it is not my intention to do anything of that kind, for the reason that we have the greatest abundance of occupations and opportunities to teach the Indians the arts and industries of civilized life which will have some influence to lead them into those arts and industries and so away with Indianism. The perpetuation of the puttering basket and bead work as a venture by the Government is unbecoming and belittling to its own work and calculated to keep up the distinction between the races and to produce no prospective permanent income worth contending for. The pictures I have of bedraggled Indians at some of our watering and summer resorts, Saratoga and elsewhere, at this sort of work all condemn it to me with so much emphasis as to keep me from going into it at all.[30]
>
> If I could have had half as much time with the President as the basket and bead-workers' trust had [,] he would never have said one word about the matter in his message, or if he did would have condemned it.[31] If the Indian Industrial School work is to be dominated by fads of this kind it has no further use for me, and I warn you now that I shall not only continue to speak against it but shall continue to write against it also.
>
> You can use this letter in any way you see fit.[32]

Pratt's obstinance on the direction of Indian education would shortly result in the Indian Office having "no further use for" him—as he predicted.

Pratt was not the only critic of Reel's new *Course of Study*. Former commissioner Thomas Jefferson Morgan, also an old assimilationist, told the American Social Science Association in 1902 that he saw in her plan an effort to "discredit the whole Indian school system and to call for its abandonment." Morgan called her curriculum the design for "an inferior training" that doomed an Indian child "to failure in the struggle for existence." Historian Frederick Hoxie writes that Morgan's "outrage revealed the distance between the assimilationist zeal of his administration and the 'realism' of Estelle Reel."[33]

More dispassionate criticism eventually arose that questioned the validity of having a course of study that addressed all the needs of each separate tribe. Professor Ernest W. Coffin of Clark University published an article in 1908 titled "On the Education of Backward Races" in which he provided a historical and critical—albeit ethnocentric—discussion of Indian education in the United States in a section called "Our Indian Problem."[34] Referring directly to Estelle Reel's uniform course of study, Coffin asked,

> Can there be a uniform provision made for the three hundred schools at present among the Indians? Some fifty-nine linguistic stocks have been recognized in North America . . . ; customs differ widely; each great nation has been studied by some specialist in that field. . . . Yet the Department of Interior meets the needs of all at once by a blanket curriculum administered by its employees, four-fifths of whom are white, while the actual teachers are prepared by no special training in the needs of the situation they have to deal with.

"The great diversity among the aborigines of America," he concluded, "makes it impossible to prescribe a course of studies that shall be uniformly suitable for all tribes."[35] Such criticisms, however, lay in the future, not in Detroit in 1901.

Reel's enthusiasm for her *Course of Study* remained unabated in Detroit, with, as mentioned, three separate sessions devoted to instructing her educators on its implementation. It is safe to say that educators' adherence to its curriculum varied from school to school, with evidence pointing to Indian school workers embracing its industrial and vocational bent. Certainly exceptions, such as Pratt, remained unconvinced of its value, although his open defiance was unique. Scholar Adrea Lawrence has found that, in northern New Mexico, while there was general adherence to Reel's *Course of Study*, over time that fidelity "softened and faded into the background of the day-to-day needs of the day school teacher and the community."[36] No doubt what Lawrence discovered in her research would be true across the vast Indian school service. Eventually Reel's *Course of Study* ran its course, probably by 1910, and was replaced by a new curriculum in 1916.[37] That occurrence, however, was a long way off from her unveiling of her curriculum at the NEA meeting in Detroit.

Reel also suggested that during that meeting educators plan to visit Buffalo, New York, for the Pan-American Exposition of 1901.[38] There educators found a student display similar to Reel's in Detroit. "Although the exhibit [at Buffalo] continued to focus on students' training," historian Robert Trennert explains, "a separate segment on 'the native ability of the Indian' presented examples of traditional Indian craft work"—a clear break from past exhibits.[39] Reel's curriculum, which downplayed the intellectual abilities of her Native students; her planned student display and agenda in Detroit; and the Buffalo exhibit all reflected the emerging shift in American policy from assimilating Indians as equals in society to marginalizing them, where they would be relegated to "experiencing life on the fringes of what had come to be regarded as a 'white man's land.'"[40]

Reel undoubtedly took great pride in the reception she received for her part in that shift. She won numerous accolades for her display, which attracted throngs to the writing room of the Cadillac Hotel on Michigan Avenue to admire the work "done by the children of the forest."[41] Following the Detroit meeting, the editor of the *Journal of Education* lavished praise on her, declaring that she "was the busiest person in Detroit, and demonstrated that a woman is fully the equal of any man as an organizer and administrator. Her department had the most sessions and the largest audiences, while her exhibit was the most fetching." Furthermore, her emphasis on revitalizing the Native art on display was important because it belonged "to an ancient civilization, the last vestiges of which are passing away."[42] Another correspondent complimented Reel's attention given to the practical education of the American Indian student, "which will make him self-supporting."[43] A separate reporter opined that the sale of the revitalized arts "will open up another avenue for making the Indians self-supporting, this being the keynote of Miss Reel's whole plan of Indian education."[44] "It is evident," the editor of the *Southern Workman* mused, "that the education given in the Indian schools is of a most practical character. The thought expressed in a number of papers that the system of education followed in these institutions has great advantages over the public school system of the country seems not without ground."[45] Reel's student exhibit, agenda for the meeting, and *Course of Study* had convinced observers that she had charted the right course for Indian education, and that, maybe, it was the right course for the rest of the country.

# 8 | President's Address

## *Learning by Doing*

H. B. FRISSELL, *Principal, Hampton Normal and Agricultural Institute, Hampton, Virginia*

**Source:** *NEA Proceedings*, 1901, 893-96, is "An Abstract." A full version of Frissell's address, which is reprinted here, was published in *School Journal* (New York) 63, no. 3 (July 20, 1901): 73–77.

Hollis Burke Frissell served as president of the NEA Department of Indian Education in 1901. When, in 1900, Pratt served as president of that department—but did not attend the first annual meeting—there was no president's address. Frissell's president's address in Detroit is the first for the Department of Indian Education. It is also the third paper he delivered to the gathered educators. He gave two at the inaugural meeting in 1900, the current paper in 1901, and a fourth in 1903. (For a full biographical sketch of Frissell, see his paper in part 1 chapter 1.)

The opening paragraph of this current paper identifies the trend of public school educators being attracted to the Indian school service's emphasis on manual and industrial training. That tendency will be seen again, and more dramatically, in later years. Frissell also intoned the scientific racism that relegated Indians to a "child race" to which progressive educators believed Anglo-Saxon teachers must impart "civilizing" characteristics such as working and saving—a familiar theme to his listeners.

Frissell also explained to his 1901 audience the "symmetrical training of head, hand, and heart"—in other words, intellectual, manual, and moral training, accomplished through the half-day-school, half-day-work-school schedule. British historian Jacqueline Fear-Segal points out that there were utilitarian, not necessarily educational, reasons for this scheduling of the school day. "The division of the day into two halves, one for study and the other for practical work," she writes, "served a triple function: the children learnt their lessons, were taught a trade and simultaneously provided most of the goods and services necessary to run the schools. The manual labor and farming programmes thus served a pedagogical purpose, and also supplied shoes, clothes, bread, cereals, fruit and vegetables as well as meat for the table."[46] In the following address, Frissell justified a well-established system that used the pretense of education to sustain itself: a system that under the guise of educational development needed and used Native students as laborers.

THE SYSTEM OF EDUCATION WHICH has been adopted in the Indian schools is one that is commanding the respect and confidence of all who are interested in education. It is a system which lays more emphasis upon things than upon words, which gives more prominence to the production of self-supporting citizens than to the making of scholars. It teaches its pupils to learn by doing. It makes the book merely a tool. It lays much more stress upon the active than upon the passive side of education.

The story is told of a long-headed Indian chief who, when he was asked by the commissioner of education in Virginia to let his son go to college, said that the education which the white man gave would not fit his son to kill a deer, to build a wigwam, or to endure cold or heat. He, on his part, offered to take the white man's son into the forest and make a man of him![47] We are beginning to believe in the Indian's idea of education. We are coming to understand that character is much more important than the acquisition of knowledge. Christ said when he came into the world, "I am come that ye might have life, and that ye might have it more abundantly."[48] When he was going to fit himself to do his great life work, he did not go into the schools of the Pharisees and the scribes of Jerusalem, but he went into the carpenter shop at Nazareth. There he learned the lessons of life, there he learned how to help others, how to have life and have it more abundantly. When he chose those to whom he would communicate the greatest truths that were ever given to men he selected fishermen from the sea of Galilee, men who had to struggle with their hands for their daily bread—and the same thing is true to-day [sic]. When God would choose the men who are to head great enterprises in the great work of life he selects those who, whatever they may have received of classical learning, have also come thru toil, those who have learned obedience by the things which they have suffered. And so, however we who gather here may differ as to methods, I am sure that we are all united in the thought that the true way to learn is by doing.

## Developing a Habit of Work

It is no new method that we are advocating and carrying on. Those of you who are familiar, as many of you are, with Quick's valuable book on "Educational Reformers," remember how he shows that thru the centuries there have been those who have stood for practical education.[49] Montaigne revolted against the theory that mere knowledge is power, a theory that those who have to do with child races continually see refuted.[50] Mere knowledge without the ability to use it is not power. It is like food given to a man with a poor digestion—the more he eats the greater his misery. What we need to give is the power to digest knowledge. Montaigne says, "Knowledge is not even an aid to power in all cases, seeing that useless knowledge, which is no uncommon article in our popular schools, has no relation to power." "A man's success in life," he says, "depends incomparably more upon his capacities for useful action than upon his acquirements in knowledge, and the education of the young should, therefore, be directed to the development of faculties and valuable qualities rather than to the acquisition of knowledge. Men of capacity, and possessing qualities for useful action, are at a premium all over the world, while men of mere education are at a deplorable discount."[51] The wise Seneca said, "It is better to know a few things and have the right use of them than to know many things which you cannot use at all."[52] Rousseau had the same respect for manual training that we have come to have.[53] He says: "If instead of making a child stick to his books I employ him in a workshop, his hands work to the advantage of his intellect; he becomes a philosopher while he thinks he is becoming simply an artisan." Again he writes: "Beyond contradiction we get much more clear and certain notions of the things we learn ourselves than from those we derive from other people's instruction."[54] Froebel, too, lays the greatest stress upon the active side of education. "We become truly God-like," he says, "in diligence and industry by working and doing. God creates and works productively in uninterrupted continuity. Each thought of God is a work, a deed."[55] This prominence which Froebel gave to thought of "the formative and creative instinct" in children led to the kindergarten, and the kindergarten has taught us that children of a larger growth also need activity in education, and has made us feel that man is pre-eminently [*sic*] a doer, a creator, and that he learns only thru self-activity. He recognized, too, that as children belong to the family and to society, they should prepare for society by spending some hours of the day in a common life and in well-organized common employments. (See Dewey's "School and Society.")[56]

And this thought of training youth to do their part in the great world, in society, and in the family is one that ought to enter into all our work. The school ought to be a miniature community. It is because this has been to some extent accomplished in our Indian schools that they are in many respects superior to the common schools of the country. There are certain definite things which we are trying to bring about by our peculiar system. The first, and perhaps the most important, is the formation of a habit of work. We are dealing with a people that has not been accustomed to regular habits of industry. They have thought that it was well enough for the white man to work, but that the Indian should be free from toil. The first, and perhaps most important lesson, then, and the one without which all other lessons will be of little value, is the necessity and dignity of labor. We of the Anglo-Saxon race have received toil as our natural inheritance. We do not need to be taught that "Labor must be." But our country is now dealing with many races that have a different conception of the matter.

It is, then, of vital importance that our educational system lay stress on the active side of education, that the work of the hands be given special prominence. In some of our schools, from the time the children enter the kindergarten, an endeavor is made to cultivate a love for the regular occupations of life. On Monday the wash-tub [*sic*] is introduced, and on Tuesday the ironing-board [*sic*] is introduced. The little children are taught to find pleasure in work. From their earliest days their constructive powers are trained and they learn to *do*. Dolls' houses are built, small pieces of furniture are made, rugs and carpets woven. Each child has regular duties of his own. A sense of responsibility is cultivated and a feeling that he has a part in the work of life. When the spring time [*sic*] comes the little kindergartners, as well as the older pupils, are sent into the garden for the purpose of cultivating the soil. Two children tend a plot together. While they thus learn to work with one another, there is developed at the same time a sense of individual proprietorship in land. They are allowed to carry to their own homes the products of their little farms. In this way they gain a stimulus to their work. They realize the joys of production.

How important the creation of the work habit is we hardly appreciate. We speak about the "liberty of the sons of God."[57] That is the liberty that comes to a man from the formation of good habits which hold him to the right and away from the wrong. Among these habits there is none more important than that which makes a man unhappy unless he is at work. It is doubtful if either religion or education can accomplish much until they have created a love for labor.

We hardly realize how large a factor in the preservation of order among our people is this same habit of work. Imagine what one of our large cities would be if all classes were allowed a week's holiday. Our Monday's papers show that with all the restraints which religion throws about the Sabbath it is most difficult to preserve order when the regular occupations are suspended. If the moral value of work is thus great in the case of the Anglo-Saxon, it is at least equally so in the case of the Indian.

### Principle of the Plan of Indian Education

We hear much of the relapse of our students into habits of idleness on their return to the reservation. Undoubtedly this is too frequently true. In many cases they find it difficult to obtain work. It is by no means easy for most of the returned students to live up to the standard placed before them in the schools. But this only emphasizes the necessity of cultivating in them during their school days such a love for the labor of the hands that they will not be satisfied until they do obtain employment. In order to accomplish this our teaching of trades and agriculture must be of a high order. Not only must the students be taught to work at trades, but they must have intelligent teaching. They must be taught the principles of physics that underlie their various trades. Not only must they be taught to plow, but they must know the principles of agriculture that relate to the soil, and to plant and animal life.

In one of the schools where learning by doing is made prominent there was a boy who appeared to have no ability in the class-room [*sic*] and seemed to his teachers utterly hopeless. One day the dull boy came to his teacher of agriculture and said that he had something to show him. He took him to a distant part of the school grounds and there showed him a small rough green house, which he had constructed with his own hands from bits of board and glass that he had picked up. He had made a lamp out of an old tomato can, and all thru the cold winter months, unknown to his teachers or his fellow students, he had tended these plants that had become to him as dear as his own life. He had been making experiments in regard to the effect of different sorts of soil upon the growth of plants. He had tried to find out what sorts of soil best retain moisture. He was learning by his own experience under what conditions the plant germinates most readily. Do you suppose that that dull youth will ever lose his love of plant life? It is most essential that work should be intelligent and interesting. It is made so interesting in some of the Indian schools that I have known that it is no rare thing for the boys to work on their holidays. One of them was heard to say that he hoped Heaven would be a place where there would be something to do.

### Dignifying the Common Things of Life

Very closely connected with the creation of the work habit is the dignifying of common things. Education and religion have been too much in the air. They have not been harnessed to the things of every-day [*sic*] life. Learning by doing gives an opportunity to teach Indian youth to care for the things about them. Life on a reservation is in many respects the poorest life that a human being can live. It has less of incentive, less of interest than almost any other. If our boys and girls must go back to these reservations in order to work for and with their own people, we must teach them how to create around them objects of interest. The Indian has a real love for his home. So far as possible, therefore, this love should be used as an incentive to the improvement of the family and the community. Every Indian boy ought to gain sufficient knowledge of carpentry at school to be able to put up a plain house. In some of our Indian schools the girls are taught to make simple pieces of furniture, to weave rugs, and to make mattresses. They are encouraged to make ornamental and useful things for their rooms. There is thus created at the same time a love for beautiful objects and the power to produce them. These girls are also taught how to raise chickens and care for other domestic animals, as well as how to work their own plots of land; and they have even been sent out to study and criticize the farms and homes of the community about them. In some cases they have attempted the reconstruction of the gardens and yards belonging to old and infirm people, clearing out the rubbish, planting seeds and vines, making plans for improved conditions and then carrying them out. It has been interesting to observe the enthusiasm that these young people have shown in this work, and the contagious influence of their enthusiasm on the people to whom they have gone.

**Taught to Earn a Living**

But it is of little use to try to dignify the common things of life, or to teach Indians to learn by doing, unless there is something quite definite for them to do on their return to their homes. There is an increasing endeavor on the part of the heads of our Indian schools to study the conditions from which the students come and to which they must return, and to adapt their work and study while in school to their needs at home. On one of our Western reservations a creamery has been started during the past year.[58] As there is good grazing land on this reservation, and an excellent market for butter and cream, there is reason to believe that, if well managed, this creamery will succeed. This industry will not only provide the Indians with a regular income, but will give them training in the care of cows, and in methods of fertilizing the land. In order to co-operate [*sic*] with this movement the principal of the school in which some of the boys from this reservation were pupils advised them to study dairying. From their summer earnings they have laid up sufficient money to buy cows for themselves, and when they return they will be in a position to help carry on that creamery. Whatever may be thought of the advisability of relating education to vocation among whites, it is quite clear that in the case of the Indians this relation ought to be very definite. It is very much to be hoped that the number of industries on the reservation may be so increased that opportunities for earning a living may be provided for all students on their return from school. If instead of spending hundreds of thousands of dollars for the purchase of supplies outside the reservation, factories might be established where the industrial training of the young people might be continued, great good would be accomplished. Native industries should also be revived and encouraged and business bureaus established for the sale of native products.

**Citizenship**

Another most important object to be gained in our system of learning by doing is the instruction of the Indian youth in citizenship. Whatever there was of good in the old tribal system—and there was much—has for the most part been done away with by the reservation. Unfortunately the issuing of rations has largely pauperized the Indian, and any system devised for his education must take into account the serious defects of character which are the natural result of depending upon the government for daily bread. It is not easy to develop in an Indian youth a sense of responsibility. It is quite natural that after years of government paternal care, for which he was obliged to make no return, that he should not take readily to caring for himself. No such system then as prevails in our public schools would meet the requirements of these young people.

**Developing Responsibility**

An Indian boarding school ought to be as largely as possible an industrial village community with its farms, stores, dwellings, churches, workshops, and school-rooms [*sic*], where the Indian youth is introduced into real life. Each student should be assigned some definite duty for the doing of which he should be held responsible. The thought of co-operation in work and study should also be developed. If an Indian is to become an American citizen, all his faculties must be carefully trained. To bring this about the school must be a small world where the youth will find himself in close proximity to nature and to life. Theory and practice must be combined—otherwise the Indian boy is utterly unable to take up the work of life as he ought when he leaves the school. In most of the Indian schools with which I am familiar, the disposition of the hours of the day is made nearly as follows:

| | |
|---|---|
| Intellectual work, | from 4 to 5 hours, |
| Manual work, | ″    4 to 5    ″ |
| Meals and recreation period, | 3 hours, |
| sleep, | 9    ″ |
| General school exercises, military drill, gymnastics, etc. | 2 hours. |

This program provides for a symmetrical training of head, hand, and heart. It gives more of the day to dealing with things than it does to reciting words about things. It gives the students an opportunity to use the knowledge they have acquired.

**Correlation in the Education of the Indian**

So far as I have been able to learn, co-operation rather than competition is being encouraged in our Indian schools. The variety of work and study which the school courses provide enable students of little aptitude in one branch to excel in another. Each year there is coming to be a closer correlation of academic, industrial, and agricultural work. The problems of the school-room are worked out in the shop and on the farm, and the problems that students meet in their industrial work are made the basis of their school-room work. Pupils are taught to survey the school grounds. They are furnished with bills from the school farm, the commissary, kitchen, workshops, and sewing-room [*sic*]. In this way an arithmetic class-room [*sic*] is made an interesting place, and figures are made to live. In order to cultivate habits of carefulness in the keeping of accounts, each student is obliged to submit at the end of each month an accurate statement of his receipts and expenditures. This is a regular part of his arithmetic work, and his statement is compared with the books of the treasury department. In this way these young people are introduced to business methods, and are made to feel that they must keep an account of their own income and outgo.

The study of the natural sciences is taught in our Indian schools with especial advantage, because the youth there gathered are used to the observation of nature. They have trained eyes and ears. It is only necessary that they be properly guided and they will excel in this line of work. The schools have too a great advantage in being located, for the most part, in the country, where the students have excellent opportunities for the gathering of specimens—minerals, vegetable, and animal. In the department of natural history it is easy to learn by doing. Frequent excursions are made in order to interest the students in every animal and plant upon the school-grounds [*sic*]. This study, instead of being a thing apart, is closely related to the most important subject in the Indian youth's curriculum; viz., agriculture.

In some of our schools no books are given to the pupil for the first three months of his stay, in order that his thought may be centered, as it ought to be, on things rather than on words. In addition to the study of the soil and of plant and animal life, the students are asked to perform simple experiments in the laboratory with water, air, and heat. They then talk with one another and with the teacher about these experiments. Next they write out a statement of what they have seen and done, and then later they are allowed to consult books in order to compare their own thoughts and experiences with those of others. It is not necessary to explain how interesting a subject geography becomes with such handling, how closely it relates itself to the practical work that the young people are doing.

### Geography and History

A large Indian school is a fine laboratory for the study of geography. Beginning with a careful study of the school grounds—soil, water, drainage, etc., they may proceed to inform themselves in regard to the products of the farm and the school's industries. With the conditions right about them as a basis of comparison they may then go on to learn about those in other parts of our country and in the various other countries of the world. Every Indian school ought to have a museum which its students should help to form and to which its graduates should contribute, in order that the pupils may become familiar with the products of their own civilization. While we are striving to make the Indians more like other men in some respects than they are, it is of vital importance that we at the same time study carefully whatever they have that is good, and strive to develop it. The endeavor that is now being made to revive blanketry, basketry, and pottery is in the right direction.

In the same way that geography is made to begin with the school grounds and thence extend to every part of the globe, so the history of the Indian race should be the center from which to study other history. It is not fair to shove down the Indian's throat the statements made in histories written by white men in regard to their brothers in red. He ought to be encouraged, as in geography, to make his own investigations and deductions. Some of our schools are most fortunately situated for the teaching of history. They are on historic ground which is closely related to the struggles with the Indians. It is of the greatest importance that we make use of these surroundings and help our students to gain the true meaning of their history, so that while they prize the good traits of their people they recognize their weaknesses and hold themselves open to new ideas.

### Mathematics by Doing

The help which the trade department of an institution may render its academic department by making clear problems that in the class-room may be incomprehensible, is illustrated by the work in the sheet metal room at Hampton. Here the student first draws a square, then cuts it out of tin and finally computes its area. He does the same with a rectangle, a triangle, a trapezoid, a trapezium, a polygon, and a circle. He learns how to draw a triangle or a polygon from a given side, and how to find the center from which a given circle has been struck, how to bisect lines and angles, how to draw a circle thru a given point, and in a practical way learns other simple geometrical propositions concerning surfaces. He then applies all these in roof measurements in sheet metal. Continuing, he draws the plan and elevation of a cone, develops the pattern and constructs it of tin. Then he computes its surface and volume. He does the same with a cylinder. Having the diameter of the base given, he draws the plan and elevation and then computes the height necessary for it to hold a pint or a quart, then he makes a pint or quart cup and tests it. The students have in this way about twenty-five geometrical propositions, no one of them being without its application to some useful article which they make of sheet metal.

### Morals and Religion by Doing

While we believe that learning by doing is the right method of procedure in every department of school life, there is one department more important than any other, to which this method is especially applicable, and that is the department of morals and religion. Christ said: "He that *doeth* the will of my Father shall know Him."[59] Here certainly is an opportunity for learning by doing. I do not underrate the value of the spoken word or of the outward ordinances of religion, but I do think that our Indian schools, bringing together as they do men and women of different creeds from different schools and different parts of the country, give us a fine chance to manifest God's truth not only with our lips but in our lives. Unless the Indian gains while in school the Christian thought of service and mutual helpfulness, very little has been accomplished. In order that this may be accomplished there must be an atmosphere of co-operation among both students and teachers. There is no place where bickerings [*sic*] and jealousies are more out of place than in an Indian school where representatives of the white race are endeavoring to show the members of a child race how to live a civilized Christian life. There are Indian schools, and I believe not a few where the one thing insisted upon is that both students and teachers shall live together in unity. The teaching of a practical, everyday religion which enters into the workshop and goes on to the farm, which both Catholic and Protestant can approve, which makes itself felt in actions more than in words, is most important.

In some of our institutions not only are the young people made to feel that their religion is a part of their everyday life, but they are interested in work for the poor and sick, they give of their time and thought to make life easier for the old people in the poor-house [*sic*] and in the cabins. The pauperizing, hardening influences of the reservation which causes the Indian to be thoroly [*sic*] self-centered can only be overcome as they are thoroly imbued with the Christian idea of service for others. This sort of Christianity can only be learned by doing.

**Learning to Provide for the Morrow**

Closely connected with the idea of serving is that of saving. It is doubtful if rapid progress can be made toward civilization on the part of the Indian youth without it. The thought of having all things in common must be overcome and the Indian taught, that in order to serve effectually he must save. In a number of our Indian schools, savings banks and provident funds have been established, and with the enlargement of the outing system the yearly earnings of our Indian pupils become quite considerable. It is of vital importance that these funds, which are usually held by the school authorities, should be expended on the return of the students to their homes in such a way as to give them a real start in business or on their farms. The old Indian customs which make it necessary for an Indian boy to share whatever he has earned with the whole tribe in a feast or a frolic, must be given up, or there will be little progress.

**One Effect of Industrial Training**

An interesting investigation has recently been made by Miss Louisa McDermott, a teacher in the Ft. Lewis Indian School in Colorado, which shows the effect of the training given in six of our leading Indian boarding schools upon the ambitions of the pupils. The results are given in the *Southern Workman*.[60] Of the 975 male pupils reporting, 11 did not know what they wanted to be. The 964 remaining named 61 different occupations; 87 per cent. [*sic*] chose lines of work distinctly industrial. Of the 841 choosing industrial occupations, there were 222 farmers or 23 per cent. In a similar investigation made by Professor Luckey, of Nebraska, among white boys of the public schools only 2 per cent. wanted to be farmers.[61] Of the 658 female pupils, one did not know what she wanted; 69 per cent. chose industrial lines of work. Of these 106 desired to be housekeepers, 92, cooks, and 92 seamstresses, while in Professor Luckey's study of white girls in the public schools, only 9 per cent. of the girls wished to sew and 2 per cent. wanted to be housekeepers. It will not do to lay too much stress upon the results of Miss McDermott's investigations. In many cases these young people chose the only occupation with which they had any intimate acquaintance. But it is interesting when there is such a decided movement from the country to the city, to observe the fact that an education which lays emphasis upon doing and brings young people of the red race in contact with nature and rural life, creates a desire on their part to remain in the country, and follow industrial pursuits. In certain parts of the South where the same sort of education has been adopted among the blacks [*sic*] the movement from the country to the city has been almost completely stopped and the young people have settled down contentedly upon the land.

**Progress in Indian Education**

I have endeavored to give a brief outline of the plan of work that has been adopted in our Indian schools. While much remains to be done, I consider that an excellent start has been made and that a real interest has been created in the subject of education, not only among the Indian youth, but among their parents. In the "Indians of To-day" George Bird Grinnell, than whom no man is better entitled to speak for the red man both because of sympathetic interest in his welfare and intelligent knowledge of the facts of the case, says, "A vast change has come over the people of the camp. Insensibly and all unknown to himself, even the most conservative of the old Indians has changed and to-day views things from a point wholly different from that of twenty-five years ago. To-day, practically all appreciate the benefits of education and desire to have their children taught. The growth of Indian education is like the growth of any organic thing. Watch the sapling from day to day; it does not seem to change. Yet if we go away and return after the lapse of ten years we find that the sapling has become a tree. So with the education of any tribe of Indians; from day to day the work is hard and discouraging and no progress seems to have been made, but if we look back five or ten or twenty years and compare the conditions of to-day with those of the past, we may find satisfaction and encouragement to continued effort in the vast improvement which has taken place."[62]

# 9 | Civilization and Higher Education

WILLIAM T. HARRIS, *U.S. Commissioner of Education, Washington* DC

Source: *NEA Proceedings*, 1901, 896–99, is an NEA-edited version. The original text of the speech, and the version reprinted here, is found in the William Torrey Harris Papers, 1865–1908, ID no. MSS25056, box 41, folder 749, "Civilization and Higher Education [Address, NEA, Department of Indian Education, 1901]," Manuscript Division, Library of Congress, Washington DC.

William Torrey Harris (1835–1909) was born in Connecticut, where he began his checkered and varied education at a rural school. Nine-year-old William moved with his family to Rhode Island, where he enrolled in a city school in Providence. He was trekking his way among New England academies by age thirteen, by which time he had attended at least six in as many years. He attended Yale University in 1854 but left two years later without completing a degree. Determined to try his hand at teaching, in 1857 he moved to St. Louis, Missouri, where he took an examination required to teach in the St. Louis public school system. Hired at a grammar school there, he now began an illustrious career as an educator and philosopher.

After only one year in the classroom, he became principal of a school, a position he held until 1867, when he became the system's first assistant superintendent. In 1868 the failing health of the superintendent resulted in Harris being promoted to that position, where he remained until 1880. He is credited during this time with establishing the first public school kindergarten. Although noted as an educator for his school administration accomplishments, he intellectually moved easily in the world of philosophy. He helped establish the St. Louis Philosophical Society in 1866 and the next year founded and edited the *Journal of Speculative Philosophy*. He also served as president of the NEA in 1875.

In 1880 Harris returned to New England, where he wrote and lectured on education and philosophy and, for a short time, held the position of superintendent of the school system in Concord, Massachusetts. He became the fourth U.S. commissioner of education in 1889, a position he held until 1906. Although little known today, by the time he died he had nearly five hundred publications and was regarded as "America's first great educational philosopher."[63] When Estelle Reel stated that she wanted her Indian service educators to be part of the NEA so that they may hear "eminent scholars discuss pedagogic questions," a scholar such as Harris fit the bill, and his prestige among educators is undoubtedly the reason she invited him back to address her educators in 1902.[64] Consistent in his 1901 address is the contemporary idea that a movement away from nature by dominating it is a movement toward civilization. Harris's argument makes it clear that he took seriously the biblical injunction to subdue the earth and have dominion over it.[65]

THERE ARE TWO METHODS OF teaching other races than our own. One method is to take advantage of them, to use them selfishly for our advantage and against our own interest. In short to exterminate them or convert them into bond slaves. The other method is to take them and put them in such training that they can participate in our civilization and learn to do what we are doing, namely to conquer nature by science and art.

If we come in contact with other races than our own through our worst elements, through our adventurers, we are likely to put into effect the first method named. [If we come in contact with those races thru the agencies of our government, we are more likely to adopt the second method,] for it may be said to be the policy of our government to provide schools for the dependent races which come to us in newly acquired territory.*[66] In those schools we endeavor to teach the children of other races letters and science, letters which make intercommunication possible and which open to all who possess them an acquaintance with the literature of our English-speaking races a literature which has revealed through its poets and prose writers the lofty aspirations and the hunger for individual freedom which our race throughout its history has possessed. We impart in our literature also our view of the world revealed in the religion of the divine human God, a heavenly Father to whom all races of men are brethren. For the highest expression of our world view is found in the words of the Evangel, Glory to God in the highest, and on the earth peace and good will to man.

It is important for the teachers of the children of a people who are in the tribal relation or who are making progress out of the tribal relation into a condition of productive industry and representative government, to ask themselves what is civilization. They should ask this question often and keep its answer in view as a kind of pole-star [*sic*] by which to direct their course. I have often heard it said among amateur students of ethnology that the white man's civilization is no better than the red man's civilization or the yellow man's civilization. A teacher of Indian youth who sincerely believed the truth of these assertions would naturally feel compunctions in carrying out the program of his day's work.

Let us attempt to define civilization by saying that in proportion to its degree the higher civilization shows its advantage over the lower civilization by producing a higher order of individualism and the greater distribution of local self government [*sic*], and at the same time a greater participation of the masses of the people in the products of the industry of its own community, and of all communities of the world, by means of commerce, and more than this a participation in the intellectual and spiritual products of all mankind.

Measured by this standard it will be seen how small is the realization which a tribal community has of the benefits of civilization. For the tribe consists of a small number of people mostly connected by family ties and governed by autocratic authority of the chief of his council. The tribe has kept a jealous watch upon its frontier lest some one or all of the neighboring tribes approach it with hostile intent. The tribe has to give a narrow education in hunting and war to its people and teach them the mythical traditions which furnish a sort of superstitious explanation to its manners and customs, and to the phenomena of nature in its vicinity. It must be a principle of the tribe to shut out communication with its neighbors. All of its people are educated into distrust of the people of neighboring tribes. Under these conditions the tribal knowledge of the races of mankind can amount to but little. And the concentration of all the nervous energy of the tribe upon defense and the [pr]ocurement of subsistence renders literature, science and art next to impossible.

Not only does tribal life prevent intercourse with the present and past history of the human race but it prevents that division of labor which makes possible any degree of productivity in the industries. Its agriculture and manufactures are conducted by the women and superannuated men,—the young warrior despises an industrial occupation.

Now if we count the value of the industry of the tribe in ordinary conditions we shall find that its money value is something less than three cents a day apiece for each man, woman and child, while while [*sic*] that of the highest civilization amounts to nearly twenty times that amount,— say from ten times that amount in the nations of the extreme north or extreme south of Europe to 20 times that amount in the industrial centers of England and Scotland. Moreover in the centers of civilization all persons participate in the world market and have more or less knowledge of all the peoples of the world, and are constantly learning regarding their doings, whether in the realm of material production or in the realm of spiritual production. The most highly civilized people in fact commence each day of their lives by a survey, more or less hasty, but quite effective, of the doings of nations as collected by telegraph and spread out before them in the morning newspaper. I can compare this survey of the entire world in its effect on human disposition only to a daily religious ceremony. For it presupposes a peaceable and cooperative relation of all peoples to one another throughout the world, all being engaged for the most part in the one great business of conquering nature and turning its products to human uses, and the making of all observation and reflection of mankind accessible to each individual citizen of the world.

The teacher of the youth of a tribal people will believe in the potency of the highest civilization and try to make his pupils learn, first, the arts of intercommunication, reading and writing; and secondly, the arts and sciences which make him acquainted with his fellow men near and far off, such as geography and history; and thirdly, to form acquaintance with those tools of thought by the aid of which man has conquered nature; branches of mathematics, physics, and chemistry, geology and astronomy, and the sciences that relate to living beings such as plants and animals. The civilized arts of life will not be neglected.

Each question that comes up regarding the course of study and discipline or moral education will be referred for answer to the principles of civilization: Does this branch aid the Indian child in acquiring a knowledge of the human race and the purposes of the several instruments of civilization? Does each discipline help him participate in the industrial civilization to which he belongs? If not, the branch of study or the discipline has no place in the programme [*sic*]. If yes, then it ought to be introduced but not to the exclusion of something having a greater claim based on the same principle.

We teach to the children of Indian tribes or Malay tribes certain elementary branches which we teach in the elementary schools of our country to the children of our citizens. The significance of these branches of the common course of study does not always occur to us with its full force when we hear those branches named in a bare series as reading, writing, arithmetic, geography and history. It is only when we state to ourselves the significance of these branches one after another that we see what instruments of power are placed in the hand of the pupil by their acquirement. Let the child learn to read and write. This is of little importance unless he uses the arts of reading and writing; if he does not use them he depends throughout his life upon his own narrow experience limited by time and space, and upon which scraps of information which he may overhear in the conversation of his fellowmen [*sic*] about him; but if he uses constantly these arts he from time to time reinforces his own narrow experience by the wide experience of his race, coming to him after much sifting in the daily newspaper; coming to him after as much more sifting in the pages of the magazine and popular book; coming to him with a third and much more sifting in the pages of the scientific book and the book of literature, of history; books which belong to what is called standard literature and science. Again, looking upon the common school branch of arithmetic: It begins with counting and producing through various processes of abridging numerical calculations up to the vestibule of the higher and more wonderful arts of mathematics, namely, geometry, algebra, trigonometry, and other arts of measurement based on a knowledge of the triangle, the calculus of variations. Arithmetic opens the door of all these things—to a knowledge of the laws of matter and motion in time and space. The savage who can count only up to 5 or 10, and who has no knowledge of the decimal system of numeration, nor of the arts of calculation, he has very little power to combine matter and motion and to make the forces of nature serve him.

Then from his geography he studies the relation of one's habitat to the rest of the world; learning the lesson of commerce, the exchange of what one's habitat produces, what is useful to the rest of mankind for the products of all places on the globe inhabited by men. Geography shows us the spectacle of the individual supplementing himself and his feeble endeavors and the scanty list of his home productions by means of the world market produced by commerce. This is a process of converting the individual into a giant by reinforcing him through the labor of mankind.

Then there is history in the common school which reveals the nature not of particular individuals so much as of the races of men. History shows the permanent characteristics; shows the margin of variation from the lowest degree to th[e] highest degree of manifestation of power and enterprise; of hum[an] passions and violence in action. It gives to each individua[l] a prospective showing himself not a mere individual but as a s[oc]ial whole, vast combinations of men united into nations and man[if] esting certain purposes and producing necessary or unnecessary collisions one with another. History is the revelation of the will power of mankind.

In our common schools, even in those offered to the savage tribes who come within the control of our national government, we offer these important branches of general culture. All of them tending to the emancipation of the individual; all of them tending to give him power to combine on rational terms with his fellow men.

# 10

# The Reservation Day School Should Be the Prime Factor in Indian Education

C. C. COVEY, *Teacher, Pine Ridge Indian School, Pine Ridge, South Dakota*

**Source:** NEA *Proceedings*, 1901, 900–901, is "An Abstract." However, a more complete paper was published in ARCIA, 1901, 467–69, and is reprinted here.

Indianian Claude C. Covey (1872–1923) began his career with the Indian school service as a teacher at Pine Ridge Day School no. 31, South Dakota, in 1900, the position he held when delivering the current paper. He moved quickly from a position as a teacher in South Dakota to superintendencies in Colorado, Washington, Idaho, and Oregon. In 1912, after seven years at the Warm Springs Reservation, he left the Indian school service, homesteaded, and tried his hand unsuccessfully at Oregon politics. He returned to the Indian school service and was back in Colorado in that capacity by 1914, when he was reassigned as superintendent for the Standing Rock Reservation in the Dakotas. Covey moved from school service with the Indian Office in 1917 to become the Indian service agent at Rosebud Reservation, South Dakota. He had once again left the Indian service by 1920 to pursue economic interests, including the sale of former Native lands as a partner in a realty company and as a member of the South Dakota Development Association, for which he also served on the highway development committee. He became an inspector for the South Dakota Highway Commission in 1921, a position he resigned in 1922 due to ill health. He returned to his boyhood home in Martinsdale, Indiana, where he died in 1923.[67]

The significance of Covey's address is its complete break from the old assimilationist ideal of educating American Indians "as remote from the tribe as possible."[68] Covey said that the reservation day school touched not only the child but also the parents, an argument common among the proponents of the reservation schools. Covey also attacked the boarding schools for having less influence on "civilizing" Indians. When he made that bold argument, government and mission boarding schools accounted for over 22,000 Native students, whereas day schools enrolled fewer than 5,200.[69]

THE AIM IN INDIAN EDUCATION is twofold—to elevate the Indian in character and enable him to live in and cope with advanced civilization. This is in reality but one result. Give the Indian, or any man, the fully developed character and all things else will be included. But most of our Indians lack so much, the casual observer is prone to pronounce the task of civilization a hopeless one. He is deficient in all the institutional ideas, but has made great strides in the last generation. If we will but investigate the history of the best civilization of a few hundred years ago, we will find that it will not stand a comparison with that of the Indian of to-day [sic]. Much of this advance must be due to education. Taking for granted, then, that the education of the Indian is a possibility, the first question is, "In what way shall we accomplish this?"

Our aim is to bring before this body of Indian educators what we consider one of the most effective means under present conditions of bringing about the desired end—the education and civilization of the Indian to the point where he will be able to become a complete American citizen, be swallowed up, as it were, in the body politic and the vexing Indian problem be forever solved.

This factor is the reservation day school as it is now conducted and as it will be improved. We believe it should be made the prime factor. "The common schools are the hope of our country," whether the inhabitants of that country be white or red.

The purpose of all education is to strengthen the institutional life of the community. The Indian has a stronger regard for his home than for any other institution. Then why not pursue a pedagogical course, take advantage of this little beginning, and implant around it the other elements that will make the pupil a useful citizen? The worst savage will lose something which the best equipped institution in our land can not replace if taken from his home in his infancy. Let us not drag the child away from all he has, but rather take what we have to him, there nourish the tender shoot, plant other seed, and after a while, when the proper time comes, he will gladly go of his own free will to seek further knowledge wherever it may be found.

This is the work of the day school—to go into the savage camp; to further the child's love for his home and the parents' love for their child; to improve that home as well as all its occupants. Insignificant as this work may seem, the Indian can not see the teacher and his family go about their work in a regular way, keeping themselves and their house in order, cultivating their little garden, milking their cows, ringing bells, and doing a thousand things on time, without himself absorbing some of their regularity. He himself must rise and prepare his meals at a certain time, that his child may not be late at school. He must have a fixed habitation for at least ten months in the year. All this will eventually cause him to form more regular habits of living and give him some conception of the value of time, counteract some of his laziness, and start him on the road to civilization. The day-school home is to the Indian camp what a model farm is to an agricultural community in the midst of which it may be placed. If properly conducted, it incites the Indian to emulate the example constantly set before him. But the greatest influence is on the young; the child is taught the English language, his education is begun, he is made to work, to keep clean, until finally, when he is ready to go to a higher school, he does these things from force of habit or from a realization of their value.

In the preparation of this paper I have consulted over thirty men who have had years of experience in the Indian school service. They have all held positions in both boarding and day schools. Some are now superintendents of boarding schools. When asked if they would affirm or deny this proposition, "*Resolved*, That the reservation day school should be made the prime factor in Indian education," all but two affirmed.

Some of the arguments given in support of the continuance of the day school were that as early impressions are lasting, one need not expect to force the child to believe that all the teachings and practices of his parents are wrong, since the parent has so much influence over the child. We must reach the home, and this can best be done through the day school. It is the only school that is doing effective work in carrying civilization to the Indian home. The change in the child's condition is so gradual that when the parent sees it every day there is no desire to nullify the whole effect of the education received, but rather a desire to help the teacher in his work. The day school comes nearer the home and heart of an Indian than any boarding school. He sees his children go to school every morning, dirty, perhaps, but when they return of an evening they are neat and clean. This must exert a great influence for good at home.

Some of the hindrances to effective work in the day school were lack of equipment, insufficient buildings, the meager compensation of the patient housekeeper, coolness on the part of government officials, and the language, customs, and dress of the Indians.

In answer to the question, "Which is the most effective, considering the cost, the day, boarding, or nonreservation school?" all but three favored the day school. Some favored it even though its costs were doubled, and others restricted its effectiveness to children under 12. One reply said: "Admitted that the boarding school will send home pupils who will for a short time speak better English, have a neater appearance, and know more about books than the day-school pupil: admitted that the nonreservation school will send home polished and perhaps refined students, we who have come in contact with the returned students know that nine-tenths of them are idle because the education the Government has given them can not be applied to anything they find to do on the reservation. They were taught to wash by steam at school, but they find no steam washers or steam wringers at home." And so in many other respects their education has been on too large a scale.

Finally, then, we will say that the more we have investigated the more we are convinced that the day school is the school best adapted to the needs of the Indian. The nonreservation school may fit him to compete with the white man; but if he will not do this, if he will not stay in the East, we must improve him where we find him, and fit him for life in his own home.

Our field matrons and nearly all officials who have had the opportunity to investigate, are awakening to the fact that the day school is the coming school. Let the children be taught in the day school till 12 or 14 years of age, then let those who are capable be sent to the boarding school, and from there promoted to the nonreservation school. There is no occasion for jealousy or friction; there is work for all; but let each do its own work and not try to usurp the place of the other, and after a while, when that happy time shall have come when reservation lines are no more and the Indians become citizens of their respective States, they will have an ample school system ready to turn over to their own local government.

# 11

# The Unification of Industrial and Academic Features of the Indian School

O. H. BAKELESS, *Carlisle Indian Industrial School, Carlisle, Pennsylvania*

Source: *NEA Proceedings*, 1901, 902–4 is "An Abstract." However, his entire paper "How Can We Secure a Better Unification of Industrial and Academic Features of the Indian Schools?" was published in the *Red Man and Helper* 2, no. 1 (August 2, 1901): 1, 4. That version is reprinted here.

Pennsylvanian Oscar Hugh Bakeless (1858–1933) graduated from Blooms-burg Normal School, Bloomsburg, Pennsylvania, in 1879. He served as faculty at his alma mater from 1890 until 1893, when he received an appointment to Carlisle Indian Industrial School. Bakeless held the position as head of Carlisle's academic department from 1893 until 1902, his station when delivering the current paper. He resigned from Carlisle in 1902 and became a professor in the Department of Pedagogy, again back at Bloomsburg.[70] In his 1902 letter of resignation to Pratt, Bakeless expressed his frustration with the trend in Indian education that he believed was marginalizing the Native students. "I am more and more impressed with the fact," he wrote, "that it is not the intention nor the policy of the Indian management to put the Red Man quickly and permanently upon his feet as an independent and self-supporting man, and thus end the work and the necessity of an Indian Service; but rather to prolong the process indefinitely." His attendance at the 1902 NEA annual meeting in Minneapolis, one year after he delivered the current paper and a mere month before his resignation, "greatly strength-ened" his conviction that there existed no policy roadmap for "any definite line of action tending to lead the Indian out into the larger life of the nation." He lamented, "This is a discouraging feature of the work."

He also expressed his faith and confidence in the abilities of Native stu-dents: "The children appeal to me strongly. They are kind, responsive, teach-able, frank and honest in expressing their deeper convictions, and ready to recognize what is for their best good. I have the profoundest faith in the capabilities of this race, and under right conditions, believe the future of the Indian is a hopeful one."

Bakeless then invoked Pratt's "Kill the Indian" mantra when he wrote, "Turned into the public schools, brought into contact with our people, and utilized in ou[r] general industries, the Indian as a question will disappear quickly, and reappear as a useful citizen."[71]

Pratt would have completely agreed with Bakeless, and it is likely the two gentlemen had discussed this very issue. In *Battlefield and Classroom* Pratt wrote that by 1900 he had concluded that "the permanent double-headed Bureau oligarchy," which included "both the Bureaus of Indian Affairs and of Ethnology," had worked for their own perpetuation by "keeping the Indians carefully laid away in the dark drawers of their tribal reservations."[72] Bakeless captured with his resignation letter the tension between the Prattian and Reelian views of Native Americans. The first view saw them as capable human beings who, once they stopped being American Indians, could become productive American citizens, a process impeded by the federal bureaucracy. The opposing view of the progressive educators held that, while there was much to be admired in Native culture, they were racially inferior to whites and incapable of reappearing as "equal" citizens. American Indians might be "useful" in industrial or domestic enterprises—to which ends the Indian service educators labored—but they were incapable of being equal to the white citizenry. Bakeless was seeing in 1901 and would see again in 1902 that the Prattian view was all but moribund, causing him to lament the "discouraging feature of the work." A frustrated Bakeless left Carlisle and assumed his new job at Bloomsburg, a position he held until his retirement in 1929. He succumbed to a heart attack on his birthday in 1933 while conducting Bible study at his church.[73]

Assuming his delivery replicated the printed version of his address, listeners would have heard a jumble of fragmentary ideas, sometimes halting, that resulted in an object lesson consistent with contemporary Indian school pedagogy—that is, Indian schools were designed to train the head and hand together to create a self-supporting citizen. Bakeless also addressed the apparent conflict between those educators focused on the head and those focused on the hand and encouraged them to cooperate in their objectives.

THEORY AND PRACTICE SHOULD UNITE at every step of the educational process. A divorcement of them makes theory autocratic and helpless, and practice slavish and ineffective.

That antiquated educational ideals and methods still hold sway in our school-rooms [*sic*] needs no defense. Too often is the teacher handicapped in his work by tradition, and biased by his early training against better processes.

To too great an extent are we slaves of the book.

We are unable to interpret the spirit of the new education that would have the school touch the life and soul of society on every side. These days call for schools that are not secluded places at work on dead forms, but LIVING ones in which the individual pupil has actual participation in the life and work of his community.

**Send the Whole Child to School.**

The Indian School, planned to lift in a single generation a people from the middle and lower stages of barbarism into civilization and citizenship, is planned along these broad lines of "sending the whole child to school." The old school had use only for the intellect.

The child's institution life becomes practically home and community life to him.

The school-room, here as everywhere, with its traditional "culture" as a thing apart from and above work, with the book as its symbol, at once arrogates to itself the superior place, and in fact, if not in intent, stands aloof from the dust and din of the shop.

Here enters this problem of unification.

With the academic teacher, trained more or less along the old school ideals, the humanistic and theoretic predominate.

He has little knowledge of business life, industry and its processes.

We hear too often with truth that "teachers are not practical people."

**The Artisan is not a Teacher.**

This is one side. Now briefly the other:

The artisan in the shop is frequently illiterate, though seldom wanting in good common-sense [*sic*], and frequently with a sound, homely philosophy. He is not usually a thinker, nor much of a student. He may be well versed in his own craft and its processes.

He has little or no knowledge, however, of the teacher's art of imparting instruction; little power of organizing and systematizing the work.

The untrained observation of the student-apprentice is the chief or only power relied on in gaining a knowledge of the craft or skill in the work he is expected to learn.

Here we have the situation to be met and mastered in the Indian Industrial School. These two great fields must become united; mutually helpful; must mutually stimulate each other.

There must be in both school and shop[.]

### Singleness of Aim,

unification of purpose, economy of time and effort in bringing about results.

The educative processes at both places must be life processes.

We must get rid of the theoretical flavor of the school-room and the peculiar tendency on the part of the teacher to want all bright pupils to prepare for the so-called "professions."

Natural inclination and gifts, and not a teacher's preferences should shape somewhat a pupil's destiny.

On the part of the shop we want less prejudice against theory and the processes of the school-room, and a willingness to grow. Knowledge and skill in the same man always make for power.

### What the Indian Needs.

The head that guides the academic work must be a student of education, broad enough to see, beyond the school room, society with its demands in which the student will have to live and to which he will have to conform in some degree.

He will prepare his pupils for that life.

The work of the school-room is a means to an end; and that end the training of men as workers good for something in community life, and willing as workers to do faithful service.

It is THIS that the Indian needs to enable him to stand alone.

### Arrested Development.

The great majority of people (and Indians are no exception) have not the intellectual interest dominant.

They do have the so-called practical impulse and disposition, and the school and the shop uniting to foster this, will send out a strong, useful character.

But let the instructor harass such a pupil by the old school tradition, thus deadening interest, and you have a case of arrested development.

Teachers and educators talk wisely often of culture and development of personality, etc., while the great mass of their pupils are only tolerating the school room in order to get merely enough of the elements of knowledge to help them, from a business point of view, in gaining a livelihood.

It is with such pupils that the correlating and unifying of the shop and the schools count most.

**Both the Shop and the School are Profoundly Educational.**

The hold of the school will be more vital and prolonged because it has recognized the power of the shop as a preparation for life.

Ideal industrial schools ought to do systematically in an intelligent and competent way, what the home, the shop, the factory and the farm disconnectedly do in a comparatively meager and haphazard way.

Guided by the united effort of shop and school, every step of the training of the Indian youth ought to be intelligent, thoughtful, scientific.

Stimulus to work will be greater in school because of this mutual dependence.

Children are active. Direct activity intelligently, and the boy will be held in school longer.

**The Greatest Waste.**

Perhaps the greatest waste in our school rooms to-day [*sic*] is that resulting from not allowing the children to utilize the experience they get out of school.

Teachers do not know the experiences of their pupils; do not try to explore this domain[.]

Facts often taught are irrelevant ones; forgotten as soon as learned or valueless if retained.

**The Shop Instructor Must Recognize Educative Processes.**

The Industrial Director must see in all the shop and industrial work, something more than the mere getting of work done, chores finished.

He must realize it is a school process, educative, and that he is an educator as well as instructor; that his processes develop manhood and character.

Here is the weakness in the system, that an industrial instructor is tacitly ranked below the academic teacher. He does not look at his calling as anything but that of an artisan's.

### The Two Complemental.

These two men, the heads of the Academic and Industrial work, then, must see that they work complemental to each other; that their respective departments are equally necessary to a youth's best development.

The former approaches the practical through the theoretical, weighing every process and giving keener power of analysis, more enthusiasm, intelligence and zeal to his pupils as workers; inculcating greater respect for labor whether of the brain, the so-called professional callings; or of the hand, manual labor.

"Work is WORK, do it well and it will make a MAN of you," is his charge to his pupils.

The Industrial Director, working from the practical side, should be constantly studying the theoretic and thus enlarging his power to do his best work.

Each department is stronger for the other; each less useful without the other.

The highest success of each rests upon this mutual dependence.

The processes have one end in view, shaping young lives to usefulness, and noble living.

Each director must be large enough to measure the import of the other's work truly.

### The Shop Instructors Should Meet and Discuss Ways and Means.

The teachers in the schools usually organize and meet weekly to discuss and study every phase of real live modern education as related to their branch of work.

The problems of adolescent life, discipline, etc., come under their careful scrutiny.

The instructors in the shop should do the same.

The teachers from the Academic side in this study should be constantly reaching out to the industrial and into the larger life of the world; more practical, original, less dependent on books.

The instructors in the shop, from the side of the process of work, the trades, should reach up to the theoretic, to the scientific principles involved in the work, the art of teaching, a wider intelligence, a broader culture.

### Artisans Should be Students.

All artisans in charge of industries, as instructors in, and teachers of their craft should be students, advancing in intelligence, in skill in their departments, and in their power to help and uplift the children under them.

Frequently the morals and habits of such employees are not above reproach.

Only CLEAN men, who are enthusiastic and eager to grow should be retained in the service.

Visits to progressive institutions and a study of their work and methods will do much towards keeping this spirit of progress and growth alive.

### A Monthly Union Meeting Advisable.

A union meeting of all teachers and instructors once a month under an efficient presiding officer to discuss the general features of the work, compare notes, consider subjects of education, of discipline, and other vital questions relating to the work, would do much toward unifying the two phases of the work under discussion.

It would bring all the employees into a sympathetic appreciation of the difficulties met in the various departments; of abuses growing up and changes needed. It would stimulate healthy growth on every side.

### Literary Clubs Should be Encouraged.

Much may be done incidentally and indirectly in this matter of growth and unification, as well as for general culture, by organization of clubs, small groups of congenial people to read and discuss together, weekly, according to their tastes, education, literature, history, philosophy, art, architecture, drawing, or technical work.

A number of such clubs composed of from two to ten members have been in existence in one school for a number of years.

They have been wonderfully effective in intellectually quickening the members,

### Broadening and Sweetening Their Lives

and enlarging their usefulness in the school and among the pupils.

Growth started along the line will almost invariably result in enlargement everywhere.

The companionship of the fellow worker as a fellow student is exhilarating and wholesome, and will insure [*sic*] a tendency to make the departments represented grow together.

There is a mutual goodwill that isolation and lack of common interests does not insure.

"We cannot enlarge our mental vision without re-adjusting our mental furnishings."

### Industries May Furnish Teaching Material.

The teachers in the school rooms can often get their best material for classwork in the shop and thus draw closer and more sympathetically to it.

Conditions arising in the shops, the sewing room, the kitchen and on the farm, will furnish material for right teaching of Arithmetic.

The most practical suggestion this year for Arithmetic work came from a ten-minute talk with the carpenter.

The class that does not get much of its data in this practical way for this subject, is wasting time, and is being cramped by wrong teaching.

Such a teacher is a helpless traditionalist.

Language teaching can in every way be strengthened by gathering material for it from the shop, or the places of work; and both school and shop will be helped by the process.

The implements and processes of the industries will furnish an unlimited amount of material for essays and oral exercises; all, too, coming within the knowledge domain of the pupil.

### Why not in all the Shops?

The director of our printing office has prepared a series of talks on the craft of printing and its history.

These are given to her classes.

Many questions and topics follow for discussion; and later, carefully worked out by each pupil, in a series of essays.

What more practical work in expression could be had for a body of printers?

The printing office is thus made the point of vantage from which the pupil can trace and follow the progress of civilized man in this craft, getting an insight into the material used, and the mechanical principles involved, practical exercises full of vitality and mental stimulus.

What hinders a similar plan being followed in other industries?

Physics, chemistry and many other subjects of learning are helped by the teacher's intimate knowledge of the shop.

Her work must suffer if she have not this knowledge.

Every fact gathered in this way will remain a permanent possession of the pupil.

**The Farm may Furnish Material for Nature-Study [*sic*].**

Nature-study will get its most helpful material from the farm and the farmer.

These men are wise in their own way, and we pedagogues want to learn that neither wisdom nor knowledge will ever die with the mere school man.

Teachers, we arrogate too much to ourselves!

Where pupils and teachers live close to the farm and the garden, and in friendly companionship with the farmer, nature-study becomes a real thing and not a fiction.

Nature-study of the kind that makes the pupil love the woods and the fields is what we strive for.

No study of nature can give young people that appreciation for her, gotten by working with her and living a simple life surrounded by her, as is so beautifully shown by the honored President of Tuskegee in a recent article in the Outlook.[74]

No object lesson gotten up as an object lesson for the sake of giving information can afford even the shadow of a substitute for acquaintance with plants and animals of the farm and garden acquired through actual living among them and caring for them.

No attempt at training of the senses in the school can compare with the alertness and fullness of sense life that comes with daily intimacy with familiar occupations, working with a purpose, under a thoughtful, skilled man as an instructor.

### The Drawing Teacher and the Shop Instructors Must Know Each Other

to be useful in their respective work.

The carpenter and black-smith [*sic*] can make necessary more mechanical drawing than time will permit of, and in the doing of it most practical arithmetical problems and calculations would constantly arise.

It is waste of energy to neglect these places of unifying, and the opportunity of turning the young people loose on live things.

Pupils at trade should work from sketch and drawing, if necessary, made for them until they are able to do it for themselves.

### How the Teacher may Humble Himself.

Frequent visits of school classes to the shop with the teacher as a learner will do much toward keeping the pedagogue humble at the profundity of his ignorance in the domain of the trades and arts.

Both instructors will thus have a greater respect for the other's efforts. We want thus to meet often and intimately workers in other fields, with minds open to receive the best they have to give.

We want to project ourselves into their lives, appreciate their difficulties, and thus grow into sympathy with them, as we profit by the best they can give.

### Lecture-Talks [*sic*] Valuable.

Talks and lectures by the heads of the departments on the inter-dependence [*sic*] of the various subjects of studies and industries would do much toward helping all to see the educational content and value of each.

We would learn the lesson that Emerson's squirrel teaches: "If I cannot carry a forest on my back, neither can you crack a nut," and in the knowledge is borne mutual respect and sympathy.[75]

### How can we Unify?

Simply unify! All are teachers from the practical or theoretical side, whether at work in the shop or school room.

Grow, grow together!

Help to stimulate the less fortunate to broaden in his work!

Learn from the shop-man [*sic*] what he has to teach!

Have him feel that for you, with your subjective training and life, he has much to give that is helpful.

If in the shops, learn how to impart instruction; all about the art of teaching.

Formulate principles upon which your work is based!

Systematize every process!

Be content with only the best for the student!

Again I say, GROW!

**Profound Respect for Labor of all Kinds Must be Formed.**

Down with the old notion that some callings are more respectable than others!

Inculcate the thought that man graces the work, not the work the man!

One of the most stimulating sights to me a few months ago was that of a bright, intelligent young man, an Indian with shop training, a most forceful teacher, who won the esteem and affection of his pupils by his earnest work, dropping his teaching for a week to lead a group of boys in some necessary repair work. With sleeves rolled up in the van of the work he led; working with the crowd of workers, and never a moment of self-consciousness, because his mind was intent upon having the work well done. This, when a skilled mechanic failed to get results because he could not lead. Such power over men and material, such a personality would do more toward unifying and intensifying the work of an Industrial School than any influence I can think of.

**Success Lies in the Spirit of the Workers, and not in Material Conditions.**

The Indian child must bring his whole mind, his whole body to the school and the shop as one institution; and we as teachers want to see that he takes away a well-stored, well-developed mind, and a healthy body, well-trained to take up the duty of self-support.

THE GOVERNMENT INDUSTRIAL SCHOOL HAS BEEN IN VAIN IF IT FAILS TO DO THIS FOR INDIAN YOUTH.

# 12

# What Shall Be Taught in an Indian School?

CALVIN M. WOODWARD, *Director, Manual Training School of Washington University, St. Louis, Missouri*

**Source:** *NEA Proceedings,* 1901, 904–9, is "An Abstract." Woodward's paper was also printed in ARCIA, 1901, 471–73, and the *Southern Workman* 30, no. 8 (August 1901): 429–35. A more complete version is reprinted here by combining all three sources. Text from the *Annual Report* is underscored. That from the *Southern Workman* is bracketed and underscored.

---

Calvin Milton Woodward (1837–1914) graduated from Harvard University, class of 1860, in his home state of Massachusetts. He served in the Union Army during the Civil War, then joined the staff at Washington University, St. Louis, Missouri. He became founding director of that university's manual training school in 1880, the position he held when delivering the current paper. Woodward died in 1914, and, in recognition for his work on the St. Louis Board of Education, a grade school was named in his honor. Originally "three portable frame buildings" comprised the school, but a new facility erected in 1922 was dedicated in his honor. It still serves students as St. Louis's Woodward Elementary School.[76]

Woodward was considered the "father of manual training," an appellation that evolved from his "assertion that training in the manual arts was desirable and advantageous for all pupils, regardless of their educational aims."[77] "He put his whole soul into the cause [of manual training]," wrote a machine shop practice instructor in 1923, "and what he did contributed very materially toward creating a popular sentiment that later on became strong enough to make the establishment of public manual training schools a possibility."[78] It is no surprise that Reel included him in the 1901 meeting during which she unveiled her *Course of Study,* which is basically a treatise on manual training.

One Carlisle Indian Industrial School attendee who heard Woodward's address reported back to Carlisle, "Our mental equilibrium was somewhat disturbed this morning by the address of Prof. Woodward. . . . This gentleman has done very much for Manual Training, but he does not know anything about Indians. . . . There were some ruffled feelings in the audience before he had finished, and had discussion of the paper been allowed a good many opinions would have been expressed that would have surprised [him]." Woodward's biggest transgression, this correspondent proposed, was expressing "his opinion, [that] Indians must be educated on their reservations, their text books [*sic*] must be written for them, [and] their own history and traditions taught them."[79] Such observations by Woodward reflected a consistency with Reel's thinking evidenced by her agenda for the 1901 meeting. Nevertheless, as one reads Woodward's paper, one can only imagine the vexation it caused educators who worked at an institution bent on eradicating "Indianness" from its Native pupils. Such disapproval, however, was not universal among Indian boarding school correspondents. Oklahoma's Chilocco Indian School's representative had quite a different take on Woodward's address. The *Chilocco Beacon* reported that Professor Woodward gave a "practical and scholarly address which was warmly applauded."[80]

Woodward also broached the topic of the education of colonized peoples elsewhere on the globe. Comparing and contrasting the challenges of educating people of color regardless of their geographical location grew as a theme at the NEA meetings and among "friends of the Indians."[81] This most certainly affected the thinking of members of the Department of Indian Education who were now considered a part of the global "White Man's Burden."

NEVER WAS SPENCER'S EARLY QUESTION more timely than just now, as we face the practical problem of Indian education: "What knowledge is of most worth?"[82]

You remember that Spencer insists, in his reply to his own question, that education must first be directed to developing the power of providing *food, clothing,* and *shelter* for one's self and one's family. Self-support is the corner-stone of all good citizenship. Without this there can be no good citizen, no sound basis for society, no reasonable hope for civilization and culture.

[As I look at it, the problem of Indian education is far more complicated than that of Porto Rico (*sic*), and even than that of the Philippines. In the latter cases there are no obstructive presumptions, the result of long-continued government mismanagement, and there can be but one aim. In our past treatment of the Indians there appear to be two widely divergent purposes underlying the government's policies. I must make this matter clear, and in my endeavor to present matters clearly, I shall not hesitate to deal frankly with the policy of the general government, and with that of individual managers.]

[First, what is the aim of Indian education, and how does it differ from the aim, say in the Philippines? In the Philippines it is to build up a people; to make them self-supporting, self-respecting, self-governing; to erect a new and higher civilization on the ruins of an old and lower one. In this case it is easy to see how to go to work with a moral certainty of ultimate success. The Filipinos are to be educated to usefulness and good citizenship just where they are, among their own people, wholly within their present environment. The youth of the islands are not to be trained for American or European employment or for American or European citizenship, but for home employment and for home citizenship.]

[Our policy in regard to Indian youth is in great part entirely different.] I was told last week by the educated young Indian in charge of the government exhibit of Indian schools at Buffalo that the purpose of the Carlisle school was to train individuals for lives of practical usefulness, not among their own people on the reservations, but in American industrial and commercial life.[83] Of course, this object is often defeated, and the graduate drifts back to his early home, and when there he frequently lapses into a life of idleness and hopeless discontent. Doubtless such cases have a faint influence on Indian civilization, but the chief fruit is individual. The number of the nation's wards is diminished by the number of people who thus desert their parents and early surroundings, but the problem of the education of the race to a better and higher civilization is left *in statu quo*. I am not sure but this depopulation leaves the tribe worse off than ever. The loss of the brightest and most promising minds must degrade the remnant.

In the case of schools on the reservations, the aim is, I suppose, quite different, but in so far as they prepare the children for lives of usefulness outside the Indian community, the effect must be bad on those that remain. The ultimate success of a scheme of educating Indian children away from all the tribes and traditions of their ancestors involves the complete depopulation and final extinction of the tribes. I do not assume that this plan has been definitely adopted nor that it ever will be, but, if it should be, it should be carried out relentlessly; every child should be withdrawn, and none should ever be allowed to go back. The government can then maintain the forlorn and useless adults in luxurious idleness and depravity until old age and disease wipe them out of existence forever. Such is the logical outcome of the scheme of government support and individual education away from the tribes. I cannot condemn this course too strongly. The Indian tribes will never amount to anything so long as they are supported in idleness while their children are educated elsewhere. No progress toward a better civilization, including self-support, is possible under such conditions.

The policy of generous allotments of land on which the Indians must support themselves must ultimately become general. This should include a system of Indian education carefully devised to deal with Indian civilization as it now exists, and gradually to raise it to the plane of respectable American citizenship. In other words, we should deal with the Indians just as we are going to deal with the people of Porto Rico and the Philippine Islands.

In the first place, the school and all it contains must be within the circle of Indian sympathies. The training must be of such a simple and practical character as to win the approval of the Indian people. Hence it must not run violently against their traditions, and it must keep in view the peculiar environment of the future lives of the children. In my judgment the course of study, text-books [*sic*], and manual features of the schools of Boston or Detroit are out of place in an Indian community. Of course, the children should learn to read, write, and speak the English language, and they should learn to translate household English into the vernacular of their homes, so as to help bridge over the gulf between our civilization and theirs. They should learn the fundamental operations of arithmetic, the tables of weights and measures (I mean avoirdupois weight, the bushels by weight, the wine gallon, and the English measures of length, surface, and volume); but avoid the confusion which results from the introduction of other tables. These should be learned practically until every child has a trained judgment and a personal consciousness of a pound and ten pounds; of a foot and one hundred feet; of an acre and ten acres; a quart, two gallons, etc. They should know how to keep simple accounts and how to make out bills. The nature, meaning, and use of fractions should be made clear by abundant practical examples. Mental arithmetic with clear oral analysis is invaluable. For the common initial school, mathematical study should stop there. The puzzles of banking, exchange, proportion, etc., and the subjects of algebra and geometry, are too remote and out of the present reach of Indian sympathy, and should be omitted.

Geography should be largely local. I doubt if at first it should go much beyond the United States. Above all, geography should be an Indian geography, specially prepared for Indian schools, giving all possible information in regard to Indian tribes, their location, their extent, their improvements, their growth and history. This combined history and geography should furnish reading lessons, should stimulate pride and ambition, and should enhance the value of social and public improvements. Neither the teacher nor the publisher should ever forget that the children are Indians, that they go home to Indian parents at night or every few weeks, and that they report at home continually what they learn at school. Thus the Indian children are to become the teachers and inspirers of their parents. In this way the whole community should be reached.

It is not greatly so in your community and mine. Our children learn more at home than they do at school. We supplement their school teaching by books and constant instruction. In the Indian house or cabin the ignorant mother and father will sit at the feet of their own child, and we must keep their intellectual and social status continually in our minds.

When it comes to the reading-books they, too, should be written for the Indian schools by people who are thoroly [sic] familiar with Indian history and biography and, above all, with the traditions which are handed down from father to son and which white men rarely hear. I fancy that the stories told of famous Indians are now so told as to keep alive a certain amount of race pride and the traditional hatred of the white man. Who will write the stories of Black Hawk, Tecumseh, Pontiac, Geronimo, Sitting Bull, and scores of other heroes in such a way as to disarm them and to bring out the nobler qualities, and the triumphs of peace as well as war. In American history there are numerous episodes well calculated to teach the worth of Indian fair dealing, of loyalty, of industry, public spirit, of education, of tribal and national intercourse, etc., Write up the stories of William Penn, of Pocahontas, and others calculated to remove prejudice and establish a feeling of confidence and good will toward our Government and ourselves.

I am well aware that some of you will not agree with me here. You are disposed to think that the children should know as little as possible of the Indian history, and that they should cherish no Indian heroes. Such a course I cannot approve. Can you secure a feeling of self-respect and self-reliance by giving the Indian boy to understand that you have no respect for his father or grandfather? that you regard them as worthless and too degraded to be worthy of recognition? Does the commandment, "Honor thy father and they mother," not apply to Indians? Can you expect to cultivate a spirit of loyalty, reverence, and chivalry in the hearts of Indian youths who are taught to forget and despise their ancestors? There is plenty of good literature touching the finer characteristics of the red man, with which to make up the Indian readers. Think of Charles Sprague, Fenimore Cooper, Hellen [*sic*] Hunt, Catlin, Longfellow, and others too numerous to mention.

But I have said enough in reference to the peculiar character of Indian text-books. I doubt if beyond our first and second readers we have any books suitable for use in an Indian community. Let Shakespeare and Tennyson and Browning wait for twenty years.

My rejection of American schoolbooks and courses of study for Indian use is no criticism on the books. Their very high merit for our use unfits them for the Indian home. In all matters we must keep well within the circle of Indian sympathy and approval, and then we must gradually enlarge that circle without snapping the chords.

It goes without saying that we must have teachers who are educated Indians, of originality and judgment, or we must have whites of rare tact and skill. Restraint, restraint, and still more restraint must be their watchword.

When we come to the manual and industrial features, we come to a subject where we have only general principles to guide us. Were I to attempt an outline of manual work for either girls or boys in a given community, I should wish to spend a year in that community to find first what manual accomplishments are most highly appreciated and useful, and what may be added with promise of success. The successful business of an Indian community may take a variety of forms besides those of providing food and shelter, which must of course stand first. But every self-supporting community must export something to balance the imports which it needs and cannot produce. The strong point of a community may be agriculture, or stock-raising, or fish culture, or poultry, or some peculiar manufacture.

In my judgment the government should send an expert to every reservation to study the peculiar conditions which surround the community, and point out an industry which may be successfully inaugurated there; then the educational forces should combine to establish and promote it. I was glad to hear that Miss Reel proposes to introduce the cultivation of grasses and reeds suitable for basket-making, with a view to promoting that industry among certain tribes. I was glad also to learn that Dr. Frissell is preparing some Oneida boys, who have been with him three years, for practical work in a creamery which has been established on their reservation, so that they may be fitted for positions of leadership among their own people. Whatever the strong point is, or promises to be, must be squarely and directly recognized in the industrial training. No such general culture over several wide fields of universal industry as is given in the St. Louis Manual Training School would be at all appropriate for Indian youth. Of course, the theory and use of the tools in common use should be taught, with the added points of method and precision, and all upon the material at hand. Household furniture, plain houses and barns and shelters, fences and gates, culverts and wooden bridges, the woodwork of wagons and carts, the woodwork of agricultural implements, the making of boats and canoes—such work should be within the reach of a young man properly trained in an Indian community, i.e., one or more lines of such work; and the shop work of an Indian school of boys from fourteen to twenty years of age should be planned accordingly. Of course, as a part of the exact and systematic work, the simplest rudiments of drafting should be taught in even step with the tool-work [*sic*].

Another very important subject, and one never yet introduced into a school, is that of a systematic use of such hardware as is needed in the building of a wooden house or in the repair of implements and tools. Costly articles, even in a white community, are thrown away and lost because the owner is unable to repair a simple break, which one familiar with tools and supplied with a little hardware would completely restore in a few moments and at slight expense. There is nothing like training in the arts of preservation and repair to promote thrift and independence, and a laudable personal pride. This should have large place in the manual training of an Indian community.

In all such manual work I should insist upon the invaluable habit of analysis into the elements of construction, and I should teach those elements as such, because they are of universal application. But the applications should be frequent, far more frequent than is necessary in a white community, for the reason that the home circle is apt to value the training in exact proportion to the useful products.

I doubt the wisdom of introducing at first ideas of art in either drawing or tool-work, as we understand art and according to our standards. An Indian has his own long-cherished ideas of art, which are widely different from ours, and he is quite sure to scorn any decided attempts to introduce our higher notions. We must reserve our pearls till a higher plane has been reached. Thrift, industry, comfort, and cleanliness are absolutely essential to any real progress. The chief difficulty is in the beginning. It is hard to begin low enough. I spent several hours among the representatives of forty-two tribes at Buffalo. I came away with the conviction that the earliest school for Indians should have a great deal of Indian and not much white man in it. Our civilization must enter as a wedge with a very thin edge. To attempt the refinements of literature and art would be to sow seed on stony ground. I do not mean that the Indian child is without capacity, but that the Indian community cannot receive and cherish it. If we aim too high, we shall not hit them, and they will remain just where they have stood for a hundred years. Hence, in all the manual work skill must be aimed at to an unusual degree, and the range of work must be extremely practical. In white schools the aim is intelligence, not skill; here we must aim at both. To be sure, the elements must be slowly and thoroly [*sic*] taught, but their application to a useful product must be encouraged, and even school furniture and appliances must not be too fine.

In the education of Indian girls, domestic science and household economy should hold the larger place, but even here the arts and customs of our homes must be introduced slowly and with great discretion. A girl's training must recommend itself to the Indian mother. I need not enlarge upon the training which is of most worth to an Indian girl who is soon to have a home and children, and to live with or beside her parents. Her parents and her husband must be proud of her. The value of what she got at school must be self-evident. She will not quarrel with her father's paint and feathers, if he prefers such evidence of blue blood and a renowned ancestry, but she will cheerfully consent to a better schooling for her girls than she herself received. In matters of dress and food much may be conceded to Indian fashion and fancy. They are largely matters of sentiment and involve no principles half as important as that of respect and consideration for one's parents. The needlework taught at school should be plain and should quickly culminate in garments, bedding, rugs, etc. The cooking should include every good point in the culinary arts of the Indians, with judicious advances. <u>And so on.</u>

You who have lived among the Indians can see where you have succeeded and where you have failed. Above all, do not lose your faith in progress, tho [*sic*] it be very slow. There is nothing more tenacious than inherited tastes and fancies, and nothing is more suicidal than a spirit of intolerance in matters of pure sentiment. <u>If these suggestions shall serve to strengthen anyone in the right course, or to make the right course seem more clearly right, my object will have been accomplished.</u>

## 13 | An All-Around Mechanical Training for Indians

FRANK K. ROGERS, *Director, Armstrong-Slater Memorial Trade School, Hampton Normal and Agricultural Institute, Hampton, Virginia*

**Source:** NEA *Proceedings*, 1901, 909–10, is "An Abstract." Rogers's complete paper, titled "An All-round Mechanical Training for Indians," was published in the *Chilocco Beacon*, 1, no. 11 (September 1901): 176–79, which is reprinted here.

Hampton Institute promoted instruction for "all-around mechanical training" for both its African American and American Indian students because it was "so greatly needed in the isolated country districts of the South and West."[84] Rogers argued that such training for Native boys and girls was necessary because the purpose of Indian education was to return the students to their homes in the West. Such an argument demonstrates the philosophical differences between the Hampton Institute and the Carlisle Indian Industrial School with its stated mission to integrate its students into white society as remote as possible from their families and home.[85] (For biographical information on Rogers, see his paper in part 1 chapter 5.)

IN THE PRESENT DAY THE civilization and aggregation of Anglo-Saxons demand expert skill of mechanics, as well as of professional men. To such an extent is this demand carried that we find the different trades divided up and mechanics becoming more and more specialists. For instance, in carpentry we find framers, finishers, stairbuilders [*sic*], etc.; in the machinist's trade, lathe, planer, or milling-machine hands; in blacksmithing, tool-makers, horseshoers, carriage and wagon blacksmiths.

In the earlier days of the white man's ascendency, and especially during the time when in America those hardy men called pioneers were reaching out toward the frontier, the mechanic was one who had more of an all-round training at his trade—in fact, he often knew much of two or more trades. This knowledge of different handicrafts, together with that trait called "gumption," was what made possible the great colonizing and pioneering feats which laid the foundation of the American Republic. The small communities which grew up about these earlier settlements probably could not boast of a stairbuilder who, as such, was not able quite as well to turn his hand to other things. There was no need of such a specialist those days, and in fact, there would have been found very few all-round carpenters who could not lay a few bricks or stone, and in times when there was no work to be had at carpentry, make pretty good farmers.

The mothers, too, had an almost endless variety of arts which they could practice with much skill, such as butter and cheese making, soap making, spinning and weaving, sewing, tailoring and dressmaking. There are few men and women left to-day [*sic*] who can remember when these conditions held, tho' [*sic*] in the more remote and thinly settled districts, owing to the nature of the conditions, a knowledge of these arts is still a part of a housewife's training.

Will not these conditions exist in some localities and among some people for many years to come, and will they not be especially true of Indians as they come out from government care and support? Will the young man who may go back to Rosebud or Darlington, knowing only carpentry, be likely to succeed as a carpenter? Should he not, in addition to knowing something of housebuilding, also know something of plastering, painting, mixing mortar, and chimney making? Should not the wheelwright know something of blacksmithing and painting, and would it be amiss if he also knew a little about mending harness? Should not the farmer know a little of carpentry and wagon repairing, and enough blacksmithing so that with a hand forge he could mend a broken chain or bolt, and save a long drive to the village? It is true that if the spirit of thrift is lacking, these various accomplishments will amount to little, but this is not altogether the case, and one of the things which will encourage an Indian to copy his white brother's thrift is the sense of power which comes to him from knowing how to do things as the white man does.

The Indian boy and girl on going back to their own people must of a necessity be, in a more or less marked degree, pioneers in the advancement of their people. If in educating an Indian, one believes in sending him back among his own people he must be prepared in the best possible way for his environment. Hampton believes that this means for the boys a substantial training along some skilled line of handicraft, with as much of some other trades interwoven as will make well-rounded and useful mechanics; and for the girls a general knowledge of the housewife's arts, together with some other accomplishments which will make it possible for each home to become a more tidy and attractive one.

I have in mind a Cherokee boy who is about to go back to his reservation, who can do a very good job at house-building, and in addition some bricklaying, plastering and tin-roofing. He can roughly paint a house, barn or wagon, and has lately added to his accomplishments a little harness- and shoe-making [*sic*]. I have seen some straps which he had just made, with the buckles neatly stitched on, also a completed bridle, all of which are very creditably done. He has also half-soled and heeled his own shoes.

The class of girls who will return this summer have added in the last few months to their general knowledge of household work, a little skill in paper-hanging, mattress-making, painting and glazing. In mattress making, such homely experience as would be likely to be a part of the Indian girl's life has been practiced; for instance, the making of mattresses and pillows from corn husks and dry grass.

Applications are constantly coming in from returned students for a year's special work at the trades. One such, a Navaho, left us a year ago a very good carpenter, and during the year at home he has done excellent work, both at his trade and in other ways, and is very anxious to return to get painting, glazing, tin-roofing, gutter work, bricklaying and plastering. Of course, the amount of each trade which he can get will be very limited, but a little knowledge will go a long way in the simple buildings on his reservation. We suggested to him that painting and tin-roofing were not practiced much among the Navahoes, and were not likely to be for some time, but he said he could work for white people in his neighborhood, as well as for the Indians; if the boys who are returning can show their elders the advantages of improved houses, and can themselves make the improvements, the Indians will gradually adopt them. Then, too, there are openings for industrial teachers in Indian schools, and it is the all-round mechanic who can be the most useful in such places. To the Indian who is expected to go among whites to earn his living as a mechanic, it would be better to give a thorough training along some special line. For instance, a Sencea [*sic*] was given the machinist's trade, and at the end of three years, was able to go into a shop in one of the large cities of the

North, where he has held his position as a machinist with much credit for three years. In such cases, which are rare, it seems justifiable to allow specialization, but Hampton does not encourage it very much for Indians, believing that her trade students would either drift into the larger settlements of whites, or, not finding work at their special trades among the Indians, would become discouraged and shiftless—a drag on their people. In either case the Indian race would lose the benefit which it should get from the trained young men. I should not like to have it understood that we do not believe in being thorough in the teaching of trades. The point to be made, it seems to me, is that one trade should be learned as thoroughly as possible, and then the elements of others should be added.

# 14 | Practical Methods in Indian Education

JOSEPH W. EVANS, *Teacher, Chilocco*
*Indian School, Chilocco, Oklahoma*

**Source:** Although listed in the secretary's minutes in NEA *Proceedings*, 1901, 891 and the *Official Program*, Evans's paper was not published in the NEA journal.[86] However, it was published in the *Chilocco Beacon* 1, no. 10 (August 1901): 160–63, which is reprinted here.

Joseph W. Evans (1868–1909) was a professional educator who graduated from Buffalo Normal School in his home state of New York. After teaching in and around Alden, New York, he entered the Indian school service in 1898, accepting an appointment as a teacher at Chilocco Indian School, the position he held when delivering this paper. He married another school employee, a practice that was common in the Indian school service.[87] She was native Minnesotan Adaline O'Brien (1874–?), a Chilocco seamstress. By 1902 Joseph was serving as Chilocco's disciplinarian. He and Adaline later accepted positions at the Yainax Indian Boarding School, Oregon, where he was assistant superintendent, and she served as a seamstress. When Yainax converted to a day school in 1907, Joseph and Adaline transferred to Colville Indian School, Washington, where he served as a teacher and she as a housekeeper. Joseph died after a short illness on December 8, 1909, one day before his forty-first birthday. Adaline, now a widowed mother with an infant daughter, transferred as a housekeeper to the Fort Totten Indian School, North Dakota, but permanently resigned from the Indian school service a year later.[88]

Evans argued in his paper that Indian students should not try to compete with white students—not for lack of innate talent, but because racial discrimination against them would prevent them from getting jobs. The evidence supports Evans's argument. A compilation of Indian school service employees in 1899 shows that of over 1,100 American Indian employees, nearly half were "Indian assistants," and Native employees dominated only in the role as laundresses, while none held the position as superintendent, physician, or manual training teacher.[89] One Carlisle graduate complained, "Although I was a pretty good workman at several different kinds of labor, no one seemed to want to hire an Indian, when there were white men to do the work."[90] Evens drew the conclusion that, as a consequence of such discrimination, Native students should have lowered expectations and despite job discrimination focus on learning a manual trade or agriculture—an idea consistent with Reel's *Course of Study*. Evans's paper is instructive in providing a window into the day-to-day activities that occurred in his Indian school classroom.[91]

OUR AIM WITH INDIAN PUPILS is to make them useful citizens; to teach them to live better, more useful and nobler lives than they are now living. The business of education is the perfection of the whole human life, physically, mentally and morally. Indians do not require and are not ready to receive a finished education. Grant that they are as capable of receiving a college education, or of fitting themselves for a profession as any other race of people, there is as yet no field open for them in which to labor in those lines when they are through.

Industrial and technical education, together with mental and moral growth, will make them independent and self-supporting citizens, while with either alone the parts of their natures will not be in harmony. The student should be trained and developed in all his nature and faculties to take a useful place in the community. It is wrong to give a child more knowledge, or more power to get knowledge, without increasing his power to use it. The educational methods of the past have been too much reception and not enough execution.

Pupils have been given knowledge without taking into account why it is given to them. If either the school room [*sic*] work or the industrial training is to be neglected in the Indian's education, it should be the school room work.

Indians should not think of competing with white men in the professions and business when they leave school. Their only place will be in the trades, and agriculture.

Every school should have a dairy and garden, and pupils should be given practical examples in farming and stock raising.

During the spring and early summer, when gardening and planting are in season, the class room [*sic*] work should be set aside and pupils should be taken out and taught to prepare the ground and plant gardens and fields.

In the class room teaching English is paramount. The method to be followed should be the same as teaching reading to primary pupils in public schools, except that we have to start lower down.

The first condition is a knowledge of human nature, and particularly of child nature. The educator should be familiar with the laws governing the mental and physical development of his pupils. This is learned by a careful sympathetic study of the child. When children of civilized parents first enter school they have a general idea of the things they see around them, and have already acquired quite a vocabulary. With the Indian children it is quite different. They have no definite idea of their new surroundings, and the English language is a foreign language to them, but they have bright minds, and the memory and perceptive faculties are very active, and it is with these that the teacher has to work.

If we can take the little boys and girls, five or six years old, and put them in a kindergarten, and keep them in school until they are eighteen or nineteen years old, we can solve the problem of Indian education; but with these boys and girls who are well along in their teens we will have to pursue a different plan.

The question of giving the most useful education possible to these pupils who can remain but a short time is one that should be carefully considered. With these pupils we should not think of doing very much in the literal line, but we should use the time in giving them manual training. Four years is a short time to acquire much of an education, but it is ample time in which to learn a trade.

For the first lesson in reading, bring objects into the room; for example, a chair, cup, box, ball, knife, etc. Hold up the object, or point to it, and name it, first in concert, then individually. Do not present more than five or six objects for each lesson. Leave the articles in the room in plain view of the class until the next lesson. Review back work each day before taking up new work.

Make the lessons short, and meantime commence to teach the children the use of their hands by stick laying, paper cutting, clay modeling, etc. Have pupils draw, cut and model such forms as will be useful in the object study and reading lessons which are to follow. For the next reading lesson, after reviewing preceding lesson, add five or six new objects to the list, and do this at each succeeding lesson. After the class has learned to name a few objects, commence to connect articles, adjectives and verbs with them. Hold up a box and pronounce the word "box." Then connect the articles to the word, as "a box," "the box[,]" "a red box." Have the pupils repeat after you, in concert first and then separately. Have the objects different colored and of different sizes so that the objects and adjectives will correspond. Teach in this way the names of all objects about the room and building, parts of the body, animals, trees, flowers, etc.

Commence the study of numbers by grouping objects which they have studied.

Have them count the objects in the groups. Teach addition and subtraction by adding to or taking away from the group. Enlarge the group as the pupils become more skilled in their work.

After they have learned forty or fifty nouns and some of the verbs, commmence [*sic*] to teach writing. Hold up one of the objects with which they are familiar, and ask them its name. Then write this on the blackboard. They will see that the object, the spoken word and the written word are the same. In this way the teacher can work in a great many interesting things, pictures, a live dog, cat, bird; point out horses and cattle in the fields. Such things tend to keep up an interest. Never teach from books and pictures when you can get the real object to look at.

Take the class out walking. Call their attention to the plants, trees, stones, creeks, hills, etc., and give them the names of each. It is wonderful how quickly they will get the words. Do not think that it will require constant repetition. Their memories are very active, more so than at any other age. After the pupils have learned to recognize and write about one hundred words, you can make the transition from the written work to the printed chart and primer.

After pupils have learned to read in the first reader and understand some elementary number work, have much concert reading. It overcomes that timidity which all Indian pupils possess. Also have good drill in oral spelling; have the pupils pronounce the word both before and after spelling it, and always insist on the pupils pronouncing it as correctly as possible and in a firm tone of voice. You can make these exercises pronouncing exercises only, but I think more benefit is derived by having the spelling in connection with the other work.

The arithmetic work in the lower grades should be nearly all oral work. Give good drill on addition and multiplication. Give little problems to be worked orally. It will be necessary to make these first examples very elementary. You can not give too much stress to the importance of oral work in these grades. You don't want the written work yet. It is harmful at this period. This is the time when the pupil should be taught to talk.

In these lower grades study each pupil and find out how much he knows. Overcome his timidity and inspire confidence. You can not do any good honest work until this is done. In the advanced grades the study of reading should be placed over all other subjects because of its developing the language. Pupils should be required to get the thought. Have them read and then give the thought in their own words.

In language the work should be confined to practical speaking and writing. Be very careful about teaching rules and technical grammar. In these advanced grades you should do much oral work in language. The oral work should always come first. Have pupils read stories or poems and then tell what they have read. Then have them write what they have told about the story. Collect these papers and carefully correct, and hand them back to be rewritten. Be careful to explain each mistake, emphasizing the correct form.

Take the pupils on excursions to the fields, garden and workshops. Explain to them, or better, have the one in charge explain, the different things. They can take pencil and paper on these excursions and make notes. When they return to the school room have them tell what they saw, and then have them write it. Make these oral and written exercises the regular language work. Cut advertisements asking for help out of the papers, and have the pupils answer them. Have them write letters, ordering goods, books., etc., from different firms.

In arithmetic do not have pupils work long problems, such as are given in the text books [*sic*]. They are not practical, and the pupils work them with no thought of why they are doing it. Let them go out and measure a piece of land and figure out how many acres are in it. Have them measure a sidewalk and find out how much it would cost to lay it, at market prices. Have them find out how much it would cost to plaster, paint, paper and carpet the school rooms at the market prices. If they are digging a cellar or ditch, let them find out how many cubic yards of earth will have to be removed. The boys who work these problems will probably be the ones who will have to do the work. The work will then mean something to them.

Bring boards into the school room and have them find out how many board feet are in them; how many it would take to make a thousand feet, etc. Bring boxes into the room and have them find out how many bushels, quarts and pints they will hold. In each case have pupils make their own measurements. Have them make out bills, and buy and sell horses, cows, dairy and farm products, farm machinery, groceries and dry goods, at market prices. Let them measure a pile of wood and find its cost. Take the class out to weigh a load of coal or hay, and then return to the class room and make the computation of the cost the regular class work. The different practical examples which one may get are unlimited, and they mean something to the pupils. They can see and feel, and the names and methods are fixed in their minds.

One of our greatest difficulties in teaching Indian pupils is their small amount of knowledge. Our text books are written for boys and girls of civilized communities. How is an Indian boy to understand a story about a railroad or an engine who has never seen one? How can he understand the stories and descriptions of places and things with his limited knowledge of geography, history and literature? We should, therefore, be very careful about details and the little things, which in a white school the pupils would know from their home training, will have to be carefully explained.

I think a very good plan to increase the pupil's knowledge would be to give the last half hour of each session to silent reading. Let each pupil select a book to be taken to his desk. The teacher can explain anything not understood. This will increase their practical knowledge and give them a taste for good literature. Nothing will broaden them more than reading the newspapers and current magazines.

Do not place big boys and girls in the same classes with smaller ones. I would have a room and a teacher for backward pupils. By putting big boys or girls in a class with small ones you hurt their self respect [*sic*] and they feel that the work is belittling them; but by putting them in a class by themselves they have each other to work with. I would use the same methods in teaching these backward pupils, varied and modified only to suit the ages of the pupils. In some of our schools the pupils are composed of separate tribes, and in other schools many tribes are represented. These children bring into their school work [*sic*] the hereditary tendencies of the tribes from which they are descended. If the schools are to do the most good, and blend them into a common American type, these individual cases must be carefully studied. The home environment from which they come, and to which they intend to return, must be carefully and systematically studied.

The pupils of Indian schools, when they return home, are to give a special trend to the individual activities of their people and they are to become leaders in all progress, intellectual and economic. Their needs, therefore, demand more than the ordinary school course can supply. They need to be taught to live.

CORA M. FOLSOM, *Teacher and Indian Corresponding Secretary, Hampton Normal and Agricultural Institute, Hampton, Virginia*

Source: NEA *Proceedings*, 1901, 911–13, is "An Abstract." Folsom's complete paper, however, was published in the *Southern Workman* 30, no. 11 (November 1901): 605–10, with the title "Guiding the Indian: 'What system will best promote character building among Indian children and the courage and ability to enter and contend in the opportunities of civilized life?'" That version is reprinted here.

Cora Mae (Malinda) Folsom (1855–1943) was born in Vermont and educated in Boston, Massachusetts. General Armstrong hired her in 1880 as a nurse to tend to the needs of the American Indian students. She remained at the Hampton Institute until her retirement in 1922. Her employment at the institute covered nearly the entirety of the life of Hampton's Indian Department. Over those forty-two years, she served as a nurse, teacher, director of the Office of Indian Records, Indian news correspondent, Indian topics editor for the *Southern Workman*, and museum curator. Among the students she "mothered with skill and success" was Winnebago artist Angel De Cora, who delivered a paper at the annual NEA meeting to the Indian service educators in 1907.[92] Panegyrists credited her for making a dozen "arduous trips to the Indian territories to return students and bring back others," as well as producing student plays and musical performances that "drew large audiences in the north at which time funds were raised for the institute."[93] As previously noted, she succinctly said about the second principal of Hampton, "Frissell did not like Indians and they did not like him."[94] Regardless, he served as president of the Department of Indian Education for the 1901 meeting and read her paper to the gathered Indian school workers.[95] Folsom died in 1943 while staying at an inn in Pittsfield, Massachusetts, one month shy of her eighty-eighth birthday.[96]

Folsom's address included reflections on the failures of boarding school life—a failure she laid at the feet of the educators—and the realities of federal Indian policy. She lamented the lack of success of students leaving the institutions, as well as the fact that Native students had learned how to live in a mechanized, large-scale environment in the boarding schools, but knew little about living in the real, less industrial life that awaited them upon leaving the schools. She also pointed out that every American Indian student would have a "bit" of land and should know how to care for it—an allusion to the allotment of Indian reservations then in full swing across the west and with the full support of "friends" of the Indians. Finally, Linda Waggoner, biographer of Angel De Cora, wrote that Folsom possessed a "deep-felt empathy for her homesick students," a feeling based on her own childhood loss of her mother.[97] Even such empathy could not overcome scientific racism that led Folsom to call the whites the "more ambitious race."[98]

THE INDIAN HAS CHARACTER. NO one who has ever come in contact with that peculiar force which we see and feel in him, will ever question that. It may not merit Emerson's definition of "nature in its highest form," but it has many fine qualities that are to-day [*sic*] his best heritage to his children.[99] Courage is also his—courage to withstand and courage to endure, and a curiously combined pride and courage that makes him too truthful to lie himself out of trouble, too honest to steal from any but his natural enemies, and, imprisoned upon a reservation with his old ideals all swept away, to tell you in all sincerity that his race has never yet been conquered. Ability along the lines of his past experience the Indian certainly has. He is to-day the white man's teacher in all that pertains to a primitive life. No man is so trusty a guide through the woods or down the rapids as he, and his blankets and baskets and canoes have never been excelled.

With such an inheritance to build upon, it would seem as if we ought to send out from our schools a better quality of graduates than we do. A certain wise man believed that if a child were "trained up in the way he should go" he would not in later years "depart from it."[100] In this way he threw much of the responsibility back upon the teacher. We find our Indian pupils bright enough, skillful enough, good enough, yet when they leave us and return to the old conditions at home, we are often disappointed that they do not accomplish more among their own people, or take a higher stand in competition with the more ambitious race. This busy, rushing age of ours demands from every successful man, whatever his race, a steady, tireless purpose that cannot yield and will not bow to any obstacle, even to failure itself. We have no right to expect this of a race whose theories of life have always been as simple as ours are complex, but we do expect it, and just or unjust, the Indian will always be measured by the white man's standards. It is for this that we must fit him.

A skilled workman would be very loath to confess that he did not know the nature of the material he was working with, nor the use to which it was to be put when it was finished, yet there are many workers in our schools who have never given the human material put into their hands a thought beyond the self-evident fact that they are Indians, and that they are bright or lazy, good or bad, as the case may seem to be. Such teachers go on patiently and industriously day by day, often spending the best years of their lives in this indefinite hit-or-miss work, trusting that at the last moment some "divinity" will step in and shape their rough-hewn ends to some good purpose. One trouble has been, that because a thing is Indian we are apt to feel—and therefore to teach—that it is to be discounted, even if not despised, and strive to replace it with things that we have ourselves been taught, whether they have any bearing upon the Indian's actual needs or not. We are improving in this respect, but we have got to discriminate still more carefully between the good and bad in the Indian's character, and the valuable and worthless in his accomplishments, if we are to adapt our work with any degree of success to his peculiar needs.

For a long time to come the Indian is going to live on or near the land that belongs to him. Any system that does not take this into consideration is losing valuable time. Each Indian has his bit of land. It may not be worth much but it is the one thing that he owns; he calls it home, and it never ceases to draw him back to it, no matter how far he may be tempted away. The Indian is yet very near to nature, and nature is a slow driver. She has no idea of letting the masses follow the few individuals we have held up to her, and skip from the dead level of barbarism to the extreme heights of civilization in a single bound. A natural growth will show the race adopting the arts nearest to those of the old life, the simple ones of food and shelter—tilling the soil and building the home—taking up the life of the farmer and the carpenter.

The Indian's land is undoubtedly his stock in trade, the one thing that he has to begin life upon. In localities where a white man can make a living, an Indian should be so taught and so encouraged that he will have both the knowledge and the heart to make the attempt, rather than lease his land and look for other work. This would require a more systematic training in agriculture than many of our schools are now prepared to give, but a great deal can be done by making the study of agriculture as important and as dignified as the literary work, and by so adapting it to the condition of the Indian country that a pupil may feel within himself the power to do just as good work as his white neighbor.

I asked an Indian this spring, when he was about to leave Hampton, what he considered the best thing his education had given him.

"My independence," he said.

I thought he might be counting his new-found [*sic*] freedom from school rules his independence and so asked, "What do you mean by independence?["]

"I mean," he replied, "that I am independent because I can go anywhere I've a mind to, and earn a good living with these two hands of mine, and I don't have to ask anybody to help me either."

This boy had come to us from a Western school. He was a handsome, interesting fellow, though dull in his studies and rather lazy and spoiled. We studied the boy, his natural bent, his family and his home conditions. He came from a farming community, but thought farm work dull and monotonous. He cared nothing for tools. His best work was found to be in nature studies and he was put into the greenhouse for a year. By that time the general agriculture course that all students are obliged to take, had aroused his interest and he entered upon a special course with enthusiasm. When he got into the dairy he found what interested him still more, and as there was a demand for that particular work at home, his whole interest became centered upon fitting himself to become a pioneer in the creamery business. The money he had earned in the North he put aside to be invested in his business, and this, with one half of his earnings at school is the capital with which he begins.

With students who have a definite end to work for, those who perfect themselves in some trade, or are well trained for teaching or business, there is no problem; they have the "courage," because the "ability," to "contend in the opportunities of civilized life." But this, even in schools where every facility is at hand for advanced training, we know too well is not the rule. Every year students return home with an equipment most unsatisfactory and into a future that is at least hazy and often pretty dark. Any system that shall materially reduce this number must be, it seems to us, one that shall make a thorough study of the character and conditions of the tribe from which the student comes, then a study of the student himself, his individual character and ability, and so train him, that going back to his tribe—as ninety per cent [*sic*] will always do—or entering into competition with the white man on the white man's own ground—as quite a number are now doing—he may have a reasonable chance of holding his own.

The ideal teaching is, of course, individual teaching, whether in the little camp school or in the large industrial institutions. Perhaps it is more important in the day school, because there the whole camp is being directly influenced by the daily return of the children to their homes. The reservation boarding school, being in full sight, and in constant touch with the people, has a chance for individual study and work such as no non-reservation school can possibly have. Like our grammar school, it is the finishing school of the great majority, giving them all that they will ever receive of instruction or training, and it is therefore the most important in the whole system. The non-reservation school is more independent and has usually better facilities for individual training. Its work should be to supplement the reservation work on special pupils, and by strengthening the weak places in character and attainments, fit its pupils for some definite line of work.

We find at Hampton that students who come to us from the larger schools have often very little idea of individual responsibility, even in small matters. They have always had too much in common, and do not know how to act when thrust into positions where they have to take the initiative, and we try to remedy this defect in various ways. For instance, a girl has been taught to do the ordinary work of the dormitory, laundry or kitchen. She is neat and orderly, but has never known by experience what it is to have a room of her own—a miniature home for which she is individually responsible. We give her such a room, and she is required to make it comfortable, pleasant and pretty. Her bed-linen [*sic*] and towels are her own, marked with her name. Her clothing is also hers, and after the first is purchased, planned and made by herself. On her wash-day [*sic*] she takes her little bag of clothes and bedding to a room fitted up with individual tubs, and there does her washing and later her ironing, all without the aid of machinery. At a certain time her mending must be done, and her clothes pass inspection. Most Indian girls sew well and many can make their own clothes when they come to us, but as a rule, they lack both taste and judgment in dressing themselves. They have seldom had the experience that would teach them to get the best material for the money and to make it up in a suitable and becoming way. At Hampton every girl is given a daily task for which she is paid, and with this money much of her clothing is purchased by herself from the stores in town. In this way a girl is forced to learn something in regard to the use of money and the relative value of different materials.

In the case of the boy not so much attention is given to detail. He has a room, shared usually with another, and is entirely responsible for its care. His uniform and many of his clothes are given him, but he has to keep an account of all these things, one that shall agree with the school's statement at the end of the month. He is then credited with the government's allowance for board and clothes and with his own earnings, which are offset by his monthly charge for board and clothes, and by cash drawn from the treasury. His earnings during the four summer months in the North are in a peculiar sense his own, and he makes his deposit in one of the banks of the town and keeps his own account independent of school supervision. That this bank account seldom survives a winter unless its owner has some definite purpose in view, one can easily understand.

The value of the outing system in bringing the Indian into direct contact with an industrious and thrifty people, is well understood. At Hampton all but a few special cases spend four months every year—about one-third of their time in the East—among the farmers of New England. They set sail by steamship to New York or Boston and then scatter to the summer homes that have been chosen for them. There they are left to deal at first hand with their employers, and though they know that in case of ill-treatment or injustice the school stands back of them, the minor details of the situation are entirely in their own hands. One year a boy wrote back to the school: "I want to change my place. This man is very bad man. He scolds me every day too much in God's name." But such experiences are the exception, and by fall the young people come back refreshed in mind and body and with ideas and experiences that help them all through the school year. Some ten or twelve every year choose to remain North for a whole year of work or study, but as a rule we find that three summers out are more beneficial than as many months taken at one time.

The keynote to the Indian's character is his religion. After its teachings his whole life is modeled. It has given him many virtues; it has also given him many less hopeful characteristics; but it has made the consistent union of faith and works a far more natural matter with him than some other races seem to find it. I can never forget the earnestness of a boy who came to me in great distress of spirit to tell me that he should be obliged to postpone his public acceptance of the Christian religion for another year, because, as I afterwards found out, he had had a vigorous disagreement with a boy from another tribe. "Next year," he said, "I am going to whip that feller. I'm going to whip him till he is almost dead; then I'll be Christian."

Ask any student what he means to do when he goes home and he will tell you that he means to help his people. Ask him how, and his answer is often pitifully indefinite. He knows that they need help and his better nature responds to the call, but the how and where and when are vague in his mind. "It is very good for strength to know that some one [*sic*] needs you to be strong" and so we try to make our students feel their responsibility for the less fortunate about them. All around Hampton the Indians can find men and women situated very much as their old people are at home. To these they go out and lend a helping hand. The boys make repairs on the buildings, inside and out, mend fences, build chicken coops, set water barrels, saw wood and do a great variety of useful things. The other day I met the son of a Sioux chief coming home, cheerfully swinging his saw and hammer, from a little cabin where he had been putting up posts for a clothes-line [*sic*] to take the place of some unsightly brush that had been serving that purpose in the front yard. The girls of course, find numberless things to do in the houses, but this year have been paying special attention to the out-of-door work. With spade and hoe and rake they have laid out grass plots, flower beds, path and vegetable gardens where only weeds had grown before, and made the shabby little yards to blossom literally as the rose—and the cabbage.

When our students have completed with fair success the round of our school system, what then? Our record shows us that about three-fourths do well under the tremendous difficulties that confront them, and yet are they not very much like the little toy engines that a child winds up and sets going on the floor? Sometimes one will go straight through a room full of dangers, but quite as often it goes bumping about among the chair- and table-legs [*sic*] and then rushes off into some dark corner where it expends its force struggling against too great odds or gives its friends no end of trouble getting it out again. Put on a reasonably good track it would be saved many destructive knocks and its friends much anxiety.

If the school system could add another department to its work, and employ among the more needy tribes one or more men or women to act as guides to our freshly wound-up students, much of the work that is now being lost might be saved to us. Our schools teach many things that might be made valuable under skillful management, and we might teach many more. At Hampton we are teaching basketry, lace- and bead-work, so that when nothing better presents itself our students can have something always marketable to busy themselves about. Fruit drying and preserving and other local industries, besides what we call the native industries, might be made to keep busy the idle hands and bring in quite an income, could there be established a reliable medium of exchange between manufacturer and market. The experiment at Mohonk Lodge in the Seger Colony seems to be proving a success and would be a great blessing on almost every reservation.[101]

If Hampton has had a measure of success in educating the Negro race, it is because its work has been made to minister to the people rather than to the pupil; and we cannot but believe that the same principle applied to the Western schools would be equally successful in its results among the Indians. Such a school would have to be situated, as the reservation boarding schools are now, directly among the people it is designed to help. It would be simple, with little expensive machinery, and small enough to be counted a household rather than an institution. As it is the teacher that makes the school, the instructors would have to be men and women of intelligence, capable, devoted, and united. They would keep in constant touch with the people about them and, regardless of scholarship, aim to fit each pupil for some work that they know will be immediately practicable. The school would have shops where the more serviceable trades would be taught, but its strong point would be its farm. This would include a stock farm, a dairy and a poultry yard, that would be an everyday object lesson to the people of the reservation. A distinction would be made between old customs demoralizing in their tendencies, and those that are harmless; also between civilized customs that are helpful and those that are harmful in the present stage of Indian development. As many occasions as possible would be created to bring the people directly under the school's influence, mothers' meetings, conferences and young people's social gatherings being held at the school in the presence of the pupils, who would, as fast [as] they were found competent, be sent out among them to help in various ways. The plan of the school would be to give each member of the household just as much of home life as possible, thus fitting them for the life that the great majority must follow when their school days are ended.

# 16 | The Day School

## *The Gradual Uplifter of the Tribe*

MACARIA MURPHY, *Teacher, Odanah*
*Day School, Odanah, Wisconsin*

**Source:** NEA *Proceedings*, 1901, 913–14, is "An Abstract." A more complete version of Murphy's paper was printed in ARCIA, 1901, 481–82. That latter version is reprinted here.

Sister M. Macaria (Joanna) Murphy (1873–1951) entered the St. Rose Convent, La Crosse, Wisconsin, in 1890 at the age of seventeen. She had not yet completed grade school. Over the next five years, she completed the eighth grade and high school, entered the novitiate, and, upon professing her vows, became the 267th member of the Franciscan Sisters of Perpetual Adoration. The sisters had opened a school at Odanah, Wisconsin, on the Bad River Reservation of the Chippewa (Ojibwe) in 1883. Although the federal government recognized it as the Odanah Day School, the sisters served both boarding and day school students and called it St. Mary's Indian School.[102] In 1895 Sister Macaria became its principal teacher and chief administrator, a position she held "almost uninterruptedly," until 1936, although she continued her involvement in the school to 1946.[103]

Recognized as an employee in the Indian school service in 1897, Sister Macaria and her assistant teacher, also a nun, received federal salaries from that year until the federal government stopped such recognition in 1915. When delivering the current paper in 1901, Sister Macaria was both a nun and a federal employee.[104] Her emphasis on the "powerful uplifting influence" of day schools on the American Indian people they served fit well into the agenda for the 1901 annual meeting.

After giving up her position as the principal teacher at St. Mary's Indian School, Sister Macaria continued engagement with the Ojibwe people. In 1935 she received a federal Works Progress Administration (WPA) grant with which she directed the WPA Indian Research Project from 1936 to 1940. Her research papers from that initiative are today held at the Viterbo University Archives, in La Crosse, Wisconsin.[105] Ojibwe writer Mary Annette Pember has concluded that the essays in this collection reflect more about Sister Macaria as a Catholic nun than the Ojibwe people. "Most of the essays on culture," Pember writes, "are framed by stereotypical ethnological studies of the day that emphasized that Native traditions were part of a rapidly dying primitive past that was giving way to the modern assimilated Native American."[106] Sister Macaria's 1901 paper was similarly framed.

TO JUDGE OF THE PROGRESS of a nation, race, or tribe, a knowledge of its past history is essential. Twenty years ago this reservation was comparatively a wilderness, the wigwam, whose inhabitants lived much after the manner described in our school histories, being the only form of habitation. But a great change was soon to be effected—the doors of a little log schoolhouse were thrown open and with their opening dawned an era of civilization for the reservation tribe.

To-day [*sic*] the reservation presents a scene of beauty and civilization. Almost as far as the eye can reach we see looming up everywhere neat dwellings surrounded in many instances by well cultivated gardens, and we exclaim: "The hand of progress has been here." In vain does the tourist look about for wigwams; these are a thing of the past; no more moving caravans in the schoolroom. On entering a dwelling one is convinced that the occupants have been trained—mind, heart, and hand; in other words, that their educators' purpose was what every true educator's aim ought to be, whether it be the white, black, or red race that is in question, viz: "To cultivate, to train, to develop, to strengthen, and to polish all the faculties—physical, intellectual, moral, and religious." To descend to details illustrating this statement would be superfluous here; suffice it to say that many of the homes here are model ones.

After all, for what are the majority of our Indian youth to be trained, if it be not for the home or family life? This admitted, that school which trains most effectually for this life is the school which does most toward the uplifting of the tribe, and this is no other than the school which is in close contact, in living sympathy with the members of the reservation— the reservation school.

What do the average Indian youth do on leaving school? They marry and devote themselves to family life. Is it necessary they should know algebra or rhetoric or have been the captain of a ball team, for this purpose?

Think not that I wish to disparage higher education or literary training—never. The reservation school should give its pupils a thorough knowledge of the common branches, yea more, it should inculcate a taste for the higher; especially should it foster a relish for good, sound literature, which whilst affording innocent amusement, prevents desires for the forbidden and aids so powerfully in character molding. But whilst literary pursuits receive special attention, the industrial must never be neglected. Hence every day school conducted according to the wise "Rules for the Indian School Service," familiar to you all, must prove one of the greatest factors in the uplifting of the reservation tribe.[107] But to comply with these is no easy task, and if there is any one position in the Indian school service in which devoted, self-sacrificing men and women are more than in any other place a desideratum, it is in the day school.

To conclude, I repeat, every day school conducted according to the Rules of the Indian School Service exerts a powerfully uplifting influence on the tribe.

# The Necessity for a Large Agricultural School in the Indian Service

C. W. GOODMAN, *Superintendent, Chilocco Indian School, Chilocco, Oklahoma*

**Source:** NEA *Proceedings*, 1901, 921–22, is an abstract. The *Chilocco Beacon* 1, no. 10 (August 1901): 156–59, published the entire paper, which is reprinted here.

Chicagoan Charles W. Goodman (1860–1932) was a professional educator who received his degree from the Kansas State Normal School, today's Emporia State University. From 1889 to 1892 he taught in and served as principal of schools in St. John's City, Kansas. He began his career in the Indian school service in 1893, first as a field supervisor, but quickly rose to top administrative positions. On September 1, 1898, he assumed his position as superintendent of Chilocco Indian School. He did not attend the 1901 annual meeting, but had the current paper read to the gathered educators. By January 1902 Goodman moved on to take charge of the Phoenix Indian School, where he would spend the remainder of his time with the Indian school service. In 1914 he resigned his position as superintendent but remained in the Phoenix area, where he became president of a shoe company. While recuperating from surgery in California, he died on April 26, 1932.[108]

Chilocco Indian School was established in 1884, specifically as an agricultural school. However, as K. Tsianina Lomawaima insightfully points out, "agricultural education was an incidental by-product of the work students did to keep the school self-sufficient."[109] In other words, Chilocco students labored in agriculture not for educational value, but to support the school. Lomawaima's position is completely validated by Goodman, who offered a tepid introduction to his topic and recommended that a course of study in agriculture "should be established." Moreover, what he described in his paper is not agricultural education, but farm work being done by Chilocco's male students. As will be seen, the following year his successor at Chilocco, Samuel M. McCowan, stated that Chilocco "is where a large agricultural school in the Indian service might be valuable."[110]

Nearly twenty years of operation had not moved Chilocco any closer to being an Indian agricultural school, the very principle upon which it had been established. The 1907 *Rules and Regulations of the Department of Interior* admitted as much: "Great stress has been laid upon the practical teaching of agriculture, stock raising, and kindred pursuits at all Indian schools wherever practicable. The efforts of the past do not seem to have produced adequate results along these lines; therefore a new departure must be inaugurated." The "new departure" was nothing more than ensuring adequate employees and students were available, even during vacation periods, so as not to "conflict with duties which are to be performed during the spring, summer, and autumn months." Regardless of this requirement, the regulations cautioned that pupils "should not be placed in the fields merely for drudgery or manual labor alone." In the end, however, results counted, and, while the production achieved in the fields was "secondary to the instruction, yet they will represent a fair standard by which to judge" success.[111] An adequate farming operation, not an agricultural school, is what government administrators sought. Not until 1923 did administrators finally establish "a structured vocational educational program in agriculture" at Chilocco.[112]

THE SUBJECT ASSIGNED WOULD SEEM to imply the necessity of a large agricultural school, but as to the plan and the method of conducting it there is ample room for discussion. This subject is perhaps assigned to me because I happen to have charge of a school well located and reasonably well equipped for teaching agricultural industries, so that I hope some reference to Chilocco may be excusable.

A large agricultural school for Indians is a necessity: (1) Because the large majority of Indian boys will need a practical knowledge of agriculture; (2) because a large, well equipped school of this kind, in an agricultural region can teach farming and the kindred industries more thoroughly and more economically than other schools.

1. The large majority of Indian boys will need a practical knowledge of agriculture. Tilling the soil and caring for stock are the primary methods of earning a livelihood, and it is upon the industries that supply mankind with food that all the other industries, trades and professions are finally

dependent. The Indians especially should learn farming and stock raising, rather than trades, because they own land. Nearly all are receiving individual tracts of land which they should learn to care for and make the most of. Much of the Indian land is rich and fertile, as they had first choice when allotments were assigned. Some have holdings in the arid regions where irrigation is practised [*sic*] exclusively, and most of the land still held in common lies in the semi-arid belt where stock raising is the principal industry. Most Indian boys should work at farming in some form, as it is the natural employment for them, and insures [*sic*] the most independent as well as the most healthful life. Boys who would not live a year in a shoe or tailor shop may have many years of usefulness and happiness in the open air life of their western farms. The Indians live near to nature, but not so near as to have discovered all her secrets, so that a thorough agricultural training is essential to success. It is well for these boys to know something of carpentering, blacksmithing, painting, plastering, stone laying, engineering, etc., and some may be called to teach or to preach, or practice law or medicine, but of those who own land many more can make a comfortable living on farm or ranch than will succeed at a trade or in a profession.

2. A large, well equipped school in an agricultural region can teach farming and the kindred industries more thoroughly and more economically than other schools. While nearly all the large schools have farms, they do not make farming the important feature. Some are not in an agricultural region; some have unproductive soil; and few, if any, have a sufficient quantity of tillable land. Some make a specialty of the trades and turn out quantities of wagons, buggies, harness, shoes, clothing, tinware, etc., for the general market and the Indian service. Some emphasize their high school, normal, commercial, musical and art courses, and each of these schools is doing well the work to which it is perhaps best adapted. But Chilocco should be the great agricultural school. It is centrally located, in the rich farming region of Oklahoma, where the conditions are similar to those that surround the Indians of a large area. There are about 80,000 Indians, exclusive of the five tribes, within a radius of 600 miles. The climate is fine. Being in latitude 37 degrees, the winters are mild; situated in longitude 97, and at an altitude of 1,000 feet, the air is dry and the climate safe and healthful alike for the Indians of the north or those of the southwest.

The equipment is good. Chilocco has a tract of 8,600 acres of land as choice as is found in the Cherokee outlet. The buildings are capacious and modern; the large barns, sheds, granaries, corrals and stock yards [*sic*] are well suited to the requirements of such a school. Much money is invested in horses and mules, cattle and hogs, and improved farm machinery. Being on the border between the north and the south, and near to the uncertain boundary line of the semi-arid regions, the crops and methods of caring for them, partake of the nature of all the areas. Wheat is harvested with both binder and header; corn is planted with check rower and lister. We can raise the southern crops of cotton and castor beans; the northern products of flax, broom corn and oats; corn and clover for the East, and alfalfa, barley, millet and sorghum for the West; peaches, apples, grapes and cherries for everybody; and cattle and wheat for the world.

In an agricultural school, as much as elsewhere, a strong common school course of study is necessary. This should be co-ordinated [*sic*] to the principal industries and the instruction should be given by practical and experienced teachers. The successful farmer needs at least a good grammar school education, and any training that will develop his faculties and give him confidence in himself is of value. The Indian boy must first know and then know that he knows. Well equipped [*sic*] shops are also required to do the necessary work of keeping up the plant and making improvements. All the principal trades are taught and practised at Chilocco but the produce of all the shops is used in the institution. This includes carpentering, blacksmithing, wagon making, harness making, painting and paper hanging, shoemaking, quarrying, stone and brick laying [*sic*], plastering, stone cutting, tailoring, baking, steam laundering, printing, broom making, plumbing, steam fitting operating engines, dynamos and ice making machinery. The largest details however are given to the farmer, the herder and butcher, the gardener and dairyman, and the nurseryman. The boys have practical training in care of teams, of beef cattle and dairy cows, in butchering cattle and hogs, raising grain and forage crops, raising and caring for broom corn, gardening, caring for orchards, vineyards, small fruits, flowers and lawns. Large quantities of fruit trees, shrubs and plants are raised and furnished to other schools and to Indians living on their allotments. About 100,000 young fruit trees and vines are now growing in the Chilocco nursery.

But to the ordinary farm detail the most thorough and systematic instruction cannot be given. The afternoon boys finish what the morning boys began. The hours are short. Two or more boys handle the same team. For various reasons the boys on the detail are changed too frequently. Freighting, yard work and miscellaneous requirements of the institution interfere with steady, daily farm labor. The work is so varied and scattered that more supervision is required. For thorough instruction there should be established at the school a special agricultural course of two years on the plan of the special normal course at other schools. The requirements for admission to this department might be the completion of the eighth grade, good health, evidence that habits of industry and carefulness are being formed, and an agreement to complete the course entered upon. This would include graduates and undergraduates of other schools who desire to prepare themselves more fully for successful life. The boys taking this course should occupy a "farmers home" apart from the rest of the school, should be excused from ordinary roll calls and drills, should have breakfast earlier and supper later than the main school and expect to work more like their neighbors of the surrounding country. Eight hours a day will not suffice for a successful farmer, white or Indian, during the growing season. During the winter months text-book [*sic*] courses should be given in the various departments of agriculture. This school would differ from the agricultural college increasing the practical and limiting the theoretical teaching. The boys would learn to do by doing, under the direction of a sufficient number of competent, educated farmers to insure thorough work. As most of the work would be productive, pupils should be paid on a graduated scale perhaps from three to ten or twelve dollars a month, and their board, for faithful service. Furnish each boy the uniform of the school but let him buy his other clothes, that he may learn to value what he gets by the amount of labor required to earn it. The instructors and pupils could doubtless be paid from the proceeds of their labor, taken up as Miscellaneous Receipts, Class IV, the equipment and rations being furnished the school from the regular appropriation.[113]

This plan, modified as experience might dictate, could be inaugurated at Chilocco at small expense, and is capable of indefinite expansion as rapidly as results would justify.

**FIG 1.** Estelle Reel was superintendent of Indian schools from 1898 to 1910. She was the first woman outside of the U.S. Postal Service to serve as a presidential appointee requiring U.S. Senate confirmation. As a director of the NEA, she made the motion in 1899 to create a Department of Indian Education and served as that department's secretary from 1902 through the last meeting in 1909, when it was disbanded. She developed agendas for each annual meeting and selected and edited Indian educators' papers for inclusion in the NEA's *Journal of Proceedings and Addresses* for each annual meeting. No one had a greater influence over the Department of Indian Education. Undated photograph courtesy of Library of Congress. Bain News Service, publisher. https://www.loc.gov /item/2014683701/.

FIG 2. Irwin Shepard served as a part-time secretary (1893–98), then the first full-time secretary (1898–1912) for the NEA. He maintained an office in his home in Winona, Minnesota, where he served as president of the State Normal School (1879–98), a position he resigned upon being elected as NEA's full-time secretary. He collaborated with Estelle Reel to invite the Indian school educators to their first joint meeting with the NEA held in Los Angeles in 1899, where he welcomed them into the national organization. Photo courtesy of the NEA Archives, NEA Records Governance (NEA1001), Office of Governance and Policy, 1857–2002, box 699, folder 20, Gelman Library, George Washington University.

FIG 3. The first meeting of the NEA Department of Indian Education was held in 1900 at Freundschaftsbund Hall in Charleston, South Carolina. Such a venue was a long way from the isolated and rural environments Estelle Reel often invoked as a reason for the Indian school educators to meet with the NEA. These settings helped to promote Indian education as a worthy endeavor within the national education scene. Photo courtesy of Historic Charleston Foundation, South Carolina Historical Society, Charleston in 1883, no. F279 C48 A26 1983.

Hotel Cadillac, Detroit, Mich

202.269. (JV.)

FIG 4. Estelle Reel's student display that included "practical" work of the students as well as Native arts brought throngs of people to the writing room of the Cadillac Hotel on Michigan Avenue during the 1901 NEA meeting in Detroit, Michigan. Photo courtesy of Detroit Historical Society, #2012.044.939.

FIG 5. "West Hotel, Fifth Street and Hennepin Avenue, Minneapolis," ca. 1897. The Department of Indian Education met at the Plymouth Congregational Church during the 1902 meeting in Minneapolis, Minnesota, but the student exhibit in the West Hotel garnered the most attention from press and a host of spectators. Photo courtesy of Minnesota Historical Society, MH5.9 MP3.1W r29.

FIG 6. "Massachusetts Institute of Technology, Rogers Building, March 2, 1905." Due to Estelle Reel's illness during the 1903 NEA meeting in Boston, Massachusetts, her clerk, Lillie S. McCoy, arranged the student exhibit and oversaw the crowds of visitors to it in the Rogers Building on the campus of the Massachusetts Institute of Technology. Photo courtesy of Digital Commonwealth Massachusetts Collections online, https://ark.digitalcommonwealth.org/ark:/50959/37720r92v.

FIG 7. (*below*) Chilocco Indian School Superintendent Samuel McCowan, who ran the "Government Indian Exhibit" for the exposition, is the man in the front row looking to his right with his left elbow resting on his wife's knee. Immediately to his wife's left is Estelle Reel. The photograph is from the 1904 St. Louis World's Fair meeting of the Department of Indian Education. It appears to have been taken on the front steps of the U.S. Indian School building. From *History of the Louisiana Purchase Exposition*, edited by Mark Bennitt, courtesy of Illinois State Library, Springfield.

THE 1902 MINNEAPOLIS MEETING DEMONSTRATED the continued divide on *where* American Indian students should be educated, and the growing vitriol between the on-reservation versus off-reservation advocates, as well as the old assimilationist and the new progressive educators.[1] As noted in part 2, the unveiling of Estelle Reel's *Course of Study* and her student exhibit in 1901 sounded the death knell of the old assimilationist imperative to vanquish from the earth any semblance of "Indianness." Rather, Reel was promoting Indianness, if only for the marketplace and her hoped-for Native self-sufficiency. Regardless, that American Indians would remain American Indians dominated the Minneapolis discussions. This thrust in Indian education convinced Professor Oscar Bakeless of the hopelessness of his work at Carlisle Indian Industrial School, and he resigned within a month of attending the 1902 meeting.[2]

Reel had established a standard administrative routine to manage NEA meetings by the time she was planning this third convocation of the NEA Department of Indian Education. She informed all agents and superintendents in a letter of May 1902 signed by Acting Commissioner A. C. Tonner about the upcoming meeting of the department in Minneapolis, as well as "summer schools" to be held at other locations around the country. In addition to Minneapolis, there would be summer institutes at Hampton, Virginia; "Pineridge" [*sic*], South Dakota; "Flandrau" [*sic*], South Dakota; and, Newport, Oregon. She provided information on the NEA-negotiated railroad rates, the dates those rates would apply, and validation requirements to obtain them. She informed her educators that "all railroad and steamship lines have offered greatly reduced rates for a large variety of side trips to the many attractive resorts and beautiful lake regions of Minnesota, Wisconsin, Michigan, and Lower Canada, which will afford a delightful outing at very reasonable expense to those taking advantage of them."[3]

The thrust of the letter, however, was officially to encourage participation: "In view of the value to the school service of these meetings, it has been decided to detail such of the agency and school employees as can be spared from their work and desire to attend (except day-school employees, who have vacation during July and August), to such of the local summer schools as they may choose, and to the meeting of the [NEA] Department of Indian Education under the regular pay of their respective positions." Instructions followed asking for lists of employees who would attend these meetings and explaining how such participation would be validated. The capstone of this encouragement was that employees would continue to receive their "regular pay" while attending these meetings.[4]

Reel had also been thinking about the very popular "display of school work [*sic*]" that she organized for the NEA meetings. She provided to agents and superintendents in February specific instructions with a detailed diagram of what she wanted for her exhibit: "Please have the work prepared in the schools under your charge carefully mounted as follows: From heavy white card-board [*sic*], prepare three cards, each 24 X 30 inches, fastened together with white tape as per illustration. Place the name of the school at the top of the card in letters 1–1/2 inches high, as shown. On these cards will be mounted the entire exhibit of the school."[5]

Card no. 1 was to hold drawings, paintings, and other "color work"; card no. 2 would contain classroom work and photographs; and card no. 3 was for needlework. The classroom work, she instructed, "shall correlate with the industrial work, as set forth in the Course of Study." Her desire for photographs had little to do with pedagogy, but much to do with her aim that the exhibit would "show the results of practical training and diligent effort," which were central to the Indian school mission. She wanted photographs "showing pupils at work in the different departments, for example, sweeping and scrubbing floors, washing with tubs and boards, kneading bread, shoeing horses, cutting and fitting garments from measurements and illustrations on the board, making gardens, gathering crops, etc." All the exhibit materials, she wrote, must be sent to her "care of the West Hotel, Minneapolis, Minnesota, and must reach that hotel not later than July 1st."[6]

Little could she have known when sending those instructions that she would encounter headwinds as she planned her own departure to Minneapolis. She found herself in trouble with the civil service commission shortly before she was due to leave Washington. That commission was responsible for ferreting out the spoils system of government patronage by establishing civil service rules and regulations for appointments to government service jobs.[7] In the process of hiring a stenographer and a typewriter for her office, Reel sent letters to the applicants asking three additional questions of each, questions not authorized by civil service rules.[8] The secretary of the interior sent a missive on June 16 to the commissioner of Indian affairs inquiring into Reel's use of the unauthorized questions. The acting commissioner responded on June 23 and enclosed Reel's letter to the Indian commissioner to explain her rationale for each question.

Two of her questions asked if the applicants could be "strictly loyal in every respect" to Reel's "interests and to the rules of the Department" and would they "agree to resign at any time" should their "services not be satisfactory." Reel explained that these questions were to ensure employees were not "disloyal to the interests of the Indian educational service," and, if they were, a resignation was in the best interests of the employee. She would rather that an employee resign, she stated, than prefer "charges of inefficiency" against someone, thus jeopardizing that individual's employment elsewhere in government.[9]

Of the three questions, the acting commissioner only commented on one: whether it would be "disagreeable" for an applicant to take "instructions from the chief clerk (colored), who," Reel said, "acts in my place when I am absent, and also frequently when I am here." The acting commissioner told the secretary, "The fact that her chief clerk is a colored man, and difficulties which had heretofore occurred in her office during her absence, in the way of giving out information to the injury of the service, made the questions which she openly propounded to the applicants appear to her to be in the line of good policy in obtaining efficient office service."[10] Reel stated in her letter, "My chief clerk is a colored man, an efficient and capable official, but several applicants have stated that it would be disagreeable to receive instruction from him on account of his race."[11]

George H. Benjamin had always been an "efficient and capable" individual. Born in Nebraska in 1871, he was raised in Cheyenne, Wyoming, where his father, Edward, a Civil War veteran, relocated to serve in the Indian wars with soldiers assigned to Fort D. A. Russell, today's Francis E. Warren Air Force Base.[12] In 1888 young Benjamin became the first Black student to receive a diploma from a Wyoming school. The *Cheyenne Sun* reported that during his high school graduation ceremony he was greeted "with a perfect hurricane of applause as he stepped upon the stage to deliver his oration on 'The New Emancipation,'" an appeal for education and employment for African Americans. Benjamin worked as a stenographer in the U.S. General Land Office in the late 1890s. Reel wasted little time in getting this "bright" young man from Cheyenne into her office. Benjamin transferred from the general land office to become Reel's chief clerk five months after she became superintendent.[13] He then served as acting secretary for the inaugural meeting of the Department of Indian Education in Charleston.[14]

Benjamin was obviously talented and intellectually aggressive. In addition to the trust Reel placed in him, he enrolled in night school as a law student at Howard University in 1899, a fact reported with pride by his hometown newspaper, which declared him "one of the brightest young colored men in the country" who ranked "high in his class."[15] Benjamin completed his law degree in 1901 while working full time in Reel's office and attending night classes "each weekday evening from October 1 to May 25." Similar to his high school graduation, he was selected to offer a graduation oration during Howard's commencement exercises.[16]

Reel had unqualified confidence in Benjamin. She unapologetically told the typewriter and stenographer applicants that he acted in her place whether she was absent *or not*. Reel became contrite, however, when called upon to justify to the civil service commission her use of questions outside the parameters of the process. In the letter in which she had explained her logic in asking those questions, she added a postscript: "There was no intention on my part to infringe or evade any of the Civil Service Rules."[17] The acting commissioner of Indian affairs also assured the secretary of the interior that neither he nor the commissioner believed "there was any intention to disregard civil service rules."[18]

Reel took her arguments directly to the civil service commission by visiting the office of James R. Garfield, civil service commissioner, son of the assassinated president James A. Garfield, and future secretary of the interior (1907–9), when she was under pressure to leave for Minneapolis.[19] She found him out of the city and, because "official duties call me into the field," wrote an explanatory letter directly to him. Using nearly the same language she had used in her previous letter to the commissioner of Indian affairs, she acknowledged that "difficulties . . . have heretofore occurred in my office during my absences in the field" when she left Chief Clerk George Benjamin in charge of the office, difficulties occurring "on account of his race." She reiterated that she had no intention "to infringe upon or violate any of the rules and regulations of the Civil Service Commission." She emphasized to Garfield that she had "always loyally and faithfully upheld the Civil Service rules" and enclosed as evidence a copy of her 1901 annual report containing a resolution from the NEA meeting in Detroit the year before in which the Indian school educators expressed the opinion that "all employees in the Indian service should be subject to the civil service," including "Indian students who desire to enter the service as regular employees."[20] This disingenuous evidence only addressed the issue of American Indians being exempt from competitive testing requirements. The civil service rules allowed them to accept appointments at Indian schools after taking a noncompetitive examination.[21] Such a resolution had nothing to do with Reel's infraction of the rules by asking unauthorized questions of the applicants.

More telling of Reel's position on civil service rules are her own reported words. At the 1899 Los Angeles meeting, a school superintendent complained about a farmer at his school "who could not hitch up a team of horses nor plow a furrow; in fact, he learned all that he knew about farming in a grocery store, but nevertheless he passed the civil-service examination." In response to this complaint, "Reel said that she wished the whole civil-service system of procuring teachers for the Indian schools could be done away with, as she thought the results of the system were very unsatisfactory."[22] Despite her pronouncements to Commissioner Garfield, Reel possessed questionable fidelity to civil service rules.

The explanations she provided Garfield, the secretary of the interior, and the commissioner of Indian affairs appear to have assuaged the situation. There is no report of any further investigation by the civil service commission.[23] However, there remained a lingering effect from her run-in with the commission. It is certainly not a coincidence that the secretary of the commission addressed the Department of Indian Education at the 1903 and 1904 NEA meetings, or that Reel excised most criticism of the commission in later NEA published papers. Garfield became secretary of the interior in 1907, and she believed that difficulties between the two of them stemmed from her troubles with him as a civil service commissioner.[24]

The most enduring consequence of the "difficulties" in her office resulting in the civil service inquiry, however, was the departure of the "efficient and capable" George H. Benjamin. He returned to his former position as a stenographer in the general land office early in the spring of 1903. He eventually left government service, moved first to the West Coast and then to the Midwest, where he died in an automobile accident in 1937.[25] The nation had been denied the talents of the incredibly bright young man from Cheyenne "on account of his race." This incident does, however, demonstrate the complexity of Estelle Reel. Despite her obvious embrace of scientific racism when judging the capabilities of her Native students, she had complete faith in the capabilities of her African American chief clerk to include delegating to him the authority to provide instruction to her white employees, whether she was absent *or not*. Regrettably, historical documentation is mute on her reasoning that resulted in this contradiction and the subsequent civil service action.[26]

Having responded to the inquiry, Reel no doubt relished in the attention her Department of Indian Education received once she arrived in Minneapolis. As Minnesotans hosted an "Army of Teachers" in their "Flour City," the *Minneapolis Journal* reported, "One of the most important branches of the National Educational association [*sic*] and the one most interesting to the general public, is that devoted to the education of the Indian. This department is under the supervision of the national superintendent of Indian schools, and is one of the largest departments of the National Educational association."[27] The sessions involving the roughly three hundred Indian service educators held at the Plymouth Congregational Church attracted much attention, but the exhibit of student work at the West Hotel garnered the most enthusiastic media coverage. The *Minneapolis Journal* trumpeted: "The room is thronged with curious and interested spectators who marvel at the high standard of excellence attained in all the work shown."[28] News stories described the wonderful and intricate work in sewing, embroidery, woodwork, painting, lace, metal, leather, water coloring, and the Native arts, including work "adapted to the traditions and aptitudes of various tribes . . . shown in the clever basket work, rug weaving, manipulation of birch bark and intricate bead work."[29] The student exhibit had the desired result of showing the practical skills foundational to the *Course of Study* and the preservation of Native traditional industries.

The papers of the meeting focused on "practical education," to include industrial and agricultural training. The *Southern Workman* summarized the addresses given at the meeting: "The Indian should be taught to do something and should then be expected to become self-supporting through his own industry."[30] Such training and the reservation day school figured prominently at the meeting. Edgar A. Allen, Carlisle Indian Industrial School assistant superintendent, mounted a vigorous defense of the eastern boarding school, but clearly the idea of amputating Indian students from tribal relations in order to educate them had attracted increasing criticism by 1902. Unfortunately, such criticism and acknowledgment of the negative effects such institutions had on Native students did nothing to mitigate the situation for them or their families.[31]

A resolution passed by the department clarified the prevailing goal of Indian service educators. Indian school workers routinely passed resolutions at their summer institutes that established positions on social, educational, or policy issues, or, more mundanely, thanked organizers for a successful event. The commissioner of Indian affairs noted in 1895 that such resolutions were "characterized by a spirit of wise moderation, coupled with great insight into the needs of the Indian school work."[32] In Minneapolis the educators looked to the 1902 annual message of President Theodore Roosevelt for inspiration and passed a resolution in support of his stated national goals for American Indians, which they believed to be their lives' work. They resolved, "We should treat the Indian as an individual, not as a member of a tribe; . . . the reservation and ration systems are barriers to progress and should be abolished; and . . . we should preserve the Indian from the evils of the liquor traffic."[33]

At the conclusion of the 1902 meeting, Reel could take satisfaction in the positive reviews her efforts once again garnered. "Miss Estelle Reel's meetings in behalf of the Indians," the *Journal of Education* reported, "were by far the largest, most enthusiastic, and useful of all the departments. There were eight sessions of this department, which was four times as many as the other departments. She always had a full house and an inspiring program."[34] The *Southern Workman* agreed. "The annual meeting of the Department of Indian Education at Minneapolis last month," it noted, "is reported to have been one of the best in the history of the department."[35]

The preservation of "Indianness" also received rousing endorsements. The *Chilocco Farmer and Stock Grower* heralded what it noted as a change in focus of Indian education. "The importance of the Minneapolis convention," it reported, "lay in the almost universal sentiment of its individual members of making *better Indians* of our red brothers, rather than to continue to attempt the impossible feat of making good white men and women of them." Then repudiating the Carlisle model, the report continued, "Regardless of parental rights or parental affection, the offspring have been stolen or purchased or coaxed away to distant schools with the avowed intention of keeping them away forever. . . . Thank God!" Chilocco's newspaper began its summary of the conference:

> Those "good old days" are over. They will never return to vex. Times have changed! Thought has changed! Sentiment is awakened! New men are in charge. From now on the Indian will be treated and regarded as a human being with human soul, human intelligence, human characteristics, human love, hope and ambitions. From now on all effort, all thought, will be toward the planting in the Indian soul of a higher conception of life and life's duties—a higher conception of his duty to humanity and to his God—and then allow him to remain an Indian.[36]

Not surprisingly, Carlisle's *Red Man and Helper* disagreed with all the positive postconference reports. Its correspondent lamented that more dialogue was not allowed to counter "ideas and theories the most antagonistic, at times even contradictory, [that] were equally applauded and allowed to pass without discussion." Furthermore, "there was more than the usual amount of hysterical maundering against the non-reservation schools, eastern schools, Carlisle."[37]

S. M. MCCOWAN, *Superintendent, Chilocco*
*Indian School, Chilocco, Oklahoma*

**Source:** NEA *Proceedings*, 1902, 861–62, contains an abstract of McCowan's paper.
The entire address was published in the *Chilocco Farmer and Stock Grower* 2, no.
9 (July 1902): 259–64, as "The President's Address, Delivered by President S. M.
McCowan at Minneapolis, July 7, at the Session of the NEA," which is reprinted here.
In her 1902 annual report, Reel titled this address "Duty of Indian Workers."[38]

Samuel M. McCowan (1863–1925), raised in Illinois, began his professional
career as an educator after graduating in 1886 from Northern Indiana Normal
School, today's Valparaiso University. He shortly turned to the Indian school
service, which he joined in October 1889 as superintendent of the Rosebud
Day School in South Dakota. Ambitious and aggressive, he quickly became
a rising star in the Indian service when he gained favor with Commissioner
Thomas Jefferson Morgan. He then moved to Arizona, where he was superintendent of the Fort Mojave Boarding School and served as acting agent.
Anxious to advance his career, for a short time he held a superintendency at
the Albuquerque Indian Industrial School, New Mexico, before moving back
to Arizona to assume the superintendency of the Phoenix Indian School in
1897. He took over the Chilocco Indian School, Oklahoma, in January 1902,
a position he held until 1908 and the position he held when delivering two
papers at the 1902 Minneapolis NEA meeting.[39]

Indicative of his recognized "rising star" status with the Indian school
service, promoters hired him to serve as the administrator of the American Indian exhibit at the Greater American Exposition held in Omaha in
1898, and by 1902 he was actively planning an Indian model school for the
1904 Louisiana Purchase Exposition to be held in St. Louis. With both of
these exhibits, he intended to demonstrate that the educated, "civilized"
American Indian represented the future, unlike the sideshow demonstra-
tions of the "Wild West" that the Indian Office so disliked.[40] He was also

seen as a rising star by those outside of the Indian school service. Upon his leaving Phoenix in 1902, the *Phoenix Gazette* grieved, "The people of Phoenix and Arizona will greatly regret the departure of Colonel McCowan. In his leaving we will lose one of our best and most progressive citizens." The newspaper proposed that, had he stayed until statehood, which did not occur until 1912, "he could have had almost anything he wanted in the way of preferment."[41]

No one could have anticipated that McCowan's star would burn out by 1908. He retired from Chilocco Indian School the end of March that year following an investigation into the school's finances. In February 1909, under the headline "Noted Indian Authority Arrested," newspapers reported: "Samuel McCowan of DeGraff, Kansas, one of the best known Indian authorities in the country, was arrested here [Guthrie, Oklahoma] today on a federal grand jury indictment charging him with embezzlement and misappropriation of federal funds while superintendent of the Indian school at Chilocco, Okla., from 1904 [should read 1902] to 1908. He was released on bond."[42]

The case never did go to trial, due to various court proceedings and McCowan's failing health. A judge ordered payment of $8,000 from a bonding company to the federal government in 1913, and, by "agreement among the lawyers connected with it," the case was ended.[43] McCowan died in Texarkana, Arkansas, twelve years later, having never returned to the Indian school service.[44]

In 1902, all legal troubles were ahead of McCowan, and he was well respected and well received at the Minneapolis meeting. One headline declared him "One of the Star Attractions at the National Education [*sic*] Association."[45] About his president's address, another newspaper reported, "Mr. McCowan . . . drew a vivid picture of what Americans would suffer if the Chinese should conquer the country and force upon us their ideas of civilization. He showed that the red man[,] too, resented being torn from his home, forced to part with his children, his religion and his customs."[46] In this regard he was clearly criticizing the Prattian drive to "kill the Indian." Moreover, he had long held the position that one should not expect American Indians to advance quickly into civilization—another criticism of Carlisle Indian Industrial School's thrust for a quick transformation of Native students through a total immersion into white society. While superintendent at Fort Mojave Boarding School, he told the commissioner of Indian affairs in 1891, "The 'solution of the Indian problem,' as applied to the Mojaves, is simply a question of time; I am very sorry to have to state it as my honest opinion that the necessary time will probably require generations instead of months or years."[47] He reflected this personal view in the following two papers.

IT SEEMS TO ME WE have reached the crucial period in our Indian educational policy. Many tell us that our policy is bad; that the redman [*sic*] never has been and never will be a "hewer of wood and a drawer of water;" that being the pioneer on American lands he is deserving of, and entitled to, every consideration, including individual domains for homes; that we owe him a living and perquisites, and that our method of educating him is but the sequel of a long serial of dishonor, bristling with myriad forms of perfidy and brutality.[48]

And so they thunder and we quake; they roar and we tremble; they assert and we admit. They tell us the Indian is not like other men; that for him special methods and peculiar dispensations are necessary, and we wonder and by our silence give consent.

It is time we made defense or established an alibi.

Are we doing our best for the Indian?

This is a serious question and invites serious consideration.

In attempting answer to it we must brave the displeasure of those who would condemn for trying to inject into this convention some theories anent the solving of the Indian question. But, after all, is not that object the very one that calls us together?

The solving of life problems is no new study. It is as old as life itself. Adam and Eve, as they wandered hand in hand through the leafy aisles of the primeval garden; as they sat in becoming nudity unashamed and read the love lyrics in each other's eyes; as they talked in voices hushed and low of this wonder and that, and the way out and beyond, were only the children of a race solving in their halting, stumbling, simple way the problems of evolution.

And the problems they solved we solved and our task is the redman's heritage and lesson. Only this is true and to the Indian's disadvantage, that we—the white race—with our passionate mania for meddling, insists upon compelling poor Lo to evolve after our own fashion.[49] He is given no freedom of choice. We are determined to solve his problems for him, in our own way and time. We have decided that there shall be no more Indian; that we will destroy him root and branch, custom, habit, legend, all, everything akin to the race and merge him into our national plan so closely that the keenest eye can detect no trait of the Native American.

Justice, right, common human love would seem to point a better way— the way that develops the *better Indian*. But our race prejudice, aided and abetted by a morbid, unreasoning desire to dictate, steps in and discourages, aye, crushes freedom of thought and of action.

I wonder how we would like to be so supervised? I was thinking upon this point the other night when I slept and as I slept I dreamed. And in my dream I saw a strong man rise up in Orient and gather a mighty army of Chinese soldiers. I saw them drill and practice and perform and then march down to the shore and go aboard the waiting ships. The fleets were so many that they covered the waters like myriads of birds.

And after a while I saw ships sail up to our Pacific coast and, although we fought a goodly fight and crimsoned the heaving billows of the sea and gorged the monsters of the deep with the slain, yet did the demons swarm, like millions and millions of the imps of death, slashing, cutting, killing, butchering, driving our brave soldiers ever away farther and farther from the sea, across the mountains and plains burning, pillaging, destroying, until this beautiful land of ours lay bare and barren as a dead man's skull beneath the unsympathetic sun—homes gone, cities razed, farms devastated, fathers seeking their children, mothers refusing to be comforted because the boys were killed and the girls imprisoned, wives moaning and weeping because the homes were broken and loved ones gone. The air was a heavy lamentation and the death song was the national anthem.

And then I thought the broken and scattered remnants of a once proud and powerful race were gathered up by the pig-tailed [*sic*] conquerors and placed upon reservations. We were not allowed to leave the reservation without first going to our agent and getting permission. And this was no easy task for, mind you, these Agents were mighty men and powerful. Moreover they thought with their stomachs and when these organs were dyspeptic we were tantalized by doubts and misgivings and were sore afraid, and made our petitious [*sic*] in vain.

And after a time, when the conquerors were in secure possession they thought to elevate us to their standard and to civilize us. In their eyes we were savages and tormented by many barbarous customs. They decided that it was wrong to wear hair as we were wont and a decree went forth declaring that all persons on the reservation must shave the front and back hair and leave only a small patch on the top of the head which must be cultivated zealously to make it grow long and beautiful.

They looked with pity and abhorrence at the feet of our woman and marveled greatly at their proportions. This marvel caused many grave and solemn councils and it was decided finally to compel our wives and daughters to submit to swathing the feet in rolls of cloth, thereby reducing them in size and making them dainty and shapely. This order, of course, produced great commotion among us and we rebelled, which was not unnatural, for when one's feet are insulted it is time to kick.

The angriest of our people were those on the Red Headed reservation and the Irish reservation. These savages swore they would never submit to such tyranny and they attacked their agent and killed him and many others. But this outbreak did not help matters any. They were captured and taken back to the reserve and were given rations, on the theory that it was cheaper to feed than to fight them. This action made men weak because it robbed them of their manhood, and it was not long ere we became servile and vilely mean and contemptible.

And then the Government took up the question of social customs prevailing among us. The officials were horrified at some of them.

They de[c]lared that never in all their experience with savage races had they witnessed anything so barbarous and immoral as our mode of dancing. When they came to witness them—which they did occasionally out of morbid curiosity—they actually blushed with shame at the—to them—unchaste way in which our maidens glided along in the reckless abandon of the wanton to the devilishly sweet and alluring music of our uncanny and bewitched violins. How any girl could retain one speck of morality or virtue and give herself up so joyfully to a strange man's arms shocked them beyond measure and they declared that dancing should cease.

This was a terrible blow to us. For with dancing went other inherited social customs which we had practiced and reveled in all our lives, and our people before us, and which we had cherished and developed and thought pretty and wise. We rebelled and sulked, but this profited us nothing for we were weak and they were strong and seemed determined to make us over into their image. Soon an edict went forth abolishing our way of dressing, and ordering us to throw aside our national garb and adopt the loose, flowing dress, wooden shoes and queer head dress [*sic*] of their people. We were not allowed to paint any more, and that hurt some of our women sorely, besides changing many to such an extent that whereas they were once regarded as beautiful they became quite commonplace. This, however, proved valuable for a time to some of our ladies, because paintless they were not recognized and were counted twice under different numbers and received two ration tickets.

Our marriage customs were interfered with next, and this was both a joy and a sorrow to our women. A joy because marriage was made compulsory upon all men between the ages of 20 and 30; a sorrow because husbands were to be chosen by the parents, and the girl often did not see her sweetheart until the day of the marriage. This edict was, perhaps, the hardest of all to bear. Our women had ever been treated right royally by Americans. They were given all freedom, all opportunity. They came and went alone, or with company. All the bars to the green pasture of absolute freedom in the matrimonial world had been thrown down, save one, and that often slipped from its moorings.

Later, our religion and mode of burial were attacked by our oppressors. They seemed determined to not allow us a single thread of ancient custom to cling to, or a bit of loved lore or legend to cherish. We were to be shorn of all natural and inherited customs and desires as a sheep of its wool. We were to be made anew—to be born again, so to speak, not spiritually but materially and socially. Our children were taken away from us and educated in Chinese ways and language. We fought the order with voice and arms but we could do nothing but wait and moan and nurse our grief and pray until our babes were sent back to us again. And their return often opened the sore anew and made it perpetual, for many had forgot our language and could not talk to us. When we hugged them to our aching hearts and showered our love in good old-fashioned English, they grinned and blushed and swore or something back at us in odious Chinese until we thought them bereft of all sense. They had been educated in other customs, in other beliefs, in foreign opinion and alien ideas, which were all out of joint with ours, and it cut deep, deep into our hearts to see and know that our children whom we had nourished had been taught to despise us. O! those were terrible days! Terrible! And many were the hearts that broke, many the tragedies enacted!

When some of our loved ones grew sick we were compelled to send for the agent physician and give foreign medicines, and when we had a death many strangers came to view our custom of burial. And after a while, when the curiosity of the officials had been satiated, and the maggots of unrest began to stir within them and cause the womb of the brain to conceive and beget a new idea, they declared that we should no longer place flowers over the graves of our loved ones, but should place meat and drink there instead.

But the cruelest blow of all came when our religion was assailed. Our people had grown rather proud and boastful of our religion and our God. We used to tell each other that we were very wise in orthodoxy, sound on creed and safe and sure on theology generally. Some of us were sure that we knew all about the creation, the crucifixion, immaculate conception, original sin, the location of heaven and depths of hell. Many of us had grown so egotistical that we became confidential and patronized the Lord right shamefully. Some of us gave our religion as well as property into the wife's keeping, which was surely wise. Some became religious drones and prayed perfunctorily. I knew one man, myself, who had learned one tiny prayer of three lines when he married and had used it on an average of six times a day for 40 years, making a total of 87600 times he had fired that billet at the good, long suffering Father, who must have closed his ears when he heard it coming. His wife, being human, was driven insane by it and languished in a dungeon vile, ever alert to hear and see the triple lines that, personified, glowered at her from the corners like demons fierce and wild.

But our masters ridiculed our faith and jeered our religious practice. They could not understand how a people could be so silly as to bend the knee and petition in reverent, believing attitude an unknown God. Some of the best hearted and most intelligent among them advocated the liberal policy of leaving us alone with our religion, seeing that it was harmless to them and helpful to us, seeming to give us much comfort and solace; but the stronger party would not listen to such arguments. The Liberals claimed that no nation could be lifted up and made better and nobler by teaching its young to despise its lowly beginnings, nor were any individuals improved by being taught to despise their people or their God. But others said we were savages and unfit to judge of right or wrong; that our religion was vile in the sight of their God, and that our practices were unsaintly and unwise, not to say obnoxious to their higher civilization, and that we must be educated out and away from our degradation into a higher standard, etc.

So they undertook to solve our problem for us, instead of helping us to solve it for ourselves, and just before I awoke in agony of turmoil and a pool of perspiration, I beheld a vision of our talented and beloved Superintendent, in gaudy and costly loose flowing trousers and wooden shoes—her once honest and natural Western feet now only three inches long—bravely herding a long, long row of former Indian teachers in a gay oriental temple and all salaaming artistically and devoutly before a brass image of a Man! I saw Supt. Allen, once a handsome and polished gentleman of position and influence, fast losing his elegantly carved avoirdupois trying to maintain his dignity and at the same time establish a current of rice between his plate and his mouth by chop-stick [*sic*] device.[50] I saw the devout Superintendent of Haskell Institute, arrayed in priestly garb and hairless as a Mexican dog, with the exception of a beautifully braided and glistening cue that swept the floor as he walked, mount upon a ladder and crack a hole in the head of the nation's rain God and put therein an immense scorpion in order to stir him up to a realizing sense of his duty and make him give the people rain.[51]

I saw many other equally strange and ludicrous tragedies—tragedies heart-breaking [*sic*] and sad beyond the telling to participants, yet mixed with a strain of the ridiculous so simple as to be amusing to an outsider.

When I awoke and the vision cleared the lesson illumined some dark places in my experience, and I saw our Indian policy from the Indians' view point [*sic*]. What the foreign foe did to us in my dream we have done to our red brothers for generations. What hurt us had hurt them. Our policy had been domination or death. That is a chief tenet in Saxon creed. And in following such policy we were blind to charity and had thrown away all weapons or aids but force. We have acted like novices in knowledge of common human philosophy; like kindergartners in the study of social and intellectual evolution. Evolution cannot proceed faster than understanding. Until understanding is firmly established progress will halt, stumble and retreat. It is tormented by timid doubts and doubts do not beget strenuous endeavor.

For generations we fought our red brother, then we carroled [*sic*] him; then we changed our tactics and fed him and schooled him. For a generation we have tried to educate him. Defying all natural laws and thinking to annihilate time, we have fully expected to transform the 14th century into the 20th by the simple process of daily doeses [*sic*] of the three R's.

Results have not met our expectations and in our disappointment we blame the Indian. We forget that the two-minute horse was not evolved in a generation. We neglect to remember that centuries intervened between the cayuse and the palace car.

I repeat: Evolution can proceed no faster than understanding. To illustrate: There is a certain lady in the service who was zealous in endeavors to christianize [*sic*] her class. A year ago she gloried in her triumph. She had routed the imps of sin and offered the entire class to the Lord as her portion of incense and myrrh. Sometime after she had done this she was walking along a sheltered path when she was shocked to hear one of her best boys say, in tones of deep reproach and insult: "Your no good. Your'e a Christian!" "I aint neither," retorted the other angrily, and leaping to his feet in attitude of offense. "I ain't a Christian 'n I kin lick the stuffin' out of anybody what calls me one."

Now, those boys were not bad. They did not understand. A Christian cannot be evolved in [a] minute, I think, notwithstanding many dissenting vocies [*sic*] to this statement. The love of God cannot be understood in a minute, and until we understand we cannot follow intelligently.

And neither can our Indians understand our civilization in a minute, or a generation. And not understanding it they cannot appreciate it and will not follow it. And why should we wonder at this condition? Why marvel? Why this hue and cry of insult to our endeavor; of condemnation of our effort and labor?

I preach today the gospel of peace and good will [*sic*]. I would that in our work among this red race we follow the promptings of love and common sense. They cannot understand us or our times now. They are blind and grope in the dark for the stairs to climb—this people so patient under insult, so meek under the whip; this people with the hateless resentment and tongueless reproach.

I preach the gospel of peace and charity, and I wonder if we know that it is only the simplest conditions in life that are worth striving for. The complexities of our modern civilization are not heaven-born. They are of human invention. God made us loving and lovable, honest and natural, kindly and charitable. He did not, I think, plant in the human heart the tree of intolerance nor scatter the seeds of discord there.

If we, the actual workers among the Indians, will perform our duty to the best of our knowledge we need not mind the criticisms of those whose mission it seems to be to taunt and denounce. The hardships and toil of the pioneer must be irksome always. And this is very true of civilization's pioneers. But by following the policy now in practice of educating the younger generation of our red brothers in industrial pursuits the friutage [*sic*] of our toil will be large and comforting. The only danger to this policy is the inclination of some to idolize and idealize the Indian. This danger is real and present and fearful. It is a danger I cannot understand, because I can see nothing in him to either idolize or idealize. To me he is simply a crude bit of humanity, very crude, intensely human, intolerant of restraint, leisure-loving, dreamy-eyed, mildly antagonistic, passive, non-progressive. And my mission seems to me to be to take this crude bit of humanity and by my counsel and example help to make it better and happier.

# The Value of an Agricultural School in the Indian Service

S. M. MCCOWAN, *Superintendent, Chilocco Indian School, Chilocco, Oklahoma*

**Source:** *NEA Proceedings*, 1902, 869–70, contains an abstract of McCowan's paper. The entire paper under the title "The Value of an Agricultural School to the Indian" was printed in the *Southern Workman* 31, no. 9 (September 1902): 494–95. That version is reprinted here.

Chilocco Indian School was founded as an agricultural school in 1884, but in 1901 and 1902 the superintendents of that school continued to argue why it should become an agricultural school because the school had never developed an agricultural curriculum. Such arguments demonstrate the failure of the original vision for Chilocco.[52]

CHILDHOOD IS A MOST PLIABLE condition, but if we would mould [*sic*] aright we should follow, as nearly as possible, the child's natural desires and inclinations as to his future avocation, and develop along simple evolutionary lines. By following the child's natural bent; by adhering to his native gifts and aptitudes, we may guide him along the path for which he is best fitted, and in which he can find the most happiness and the best success.

This is entirely true as regards the natural, unspoiled Indian child. His horizon is close to the ground. It has not been lifted by home influences and elevating environment. He has ambitions, it is true, but they are wingless. They do not attempt wanton flight into unknown and untried realms. What his father was he is content to be. And his father, like all his ancestry back to the dawn of history, was a true son of nature. His living was obtained from the soil and the chase. He loved the earth and called it mother. He studied her moods and coaxed or petted, as his simple faith taught him was right and proper. His loyalty and fealty extended to the earth-mother's children, the elements. He confided in the winds and personified them. When it thundered and the lighting [*sic*] flashed he shivered in fear, not of annihilation but of the spirit's displeasure. A drouth was a sure sign of the earth's anger which could be dispelled only by penance, prayer and sacrifices.

Whatever may be thought of such faith and practice, the fact looms prominent that it gave large experience of natural phenomena and laws; of the soil's values, and knowledge of climate and conditions[.] He became wise in weather signs and lore, which profited him much in the growing of crops, in preparing for storms, or in selecting his habitation. This knowledge is a part of the modern Indian's inheritance. In natural laws he is an expert. He does not need to consult an almanac nor a weather report to tell whether it is going to rain or be dry. In the essentials of agriculture he is wise. He cannot tell you in scientific terms, perhaps, how to cultivate, nor where nor when; but he himself understands the how, the where and the when quite perfectly and follows farming successfully.

Unfortunately for the Indian however, he has other endowments and attainments besides a knowledge of climatic conditions and selection of soil. He has inherited largely of sloth and mental indolence and peonage to passion. His will lags and his ambition sleeps in the lap of ease. He would rather hunt shade than saw wood, which is a trait not altogether peculiar to the red race. He is a stranger to thrift and not on speaking terms with economy of time or labor, of industrial or domestic resources. Here, then, is where a large agricultural school in the Indian service might be valuable. If properly conducted such a school can and will inculcate habits of thrift, awaken ambitions, put the spur of energy to the lagging will, purify the passions, enthuse the mind and banish sloth. Moreover when the Indian settles on his allotment, where the genius of earth-craft must needs be keen, enterprising and sure, then scientific knowledge will be essential to even meagre success.

From the trail of the deer to the trail of the plow is a long road strewn with the bones of countless dead hopes and ideals. And yet they are close akin. Both are wearisome and backbreaking. Either is rough, long and strenuous. Pursuit of deer or plow call into play identical talents. On the trail of the deer one must keep one's ear to the ground for sounds, and one's eyes alert for signs. All the senses must be keyed to keen, attentive pitch. When trailing the plow one's ears must be strained to detect the first cry or sign of distress from the soil. Is it thirsty? Then it must be watered or worked. Is it hungry? Then it must be fed. One must be a wise doctor to diagnose the earth's complaints and tell the ailment by results. He must be a wise nurse to understand the management and know what to feed and when and how much.

And agricultural school should stimulate and enthuse the Indian's natural inclination and desire to raise grains and stock and prepare him to realize the most from the labor of his hands and brain. It should teach him *how to make his farm pay*. You cannot chain an Indian child to books and graduate a successful farmer, but daily practice at hand labor, intelligently directed, will not only produce a skillful workman but will profit the soul and unconsciously change a common laborer into a philosopher; a pauper into a producer.

The school that does the best for the Indian is the one that cuts away all educational millinery, that discourages the easy life, that compels hard manual labor, that holds out the promise of competency to those who toil, and assures the lazy and the indifferent of an ample punishment.

LAURA JACKSON, *Girls' Manager, Carlisle Indian Industrial School, Carlisle, Pennsylvania*

**Source:** *NEA* Proceedings, 1902, 864–65, contains an abstract of Jackson's paper. The *Red Man and Helper* 2, no. 49 (July 18, 1902): 1 published the paper subtitled "Paper Read by Miss Jackson before the Minneapolis Convention of Indian School Superintendents and Teachers, last week." That latter version is reprinted here.

Laura Jackson (1846–1936), from New Hampshire, taught French at Metzger Academy in Carlisle before taking a position in 1890 as a teacher at the Carlisle Indian Industrial School.[53] She became the girls' manager in "charge of girls in the country homes" within two years of her appointment. When that position was abolished, she was then named outing matron, a position she began only two and a half months prior to the Minneapolis meeting.[54] Jackson moved by 1907 to Berkeley, California, where she became involved in real estate. She died there in 1936, seven days before her ninetieth birthday.[55]

In the following paper, Jackson provided a history of the outing system and explained what its strengths for the students were, particularly young women. She began her presentation wondering why there was a need to defend Carlisle's outing system, implying that there had been questions about its value. Reel had demonstrated faith in the Carlisle Outing System and included it in her *Course of Study*, even though Pratt believed such a system would fail in the west. Jackson's opening comment shows that Carlisle was by this time coming under increasing criticism. Only three representatives from Carlisle—the Indian school service's largest institution—attended the Minneapolis meeting.[56] They were Professor Oscar H. Bakeless, head of Carlisle's academic department, who resigned in frustration over the direction of federal Indian education one month after the 1902 meeting; Assistant Superintendent Edgar A. Allen, whose vigorous defense of off-reservation boarding schools follows; and Laura Jackson.[57]

IT SEEMS A LITTLE SINGULAR that this subject should need to be explained or defended or presented in any way in such a community and before such an audience as this.

The idea of the influence of association is not new, and the so called [*sic*] Outing System did not originate with Col. Pratt nor in the Carlisle Indian School. He may have been the first to send Indian children out from school into families as is now so generally done. I have certainly no desire to take a single leaf from the well earned [*sic*] laurels with which Col. Pratt is crowned, but since the history of man, it has been well known that the association of different nations and peoples made those nations and peoples more alike; that the association of the ignorant with the cultivated, of the lower classes with the higher has always elevated the ignorant and the lower classes even if the higher were in such inferior numbers as to become incorporated with them. Children, for the same reason, are urged to associate with their equals or with those in higher walks in life than themselves, and how quickly a child shows what his associates are! How many people keep their children from public schools because they dread the influence upon them of the lower class of children who are always to be found there.

A savage nation brought into contact with a civilized one is always elevated by this contact. Compare the condition of the negroes, brought here as slaves, even with the condition of those who have remained by themselves in their own country. The condition of many of them in this country is degraded enough still to make them a very discouraging problem to contemplate, but it is vastly superior to that from which they were taken.

Some of them, here, by association with the white man, have risen to places of eminence and distinction. None, to my knowledge, have accomplished this by themselves, nor could they have done it here, had they been put upon certain tracts of land and forced to remain there apart from their white masters. The same might be said of all the other foreign elements flocking to this country. They all associate intimately with the American from the first, and for this reason, in an incredibly short time, are American themselves.

Not long ago, a group of people were amusing themselves by making guesses upon the nationality or rather upon the part of the country from which each member came. Some were judged from the South, others from the West and so on. Finally one young woman was unanimously voted to be from New England, but she laughingly shook her head, and, after a little further discussion, said she was born in Ohio, but that her mother was a German and her father an Irishman. She, the child of foreign parents, but reared in a section of Ohio that was settled by eastern people, was apparently a type of New England, the most American part of our American Continent.

The Indian, the native American, is the only one we have shut up on a reservation by himself and have expected him to become a civilized enlightened and useful citizen in this way.

Colonel Pratt, in adopting the so called Outing System, was simply applying the same idea to the Indian that has always been applied to everybody else. His practice of this idea commenced in the spring of 1875, when he was sent to Florida with a party of Indian prisoners. He took a second step in the same direction at Hampton in 1877 and a third, in 1879, when he brought eighty-two untrained Sioux boys and girls from their homes in Dakota and formed for them a school in the midst of a college community in Carlisle PA. He carried this idea only a little farther, when in 1880, the next year, he sent six girls and eighteen boys out into families. This experiment was so satisfactory that he has been increasing the application of it every year since, until, at the present time, he has three hundred and thirty-one girls and three hundred and seventy-five boys scattered about in families over eastern Pennsylvania, New Jersey, Delaware, and Maryland and a few in other states.

The families into which these children are sent, are very carefully selected, each new applicant being required to furnish three good references, unless he is known to the school, and it is understood that these boys and girls are sent out as students to be trained in right ways of living as well as in right ways of working. They are not sent out as ordinary servants, though even that would be a blessing to them. They are sent out to become members of the families into which they go and to attend school with the children of the family.

At the present time there are so many more applicants for students than the school is able to supply, that less than one half can be considered, and, of course, only what appear to be the best places are chosen. After a girl is placed in a family, a monthly report of her progress and conduct is sent to the school, and she is visited by some one [*sic*] from the school in the family where she lives, at least twice a year, if she remains out that length of time. In this way, there is a second culling out and selecting of places, for, if the visiting agent discovers that there are objectionable influences in the home or in the surroundings of the home, such a family is dropped from the list of school patrons. Sometimes whole communities are dropped. With this care to the selection of her surroundings even the crudest girl cannot fail to absorb much that is refining and that must bear fruit in her after life.

The girls are usually found happy in their country homes, as they are called, and some prefer to remain out rather than to return to the school, though they always regard that as their home, and it is often touching to witness their fondness for it and their loyalty to it. But, like all other people, these Indian girls like and need a change. So, after commencement, as the school year draws to a close, there is always a clamoring among them to "sign for the country," as they call it, and they are eager to go. On their return in the fall, they come back a laughing, happy band, and, as most of them come on the same day, there is great excitement and rivalry among them as they tell of the good times they have had. They almost invariably come back in better health than they went out; fleshier, with clearer, better complexions, and, with the new clothes they have earned and usually made themselves, they have quite the appearance of a party of white girls. Some have grown so rapidly and become so fleshy in the four or five months they have been absent from the school, as to be scarcely recognizable. Their manners also are changed, and we can judge a good deal of the families from the manners of the girls who have lived in them. Expressions like this are frequently heard at Carlisle. "That girl has had a good country home and she shows it." "It is easy to see that that girl has been with refined people." "How that girl has improved." Etc., etc.

While absent from the school at Carlisle, students are required to attend the public school at least one hundred consecutive days in the year, and many of them go the whole school year. In this way, they have the same advantages as the white children of the community in which they live. They are obliged to take their places beside them upon the same social and intellectual basis and to compete with them in class work from day to day. This is certainly invaluable to an Indian girl. She is the constant companion of her white sister and forms many warm friendships with her. She also grows to look upon herself as a girl and not as an Indian. Some of them are very popular with their school friends.

One of the greatest improvements is in their use of the English language. They have heard nothing else, consequently have been able to speak nothing else, and they have necessarily imitated the speech of those by whom they have been surrounded. Some of them learn very slowly, it is true, but they all learn. Occasionally, a girl who comes to the school at the present time, has never spoken any thing [*sic*] but English, but her English is usually very faulty. On the other hand, there are, even now, quite a goodly number of girls who can speak almost no English when they come, and but very little when they go out to their first country home. These, of course, when they hear nothing else, are obliged to express themselves in English the same as we are obliged to express ourselves in French or German when we place ourselves in a French or German family for that purpose.

Not long ago, in conversation with a white girl from the state of New York, who has a certain amount of Indian blood in her veins and who might now be supposed never to have spoken any thing but English, I was surprised to learn that when she entered the school she could speak no English, and almost none when she went out from the school for the first time. And speaking of this girl, leads me to mention another fact which seems remarkable; that is, that the most ignorant girls who come to us, many of them apparently white, are from this same state of New York. These girls have grown up in the midst of civilization and cultivation and yet have been so completely isolated from both, that they come to us sometimes with but the slightest knowledge of either, or of the English language, thus proving that even their white fathers or mothers have become so completely Indianized, by association as to have dropped the use of their mother tongue even in the state of New York, and their children have no knowledge of it.

As is well known, the school at Carlisle is an industrial school, and the girls learn there how to keep a house clean and in order, how to do laundry work, dining room work, teaching, dress-making and even cooking to a certain extent, but in so large a school, their knowledge of cooking is largely theoretical, the actual practice coming to them in the homes to which they go, where many of them become good practical cooks. Last year, two of the girls did the cooking for a summer hotel at Ocean City. They also learn general housekeeping and that most necessary of all arts, the art of home making, as they could not learn them in a school.

The girls frequently become Christians and connect themselves with the churches they attend while in their country homes, and some of them become very active workers in Christian Endeavor societies[,]Sunday Schools, etc.

In many cases people have expressed a wish to adopt the girl living with them and since the opening of the school, several girls who had no other homes have been so adopted, some even to the extent of inheriting property.

While students go out only upon their own written request, it is rather expected that each one will spend two winters of the five for which she enters the school in a family. Of course, some do not spend this length of time, while many spend much more, sometimes remaining from two to five and six years in the same place. A few have been out even longer than this.

This leads to another important benefit arising from the system not yet mentioned. These girls are earning wages that vary from their board and car fare to sixteen dollars a month, according to their age and ability. Of their earnings, they are at present required to save one half, while they are allowed to spend, under the supervision of the school, the other half. This training alone, though the last mentioned, would be a sufficient recommendation of the Outing System, as it is well known that the Indian does not know the value of money nor how to use it. On the contrary he is proverbially improvident, made so first by nature, perhaps, and secondly by the treatment he has received at the hands of the United States government. This well directed use of the money which they themselves have earned, teaches them what is most needful for them to learn:—namely, to depend upon themselves, or independence instead of dependence,—or instead of waiting for the annuities they and their parents have so long depended upon, and which, though granted in kindness and in a spirit of recompense for past wrongs, have contributed largely toward keeping the Indian from independence and advancement. It is a real beginning toward self support [*sic*].

It may be interesting and possibly surprising to some to learn that from the small amount earned in 1880, of which I could find no record, the sum has increased from year to year, with some fluctuations, until in 1891 the wages earned amounted to $28,741.69, and that the aggregate earnings of the boys and girls at Carlisle have reached the modest sum of $253,595.90 during the last twelve years.

What they do not spend, is cared for by the school, and as soon as they have twenty dollars, it is placed on interest for them and added to from time to time as they earn more. In this way many of them have quite a sum of money to take with them when they leave the school. A number of those who left since the first of July took $100 or more apiece with them.

# 21 | What Is Our Aim?

E. A. ALLEN, *Assistant Superintendent, Carlisle Indian Industrial School, Carlisle, Pennsylvania*

**Source:** NEA *Proceedings,* 1902, 870–71, contains an abstract of Allen's paper. Carlisle's *Red Man and Helper* 17, no. 52 (July 11, 1902): 1, 4 published the entire paper, subtitled "Paper Read by Mr. E. A. Allen, before the Minneapolis Convention of Indian School Superintendents and Teachers." That version is reprinted here.

Kansan Edgar A. Allen (1866–1939), a lawyer by academic training, began his nearly forty-year career with the Indian school service as the principal teacher at the Herbert Welsh Institute, Fort Mojave, Arizona, where he worked for Samuel M. McCowan, president of the Department of Indian Education during the 1902 NEA meeting. The U.S. Army occupied Fort Mojave until August 1890, when it transferred to the Department of the Interior, and an Indian school, named after Indian Rights Association founder and long-time principal agent Herbert Welsh, opened at that location with McCowan as superintendent.[58] In 1893 Allen arrived to take the position as principal teacher, but he found the conditions there unacceptable and desired a transfer. To the commissioner of Indian affairs he wrote, "My reasons for asking for a transfer are, first, there being no employes' [*sic*] mess maintained I am compelled to do my own cooking; second, the salary as teacher at this school is insufficient."[59] A transfer followed, and he began his perambulation through many schools and positions within the Indian school service. Along the way he married one of his former Chilocco Indian School students, Ida Johnson (Wyandotte), who then transferred with him, as a matron, assistant teacher, or teacher at their various schools.[60] In October 1901 Allen assumed the position as assistant superintendent at Carlisle, the office he was holding when he delivered the following address. Allen continued as the assistant superintendent after Pratt's dismissal from Carlisle in 1904, but he desired to move on, which he did in September 1904, as a special agent for the Indian school service.[61] By 1911 he was superintendent back at Chilocco

Indian School.[62] Allen retired from the Indian school service in 1930, and moved to a fruit farm in Raymore, Missouri, where he died in 1939.[63]

Allen, who served mainly at large off-reservation boarding schools, defended the separation of the child from tribe and family to reside at a boarding school. As previously noted, the years from 1900 to 1904 mark the time during which the proponents of the off-reservation boarding clashed most openly with the proponents of reservation boarding and day schools. Allen's address represented a vigorous defense of the off-reservation boarding school and its role in civilizing and assimilating Native students. He vigorously assailed civilization efforts that did not amputate the child from tribal and familial connections.

DURING THE PAST FEW MONTHS, encouraged by the speeches made by a couple of members of Congress, a band of tearful humanitarians, champions of the picturesque Indian, have come forward with most lachrymal pleas against sending the child away from the protecting care of the parent to a school where he will be educated away from those qualities and ideals of his tribe that are responsible for all the phenomenal strides made in civilization on the reservation. Also men who have retired from active Indian service to allow recuperation to badly jaded reputations, have come gasping to the surface again with preachments on the same subject. An ex-inspector, the patron of cheap saloons and all that accompanies them, while in office, has during the winter been most active in pointing out the right way and deploring the immorality of most all Indian workers but himself, while a sage of the Pacific slope who, as Indian agent, located a school in his country and found in his stocking a deed to a ranch beside it, has lately been denouncing the cruelty of taking children away from home to school.[64] We even find ourselves buying a new reservation for the Agua Caliente Indians instead of ranches, while we are on the other hand endeavoring, we say, to break up the reservations we have.[65] Surely our left hand does not know what our right hand is doing.

Educate the Indian at home but do not educate him away from his people. Do not let the child run in the light of our best Christian civilization because he will leave his grandmother stumbling in the darkness of the barbarism she will not leave. In 1850 and for a number of years thereafter, a Missionary, one of the most prominent educators of Indians, worked among the Peorias and Miamis. Most excellent reports were made of his school, all showing great progress in both literary and industrial lines made by the students. These statements read very much as do those optimistic ones we make in these more modern times of the gratifying advancement noted and modestly observed to have its inception contemporaneously with our connection with affairs. Mr. Lykins was a most able and excellent man who labored hard to accomplish the impossible.[66] Instead of making industrious citizens of the people he labored with, he found his children and grand children [*sic*], without having any mixture of Indian blood, taking on Indian characteristics. They "went back."

By some legerdemain they succeeded in securing adoption into the Peoria tribe and a numerous family has secured allotments of two hundred acres each. They rent their lands, sell them when the restrictions are removed, have been hauling their children to the Government school each autumn and are notoriously the most clamorous for payments. It is true that some of the white man's enterprise is shown by one having some local influence, in that he has secured for his wife, the mother of some eight or ten children, a place as a teacher in the village school.

In 1820, it is reported of one Richardville, a Miami chief, by a special Commissioner, that he is a man of good sense and manners like those of our respectable farmers.[67] He also reports that a missionary named McCoy, a Baptist, preached to the Miamis and kept a school for the children, and that a great majority of the people were friendly to civilization.[68] He thought it a good plan to collect the Indians for purposes of education. You can say this of the situation to-day of all the Miamis who have remained "collected," and you can [not] say more. A descendent of that same Richardville, and bearing the same name is still chief, and they have the same friendliness toward civilization.[69] But this friendship has not made them educated. In the beginning of last century the so-called civilized tribes had their schools and academies among themselves, and they still have them. But everyone knows that the term "civilized" is a misnomer. Precious few, if any, educated Indians came out of the doors of those schools, and so scandalous did their institutions become that at last, within the past few years, the Government has been obliged to assume supervision. The fullbloods still live in the hills and brakes and with few exceptions the reputation for civilization is made by the mixed bloods and adopted whites among them. Even the Osages had two schools as long ago as 1820. Listen to an extract from a report on one of them, made by the Superintendent: "The male department is conducted by three Catholic clergymen and seven lay brothers; one of these, being a good scholar, is employed as assistant teacher; the others accompany the children during the hours of agricultural instruction, or such other employments as are calculated to instill into their minds industry and perseverance. As to the progress in learning made by these pupils, a considerable number can read well; they acquire a knowledge of penmanship more readily than the generality of white children; in the study of arithmetic, they exhibit a great degree of emulation. Sometimes the half-breeds, at other times the unmixed Osages, surpass one another. The other branches of common learning, such as geography and grammar, are also regularly taught.

["]With regard to the female department, nothing has been left undone to insure [*sic*] permanent success; being well aware that the progress of civilization and the welfare of a rising nation greatly depend upon the female members of society, for they are to instill the first principles of virtue and morals, the foundations of a future happy generation. The pupils are educated under the careful guidance of six religious ladies, who devote all their attention to the mental and moral improvement of their pupils. They are taught spelling, reading, writing, arithmetic and geography, and besides, certain hours are set apart for knitting, sewing, marking, embroidery, etc. Between school hours they are engaged in occupations of domestic economy."[70] What is the name of the Osage who carries the marks of any part of this training, provided for nearly a century?

There were industrial schools among the Indians long before the first birthday of any in this presence, and all on the reservation, while day schools were numerous. Schools and missionaries have been established among the Indians of New York, and the best civilization the world knows has been just outside the borders of their reservation for more than a century, but they are not appreciably nearer to being a part of that civilization to-day than they were when the first teacher said to the first pappoose [*sic*], "the primer class will now recite."

Indian Rights Associations, yea, and Sequoyia [*sic*] Leagues, with a better organization, as extended an acquaintance with and as large a measure of love for the Indian, as those of this day, were not unknown to our fathers.[71] During the presidency of James Monroe there was founded, to use their own phraseology, "A society for promoting the civilization and general improvement of the Indian tribes of the United States."[72] It had a

Washington office and a Washington agent. It's [*sic*] membership included the most patriotic and philanthropic people of the time; it was officered by such men as John Adams, Thomas Jefferson and James Madison, and there appeared upon its rolls the names of John Jay, Charles C. Pinckney, Andrew Jackson, Henry Clay, William Wirt, Francis S. Key, none of them unknown to us. The association has passed into history and the last ripple it caused in Indian barbarism has grown fainter and fainter until it is lost in the sea of ignorance in which the reservation Indian is still immersed. To all those people who, standing on the outside, wish to form a board of strategy for the President, the Secretary and the Commissioner, a quotation from Levy seems in place, "Lucius Emelius Paulus, a Roman Consul, who had been selected to conduct the war with the Macedonians, BC 168, went out from the Senate House in the assembly of the people and addressed them as follows:

"In every circle and truly at every table, there are people who lead armies into Macedonia; who know where the camp ought to be placed; what posts ought to be occupied by troops; when and through what pass Macedonia should be entered; where magazines should be formed; how provisions should be conveyed by land and sea; and when it is proper to engage the enemy, when to lie quiet. And they not only determine what is best to be done, but if anything is done in any other manner than what they have pointed out they arraign the Consul as if he were on his trial. These are great impediments to those who have the management of affairs; for every one cannot encounter injurious reports with the same constancy and firmness of mind as Fabius did, who chose to let his own authority be diminished through the folly of the people, rather than to mis-manage [*sic*] the public business with a high reputation.

["]I am not one of those who think that commanders ought never to receive advice; on the contrary, I should deem that man more proud than wise, who did everything of his own single judgment. What, then, is my opinion? That commanders should be counselled chiefly by persons of known talent; by those, especially, who are skilled in the art of war, and who have been taught by experience, and next, by those who are present at the scene of action, who see the country, who see the enemy, who see the advantages that occasions offer, and who embarked, as it were, in the same ship are sharers of the danger. If, therefore, anyone thinks himself qualified to give advice respecting the war which I am to conduct, which may prove advantageous to the public, let him not refuse his assistance to the state, but let him come with me into Macedonia. But if he thinks this too much trouble and prefers the repose of a city life to the toils of war, let him not on land assume the office of a pilot. The city in itself furnishes abundance of topic for conversation, and we shall be content with such councils as shall be framed within our camp."[73]

A delegate in Congress from Arizona made, in the House last winter an attack upon all eastern schools for Indians in general and Carlisle, as a somewhat conspicuous example, in particular, in which there was much animal heat.[74] He does not stop to consider that the large school at Phoenix, in whose appropriations he is much interested, is transporting children from almost as far as Carlisle does and from as different material conditions of life. He says that it is cruel to separate the child from his home environment, educate, him, [*sic*] as he and Hamlin Garland are so fond of saying, in Latin and Greek, and send him back.[75] We have tried, as the charge has been reiterated by the gentleman often, to ascertain what in our curriculum is as Latin and Greek to them, and are forced to the conclusion that they must refer to our study of the decalogue. Not one of the gentlemen who are deploring the unwisdom of schools in the midst of our best civilization has ever graced Carlisle with a visit though many times invited and entertainment gladly offered. What is there admirable or worthy of preservation about the environment of the average Indian home except the appropriation distributed annually, and in the eyes of the novelist, the picturesqueness that is enfolded in the blanket smeared with paint and that exhibits itself in the sun dance. Moses, for all his years of toil, was rewarded with a glimpse of the promised land and died happier and more richly rewarded than if he had remained to bask in the presence of Pharaoh's daughter. If knowledge makes us miserable, then we are destined to be so, for our Creator ordains that we shall know. But to be conscious of better things than our fathers knew is not to gather unhappiness, for all good is obtained to him who persists in its pursuit, no matter what his nativity or ancestry. The president of one of the largest schools for colored youth in the south, a man born a slave, and, as he says, a "full blood", said in our chapel last winter:—"My big hands have never been in my way; my flat nose has never been in my way; my kinky hair has never been in my way; my black skin has never been in my way—nothing is in the Negro's way but himself". If this is true of the black [*sic*] man who so lately bore the owner's brand, there must be hope for the Indian who is subject to none of the social discriminations of the other man, but is welcomed among the best people and given all the opportunities that the twentieth century brings to us. Some people are intermarried with these "stone age" folks in apparent indifference to Mr. Garland's opinion as to its inadvisability. But the necessary conditions for growth do not obtain within the limits of any reservation in the world. The white man and the Indian, alike, who go there, "go back." The opportunities for laziness are fostered there and are irresistible. We must not be guided by those whose interest is in the preservation of relics as an inspiration to the painter and novelist. The seats of the most ancient civilization of the world are now the abiding places of the most abject degradation, because people make their living there by preserving the relics and showing them to a morbid crowd.

The decree goes forth that the reservation must be broken up and immediately thereafter new schools are built and old ones enlarged to make the breaking up impossible. The sentiment is expressed that children should not be taken from home for education and the next day the remote schools are given greatly increased appropriations. The painter, the writer of fiction and the ethnologist wish to preserve the picturesque Indian, the Congressman his appropriation and each superintendent and agent his particular school and agency. What a mess it makes. The red man is an American; let us put him where the American should be placed for his training—into our public school system, where he may, nay, must sit at the feet of the same teachers and in the same environment learn the lessons that have made men of our race; out of the public schools into our industrial life doing work, even so-called inartistic work if necessary, any work that an honest person can do, and by its fruits earning his bread. Grant that he has been robbed of his heritage. It will never be restored to him, and, more than that, he is yet being robbed with his own consent of the little yet remaining. He must meet our industrial conditions. Let him learn how to take the waves and rise with them, from those who know how. He cannot live on the memory of what he once had. A decayed aristocracy endeavoring to subsist on the proceeds of a farm rented to a white man with the certain prospect that his children will have nothing to rent, is a condition that should move us to positive action, heedless of the dreamer's talk of an artistic life. The best artist is he who weaves an honest life out of the opportunities all have, and who can paint in his own countenance the likeness of a sturdy, conscientious, self-supporting member of society. All that is worth preserving of the Native American will endure and gather strength and the rest will quickly perish from the earth it cumbers.

A. O. WRIGHT, *Supervisor of Indian Schools, Washington* DC

**Source:** NEA *Proceedings*, 1902, 872, contains an abstract of Wright's paper. The address was published in the *Chilocco Farmer and Stock Grower* 2, no. 10 (August 1902): 288–93 under the title "Some Criticisms and Some Hints," which is reprinted here.

A New Yorker by birth but educated in Wisconsin, Civil War veteran and ordained minister Albert Orville Wright (1842–1905) came to work with the Indian school service late in his life. He was not a professional educator like many of his Indian school colleagues, although he had served as president of a college and served on its board of trustees. His greatest distinction for school service rested with his philanthropic work in such organizations as the State Board of Charities and Reform in Wisconsin, the Wisconsin Conference of Charities and Corrections, the National Conference of Charities and Corrections, the National Children's Home Society, and a Soldiers' Home for Grand Army of the Republic (GAR) veterans.[76] The Department of the Interior temporarily appointed Wright as a supervisor of Indian schools in 1898 based on his experience in charitable work, although such appointments were normally reserved for former Indian school superintendents. The civil service commission was not pleased that Wright had been appointed from outside the Indian service without a competitive examination. In its *Fifteenth Report* it complained that, despite his being "eminently qualified for the position," allowing such appointments to occur would "be a return to the evils of the patronage system." Regardless, the Indian service prevailed, and in its *Sixteenth Report* the commission reported that Wright's temporary appointment had become permanent in November 1899.[77]

Despite his charitable work and inclinations, his reports as a supervisor were generally deprecating of the Native people who resided in the areas in which he traveled.[78] His last assignment was to investigate the allegations of Father Joseph Schell "regarding the sale of liquor and other forms of debauchery among the Winnebago Indians in Northern Nebraska."[79] Father Schell's reports of corruption on the reservation received national coverage, garnered him an audience in Washington with President Theodore Roosevelt, and launched an investigation to be handled by Wright.[80] En route to Nebraska, he fell ill, returned to his home in Madison, Wisconsin, and died there June 19, 1905. With his passing his hometown newspaper declared him "one of Wisconsin's most prominent educators and philanthropists."[81]

Wright's presentation hit on the themes of the 1902 meeting: that what Indian students needed were more day schools and actual industrial and agricultural training, not just laboring at schools. He complained about the institutionalizing of children in the absence of their parents, reflecting criticism levied against the large nonreservation schools. He additionally told Indian service educators that the industrial and agricultural training that they offered to their American Indian students was what the rest of the nation needed in its public school systems—a theme repeated throughout the Minneapolis meeting.

WHEN INDIAN SCHOOLS BEGAN TO be organized in earnest, it was seen at once that the conditions of the problem were different here from those among our civilized citizens. It was perfectly plain that the Indian children should be taught how to work as well as how to read. It was believed that industrial education could not be given unless they were taken away from their homes and placed in industrial boarding schools. Hence our great system of reservation and non-reservation boarding schools.

Day schools were not attempted, or if attempted were not successful except in a few places. These boarding schools were organized on the basis of half a day work and half a day study, similar to the plan of the reform schools for the white savages of our cities. It is this system which has been on trial, and it is this system with which the friends of Indian education are so largely now expressing more or less dissatisfaction. These observers do not fully analyse [sic] the cause and results. They only see that there is something wrong, and they frequently suggest inadequate remedies. But this does not prove that there is not good cause for dissatisfaction.

In my opinion the real difficulty goes deeper than any mere question of management of Indian schools. It is a part of the great revolution which is impending in our whole system of education. As society has outgrown the old simple organization of farmers and mechanics and traders, and has developed into a highly complex system of organized labor and organized capital, producing by machinery and distributing through great lines of transportation and immense mercantile establishments, a corresponding change in our methods of education is fast becoming necessary. A merely literary education is not sufficient; it must be technical also. The time is rapidly coming when our public schools will be made technical schools. Already in at least two interior states agriculture is required to be taught in common schools. Already in many of our cities, cooking and sewing are taught in the grades below the high school. Already in many cities manual training high schools are teaching the use of tools and machinery. Technical training is rapidly coming to the front.

In their literary work the Indian schools have followed the proved methods of the public schools, and have teachers trained in these methods. They are therefore successful in the literary work.

But in their industrial training they have followed the old methods of the apprentice system. The necessary work of the farm, the shops and the household, is done by details of pupils working with employes [*sic*]. Until lately there has been no attempt to teach industries as literary subjects are taught.

The employes are selected, not for their ability to teach, but for their ability to do work themselves. The consequence has been that the pupils have learned what the employes are capable of teaching. In a few instances pupils have been taught surprisingly well, but, as a rule, the teaching of industries has been merely such as the pupils can pick up as helpers of the employes. The cook, for instance, has a detail of girls to help her. But she is concerned to get the meals and therefore does the actual cooking herself, keeping the girls busy preparing vegetables, washing dishes and other work which does not teach them cooking. Further, she is not herself a cooking school teacher; she has learned to make good bread, to cook vegetables fairly well and to destroy all the natural flavor of meats, in the usual way of country cooks, and she teaches all she knows. She is also obliged to use the wholesale methods of instruction, and she puts the food on the table before the children are called, thus giving it fifteen minutes to cool before it is eaten. The pupils are thus not allowed to cook for themselves; they only see average cooking done in a wholsale [*sic*] way and not in quantities suitable for a family, and they never hear of the scientific principles of good cooking, of which the cook herself is wholly ignorant.

The same general difficulties exist with other household industries. The seamstress does not like to trust the older girls to cut and fit, and therefore does all of this herself. She cannot possibly do all the sewing herself, and therefore has a number of girls well trained to run sewing machines. She does not want to do extra work and therefore objects to taking a class of little girls in patching and darning. The result is that Indian girls, with their natural aptitude for needle work, learn to run sewing machines only. The seamstresses themselves are rarely skilled dressmakers and cannot themselves teach what they have never been taught.

In laundry work, in the care of rooms, and dining room work, there is less need of any more than routine work, and the results are not so glaringly inadequate. Everywhere however, the instruction, such as it is, is wholly by imitation, and is limited to the actual needs of the daily round of household life. There has been rarely anywhere any idea or attempt to teach household science. The result is to send out pupils from the schools who have learned the habits of cleanliness and regularity of work, who know how to keep house in an institution but who cannot cook or make good looking [*sic*] garments, and who have learned all they know of housekeeping by imitation, and not rationally. And the housekeeping they have learned is that of an institution and not that of a family. Their industrial work has not been correlated to their literary work, and there has been no vital connection between them, except that one was taught in one half day and the other in the other half day. Further, industries have been taught as merely the hand-maids [*sic*] of literature, and of inferior rank in life, thus giving a wrong conception of life.

The same thing is essentially true of the boys' work. The farm work has been taught imitatively, and the boys have been treated as farm hands not as students of agriculture, so also with the trades. These are taught by the old apprentice plan and not by that of the modern trade school. There are some notable exceptions to this, but this is the general rule.

The Indian Office has sent out to all the schools the little manual for teaching sewing to the smaller girls, which is used in all the public schools in Boston, and is admirably adapted to this use, and these books have simply been put in the library and have not been used. The office has sent out also a fairly good text book [*sic*] on agriculture, which has been treated in the same way. The inertia of routine and the difficulties of making farmers and seamstresses teach from text books has prevented anything being done. There are two or three notable exceptions to this.

The net result of all this is that the industrial side of the Indian schools has not been a failure by any means, but that it has not been such a success as it should have been. Habits of industry have been taught, and that to savages whose ideal life is idleness, especially for the boys.

Habits of cleanliness have also been taught to squalid savages. New wants for better clothing, food and housing have been created, which are the beginning of a deep desire for civilized life. But the industries have been given an inferior place to the studies, and the ambitions of youth have been excited to seek success in some pursuit that does not soil the hands. In this the Indian schools are doing precisely what the public schools are doing, but without the correctives in home life, which the public schools have. The fault is that no advantage has been taken of the great opportunity in teaching industries to instill ambitions also for success in life by means of them, that the industries have not been taught according to modern methods of systematic and scientific instruction, but according to the medieval methods of imitation, and that they have not been taught according to the methods needed for a family; but according to the methods needed for an institution. The old apprenticeship system required seven years to teach a youth a trade by imitation; while the Baron Hirsch Trades School in New York is teaching the same trade more thoroughly in six months by modern methods.[82] The Indian schools are still using the old methods. No wonder there is dissatisfaction with them.

Another very serious difficulty with the education of Indian children comes from the fact that, as a rule, with few exceptions, their education is in boarding schools. The defect is not merely that of being associated with their own people in school, though that is of itself a great disadvantage, as the influence of fellow pupils is half the education given in any school, but it is mostly from the unfavorable influences of institution life. No institution can be as good for a child as a family. Babies cannot be brought up in cold storage warehouses, which the best of institutions are inevitably. The old fashion of orphan asylums for children deprived of their parents is now passing away and is condemned by all students of social problems. As formerly Secretary and President of the National Conference of Charities and Corrections I have had abundant reasons to know this fact, which the printed volume of the proceedings of that association of persons at the head of public and private charities will fully show.

Instead of organizing day schools for younger children they have been brought into boarding schools when they were not old enough to learn industries and when they might better have been left with their mothers, as far as their health and general progress is concerned, if only day schools had been provided for them. I pass by here many side issues which could be raised about the irregular attendance at day schools, and the better opportunities to teach civilized habits in the boarding schools, all of which have some value, and only call attention to one fact, which seems to have been wholly neglected. The great objection to day schools in most places has been the distances the children have to go. Our public schools are beginning to meet this same difficulty in the public day schools by furnishing transportation for pupils who live at a distance. Massachusetts, in a majority of its towns, brings the children to a central school each day by teams. I have never heard this offered as a method for Indian day schools. But I now offer it, and urge that it be adopted wherever feasible. With this, many day schools could be carried on where they are not now.

But, as it is, the natural method of bringing up the children is ignored. This not only leads to a constant conflict between parents and school authorities in regard to bringing in children at the beginning of the school year, and taking them out for visits at home and visiting them at the school, and taking them home when sick, all of which are constant sources of irritation, but what is of more consequence it puts the children in the unnatural atmosphere of an institution and not in that of a home. Furthermore, it relieves the parents of the necessity of providing for their little children and thus encourages the very habits of idleness which we are trying to eradicate. There is no doubt that a boarding school gives better food, clothing, shelter and more healthful surroundings than the average Indian home, but it does not provide parental affection, nor does it bring any effectual influence on the parents to bring them also along the path of civilization which their children are taking.

At present it seems to be a choice of evils. Many of the younger children can be educated in the day schools at their homes. In some cases these are public schools in which white and Indian children meet, and such as they will be obliged to use when full citizenship is given the tribes, and the Indian schools are abandoned. In other cases, as on the Pine Ridge and Rosebud Reservations, there is an adequate and efficient system of day schools for Indians under compulsory education. In other cases such schools might be organized with little trouble. So that it is safe to say a large number of the Indian children under twelve years old could now be sent to day schools. Where day schools cannot be provided, it may be necessary to bring in the little children to boarding schools. But there would be no harm in letting them wait till eight or nine years old, when they can learn some of the industries.

At the age of twelve, or thereabouts, children have reached the stage when they can profitably take up industrial work and industrial instruction. These can be best taught in large schools. With the Indians this means that industrial education, except in rudimentary forms possible in small day schools, must be given in boarding schools. The reservation boarding schools now exist and are the only ones to which any compulsory educational process is applicable. They therefore form convenient half-way schools between the day schools and the non-reservation boarding schools. Enough industrial work can be given in them to fit the pupils for farmers and house-keepers [*sic*]. It will be possible to abandon several of these at an early date, leaving the public schools and the non-reservation school to teach the children, with the intention, eventually, to withdraw these children entirely from the care of the United States Government as wards of the nation and place them absolutely in the same position with regard to education as any other citizens of the States in which they live. Wherever this can be done it should be done and my official recommendations have been in accordance with it.

The non-reservation schools, especially the better equipped ones, should not receive any little children, and should not act merely as competitors or substitutes for the day schools or the reservation boarding schools. In some localities there are either no reservation schools or those that exist are entirely inadequate. In such cases it is necessary to bring these Indian children who can be induced to go to school to some non-reservation school in default of anything else. In such cases it is doubtful whether it is wise to take little children. A general rule would be a wise one forbidding non-reservation schools to receive any children under twelve, except as specially authorized by the Commissioner. Several of the non-reservation schools have already adopted this policy and are receiving no children under twelve except for special reasons. It is also unwise to allow representatives of such schools to go on the reservation in vacation time and in the absence of the superintendent of the reservation school take away such children as can be secured. Properly all transfers from reservation to non-reservation schools should be in the nature of promotions. The most advanced pupils in either industrial or literary work should be transferred from reservation boarding schools and their places supplied from the children on the reservation not in school. This convention has frequently discussed the question of transfers and also the question of wisdom of the act of Congress forbidding transfers without the consent of parents. But, I find it is not generally known that there is no law to prevent young persons of age to judge for themselves from going to a non-reservation school in their own state without the consent of their parents. This fact greatly facilitates promotions of advanced pupils to non-reservation schools.

With pupils over twelve, and who have had some fair degree of training in industry and in books at reservation schools, both day and boarding, it will be possible for non-reservation schools to become true training schools. At present the only advantage many of them have over reservation schools is in the fact that they are further from the homes of the pupils, if that is an advantage, and the fact that their pupils coming from various tribes are compelled to speak English. There are now several reservation schools which are larger, better equipped and doing better work than many non-reservation schools. These smaller non-reservation schools should either be made something or nothing. They should either be abandoned or increased in size and equipment so that they can do proper work.

I sum up this paper as follows:

1. The evils of institution life for little children should be avoided by establishing day schools wherever possible, and by providing transportation to them daily for pupils living too far to walk. They should also be avoided by not bringing into the boarding schools pupils too young. Non-reservation schools should not generally receive pupils under twelve and reservation boarding schools under eight at least. Much more ought to be made out of the "outing system" than is now made of it generally in non-reservation schools.

2. Domestic economy, agriculture and trades ought to be made the subjects of technical teaching, and not merely of imitative work. These subjects ought to be taught by competent persons, trained in agricultural

colleges or other similar institutions. Modern methods should be employed in the teaching of industries as well as in the literary work.

There is now a strong movement in this direction in several of our larger Indian schools, carried out most fully at present at Hampton and Haskell, which are good examples in many lines of technical schools, and in the new course of study prepared by the Superintendent of Indian Schools we have the high water mark [*sic*] of technical education anywhere in America for schools below the high school, and this skillfully correlated with the literary education. The rapid change which can be seen this year in many Indian schools toward the new twentieth century education shows that this course of study, just issued in October, has been taken up by receptive minds who were already prepared for it.

I believe that this portends a great change in the education in our common schools generally, as well as in the Indian schools, and that it will not be many years before we shall see agriculture, wood working and domestic economy regularly taught in all schools as they are now in some. We are thus not working only for the Indian, but we are pioneers of a broader and more fruitful education of the white children as well.

# 23 | The Value of Day Schools

JAMES J. DUNCAN, *Day School Inspector,*
*Pine Ridge, South Dakota*

Source: *NEA Proceedings*, 1902, 874, is an abstract. The *Southern Workman* 31, no. 10 (October 1902): 541–45 published an article titled "'Indian Day Schools' by J. J. Duncan [Day School Inspector in the Government Indian Service]," which is reprinted here.

Iowan James J. Duncan (1859–1924), who received his education from Monmouth College, Illinois, was a professionally trained and lifelong educator. Monmouth was a Presbyterian college, and, upon leaving there, Duncan joined the faculty at Knoxville College, Knoxville, Tennessee, where the Presbyterians had established a college for formerly enslaved African Americans. He served as agricultural instructor there from 1892 to 1894.[83] He took the superintendent's examination in 1894 to join the Indian service and began his life's work with the Indian schools at Fort Lewis Training School, Colorado, not as a superintendent, but as a teacher.[84] He transferred as superintendent to the Pottawatomie School, Kansas, in September 1898. He proved to be a harsh taskmaster. To the commissioner of Indian affairs, he complained that "it took severe punishment to break up running away" from the school. "One of the rooms in the main building," he continued, "was made into a quasi jail [*sic*]. After confining the worst cases in there for a week or two on limited rations, they generally preferred staying with us."[85] He remained in Kansas from September 1898 to February 1899, when he was transferred again, to become superintendent at Cheyenne School, Darlington, Oklahoma. The very next year he became superintendent at the Arapaho Boarding School, also in Darlington.[86] Both of these schools were under the Cheyenne-Arapaho Agency, but, because "animosity between the two tribes was such that few children were sent so long as both groups were education together," there remained two schools.[87] He transferred again in early 1901 to South Dakota as day school inspector for Pine Ridge Reservation.[88] Duncan had transferred four times in roughly three year, and served in five positions in those years. Now, however, he settled into a long tenure as Pine Ridge's day school inspector. He spent his final two years with the Indian school service as the superintendent at the Sisseton Sioux Indian School, South Dakota. There he died in December 1924.[89]

Duncan delivered two papers to the Department of Indian Education in which he promoted the value of day schools: the first in 1902, and a second paper in 1905.[90] In his first address, he credited J. George Wright, Rosebud Indian agent, for the success of day schools at that reservation. Principal Frissell of the Hampton Institute did likewise in his address at Charleston, South Carolina, in 1900.[91] However, in a 1906 report to the commissioner of Indian affairs, Estelle Reel wrote, "I am convinced that the good work on the Pine Ridge reservation is due to the close supervision given the day schools by Inspector Duncan."[92] Regardless of who got the credit, contemporarily Pine Ridge day schools set the standard by which to measure Indian day schools, and that was certainly Duncan's message at the NEA meetings. In retrospect historian Thomas G. Andrews found the history of these day schools "the most extensive system of Indian day schools in the nation—the thirty or so little schoolhouses of southwestern South Dakota's Pine Ridge reservation, . . . an illuminating counterpoint to the better-known tale of deculturation, abuse, and resistance at residential institutions during the assimilation era." In his study of them, he wrote that "day schools became important sites of cultural contact and negotiation where Oglala people struggled to subvert and resist the federal project of destroying their culture and changing their lifeways."[93] Duncan's description of the Pine Ridge day schools is, thus, only one side of that struggle.

THE DAY-SCHOOL SYSTEM OF EDUCATION began at Pine Ridge Agency in order to fulfill the treaty made with the Sioux Indians; but its growth and its success are owing largely to the faith and personal attention of J. George Wright, who was the champion of day schools while agent at Rosebud. He never lost faith in their ultimate success or in their beneficial effect upon the whole people, even during the trying times of 1890–91.[94]

The day-school work began at Pine Ridge Agency during the winter of 1881–'82. Four day schools were erected in the villages, being substantial log buildings, having a schoolroom 20 X 30 and three rooms for a residence for the teacher. The next year two more were built. Up to 1890 there were only eight schools. The year 1893 is the era of day-school building on Pine Ridge; at least sixteen were either built or rebuilt. Now there are thirty in successful operation.

Day-school work, even at Pine Ridge, has not always been encouraging. It is said that the first school was built for the purpose of making a scattering of the Indians who all persisted in staying in sight of the commissary. This was done after all other expedients had been exhausted to get them to move away from the agency. After the schoolhouse was begun, and the Indians saw what it was for, the agent "was both surprised and delighted to see the Indians fleeing in every direction."[95]

A brief description and a picture of one of the day schools will give the reader a general idea of all the day schools on the reservation. There are two main buildings, one a school building with vestibules, and the other the teachers' cottage. The cottage has four rooms, one for an industrial room for the girls, the remaining three for the exclusive use of the teacher and his family. The cost of the buildings is, in round numbers, $2000.00. The government has fenced off from 40 to 80 acres at each school for the exclusive use of the teacher. This affords plenty of pasture and hay for what cows he needs and a team of horses. The most desirable location is chosen, usually near some living stream and in the midst of an Indian camp of from two to three hundred Indians.

The literary work of the school is carried on very much as in the white district schools. One hour of the school time between nine and four is required to be devoted to industrial work. During this hour the boys saw wood, carry water, clean the premises, make gardens, etc. under the supervision of the teacher. The girls are taught sewing, washing, ironing, mending, cooking, and sometimes fancy work, under the supervision of the housekeeper. None but male teachers are employed at present on this reservation, and their wives are housekeepers. The teachers receive $600 per annum and the housekeepers $300. The average attendance here is probably as good as at any of our white district schools, and in some cases it is better.

The great value of these day schools, not only from my own observation but also from that of the employes [*sic*] in them, is that they are having an influence not only upon the children but also upon the parents. They are the leaven at work leavening the whole lump. These little homes are model Christian homes in the midst of pagan uncivilized homes. The flag that floats daily at the school teaches silently its lesson of patriotism. The schools form centers for the distribution of simple remedies to the sick. The teacher's garden, his cow and chickens, the milk seen and often used by the school children, are bound to teach these people to have similar things. In round numbers 900 visits to the pupils' homes were made by the teachers and 485 by the housekeepers during the last three months of the present fiscal year. There is probably no power on earth that can more thoroughly induce these Indians to have fixed homes and to stay in them at least ten months of the year than these very day schools. It would be a blessed thing if all the reservations had this leverage.

It has been the writer's privilege lately to spend six continuous weeks visiting the thirty day schools at Pine Ridge, spending a day and night at nearly all the schools. After the close of the regular school work [*sic*], I visited, in company with the teacher or the housekeeper, about one hundred and fifty Indian homes in different camps.

Before I started, I wrote to the teachers asking them to prepare a program, speeches, songs, etc., and I would take my gramophone, and we would ask the parents to meet at the schoolhouse during the evenings of my visits. On the whole the experiment was highly satisfactory, and it suggested a new idea to me—that these little Indian schools might be made something similar to our white country literary societies, and that sometimes two or more schools could join in these exercises, which might be held in the local churches. There are more than twenty of these at Pine Ridge, which the day schools have helped to establish. One teacher said to me, "It is not an uncommon thing for a parent to come to me and say, 'I wish you would tell my boy that he must obey me just the same as he obeys you.'" Such living lessons of respect and obedience as the teachers require are of value to the old Indians.

It is not much wonder that one so favorably situated for observation should have confidence in the work of day schools. I am aware that some isolated day schools have proved failures, but when I look over the Commissioner's Report and see that thousands of children are not yet provided for, and again when I see the pressing demand that the Indians should become self-supporting after settling upon their allotments, and when I see white people settling in among the Indians, either leasing or joining farms, I see also an increasing demand for just such schools. I believe no day school should be without supervision. Our white district schools are not without a county superintendent, even though in the midst of intelligent communities. Where the small number of schools do not justify one especially detailed for the work, I believe it would be much better to leave their supervision in the hands of the superintendent of the boarding school. The agent has enough to attend to without having charge of the day schools, and besides it is out of his line of work and interest. Where the superintendent has charge of both the boarding school, or bonded school, and the agency, it would probably be better to confer the management and grading of the day school upon the principal teacher. It will be both to the interest of the principal teacher and the superintendent to keep up the standard of these day schools in their midst, as they are the feeders for their own schools.

According to the Commissioner's Report, there are 138 day schools, with an enrollment of 4,622, and an average attendance of 3,277; or nearly one-fifth the entire enrollment in the government schools. There are 56 in South Dakota, 19 among the Pueblos, 18 in California, 12 in Washington, 9 in North Dakota, 9 in Wisconsin, 7 in Arizona, and one or two in several other states. I believe an effort will be made to establish other schools on some of the large reservations, such as the Navaho, and in other places where a few can be established in settlements and villages. The usual objection that the Indians are too scattered has been caused chiefly by expecting too large an attendance. We do not want an enrollment of over twenty-five. It will be seen that even this small attendance is maintained at far less than half the cost per pupil of those in the boarding schools.

The policy of the day school, which is a humane one, is to allow the parents to have the benefit of their children while children, as they thus live at home until they are fifteen, when they are transferred to the reservation boarding school. They are classified and the course of study is arranged with this in view. It is hoped that before the pupils are eighteen the worthy and capable ones may be induced to go to some good non-reservation school. This seems to me to be in the line of the policy pursued in the white schools of our country and the plan, if generally followed out, would result in a higher standard of education in the non-reservation schools, and a much better attendance.

WILLIAM T. HARRIS, *U.S. Commissioner of Education, Washington* DC

Source: NEA *Proceedings*, 1902, 875–77, and "Interesting Addresses by Commissioners Harris and Dr. Butler," *Star Tribune* (Minneapolis), July 9, 1902, 6. The *Star Tribune* quotations are underscored.[96]

(For biographical information on Harris, see his paper in part 2.) Harris's blinkered view of newspapers *in* Indian schools missed the import of newspapers *by* Indian schools. Estelle Reel listed thirteen Indian school papers in her 1903 *Annual Report.* She wrote, "These are of educational value to the students. . . . The editing of these journals is supervised by the superintendent or principal of the school, assisted by some of the teachers, but many of the articles are contributed by the students."[97] Scholar Jacqueline Emery writes about these publications:

> Boarding school newspapers, much like the schools themselves, were complex sites of negotiation. Whereas school authorities used the white-edited school newspapers to publicize their efforts to erase their students' Indianness by imprinting them with the markers of a white middle-class cultural identity, students often used the school newspapers to defend and preserve Native American identity and culture against the assimilationist imperatives of the boarding schools and the dominant culture. Writing for, editing, and printing school newspapers, students learned how to negotiate the demands placed on them by school authorities who oversaw these publications.[98]

Harris, not surprisingly, argued that reading a newspaper from *outside* the school would provide students with a national or worldly view, but failed to see the value to the students of producing newspapers *inside* the schools. He saw, as did most of the Indian service educators, a monochromatic world in which his culture dominated.

ONE OF THE FUNDAMENTAL METHODS of conveying knowledge and information is by means of the printed page. As soon as you have learned to read you have all human knowledge within easy reach. No personal teacher is required; each one can study and investigate for himself. There is no need of running to father, mother, brother or sister for explanations after the art of reading the printed page has been accomplished.

One of the most important, perhaps the most important, object in the school of modern times is to prepare the pupils to read the printed page. No eloquence on the part of the teachers, no talking or demonstration, no pouring out of information, is or can be a substitute for teaching the child how to read and how to understand what he reads. The child who learns how to read becomes his own teacher. By reading the printed page he can find the most systematic and the most accurate presentation of the knowledge that he seeks. He can look up information in the encyclopedia, in a history, or in an elaborate treatise. On acquiring skill in using the printed page the pupil emancipates himself from dependence on a living teacher. The lecturer goes from paragraph to paragraph, and the hearer does not have sufficient time to recall and understand. The book waits on the pupil's leisure. If he does not understand on the first reading he reads it a second time, and a third time. If he finds himself weary and dull-minded [*sic*] he lays aside the book and resumes it in the fresh period of the morning.

There are two kinds of attention: that of alertness and that of absorption. In listening to the lecturer one must be alert. He must keep up with the reading and not allow his mind to dwell on the sentence that he hears so long as to lose the sentence which follows it. This is all well enough for half of the purposes of attention. But the other half is at least quite as important. The student must learn to give an analytic attention, forgetful of what is present before him, but going down step by step into the depths of the subject, tracing back the casual chain of explanation down to the tenth, the twentieth, the fortieth step. The printed page encourages this cultivation of absorptive attention, whereas the oral method of teaching encourages alert attention, which watches carefully what is going on before it, but does not go down step by step into a consideration of the causes and explanations of what it sees and hears.

In reading the printed page one becomes "eye-minded" as well as "ear-minded." The eye-minded person thinks in printed or written words. The ear-minded person recalls sounds and tones. The eye-minded person can think accurately because he finds and learns in print a technical vocabulary that is not used in colloquial speech. The newspaper brings the citizen into a greater world of public opinion than he can find in the oral speech of his village or community. The newspaper elevates village gossip into world gossip. It follows that the newspaper reader acquires a habit of adjusting himself daily to a view of the world. The person who does not read the newspaper limits his adjustment to his immediate community.

It is a wonderful education to be able to think sympathetically on great human events. The laborer in the city of Minneapolis, thru the printed page of the daily newspaper, acquires an interest in the life of the inhabitant of China, or of Russia, or of South Africa. It is one of the best ways to educate the heart to get the person interested in his fellow-men [*sic*], for sympathy follows a knowledge of their deeds. The newspaper gives one a reflection of the sympathies of his fellow-men. He notes that one person has one class of sympathies and another a different kind. When the pupil can motive the different and strange ideas, and understand how that which is not his own method of doing things may really seem to be the best method to his fellow-men, he broadens his mind into toleration. He reinforces his mind with the ideas of other people, and the newspaper is one of the best means of this kind of education, because it continues thru the year. It makes the citizen a spectator in the great drama of life that is unfolding before him on the world-stage [*sic*].

Even the poorest paper in Minnesota, though it may be possible you have no poor papers in Minnesota, has its influence and place in educating and bringing someone to something better, and of higher and wider interest. The individual only becomes great and strong by reinforcing his own mind by the ideas of others about him. Each one gives his thought to those around him, and in turn he is affected by the opinions of all the others, so that this nation is essentially a nation of public opinion.

Every Indian school should have the newspaper. The pupil should read first that which interests him. He will go from that to the far-off events of the world, according as he grows in intellectual capacity. Pictorial newspapers are a great help to those coming up from a tribal form of government to the most civilized form. The most civilized government makes most of the individual and teaches him how to think and act for himself in the light of all human experience. Before the newspapers came into so much vogue there was more village gossip in regard to small and personal things. The worst novel is not so bad as village gossip, even the gossip that one finds in the best families. Let the Indian child read the newspapers. He works from day to day acquiring a knowledge of the public opinion of the Anglo-Saxon race, and then he comes to see how the other races think. Thru presentation by picture and by word great events can reach all classes of intellects.

You may teach the Indian scientific facts; you may teach him history and literature; but if he does not get interested in the newspaper and become a reader of it he will not come into the Anglo-Saxon world of public opinion. He will not become educated in the highest sense of the word.

BY THE TIME OF THE Boston meeting of 1903, Indian school educators and teachers of the masses, including the immigrants flooding into America's cities, were clearly seeing each other as colleagues in the same struggle. The emphasis on "practical" education, embedded in the Indian school service's *Course of Study*, had become a national trend. "Uplifting" people to work in America's burgeoning industries and to service the Anglo-Saxon needs of rapidly expanding cities united these educators in a common cause. Sitting with other educators in general and joint sessions and listening to the same speakers meant that Indian service educators had been folded into the national educational landscape and were increasingly being respected for their work in educating a "child race" for productive laboring citizenship.[1]

Great excitement surrounded this NEA meeting.[2] The city had hosted the NEA's 1872 annual meeting with a lackluster attitude that resulted in small attendance and indifferent teachers. Local organizers were anxious to ensure that did not happen again. They pulled out all of the stops, and, when over, general agreement was "that no previous meeting was so elaborately organized."[3] Charles W. Eliot, president of the NEA and Harvard University, informed NEA members prior to the meeting, "While the chief concern has been to present the best possible programs for both general and department sessions, it has been the aim also to provide ample opportunities and facilities for visiting the many points of historical, literary, and educational interest in and about Boston." Sessions were scheduled only in the mornings and evenings, to leave "the afternoons free for recreation and excursions."[4]

The appeal worked well. Not even local organizers expected such a turnout, with attendance breaking all records. The high-water mark for the NEA annual conventions was the Los Angeles convention of 1899, with just over thirteen thousand attendees. The Boston meeting nearly tripled that number, with over thirty-five thousand registered educators perambulating the city.[5] Counting the unregistered individuals who also flocked to Beantown, an observer concluded that "one is probably safe in saying that from 40,000 to 50,000 people interested in education were attracted to Boston during convention week."[6] After the meeting Charles F. Meserve, president of Shaw University, who had addressed the Department of Indian Education, wrote to a colleague, "I returned Saturday night from Boston where I attended the National Educational Association. It was one of the greatest educational meetings that I ever attended in my life."[7]

Attendees were afforded ample time to see Boston and its environs, as promised. One journal reported, "Nothing could have been more appreciated than the unusual opportunities afforded to the teachers for visiting the famous shrines of American history and of great American literary and historic figures. It was beautiful to see the joy and delight of the well-mannered throngs of shirt-waisted, guide-booked teachers at the places hallowed by the country's best tradition with which Boston is enriched."[8] Local organizers had done well.

Estelle Reel exuded an enthusiasm equal to the local organizers when planning her department's participation in the convention. "The Indian workers," she said in a preconvention news release, "are looking forward to the Boston meeting with unusual interest, and expect to receive benefit from their visit to the city (and its uplifting influence) than from any previous convention." Like the other educators set to flood the city, the Indian school educators would "visit the various educational and philanthropic institutions of Boston . . . in order to obtain material that may be of use to them upon their return to their respective schools in the West."[9]

In late October 1902, Reel solicited from the superintendents topics that were to be discussed at the meeting. Carlisle's Pratt responded to her in short order. He told her that he intended on coming to the Boston meeting; if he were there, it would be the first meeting he had attended since the Los Angeles meeting in 1899. He then told her the topics he thought "vital" for discussion. The first was that spending "money to segregate Indians and build up and strengthen their tribal life [thus, having them reside on reservations] is unwarranted." Second, he held that the "present system of home schools"—that is, day schools and reservation boarding schools—for Indians "directly hinders their transit into the national life." Finally, he wrote that industrial schools "located in the best industrial and civilized surroundings" are the "Indian schools best calculated to open the way and give real aid to Indian youth" for citizenship.[10] In other words, he proposed discussions on everything antithetical to contemporary Indian school strategies.

On an early version of the program, Reel listed Pratt for a twenty-minute discussion of his point that spending money to "strengthen tribal life" was unwarranted.[11] Then, unexpectedly, Pratt resigned from his superintendency at Carlisle Indian Industrial School after the War Department informed him that he was to be retired from military service. He just as abruptly unresigned after Commissioner Jones urged him to remain at Carlisle.[12] Reel had by now lost patience with the old warrior. He had been listed on the programs to address the Department of Indian Education for the preceding NEA conventions of 1900, 1901, and 1902, even though he did not attend any of those meetings. He was not included on the program for the 1903 convention, a fact that the *Boston Globe* did not miss: "Col Robert [should read Richard] H. Pratt, USA, retired, who was for many years at the head of the Indian school at Carlisle, Penn., and who had a place on the provisional program to speak in opposition to the government's policy of segregating Indians, has been left off the official program."[13] The article was wrong in using the past tense: Pratt was still at the head of the Carlisle Indian Industrial School, but, as the newspaper correctly noted, he was not on the official program for the 1903 NEA convention. The Pratt era was drawing to a close.

Reel made other modifications to the official program as well. She grouped papers for the first time into discussion topics as some of the other NEA departments did. She then informed speakers of the theme for their papers based on those subjects.[14] The topics for the Boston meeting were "Citizenship," "Character Building," and "Industrial and Miscellaneous Roundtable."[15] Those topics, and the speakers Reel invited, elevated the department's conversations from the day-to-day activities of education to addresses regarding early twentieth-century trends including a resolute belief in scientific racism, the broader goals of Indian policy and national education, and civil service.

There were also impromptu modifications to the agenda that may have been caused by Reel's health. She had always struggled with some issues, mainly her poor eyesight. She was also occasionally laid low from exhaustion, depression, or both.[16] In Boston, despite great enthusiasm for the meeting, she spent most of her time ill and absent from meetings. The *Chilocco Farmer and Stock Grower* noted, "To the deep regret of all

Indian workers, Miss Reel was unable to lend her cheering presence at the meetings for more than an hour or so each day. She heroically left her sick-bed [*sic*] in order to be present even that short time, but, of course, hers was the mind that directed all the arrangements, whether her body was able to work or not."[17]

Undeterred by Reel's illness, the Department of Indian Education held a joint meeting with the Departments of Manual Training and Elementary Education.[18] These are logical compatriots for the Indian service workers. The Department of Manual Training, for example, created a committee to prepare a report on the "future educational needs of the working classes in this country" and to determine what steps should be taken in the country to provide "adequate technical and industrial education for the working classes."[19] Moreover, much of Indian school work was focused on manual training and was at the elementary level, including students as young as kindergarteners at off-reservation boarding schools.[20] Thus, the issues the Departments of Manual Training and Elementary Education wrestled with were similar to those of Indian school educators. Scheduling these groups together also pointed to the growing belief that the needs of American Indian students mirrored the needs of the masses of students in an industrializing society. The *Manual Training Magazine* editors lauded the joint meeting because of the "growing importance of the manual and the vocational elements in the public-school systems of this country."[21]

Furthermore, the keynote address of the Manual Training Department's first session featured a manufacturer who argued for more and improved trades education. "It is now pretty generally agreed," he said, "[that] we must look to the schools for our future skilled workmen." Then, in discussing how the training of those workmen should look at the schools, he continued, "Is it asking too much . . . of the school board to make a half-time course, where one-half of class can be in the schoolroom one-half of the hours in a week while the other half of the class is at work in a shop?"[22] The speaker's arguments for skills training and a schedule similar to the Indian schools' half-a-day work and half-a-day study routine would have been familiar to Indian service educators. Carlisle's newspaper the *Red Man and Helper* even printed an abstract of his address.[23]

The joint meeting with the Departments of Manual Training and Elementary Education, planned from the beginning of the convention, was not the only joint meeting for the Indian school workers. For reasons unknown, but probably due to her illness, Reel canceled the session on the topic of "Industrial and Miscellaneous Roundtable" and, with no prior arrangements, led her educators into a session of the Department of Physical Education. The president of that department described what happened in a letter to Secretary Shepard: "Miss Estelle Reel, in her precipitous way, without my knowledge or any previous intimation, adjourned the section of the Department of Indian Education to our section. I knew nothing of this until about nine o'clock on the morning of the meeting [thirty minutes before his meeting started]. It became necessary to run through the programs of the two departments in a continuous session. . . . The two meetings were fused together without any previous knowledge on my part." The fusing together of the two departments became an issue when the intrusion into his department's meeting resulted in a questionable election of its officers for the next year. While the minutes of the Department of Indian Education noted this improvised joint meeting, the minutes of the Department of Physical Education did not.[24]

In addition to sessions and addresses, planned or unplanned, Reel anticipated another well-received Indian school student display in Boston. "There will also be on exhibition at the Rogers Building, [Massachusetts] Institute of Technology," she wrote, "where a large collection of industrial, literary and native Indian work from every state and territory in the union where an Indian school and tribe may be found. The past and present work of the tribes will be set forth and this convention marks the progress of the race, showing the great strides recently made from barbarism to civilization."[25] She was exceedingly proud of the exhibit at the Minneapolis meeting the year before. In bragging about it to Albert K. Smiley, founder and organizer of the Lake Mohonk Conference of the Friends of the Indians, she sent him a newspaper clipping regarding it and wrote, "I am happy to say that each year shows improvement and that our Indian teachers are beginning to see as never before the necessity of giving the Indian a practical education."[26] She wrote to him again two months later while preparing to attend the Lake Mohonk conference the end of October 1902: "It has occurred to me that a collection of work accomplished by Indian children might prove of interest to the friends at Mohonk, and I write to ask if I may bring a small exhibit for the meeting on the 22nd." Smiley agreed, and Reel took to Lake Mohonk work she had in her office that was already mounted on cards, probably left over from the Minneapolis meeting.[27] As proud as she was of that exhibit, Reel was determined to make the Boston exhibit even better.

Her instructions about preparations for the student exhibit written for agents and superintendents the year before were very detailed, including a diagram showing them how to follow the directions. She apparently found those instructions less than adequate. She far surpassed the finer details in her prior year's letter when preparing for the Boston exhibit. In 1902 she had only directed that student work be mounted on cardboard. In 1903 she told them,

> Cardboard for mounting the exhibit has been forwarded to you, also gray tape for fastening the cards together. The work is to be mounted on the light side of the cards. The holes for the tape should be punched four inches from the ends of the cards, which when hung should be about 1–4 of an inch apart, so that they will fold readily. It is desired that the name of the school be printed IN BLACK LETTERS TWO INCHES HIGH, at the top of each card, in order that the school may get credit in case it becomes necessary to detach the cards. All paper used for class-room [*sic*] work should be 6 1–2 by 8 inches, and should be mounted on the cards IN SINGLE SHEETS.

She increased the number of cards from three in 1902 to five cards for the Boston exhibit, to include one dedicated to "Native industries: beadwork, baskets, blankets, leather articles, etc." She provided detailed instructions on securing and labeling items for the cards. She had also not been satisfied with the photographs received the previous year showing students at work. "In taking photographs," she admonished, "see that pupils are looking at their work and not at the camera." She informed them again that this effort was to "show the correlation of the class room [*sic*] with the industrial work as set forth in the Course of Study."[28]

Despite her near incapacitation during the convention, the student exhibit in three large rooms of the Rogers Building at MIT proved a huge draw to Bostonians and other attendees, in large part thanks to the work of Lillie S. McCoy, Reel's clerk.[29] "[McCoy] was tireless in her devotion to the placing of the material," *Chilocco Farmer and Stock Grower* reported, "and equally tireless in explaining to and answering the questions of the throngs who visited the rooms. And nothing in the city attracted greater crowds."[30] Bostonians were invited to the exhibit under the headline

"Boston May See What Indians Can Do" with accompanying photographs of young women making bread and sewing and young men carpentering and wheelwrighting.[31] What attracted the most attention were the Native industries: "Basketry, their own indigenous pottery, birch bark, bows and arrows, beads, leather, hide and feather work."[32] At least two observers of the student display lamented the fact that Indian students were being taught white man's trades. They were being "compelled to take up the white man's burden," one sighed. These correspondents hoped that the revival of Indian industries would continue.[33]

One of the highlights of the convention for the Indian service workers was being entertained at the home of Alice Longfellow, daughter of American poet Henry Wadsworth Longfellow, who wrote *The Song of Hiawatha*. The *Southern Workman* reported the visit "one of the delightful events of the week," and that it "was interesting to see her surrounded by a company of Indian girls on her beautiful law in Cambridge adjoining the old Longfellow mansion," which had served as the headquarters for General George Washington during parts of 1775 and 1776.[34] Longfellow had an interest in Native work, the *Indian Leader* reported, and spent much time visiting the Indian school student display at MIT.[35] It is not known if Reel left her sickbed to accompany Longfellow during her visits to the Rogers Building.

The Boston meeting had more downsides than just Reel's illness. The first was low attendance by Indian school educators. Despite record numbers of educators descending upon Boston for the convention, only 125 to 150 Indian service workers arrived for it, roughly half the number who attended the 1902 convention in Minneapolis.[36] Distance may have played a part in this low turnout. Most of the Indian schools were far removed from New England. Minneapolis was much more accessible to Reel's educators.

The other downside to the meeting happened after the convention. Reel had lined up a Who's Who list of Bostonians to address the gathered Indian service workers that included luminaries such as Dr. Edward Everett Hale and Dr. Alfred E. Winship, editor of the prestigious *Journal of Education*. Reel submitted to the NEA editor for publication shortened versions of their and other prominent participants' addresses. Her section of the journal for 1903 carries the editor's footnoted lamentation: "It is a matter of regret that only abstracts of most of the following addresses were furnished by the secretary of the department."[37] Reel submitted for printing only three addresses not identified as abstracts, even though two of those were also edited for length, and she dedicated most of her allocated publication space to the president's address and the first address to Indian service educators from a member of the civil service commission. Shortened or not, the papers for the Boston convention supported the collective theme of "citizenship." In summarizing the 1903 conclave of the Department of Indian Education, one observer wrote, "Cultivating the work spirit among Indians as a means to active citizenship was the subject discussed in all its phases, both practical and philosophical."[38]

# 25 | President's Address

## Our Work, Its Progress and Needs

H. B. PEAIRS, *Superintendent, Haskell*
*Institute, Lawrence, Kansas*

Source: NEA *Proceedings*, 1903, 1044–49, is a truncated version of his paper. A complete version appeared with the title "Our Work, Its Progress and Needs" in the *Chilocco Farmer and Stock Grower* 3, no. 16 (July 15, 1903): 433–40. The latter version is reprinted here.

Born in Ohio but raised in Kansas, Hervey B. Peairs (1866–1940) received his education at the University of Kansas and Emporia State Teachers College, today's Emporia State University. After graduating in 1887, he began his lifelong career with the Indian service as a teacher at Haskell Institute, today's Haskell Indian Nations University, when it had been open only three years. He rose through the positions as industrial teacher, principal teacher, disciplinarian, assistant superintendent, then superintendent in 1898, and spent most of his forty-four years of Indian school service at Haskell.[39] As an administrator he was strict. One student accused him of breaking his leg; other students were denied the opportunity to go home when seriously ill.[40] He frequently saw students as laborers at his school. He told the commissioner of Indian affairs in 1901 that "the employees and pupils deserve great credit for the great amount of hard labor performed" at Haskell. He turned down a request in 1907 for fifty male students to work in beet fields in Colorado because their absence would "cripple" the work at his school.[41]

Peairs left Haskell in 1910 to become the chief supervisor of schools under a department reorganization by Robert G. Valentine, commissioner of Indian affairs, that eliminated the position of superintendent of Indian schools.[42] The Meriam Report of 1928, officially titled *The Problem of Indian Administration*, resulted in Peairs's removal as director in September 1930.[43] He then resumed his position as superintendent at Haskell, only to be retired the next year at age sixty-five, a congressionally mandated age limit for service. At the time of his retirement, he had completed forty-four years and three months of service.[44] He retired to his dairy farm in Lawrence, Kansas, where he died of a heart attack in September 1940.[45]

By all appearances, Peairs "remained a thoroughly old-style assimilationist" throughout his Indian school service career.[46] One wonders how he endured the philosophical changes wrought by Reel, although he would outlast her in the Indian service by many years. As will be noted in the paper, for the NEA *Proceedings* Reel excised his more controversial remarks from his president's address, as well as some of his criticism of the civil service commission. Nevertheless, his "old-style assimilationist" ideals came through during his Boston presentation.

EDUCATION HAS LONG BEEN RECOGNIZED as the chief factor in the development of humanity. Especially has this been true of American civilization. From the very beginning of colonization all attempts at reclaiming mankind from savage live[s] and manners have been through education. Thus it was in our earliest relations with the Indians. As early as 1646, Rev. John Eliot, a great-hearted, Christian man, began educational work among the Indians of New England.[47] I quote from Dr. W. N. Hailmann on the education of the Indian:

A remarkable pioneer work, of a typical character, was done by Rev. John Eliot in Massachusetts. Mr. Eliot was actuated by motives of broadest Christianity and purest philanthropy. His simple measures were chosen with consummate wisdom. In the first place, he familiarized himself with the language, disposition, and character of the Indians. Then, by according them the same, he secured their confidence and respect, and stimulated in their hearts, reverence and a sincere desire for the industry and thrift, the godliness and purity of life, of which New England communities afforded the example. Those who would follow him, he gathered in towns, where he taught them the liberties and responsibilities of township government and the device and institutions of civilized life, among which the school and the church naturally occupied places of honor. A number of choice Indian youths he induced to attend English schools that they might prepare themselves for missionary work as teachers and catechists among his own people.

"He was warmly supported in his work by 'the corporation for the propagation of the Gospel in foreign parts,' by the general court of Massachusetts, and particularly by Mr. Daniel Gookins, the official superintendent of the Indians in Massachusetts.[48] In 1674, there were fourteen towns of 'praying Indians' whose schools and churches, in the majority of instances, were administered by educated natives. At the same time an Indian college had been founded at Cambridge."[49]

Similar work was done under the direction of Rev. John Cotton[50] and Richard Bourne, in Plymouth Colony.[51]

This work was very successful and could it have been continued without interruption, certainly the NEA would be without an Indian Department, as it meets here in Boston in 1903. The Indian problem would have long since merged into the general problem of education. However, such a result was destined to be greatly delayed. Misunderstandings, disregard for the rights of the Indian, a determination on the part of early settlers to acquire territory at any cost, brought on war; and war smothered, for a time, all attempts at education.

Although feeble attempts were made from time to time by missionaries, there was a long period of inactivity. Meantime, the Indians were gradually driven back, back, westward, westward, by the advance guard of civilization. The final result is well known. The tribes, so unjustly treated, became very revengeful. Their hunting territory having been encroached upon, their means of support was gone. Under the circumstances, the only thing to do at that time, seemed to be to place the tribes on reservations under military supervision. A natural outgrowth of the reservation system were the annuity and ration systems, a very sure, although slow, process of extermination.

Thus the Indian became the "white man's burden." At this stage of the play, the selfish, non-Christian element would have said, "Exterminate the Indian and be done with him;" but Christian civilization took up the burden, accepted the duty, and said, "We must, in all fairness, in the sight of God and man, give the Indian a chance again, by offering to him educational advantages equal to the best." Systematic educational work was then begun.

"Missionaries took up the work with renewed zeal. Congress re[s]ponded in 1819 with an appropriation of $10,000.00, in addition to certain treaty obligations. In 1820, the president was authorized to apply this sum annually in aid of societies and individuals engaged in Indian education. In 1823, the sum of $80,000 was expended in 21 schools maintained by missionary bodies. $12,000.00 of this amount was contributed by the government."[52]

The number of schools increased gradually, largely under missionary control, until 1877. At this time, the government began the work of Indian education in earnest, by the establishment of day, reservation boarding, and industrial training schools. The annual appropriations have increased from $20,000 in 1877 to $3,251,254.00 in 1902. The entire amount of money expended from 1877 [to] 1902 for educational purposes has been $38,613,147.00[.]

The question naturally arises, what has been done with this large sum of money?

The report of the Hon. Commissioner of Indian Affairs for 1902, answers this question briefly as follows:

**Table 1.** Number of Indian schools and average attendance from 1877 to 1902

| | BOARDING SCHOOLS | | DAY SCHOOLS | | TOTALS | |
|---|---|---|---|---|---|---|
| YEAR | NO. | AV. ATTEN. | NO. | AV. ATTEN. | NO. | AV. ATTD. |
| 1877 | 48 | | 102 | | 150 | 3,598 |
| 1878 | 49 | | 119 | | 168 | 4,142 |
| 1879 | 52 | | 107 | | 159 | 4,448 |
| 1880 | 60 | | 109 | | 169 | 4,651 |
| 1881 | 68 | | 106 | | 174 | 4,976 |
| 1882 | 71 | 3,077 | 76 | 1,637 | 147 | 4,714 |
| 1883 | 80 | 3,793 | 88 | 1,893 | 168 | 5,686 |
| 1884 | 87 | 4,723 | 98 | 2,237 | 185 | 6,960 |
| 1885 | 114 | 6,201 | 86 | 1,942 | 200 | 8,143 |
| 1886 | 115 | 7,260 | 99 | 2,370 | 214 | 9,630 |
| 1887 | 117 | 8,020 | 110 | 2,500 | 227 | 10,520 |
| 1888 | 126 | 6,705 | 107 | 2,715 | 233 | 11,420 |
| 1889 | 136 | 9,146 | 103 | 2,406 | 239 | 11,553 |

| | | | | | |
|---|---|---|---|---|---|
| 1890 | 140 | 9,865 | 106 | 2,367 | 246 | 12,232 |
| 1891 | 146 | 11,425 | 110 | 2,163 | 256 | 13,588 |
| 1892 | 149 | 12,442 | 126 | 2,745 | 275 | 15,165 |
| 1893 | 156 | 13,633 | 119 | 2,668 | 275 | 16,303 |
| 1894 | 157 | 14,457 | 115 | 2,639 | 272 | 17,220 |
| 1895 | 157 | 15,061 | 125 | 3,127 | 282 | 18,188 |
| 1896 | 156 | 15,683 | 140 | 3,579 | 296 | 19,262 |
| 1897 | 145 | 15,026 | 143 | 3,650 | 288 | 18,676 |
| 1898 | 148 | 16,112 | 149 | 3,536 | 297 | 19,648 |
| 1899 | 149 | 16,891 | 147 | 3,631 | 286 | 20,522 |
| 1900 | 153 | 16,708 | 154 | 3,860 | 307 | 21,568 |
| 1901 | 161 | 19,464 | 143 | 3,613 | 304 | 23,077 |
| 1902 | 163 | 20,576 | 136 | 3,544 | 299 | 24,120 |

This shows that during the period in which the expenditure of $38,613,141.00 has been made for educational purposes, the number of schools has been increased from 150 to 299, and that the average attendance has increased from 3,598 in 1877 to 24,120 in 1902. The attendance averaged for 26 years, 12,682. The average annual cost per pupils has been $117.01. The capacity of all schools, including mission schools, was in 1902, 28,024. The capacity has been increased somewhat since the close of the fiscal year 1902. Therefore it will be seen that from a mere beginning in 1877, such progress has been made that at present, excellent educational accommodations are provided for almost the entire number of Indians of school age. In fact, I believe there are sufficient accommodations for every Indian child who really needs the help of the government to get an education. While appropriations for the maintenance of the school plants will need to be made annually, it is certainly cause for congratulation that such progress in establishing new institutions has been made, that that part of the work is practically done.

Not only has great progress in building been made, but at the same time the character of the building has been greatly improved. During the early years of Indian education buildings were carelessly erected. No thought was given to furnishing proper systems of ventilation, lighting, and heating. As a result, children in many schools broke down in health, sickened and died. Naturally parents became prejudiced against the schools. To overcome this prejudice has taken a long time; but as more attention has been given of late years to architecture, and as buildings have been provided with all necessary modern sanitary conveniences, the health record of the schools has greatly improved. Consequently, Indian parents are now much more willing to place their children in school. The improvement in the manner of building has also resulted in the building of better homes by returned students. The opportunity which students have had to see good homes, either at school or in the vincinity [*sic*], has resulted in many instances in their applying the knowledge thus gained in building homes of their own.

While the construction of school plants is only incidental to real work of educating and training Indian youth, it has been a necessity; and it has been accomplished wisely, and in a great degree, economically.

As is shown by the statistics given, only 3,598 children were in school in 1877. It was difficult to get even that number, as the sentiment among the Indian tribes was very strongly opposed to any educational movement. The most difficult feature of the work in the early days was to secure children for the schools; in fact, they knew nothing but the free, indolent, tribal life and therefore were satisfied to remain in such a life. The children were blameless for they knew no better. The parents were practically in the same condition; however, there were other reasons why they were unwilling to send their children to school when asked to do so. Confidence had been broken so often with them that they naturally thought that a request for their children was only another method of taking advantage of them. (They were rightfully suspicious of the white man's offer.) Under these circumstances it was extremely difficult to secure pupils. Gradually, however, the influence of the returning pupils has become stronger; and now the prejudice of the parents is almost entirely overcome in many reservations. Although some parents still object to placing their children in school, yet, considering the entire Indian population, the sentiment is now strongly in favor of schools and education. This is certainly a great step forward. A volunteer enrollment of practically 30,000 children, or six-sevenths of the children of school age, shows beyond question the change of sentiment. Public sentiment once being right, almost any result may be attained.

Not only has right sentiment been created, but at the same time very marked results of a more tangible character may be noticed. Statistics concerning Indian education are not always reliable and yet they give a general idea of its progress; therefore I shall give a few from the annual Report for 1902.

Population, exclusive of Indians in Alaska, 270,236. Of these, 84,500 belong to the Five Civilized Tribes and provide their own schools. One of the marks of progress is the greatly increased number who read and speak English. The Commissioner's Annual Report for 1902 gives as the number of Indians who read and speak English enough for ordinary purposes, 62,616, or more than one-third of the entire population with which the government is now doing educational work. This estimate is undoubtedly too low, but accepting it as correct, is it not sufficient progress to be worthy of commendation rather than condemnation?

Another mark of progress is the number who have adopted citizen's dress, wholly or in part; the total being 143,974 or more than seven-eights [*sic*] of the population. Originally, these people were without homes. There were in 1902, 26,629 dwelling houses occupied by Indians. Counting the average family to be five in number this would make a total of 133,145 or approximately two-thirds of the population in houses. These statistics show remarkable progress, most of which can be traced directly or indirectly to the work of the schools. Many other marks of progress might be mentioned, but I am also to consider briefly some of the needs of our work, therefore must hasten.

A careful study of present conditions convinces one that, although much progress has been made in some lines of the work, in others but little advance has been made.

The increase in the acreage of land cultivated by Indians has been comparatively very small. During 1902, only 361,680 acres were cultivated. Remembering that the population, exclusive of Alaska and Indian Territory, is 185,738, we find that the acreage of land cultivated is less than an average of 2 acres per person.

As the Indian's principal capital is his land, the fact that he is making so little use of it, indicates that something is radically wrong. There are a number of reasons for this condition of affairs. The government's policy of issuing rations and paying annuity money has made it possible for the Indian to live with but little work, and the possibility has been cheerfully accepted. Since the lands have been alloted [*sic*], the leasing system has been a very great obstacle to the progress of the Indian. The fact that Indians are permitted to lease their land instead of working it themselves, has naturally resulted in their continuing in idleness. A rather large acreage of Indian lands is being cultivated; but the white man is doing the work, while the Indian is sitting idly by and waiting for his small share, or for a very meagre cash rental. This system of leasing has been bad, not only for the older Indians, but especially so for the boys returned from school. Having learned how to work, they have gone to their homes with the intention of improving their allotments. Arriving at home, they find their parents leasing their land and living away from it. Although the boy may honestly wish to work his allotment, he has no place to stay and no way to get a start. The result is that he leases his lands and becomes a boarder with his parents and shares in their idleness.

In stock raising, as well as in farming, but little progress has been made. This fact, too, is greatly to be regretted, since a large part of the Indian population, especially in the Northern states, must depend almost entirely upon this industry for gaining a livelihood. Here, too, the ration and the annuity policies and the leasing system are largely responsible for the course taken by the Indians.

We hear so much about the downfall of returned students; the failure of boys and girls who have been in school for a few years. Need we wonder when we consider the reservation conditions? The failures in a very large majority of the cases are due to environment; and the environment is in a large measure due to the ration and annuity systems.

Liquor has ruined, destroyed many, many, strong, stalwart, Indian young men; but I believe I am safe in saying that the before mentioned policies have been responsible for even a larger number of wrecks among the dusky red men. In fact, had such policies not been in vogue, thus making idleness possible, worthlessness, drink, and crime would never have claimed so many victims.

I do not mean to say that the adopting of such policies could have been avoided. Conditions in the past possibly justified their adoption. However, they are largely responsible for the little progress made by the Indians toward self-support.

Conditions on reservations could not be expected to change materially under such policies. True, taking children from such conditions and placing them in schools where they have had elevating, ennobling influences about them; where they have learned to study, to work; where they have learned habits of industry, of cleanliness, of order; where they learned to respect each other's rights; where in every fibre of their natures they have been strengthened and tested; and then sending them back among their own people, have resulted in marvelous progress in some lines; nevertheless the progress toward self-support does not seem to have been given much momentum as a result of influences of returned students.

Children and young people have learned how to work, but have not learned to work in the face of such obstacles as are met on many of the reservations. Cease issuing rations and paying annuities; dispense with other systems of paying the indians [*sic*]; then rapidly indeed, will the trained young Indian men and women from the schools forge to the front in all lines of industrial work. They know how to use their heads and their hands; and brought face to face with necessity or, I believe, if given opportunity among their own people, they will intelligently, willingly, and cheerfully work.

Given the opportunity and incentive of necessity, the Indian boy or girl will work as faithfully as anyone. It is but natural, however, for any son or daughter to drift toward home and kindred; and while it may be argued that white boys and girls do not tie themselves to their mothers' apron strings, it is true that they do tie themselves to some person's apron strings. At least the boys do; and girls generally tie some boy to their heartstrings. It is just as natural for Indian boys and girls to seek among their own kindred and race for life partners. This then, brings us face to face with what seems to me to be of vital importance in our work. We can not if we would keep the Indian children from returning home from school. Conditions at their homes must therefore be changed. To change and improve the homes materially will require vigorous, persistent treatment. I make the following prescriptions and guarantee a cure if used according to directions:*[53]

Cease issuing rations (to be taken July 1st 1904.)[54]

Credit each individual Indian with his share of all moneys held in trust. (To be given in doses as large as the individual intelligence and experience will permit.)

Prohibit the leasing of lands belonging to able-bodied persons who are not steadily engaged in work other than agriculture. (This prescription to be kept on the shelf for use at any time.)

Individualize. One of the greatest mistakes made is in dealing too much with the tribes and not enough with the individual. "Individualize" should be the 20th Century motto in our work with the Indians.

Obliterate all reservation lines. Push the work of allotting lands as rapidly as possible.

Throw open all surplus lands for settlement by white people. Encourage the building of railroads, the development of mining interests and all other natural resources of the reservations. In other words, break down the barriers and permit civilization to thrust its helpful influence upon the needy; to carry light into the homes of those who have been living in darkness.

There has been much discussion about the comparative value of reservation and non-reservation schools. Permit me to suggest the way to a satisfactory solution of this much discussed question. Blot out of existence every reservation; and every reservation school will become a non-reservation school. The principal reason for the establisment [sic] of Carlisle, of Haskell, of Chilocco, of Phoenix, of Genoa, of Chemawa and other non-reservation schools was that reservation conditions rendered the best educational work impossible. Therefore, the earlier these conditions are changed by the introduction of civilization, the earlier will it be advisable to leave the work of Indian education to schools located in the vicinity of the homes of the Indians. These are vigorous measures to propose, and had such been resorted to 25 years ago, the result would probably have been ruinous. However, conditions have been changed. Education has been at work all these years, and now I believe it is time for methods to be changed. Educational work should not, I believe, be curtailed in the least. In fact, it is very essential that it be conducted very vigorously during the period while the barriers are being removed from the reservations. Let thoroughly trained, courageous, Christian men and women be employed in the schools, to guide the Indian people and to protect their rights during this time when greater responsibilities are being thrust upon them.

I would like to suggest just at this time, that, although the extension of Civil Service to positions in the Indian Service has been one of the progressive steps in Indian education and has greatly improved the character of the work, a more practical Civil Service is needed so far as the manner of selecting employes [*sic*] is concerned. It should be possible for superintendents to secure the service of persons having special qualifications for certain lines of technical work. For instance: I want a man who has had technical college training and also practical experience in farming to put in charge of the agricultural work of an institution. Under present methods there is only one chance in ten of securing a satisfactory employe. The same is true of a number of other positions, such as physical director, or disciplinarian, domestic science teacher, domestic art teacher, and manual training teacher. While heartily endorsing the spirit of the Civil Service, I as earnestly advocate some reform in this particular.

Put all children of school age in school: (This prescription to be given at once to the entire Indian population.)

Continue educational work along lines already well established. Further, emphasize domestic training for girls, especially cooking and sewing; and agriculture, stock-raising, and builders' trades for the boys.

I should like to suggest one other course of treatment that is essential, without which I would not be willing to guarantee a permanent cure: Boys and girls should both be given regularly, while in school, during that period of life when their habits are becoming fixed and character is being developed, systematic, thorough Christian training. Bible study should have an important place in the daily program. God made men in His own image. Later it became necessary to make laws for the guidance of man to enable him to avoid sin and wrong doing [*sic*], to live righteously. Boys and girls must have a knowledge of such laws if they would stand erect in the sight of God and man. A really civilized people cannot be found in the world except where the Bible has been sent, the Gospel taught; hence, we believe that the Indians must have, as an essential part of their education, Christian training. This can best be given through the schools. I wish to make a special plea for more intelligent, more earnest, religious work in Indian schools.

In closing I wish to summarize as follows:

**Progress Made:**

School accommodations for practically all Indian children are now provided. These schools are generally well equipped.

Public sentiment among the Indian has gradually come to favor educational work.

Nearly 30,000, or six-sevenths, of all Indian children are in school.

More than one-third of the Indian population are now English-speaking people; seven-eights of the Indians wear citizens' clothing, wholly or in part, and probably two-thirds live in dwelling houses.

**Things We Need To Do:**

Stop issuing rations.*[55]

Individualize all Indian moneys.

Prohibit the wholesale leasing of lands.

Abolish all reservations and permit civilization to advance.

Put all Indian children in school and keep them there.

Stop being sentimental about taking the children away from their parents. The greatest love that a parent can show for a child is to do the best for the child at any self-sacrifice. Schools have been built and equipped. The Indian child must be educated. Some parents are too ignorant to be good guardians for their own children, therefore the big-hearted government has assumed guardianship. Use the intelligence and judgment of a good guardian and see to it that the child's educational opportunities are not interfered with.

Emphasize domestic training for girls, especially cooking, sewing and home making [*sic*]; and agriculture, stock-raising and the builders' trades for boys.

Improve Civil Service regulations so that it may be possible to secure competent industrial instructors.

Emphasize for both boys and girls, religious training.

Push the educated young people out to work for themselves as rapidly as they are prepared to do so. Give them encouragement and sympathy while they are getting started in the battle of life, but do not give them anything more.

We must not become impatient, for the work cannot all be accomplished in a generation. Yet the present generation of young people should in some way be made to realize that they must soon, very soon, depend upon their own efforts for whatever they get out of life.

A careful investigation of work done reveals good results attained as well as present conditions that require earnest, vigorous work within the next few years. We should not allow ourselves to be led into impractical channels of work by the suggestions of impractical on-lookers [*sic*], but should conscientiously and vigorously prosecute our work, ever keeping in line with the best that American civilization offers until the Indian educational problem may be merged into the greater problem of general education.

**To What Degree Has the Present System of Indian Schools Been Successful in Qualifying for Citizenship?**

H. B. FRISSELL, *Principal, Hampton Normal and Agricultural Institute, Hampton, Virginia*

**Source:** NEA *Proceedings*, 1903, 1049–12, and *Chilocco Farmer and Stock Grower* 3, no. 10 (August 15, 1903): 511, each have an abstract of Frissell's paper. What is reprinted here combines those two shortened versions. Underscored text comes from the *Chilocco Farmer and Stock Grower*.

Frissell's paper was grouped under the agenda topic "Citizenship," the major theme for Indian educators at the Boston meeting.[56] The paper represents the fourth and last one that Frissell provided to the Department of Indian Education. He delivered two papers in 1900, one in 1901, and this one for 1903. In this defense of boarding schools, Frissell argued that such an environment offered Indian students the opportunity to learn the rudiments of living in a village. He used statistics from annual reports of the commissioner of Indian affairs, as well as Hampton, to make his point that Indian education had been successful.

PROMINENT AMONG EARLY INDIAN TEACHERS was Rev. John Eliot, of Massachusetts, whose practical plans of education have had an important influence upon all training of Indians in this country. Eliot received their confidence and respect, and at the same time inspired in them a sincere desire for the industry and thrift, the godliness and purity of life, which characterized the white settlers of New England. He made a careful study of the Indian language, disposition, and character. Instead of endeavoring to kill out their race characteristics, he recognized the good that there was in them, and endeavored to perpetuate it.

The Indian day schools are among the most interesting and valuable because of the instruction they give to parents as well as to children, in civilized ways. A teacher and his wife are provided, not only with a school-room, but with a house and a piece of land. During a part of each school day the boys work with the teacher on the farm, while the girls help the wife in the cooking and housekeeping. At noon all sit down together to a meal which the girls have cooked. The work of the schoolroom is closely correlated with that of the farm and kitchen. The house and farm become an object-lesson to the Indians in the vicinity. The teacher gives instruction to the farmers of the neighborhood, and his wife shows the Indian woman proper methods of keeping their homes. How much more such a school means to a child-race than does the ordinary public school it is not difficult to understand. Instead of centering the educational work upon book-learning it is made to center upon real life. The schoolroom is used to explain the farm and home, just as John Eliot, when he would help his Indians understand the ways of civilized life, took them to the towns and explained to them the store, the church, and the schoolhouse.

In the reservation boarding school the Indian is introduced to a small industrial and agricultural village. In addition to the usual teachers, there are a cook, seamstress, and laundress, whose office is not only to supervise their respective departments, but to instruct the girls in these arts. Similarly for the instruction of the boys there are a farmer, an industrial teacher, and at the larger schools, a tailor, a shoe-and-harness-maker, a carpenter, and a blacksmith. In these, as in the day schools, the emphasis is placed upon the home, the workshop, and the farm, where the study of history, geography, etc., helps the Indians to understand the place which the small industrial village of which they are a part holds in the history and geography of today. The stories told them by their fathers of the past of their own tribe are supplemented by the stories of other great men who have excelled in quite different spheres.

The training given in these schools is sometimes spoken of as that of the head, heart and hand. Any one [*sic*] who has examined Miss Reel's admirable 'Course of study for Indian Schools' will realize how much time and thought are given to preparation for the actual duties of life. Half a day in the schoolroom and half day in the shops or on the farm is the rule.

The non-reservation boarding schools have carried on the same methods, devoting half the day to work and half to study. The plan of these schools originally was that each should devote itself to some special occupation.

As, in the schools of France, certain institutions are devoted to the study and cultivation of grapes, certain others to the fishing industry, still others to dairying; so it was felt that the Indian youth of certain tribes might with advantage be taught dairying or herding, for instance, and the whole work of the school be made the center of that industry.

In all these schools undenominational religious work is carried on, and opportunity is given to both Protestants and Catholics to influence the life of the young people. In some of the schools there is cordial co-operation [*sic*] between Catholic priests and Protestant clergymen, and it is to be hoped that this will soon be true of all.

Having considered the systems of schools under which our Indian youths are being educated, let us inquire how far this system has qualified them for citizenship. When one goes to the agencies where returned students live in the greatest numbers, he finds that most of the important positions at the agency—those of interpreter, clerk, farmer, and policeman—are filled by returned students, and that nearly every place in the trade shops, except that of foreman, is filled by boys who have learned more or less of a trade at school. In the boarding schools one or more will usually be found in the class-rooms [*sic*] as teachers, and several in industrial positions. Among the camp schools—little oases in the desert of ignorance—very often an educated Indian and his wife are in charge, doing their best teaching by providing a living object-lesson to both children and parents. At several agencies societies have sprung up among the returned students, which hold the leaders together, sustain the weak, and have proved of political as well as ethical value, supplying the places made vacant in civil affairs by the deposition of the chiefs and the absence of any other guiding power.

While the progress of the Indians in adopting the white man's dress and habits, in agriculture and mechanical arts, and in willingness to have their children educated, is not altogether the result of Indian schools, there is no doubt that these have had much to do with it. Statistics given in the commissioner's report as to the advancement made along these lines will be interesting. In the year 1890 the Indians had under cultivation 288,618 acres of land; in 1901, 355,261. The number of acres fenced increased during these eleven years from 608,987 to 1,289,689. The number of families actually living on farms and cultivating their lands in severalty rose from 5,554 to 10,279. The number of horses and mules decreased from 443,244 to 343,300, while their head of cattle have increased from

170,419 to 253,397, showing that they are getting rid of worthless ponies and investing in cattle.

While the allotment of land to the Indian has had much to do with these improved conditions, it is doubtful if the allotment itself would have been possible except for the schools. The number of Indians adopting citizen's dress has increased between 1890 and 1901 from 70,095 to 98,197. The number of Indians that can read English has increased from 23,207 to 32,846, and the number of dwelling-houses from 19,104 to 26,574. It is not too much to say that the abolition of the ration system and the adoption of the work system, which Commissioner Jones has so effectively brought about have been made possible thru the government schools.

The last twenty years have seen a progress far in excess of anything that preceded it. The system of Indian schools which is in existence today is worthy of study, and its results, as shown in qualifying men and women for citizenship, have already proved its value.

The reports of the returned students of Hampton, as collected for the past year, may be considered as a fair representation of the progress that has been made.

The school has taught 938 Indian boys and girls, 673 of whom are now living. These returned students are doing work and exerting influences which, according to our best knowledge, we classify as follows: Excellent 141, good 333, fair 149, poor 42, bad 8. According to this classification, 474 returned students are entirely satisfactory, 50 have poor records, and 149 amount to but little either way. They are largely the sick and deficient.

The first three Indians were graduated from the academic course in '82. Since then 89 have been graduated. Of this number seven have died, and the others rank as follows: Excellent, 48; good, 22; fair, 7; poor, 4; bad, 1.

To some the problem of raising the Indian race seems a simple one. All that appears to necessary them is to break up the reservations and scatter the Indian population throughout the country. To others of us the problem of assimilating a semi-barbarous race seems more difficult. England, with its large experience, has not succeeded in assimilating a small Irish population. Its work in India seems to many Englishmen most unsatisfactory. While our Indian police has not been a cause of just pride, there have been ever since the day of Eliot earnest men and women who have done faithful and effective service in the cause of Indian education and civilization.

SHELDON JACKSON, *General Agent of
Education in Alaska, Washington* DC

**Source:** NEA *Proceedings*, 1903, 1052–53, is an abstract of Jackson's paper. The Presbyterian Historical Society Archives has a copy of his paper titled "An Alaskan Start Towards Citizenship."[57] That version is reprinted here.

The life of Dr. Sheldon Jackson (1834–1909), born and raised in New York, was aptly described by a biographer who titled his work *Winning the West for Christ*.[58] Educated first at Union College, Schenectady, New York, Jackson continued his education at Princeton Theological Seminary, Princeton, New Jersey, to prepare for the ministry in the Presbyterian Church. He graduated from the seminary in 1858. Upon graduation he sought missionary work in either Asia or South America but accepted the decision of the church to post him at an Indian reservation. He began his first work with Natives at a school for Choctaw boys in Indian Territory. The American Civil War intervened, and for a time he comforted Union soldiers in hospitals and Confederate prisoners of war. Returning to the missionary field after the war, Jackson spent his time in the Rocky Mountain West from New Mexico to Idaho. The Presbytery of Missouri River in 1869 designated him "Superintendent of Missions for Western Iowa, Nebraska, Dakota, Idaho, Montana, Wyoming, and Utah, or as far as our jurisdiction extends."[59] He made a trip to Alaska in 1877 fearing that Catholics, Episcopalians, and Methodists were gaining footholds in that region.[60] The result of this trip would be his life-defining work. By 1885 Jackson had picked up the moniker "Mr. Alaska" and was placed on the government payroll for the U.S. Bureau of Education as general agent of education for Alaska, the position he held when invited by Reel to attend the Boston meeting.[61] Reel was no doubt sincere in her invitational letter to him when she wrote, "The Indian workers will be delighted to have the opportunity to hear you."[62]

One issue she probably thought the educators would be interested in was Jackson's introduction of reindeer to provide Alaska Natives with a livelihood. He hatched that plan in 1890 and undertook a project to procure them. He was unsuccessful at getting Congress to appropriate funds, so he raised them privately, and by 1891 he was introducing reindeer to Alaskan Natives. The number of reindeer in his project was smaller than he had hoped, but his endeavor was getting noticed.[63] There was enough momentum to his project that the NEA endorse it with a resolution in 1895: "We heartily approve the efforts to educate Alaskans, and especially in the care and use of reindeer as an industry and as a means of saving them from starvation, and affording them food, raiment, shelter, and transportation."[64] After Congress finally provided his much-desired funding in 1898, he set off to Siberia to procure reindeer by the hundreds.

Transporting the animals to Alaska proved more than arduous, and only 141 out of 538 reindeer survived the journey. An investigation into this project was launched, which quickly expanded into looking at his alleged preference for church schools, particularly those run by Presbyterians, and his continued remittance from the Presbyterians while being paid as a government employee. The investigation, which was completed in 1906, undermined any influence he had in Alaska. He ended his work with the Bureau of Education two years later and went back to Washington DC. Shortly after his return, he underwent surgery at a hospital in North Carolina and died there in May 1909.[65]

Jackson provided in his Boston presentation an overview of the indigenous people of Alaska and his missionary activities among them. One can only speculate the emotional responses of Jackson's listening audience when he graphically described infanticide and geronticide among the Eskimos. Jackson's ethnocentric conclusion that these practices represented the lowest barbarism discounted societal norms among peoples living marginal subsistence lives. Writer Sandra Newman posited that infanticide "is mainly driven by survival concerns." Likewise, geronticide has significant societal implications, also tied to a group's survival. Professor Mike Brogden referred to "death-hastening" when "death is surrounded by ceremony, with significant others giving some semblance of consent" when the elderly voluntarily submit to ending their lives, much as Jackson described.[66] In *The World Until Yesterday*, American polymath Jared Diamond described infanticide under trying conditions where "it is difficult to see what else the societies could do" except to sanction the killing of an infant.[67] Regarding the elderly, Diamond outlined voluntary and involuntary methods, under which societies jettison "burdensome old people," what he called "senilicide." He wrote, "If there isn't enough food to keep everyone fit or just alive, the society must sacrifice its least valuable or least productive members; otherwise, everybody's survival will be endangered."[68]

More specifically, some groups of Eskimos did practice both infanticide and geronticide, although scholars debate the motives. Among motives cited are food uncertainties, inability to support unproductive members of society, a belief system that recognized a transition to life after death, ecological pressures, and others.[69] Whatever the motives, neither Jackson nor his listeners would have viewed these practices as dispassionately as more modern-day scholars.

At one point in his address Jackson simply provided his audience with his 1902 annual report to the commissioner of education. Jackson also edited his remarks to exclude the names of some of the individuals whose lives he was providing as anecdotal information for the progress of education in Alaska. Where possible, those names and associated information are provided in the accompanying citations.

THE PEOPLES STARTING. ALASKA HAS five familes [*sic*] of aboriginal peoples,

1. The Eskimo. From Labrador, on the Atlantic Ocean, to Cape Prince of Wales on Bering Strait, the arctic regions of the North American Continent are inhabited by scattered bands of Eskimos. From the international boundary line to Point Barrow, 423 miles; from Point Barrow to Bering Strait, 847 miles; from Bering Straits to the Aleutian Island, 1,637 miles; and from the Aleutian Islands to the base of Mt. St. Elias, 1,845 miles, are the habitations of approximately 15,000 Eskimos. They are the coast dwellers of Alaska.

2. The Indian. Inland from the shores of Bering Sea and of the Arctic and Pacific Oceans, along the great water-courses of the interior, are the Indians belonging to the Athabaskan family, whose hunting grounds stretch from central Alaska across the mountains to Winnipeg, north of Minnesota. They number in Alaska approximately 15,000.

3. The Thlingets [*sic*], who occupy the coasts and islands and the Alexandrian Archipeligo [*sic*]. They number about 3,000.

4. The Hydah, a small band of about 800 in number, who many years ago

in war drove the Thlinget inhabitants of Prince of Wales Island out of the southern half of the island, taking possession of the same for themselves.

5. The Aleute [*sic*] and Creoles, now but a remnant (3,500) of a once numerous people. Their scattered villages are found from Cook's Inlet on the east to Attou [*sic*], 1,600 miles to the westward.

Starting Point.

Lowest Barbarism. Polygamy, polyandry, slavery of their own people, killing of witches, often times [*sic*] with horrible cruelties, was universal, and among the Eskimos were added infanticide and the killing of the sick and aged, and these barbarities still continue in portions of Alaska outside of the influence of the various missions which have been established in different sections. Upon one occasion I had a native, young Eskimo woman as an interpreter, who, when born, by direction of her mother, had been thrown out of doors to perish with cold or to be torn in pieces and eaten by the village dogs. An older sister, taking compassion of the helpless babe, picked her up, brought her back onto the house and took care of her a few days, until becoming tired of the charge, she threw the babe out of the house the second time. A neighboring woman, taking compassion on the babe, then picked her up and adopted her as her own. Later, upon the arrival of the missionary, the child was placed in the mission school and at 16 or 18 years of age was well instructed in the rudiments of an English education and is an earnest working Christian.

A few years ago, as I was leaving Norton Sound to return to Washington after an investigation of the northern schools in Alaska, a Missionary came and plead [*sic*] with great earnestness that the Secretary of Interior should provide some way by which Eskimo parents in his vicinity could be prevented from destroying their infants.

Three winters ago a missionary lately arrived on St. Lawrence Island, in Bering Sea, was horrified to be invited to be present at the killing of an aged woman. He went, hoping to prevent the deed. An old grandmother had for some time been pleading with her child to kill her, as she no longer desired to live. They had remonstrated with her from time to time but finally importunities prevailed. The day was set, and upon its arrival the children and grandchildren gathered at the grandmother's hot pot dressed in their best clothes. When they were assembled the old lady, dressed in her best clothes, took her seat on the floor in the center of the room, adjusted a cord around her neck, then one of her sons, stepping up behind her, placed a short stick between the cord and the neck, and twisting it up, strangled his mother to death. Upon two or three similar occasions that same winter the missionary was invited to be present.

Upon one occasion, hearing of the killing of an aged person by his sons, I inquired of my interpreter, a middle-aged man, if that was common among them. "Oh yes," he said, "I killed my father; by and by when I get old my sons will kill me." IT [*sic*] was the custom of the country, and the man spoke as calmly concerning it as an eastern merchant would talk of turning his business over to his sons.

This past winter several cases have been reported through the Associated Press Dispatches from Alaska of natives tortured to death as witches, but doubtless scores were tortured in the same way concerning which no notice reached the public. The killing of witches is universal at the present time through all that country outside of the influences of Christian missions.

Without the knowledge and comfort brought to the human race by the revelation of a God of love, their darkened lives are one prolonged terror of ever imminent disaster from evil spirits. The mysterious sounds of nature, the flashing and changing of the Aurora Borealis, the forked lightning, the rumbling roaring thunder, the blazing smoking volcanoes, the quaking yawning earth under the repeated shocks of earthquakes, through centuries have reduced them to the lowest barbarism.

Helps toward making a Good Start. Notwithstanding their barbarous condition they are a strong and vigorous people physically and mentally. The children from Alaska that have been brought to eastern schools rank high. The 50 Alaskan children now in the celebrated Indian School at Carlisle, Pa., grade as follows: in scholarship, excelent [*sic*], 5; very good, 26; good, 15; medium, 3; poor, 1 (a boy recently received into the school who had not learned the English language.) For industry, excellent, 9; very good, 29; good, 11; poor, 1. For conduct, excellent, 24; very good, 18; good, 7; poor, 1.

They are industrious. They differ from the Indians of our western plains, where the men despise manual work. The necessities of their hard lives compel the Alaskan man, woman, and child to work from earliest childhood to secure sufficient food to support life.

They are also of a mechanical turn of mind. With a few pieces of driftwood and the walrus-hide they construct a canoe which will weather heavier seas than the best boats of the same size created by our highest skill. A band of Eskimo boys with the same knowledge of the English language, placed in an industrial school with an equal number of American boys, will excell [*sic*] the latter.

With health[y] bodies and a mechanical turn of mind they are good raw material from which to make good American citizens.

The start towards citizenship was made August 10, 1877, when I located a Presbyterian mission and school at Fort Wrangell in south-eastern [*sic*] Alaska, placing Mrs. A. R. McFarland in charge.[70] The following year (1879) I secured as missionary the Rev. John G. Brady, now serving his second term as Governor of Alaska, and had him sent with Miss Fannie Kellogg to open a mission and school at Sitka. The same year Rev. S. Hall Young, D. D., was sent to the assistance of Mrs. McFarland at Fort Wrangell. They were followed by others. In 1880 I secured the calling of a convention at the Methodist book rooms, in New York City, of the secretaries of the leading Home Missionary Societies of the United States. As the result of that convention the leaders of the leading ecclesiastical denominations agreed to establish schools and missions in widely different sections of Alaska. As the Presbyterians were already at work in south-eastern Alaska, that was by common consent left to them. The Baptists selected for the center of their operations Kodiak Island with the adjoining coasts of Prince William Sound, Cook's Inlet, and the Alaskan Peninsula. The Methodists went 622 miles west of the Baptists and established their headquarters at Unalaska, taking the Schumagin and Aleutian group of islands at their special field of work.[71] The Moravians went over 800 miles to the north-east [*sic*] of the Methods missions[72] and located themselves in the valleys of the Nushagak and Kuekokwim Rivers.[73] As the natives in the great Yukon Valley, hundreds of miles beyond the Moravian field, had through the visits of Canadian-English missionaries become familiar with the liturgy of the English Church, that great valley stretching across Alaska for 1,700 miles, was properly considered the special field for the Episcopal Church of the United States. 300 miles west of the Episcopal field, on Norton Sound, the Swedish Evangelical Union Mission of the United States established stations, also at the base of Mt. St. Elias. Two hundred miles west of Norton Sound the Congregationalists established themselves on Bering Straits. The Quakers, represented through the yearly meetings of the Friends in Ohio, California and Oregon, established stations in south-eastern Alaska and on Kotzebue Sound under the Arctic

Circle. And later the Luthern [*sic*] Church located a station at Port Clarence, on the Seward Peninsula. Special circumstances afterwards led the Episcopalians to Point Hope and the Presbyterians to Point Barrow and St. Lawrence Islands. The Roman Catholic Church, while not a party to the gareement [*sic*] of the Convention, have located missions in many of the leading centers of the country. Their largest schoolwrok [*sic*] among the natives being at Holy Cross Mission on the Yukon River. The Orthodox Church of Russia commenced missions among the Aleuts a century ago, and their churches can be found upon every inhabited island of the Aleutian group and along the southern coast of Alaska as far east as Juneau. These mission centers, so widely scattered, were the first starting points towards the citizenship of the native.

The older members of the National Educational Association will remember my earnest plea on the 23d of March, 1882, before the superintendents' Section of the Association, to secure a congressional appropriation of $50,000. for public schools in Alaska, to be disbursed through the National Bureau of Education. They will also remember the strong endorsement given by the Association in session at Saratoga Springs July 9 and 11; similar action having been taken by the Department Superintendents of the Massachusetts, Vermont, New Hampshire, Connecticut, and New York State Teachers' Associations, which resulted in securing in 1884 the commencement of Congressional aid for the establishment of public schools in Alaska. Printing these endorsements in the form of a circular, I distributed through the United States Bureau of Education a hundred thousand copies to as many teachers between Canada and the Gulf of Mexico, requesting them the same to circulate petitions through their school districts and return the same to their representatives in Congress. The avalanche of petitions which followed so stirred up Congress that on the 17th of May, 1884, an appropriation of $25,000. was made to the Secretary of the Interior for the establishment through the Bureau of Education of public schools in Alaska.[74] The campaign of education that secured from Congress a public school system for Alaska also secured the first extension of law and government over that section of the United States.

On the 2nd of March the Secretary of the Interior assigned the work of making provision for the education of children in Alaska to the Bureau of Education, and on the 11th of April I was appointed by the Commissioner of [E]ucation, with the approval of the Secretary of the Interior, to establish and carry forward the public schools in Alaska. Since then, between 40 and 50 public schools have been organized, and four to five thousand of the native children have been brought for a time under their influence.

In southern Alaska many of the pupils have been taught industrial pursuits in connection with the schools. In at least one of the schools the pupils are required to give three hours each school day to books and three hours to manual labor. In arctic and sub-arctic [*sic*] Alaska, to the extent of the funds provided by government for the purpose, Eskimo young men have been given a five years' course of training in the care and management of domestic reindeer. These schools and their industrial training are also centers for the start toward citizenship.

These questions are often asked, "What progress have these pupils made in the race? What becomes of the students after they leave school?"*75 They may be answered as follows: some after leaving school form habits of dissipation and soon die. The larger number take their places among their own people and by an example of better living help lift up a little way the whole of the native community; while a small number become leaders.

An annual report from the Sitka Training School gives the names and post-office addresses of recent pupils who are engaged in the following pursuits: eleven are boot and shoe makers; 3 are engaged in boat build-ing[,] 2 are carpenters, 3 coopers, 2 clerks in stores, 4 are in canneries, 2 are cooks, 4 are engaged in dress making [*sic*], 2 in paper hanger, 4 are engaged in saw-milling [*sic*], one is a silversmith, 4 are teachers in public schools, 4 are missionaries and the names of 28 young women are given who are married and preside over Christian households, while others are still unmarried but are keeping house for their parents.

In arctic and sub-arctic Alaska 44 eskimo [*sic*] young men, no longer content to live as barbarians, dependent for daily food on their daily catch of fish, or the uncertain proceeds of the chase, have made a good start towards citizenship by becoming owners of small herds of domestic reindeer which have already made them the wealthiest men among their own people.

Twelve months ago I brought from Point Barrow, the northernmost settlement on the North-American [*sic*] continent, a six year old Eskimo boy and placed him in the Sitka Training School. After six years in that school he was brought to the celebrated Indian School at Carlisle, PA, where he has been graduated with honor and will thi[s] fall enter the preparatory department of a western college. In the 80's [*sic*] a little orphan boy sought permission from his uncle to enter the recently established Mission School at Sitka, which was denied him as he was valuable to his uncle for fishing purposes. One day while they were a long way out at sea, fishing, the uncle, angered at the importunities of the boy, picked him up and with an oath threw him out of the canoe and bade him go to school. The little fellow struck out for shore, which he eventually reached but so weak that when the waves threw him on the sand they washed him out again to sea, tossing him backwards and forwards until a wave stronger than the others threw him up so far on the beach that he was able to clutch in the sand and remain. After a while, gathering strength, he crawled up to the school and was taken in. Afterwards he was the first of the pupils to give his heart to the Savior and accept of Christianity, and through his efforts his heathen uncle and aunt and other relatives were brought into the Kingdom. After a course of training in the Sitka School [he was brought East and given a course of training at Moody's School] for Boys, at Mt. Hermon, Conn. Returning to his people, he was made interpreter for the mission, and native assistant for the missionary at Juneau, and when last fall he died scores of the natives claimed him as their spiritual father.[76]

Early in the 90's [*sic*] two or three young men, leaving the Sitka school, went to the salmon canniers [*sic*], saved their wages, and after a while formed a partnership for the running of a steam-sawmill. With the money that they had saved from their wages they went to Portland, Oregon, purchased machinery, paying largely cash and giving their note for the balance. They paid the freight on the machinery to Alaska, set up the machinery themselves, not needing a machinist to put their mill together, then commenced sawing out the lumber with which to enclose their mill. With their mill in shape, one of their number became a commercial traveller [*sic*] for the firm, visiting the various salmon canneries in the vicinity and taking orders for boxes in which the canned salmon is sent to market.

At the same time two other pupils (brothers) framed a partnership, took the money that they had made by working in the canneries and started a store. The owner of the leading community store in the same village tried to induce the young men to place their goods in his store and take stock for the same. Failing to induce them to do this he put down prices so low that he thought they could not compete; but many of the natives patronized them, paying higher prices than they would have been compelled to pay at the community store. Making a few thousand dollars at store keeping [*sic*], and encouraged by the success of their comrads [*sic*] at saw-milling, they removed from the village and established a saw-mill which, when I visited some some [*sic*] months ago, was running day and night, unable to fill orders for lumber and for cannery boxes.

Another [of the] natives that left the school in the 90's went to the Klondyke [*sic*], and afterwards into Alaska, where he has made a moderate fortune in gold-mining.[77] When the great rush of '97 and '8 to the Klondyke was in progress, a number of the young men from the school earned fabulous wages in packing supplies for the white miners going over the White Pass to the headwaters of the Yukon River. They manifested the progress they had made towards citizenship by being the most reliable packers that in those days of great excitement could be found.

In 1898 a Chicago capitalist, returning from the Yukon mines, was attracted by the pretty face and intelligent demeanor of an Aleut girl in the Methodist Mission School at Unalaska.[78] Expressing a wish that he could take the girl to Chicago and give her a chance for a good English education he was informed that he could do so and the girl was placed under his charge. Arriving in Chicago she was placed in the Forestville Public School, one of the best of the kind in that city. She took her place side by side with sons and daughters of the best class of the American population in that city, entering the third grade, she passed with her associates step by step through the various grades, until, five years later, she graduated with 1,200 of Chicago's best children, at the head of the class, taking the gold medal for which, among others, it is said, that the daughter of the President of Chicago's Board of Education was a competitor. Thus a girl with no heredity of intellectual training came into a Chicago school and took the prize away from 1200 of its children, many of whom, if not all, had had centuries of hereditary training behind them.

In the 80's a young Thlinget girl was taken into the Mission School at Wrangell, afterwards was transferred to Sitka, and thence, through the interest of eastern ladies, was placed in a young ladies' boarding school of much reputation at Elizabeth NJ.[79] She spent her years in that school the trusted and loved companion of her associates, many of them dauthers [*sic*] of wealthy New Yorkers. Christmas and Easter vacations were often spent by her, on invitation, in the palatial residences of her companions in New York. She was graduated with honor, the equal of those of more than ordinary success, and has latterly reduced the Thlinget tongue to writing and produced a lexicon of the same which will soon be published by the United States Bureau of Education, and which is, I trust, the first of a series of books that this talented young woman may provide for her people.[80]

In the latter 80's Edward Marsden, a Tsimpshean, was brought to the Sitka School, where he forged ahead of all his companions in all his studies.[81] From Sitka he was brought to Carlisle, Pa., where he tarried only a short time, passing thence to Marietta College, Ohio, then under the distinguished presidency of the Hon. John Eaton, former United States Commissioner of Education. Passing through the College he went to the Presbyterian Theological Seminary, at Walnut Hills, Cincinnati, and while taking a theological course, in order that he might be more useful to his own people upon his return to his own country, he studied law. In the same season he was both ordained to the full work of the Gospel Ministry, and, I believe admitted to the bar. Returning to his own people under a commission from the Board of Home Missions of the Presbyterian Church he secured, through the contributions of his friends, a small steam launch of which he is captian [sic], pilot, engineer, and with which he is visiting eighteen villages along the coast of Alaska teaching the Gospel of the Lord Jesus Christ.

These, it is true, are but isolated instances, but they should be increased hundred of time if the educational advantages and opportunities to the Alaska aborginial [sic] races were similarly increased. The Alaskans have fine minds and simply need, by the blessings of God upon intelligent, tactful teachers, such a chance as is given the larger number of the children of the land in the older sections of the country.[82]

Have I answered the question of what progress has been made towards citizenship in Alaska? In the bill, which was before the last Congress authorizing the appointment of a delegate to represent Alaska on the floor of Congress, there was designated the qualifications of voters in that country and there was provided a way in which the educated native men of twenty-one years of age should become voters with all the rights of a voter.[83]

# The White Man's Burden versus Indigenous Development for the Lower Races

G. STANLEY HALL, *President, Clark University, Worcester, Massachusetts*

Source: *NEA Proceedings*, 1903, 1053–56.

Of all those who spoke to the gathered Indian school educators at any NEA convention, Granville Stanley Hall (1844–1924), more than any other, towered over contemporaries in the field of education. Hall was by the 1890s recognized "as a pivotal national figure and as the progenitor of the modern scientific study of education."[84] Hall became the leading progressive educator of the time, influenced by the intellectualism of Ralph Waldo Emerson, the evolutionary theories of Charles Darwin, and the Social Darwinism of Herbert Spencer. He launched and edited the *American Journal of Psychology, Pedagogical Seminary,* and *Journal of Race Development,* and he served as the first president of Clark University, in Worcester, Massachusetts, from its founding in 1888 until his retirement in 1920.[85] Today Hall's successes are overshadowed by those who at one point worked for him at Clark University or were students of his. Famed anthropologist Franz Boas ranks among the former, and educational psychologist John Dewey, whom Hall disliked, among the latter.[86]

Hall possessed distinct ideas about race and gender. Regarding the first, although he left no doubt about where "lower races" were on the evolutionary scale, he was a noted champion for "protection, support, and education of other races" in order "to honor and maintain the diversity of humankind."[87] Furthermore, he "saw race from a global perspective, seeking to safeguard and direct the upward development of humankind as his ultimate goal."[88] He sympathized with indigenous peoples who were negatively affected by encounters with whites. One observer mused about his address to Indian service workers, "It was a great surprise to everyone from the fact that it advocated measures in direct opposition to the policy now pursued by the Indian Bureau."[89]

Moreover, his position on gender directly challenged Reel as an unmarried, professional woman. Psychologist Lesley Diehl has written that Hall "clearly perceived the avoidance of heterosexuality on the part of women as a threat to the continuation of the species and, therefore, as aberrant."[90] Paradoxically, while he understood unmarried women to be those "who would not produce children and, thus, who were terminal products of evolution," he supported graduate study for women at Clark University, most of whom were unmarried, and none who had families.[91] Whether he viewed Reel as aberrant is not known, but it is likely so. Regardless of his positions on both her gender and the race of the students over whom she superintended, Reel submitted his full paper for publication in *NEA Proceedings* and invited him back to address the department meeting at Cleveland in 1908.

Hall gave two other addresses in Boston: one to the Department of Secondary Education, and the other to the Department of Child Study.[92] In his presentations, particularly that to the Department of Indian Education, he tended toward the pretentious in lavishly sprinkling his papers with esoteric erudition. A former student wrote about Hall's work, "His lecturing . . . resembled the surging rush of a swollen stream which gathers to itself both rich sediment and worthless trash and carries both vehemently to the sea."[93]

MAN IS TODAY, AND FROM the dawn of history has been, the greatest of all exterminators. The great auk, the cave bear, the woolly rhinoceros, and scores of smaller species owe their extinction to him, and several score of other species are in a slow process of extermination. The missing link that connects him in evolutionary series with the humbler forms from which he sprung he himself has destroyed. The same process is now rapidly going on with the lower races. Primitive tribes fade away at his touch. Where civilized man wishes to preserve savages he cannot do so. Many diseases, slight for him, like measles and whooping cough, are deadly to lower races. Other worse infections find the nidus of a more vigorous and deadly development in the bodies of barbarians than they have in our enfeebled systems. Often our worst is in contact with their best. The world knows the sad story of the extinction of the Tasmanians, the Boethuk [*sic*] Indians of Newfoundland;[94] has read the story of the Last of the Mohicans;

of poor Calle Shasta, the sole survivor of the Modocs;[95] of the natives of Hawaii, who dwindled from a hundred thousand to thirty thousand; of the fading tribes of the Samoieds [*sic*] of Siberia; of the Todas of India; of the natives of New Zealand and Madagascar.[96] A few of their younger men and women have taken on a little of our superficial culture, and even become limp prodigies, later to go back, ostracised [*sic*], to the bush and wish they had never left it. A great ethnologist estimates that twenty million slaves, mostly adolescent, have been sold or died in slave ships within the Christian centuries, and declares that Africa would today be better off had it never been discovered by the whites. Discovery is doom for low races, if they have committed the unpardonable crime of settling on land the mineral or vegetable product of which makes it valuable to whites. One-third of the land of the world and two-fifths of its population are today comprised in the various dependencies, colonies, or spheres of influence which, since the great international scramble which began about 1897 or 1898, has absorbed all of the inhabitable globe.

Civilization is man's attempt to domesticate himself, and the most civilized among us have not yet attained the true test of domestication, namely, breathing or self-reproduction in the captivity we have made for ourselves. We have developed the city, which is a biological furnace that intensifies individuation and reduces genesis. Culture at its best is a dim candle illuminating only a few rooms in the great city of man's soul, and leaving the rest in twilight or pitchy dark. Huxley said in substance that slum life in London was lower than among any savage race,[97] and Rancke urged that civilization was in no whit an advance over barbarism, because its lowest dragged down its highest half to a lower average;[98] and yet, with a fanaticism worthy of the Mahdi himself, we force our culture upon unwilling necks as the most holy thing on earth.[99]

What is the most precious of all things in the world? It is the native indigenous stocks or strips of men and women who are natural, vigorous, pure, abounding in health, and that have potency for posterity, which is the very best test of a race and of civilization. It carries in its bosom the great promise to Abraham, that if he kept covenant with the Divine his seed should be as the stars of heaven for multitudes. Ounces of heredity are proverbially worth pounds of education and civilization. This is the most ancient wealth and worth. It conserves thru generations the most precious things.

Now, my simple proposition today is that the lower races should first be understood, their customs studied, their language made familiar, their feelings, views of the world and life, their traditions, myths, institutions, sympathetically appreciated; and that all attempted reconstruction of their lives, thoughts, and emotions should be guided by this knowledge. The tribal system of our Indians is not unlike that on the basis of which, as Morgan has shown, Greece, Rome, or earlier civilizations were developed.[100] The policy is to break it up, instead of studying it, grafting all possible good into its vigorous stock, utilizing everything that is excellent in it, and developing it up to the point when a better culture and system shall come as naturally as a growth. Low races abhor our methods of industry, regulated by the clock that makes alike all the days for them. Longer periods of great effort alternate with those of relaxation. Between matrix and all literary culture is myth, and every well-developed myth system has in it the promise and potency of more or less highly developed art, philosophy, literature, and perhaps religion. Instead of reviving these, we ignore, or perhaps wage a war of extermination against, them. Instead of trying to make a good Indian, we try to make a wretched third-class white man.

Pritchard described traders who batten on the failings which they found, and the greater ones they made, among the Tehuelches in Patagonia.[101] Humboldt tells of the great gift of music, the wealth and depth of religious thought and feeling, among the Huichols in Mexico, all of whom are descended from a god.[102] Bolt in Nicaragua finds abundant traces of an early civilization which he deems higher than that of Cortez,[103] who exterminated it and, according to Bastian, killed one hundred and fifty thousand natives, introduced small-pox [sic] that slew eighty thousand the first year and two million in a generation, and destroyed a magnificent system of irrigation, and so left the land a waste ever since.[104] Le Plongeon thought the natives of Yucatan great builders,[105] like the Pelasgi, and that they were direct descendants from the old Egyptians.[106]

Miss Fletcher and Cushing have taught us that to know the real Indian is to love him, and suggest that we should teach that our religion is only another form of theirs; tell us that their dances are sacred passion plays, and that even the ghost dance is only a pathetic appeal for help and comfort to the denizens of their unseen world, who seem to have forsaken them.[107] Duncan has developed a new pedagogy and transformation among the Metacathlahs.[108] Is it extravagant to say that Anilco,[109] Spotted Tail,

Samoset, Massasoit, Pontiac, Black Hawk, King Philip, and many more represent a patriotism comparable to that of Winkelried?[110] General Crook, who spent much of his life among these men of the Stone Age, tells us that many of them have an eloquence that would not disgrace the halls of Congress. We are long past the stage of hunting them with dogs, as Rev. Samuel Hopkins urged Popham's men to do in Maine in 1703, and of being proud of Indian slayers in our ancestry who kept tallies on their gun stock of the heads of Indians they had killed.*[111]

Canada has no Indian problem, because it adopted the French policy, which affiliates, and sometimes even promotes intermarriage.

Thanks to the present administration of Indian education, efforts are now made to preserve, or rather revive, their wondrous art of making baskets, into which they sometimes weave in symbols the whole story of their lives. This renaissance not only gives them support—such is the demand for basketry—but teaches them self-respect. Why cannot the same thing be done with their pottery, skin-dressing, bead-work [*sic*], canoe-making, taught, where possible, by natives before they become lost arts? Why cannot all their myths and ceremonies be studied and developed? Why should we force them, in the beginning of a new century of dishonor, in the words of a young brave, "to clean the spittoons of the white man's civilization?"[112] Why, instead of making them poor, and perhaps bad, white men and women, breaking down their health, industries and social organizations, morals and spirit, shall we not try to make them good Indians?[113]

Cushing, Miss Fletcher, Fewkes, Catchet, Hough, Miller, Cyrus Thomas, and many other ethnologists have studied and know them sympathetically.[114] Why should not our bureau and schools avail themselves to the fullest extent of this knowledge, and be guided by the very practical suggestions from such sources? Now, on the reservations, in which they are impounded very like the victims of Weyler in *concentrado* camps, they cannot paint, and cannot even celebrate their dances, which are holy passion-plays, sacred worship, all their religion to them.[115] The agent should be simply a kind and fatherly adviser to these men and women still in the adolescent stage of their development. Why should not the missionary graft, instead of eradicate? Why should he not study their totemism, worship, myths, and make religion a natural growth rather than a sudden alien conquest?

Above all, the Indian is perhaps the most religious race on earth. Among many tribes, nothing is begun without asking help from on high. Children of the gods themselves, their lives center in worship. What most struck the Zunis whom Cushing brought to Boston was, as one chief said, that "they saw many men hurrying about and doing many things, but no one praying."[116]

Our country now needs to take a new and larger view of the problems of lower races, and base its treatment upon their nature, as we now study children in order to mold schools and methods to fit them. I have been told by government teachers among the Filipinos that they had no legends or customs. This, ethnological literature abundantly disproves. In fine, we ought now to consider education, religion, statesmanship, history, from a larger standpoint, because the best things have not happened yet. Often victims have been in the end the real conquerors. We may sometime need primitive stock, that our blood or institutions will dominate the far future. In later ages other stocks now obscure, and perhaps other tongues now unstudied, will occupy the center of the historic stage, appropriating the best we achieve, as we learn from Semites, Greeks, and Romans. If this be true, every vigorous race, however rude and undeveloped, is, like childhood, worthy of the maximum of reverence and care and study, and may become the chosen of a new dispensation of culture and civilization. Some of them now obscure may be the heirs of all we possess, and wield the ever-increasing resources of the world for good or evil, somewhat perhaps according as we now influence their early plastic stages.

CHARLES F. MESERVE, *President, Shaw University, Raleigh, North Carolina*

Source: *NEA Proceedings*, 1903, 1056–57, contains an abstract of Meserve's paper. The entire paper appeared in the *Chilocco Farmer and Stock Grower* 3, no. 11 (September 15, 1903): 553–57, under the title "A Survey of The Field and Another Step Forward." That version is reprinted here.

Charles Francis Meserve (1850–1936), a Massachusetts native, began his professional career as an educator after graduating from Colby College, Maine, in 1877. He started as a teacher, but quickly moved into administration, serving as principal of schools in Rockland and Springfield, Massachusetts, from 1877 to 1889. Commissioner Thomas Jefferson Morgan appointed him in 1889 to be superintendent of Haskell Institute in Lawrence, Kansas.[117] This appointment quickly became controversial and, as a local newspaper reported, "caused such a lively row between Commissioner Morgan and the two Kansas senators," when the latter "interpreted the appointment of an outsider as an infringement of their political privileges."[118] Another newspaper adjudged the controversy "ridiculous" and mused, "Evidently, we need a better civil service."[119]

In addition to political opposition to his appointment, the fact that he had never worked in Indian education attracted criticism. The *Lawrence Daily Journal* remarked about his appointment, "No indication is given that he is in the least acquainted with the distinctive work of Indian education."[120] Another reporter observed, "It is said [he] had never seen an Indian until he came to Lawrence."[121] His lacking experience with American Indians became a rub for Haskell students. Two hundred and fifty of them signed a petition nine months after he assumed his position and sent it to the secretary of the interior asking that he be removed. It read:

The undersigned Indian pupils at Haskell institute, Lawrence, Kansas, humbly ask for the removal of our superintendent, Charles F. Meserve, for the following reasons: He does not know how to treat Indians; he has called us thieves and liars in talks to us in our assembly rooms, and ever since he came he has treated us as though we were more treacherous than wild Indians. We like Haskell institute and do not like to leave it, but unless something is done we will either go home or to some other school.[122]

Commissioner Morgan quickly responded to this and other complaints from employees about Meserve and sent an investigator to Lawrence. The investigator concluded "that the opposition which has been arrayed against the superintendent has, to a very large extent, been made by discharged employes [sic], backed by a small junta of politicians who have been disgruntled because they had not been recognized in the matter of control."[123]

Meserve survived the controversy and remained at Haskell until 1894, when he was appointed the president of Shaw University in Raleigh, North Carolina. Shaw University, like Hampton Institute, was founded to provide educational opportunities for formally enslaved Blacks. Meserve remained there until his retirement in 1919. Upon retirement he stayed in Raleigh, where he died in 1936.[124]

When he spoke to the gathered Indian school educators in 1903, he launched an attack on the civil service while ironically complimenting it for improvements to the Indian schools. John T. Doyle, secretary of the civil service commission, offered a vigorous defense of civil service rules immediately following Meserve's address. The juxtaposition of the two addresses compelled one observer to note, "The two papers taken together made the session a most interesting one."[125] While Meserve's listeners in 1903 knew his criticisms of the civil service, readers of his paper in the *NEA Proceedings* did not. Reel excised those criticisms from the piece before publication.

SEVEN FORWARD STEPS HAVE BEEN taken by the United States in the last quarter of a century in the solution of the Indian problem. First, the establishing of industrial boarding schools, usually at a distance from the reservation, and also day schools. Second, the allotment of land in severalty in accordance with the provisions of the Dawes Bill. Third, the application of civil service rules to positions in the school service. Fourth, the creation of the Dawes Commission to negotiate with the five civilized tribes of the Indian Territory and break up their tribal relations, thereby making 180,000 Indians citizens of the United States and destroying the anomaly of an *imperium in imperio*. Fifth, the action of Congress in gradually reducing the appropriations to schools under demonational [*sic*] control until such aid is no longer given. Sixth, lessening, and, in some instances, withdrawing rations and thereby throwing the Indian upon his own resources. Seventh, the innauguration [*sic*] of the policy of abolishing agencies and putting all agency affairs in the hands of school superintendents.[126]

The propositions all met with opposition, but they now have the sanction and authority of public opinion. When the late Hon. Henry L. Dawes, in 1877, asked the Indian committee of which he was a member, to recommend $20,000 for the education of Indian boys and girls, he was laughed at and told that Indians could not be civilized and educated, but finally "because Dawes was such a good fellow" the item went into the Indian bill and the appropriation was made. But the appropriation for schools for the fiscal year beginning July 1st, 1903, is $3,522,950.00, and this splendid gathering of workers is only one of the many evidences of the magnificent growth of Indian schools and their good results.

The Indians are learning and many are becoming good citizens.

Again, when the allotting of Indian land and the selling of the surplus was advocated, many people said, "Indians will not work." The land on several reservations has been allotted and the surplus sold, and some of the finest fields of corn, wheat and oats I have ever seen were planted, cared for and harvested by Indians.[127] I learned recently from an Indian agent that he was daily paying out to Indians under his control $60.00 for honest manual labor.

Certain positions in the Indian school service were included in the classified civil service and it was said Indian schools would go to pieces because they were being removed from the control of practical politicians into the hands of theoretical and visionary philanthropists and school men, but the schools are more numerous and better than ever before. They give a practical education and will continue until absorbed by the states in which they are located.

It was proposed to abolish five nations doing business and exercising sovereignty on United States territory, and there went up a protest from many good people that sacred treaty rights were being violated, overlooking the fundamental principle that to have and to hold does not imply the right to block the wheels of civilization and keep locked the doors to the storehouses of Nature's great resources.[128]

The appropriation of public funds to schools established to propagate religious faith was held to be in violation of the spirit of religious liberty guaranteed by the Constitution of the United States. This idea grew and became so strong that Congress decided that such appropriations should be annually reduced until they should cease, as they did two years ago. But the opposition was so aggressive in some parts of the country at the following presidential election that the party in power was overthrown. A gallant soldier, a typical American, whose family name had been associated with our national history and progress for nearly a century, a wise and conservative statesman, a president who was such a good judge of men as to say that Theodore Roosevelt, the chairman of his civil service commission, possessed excellent presidential timber, went down in honorable defeat. But religious liberty is safer, and in all government Indian schools representatives of all denominations are free to give religious instruction to the children of their faith.[129]

The order went forth to reduce the rations or cut them off entirely. The Indians had been living in idleness and the workers of the country were being taxed to keep them in idleness, and again the sympathies of many good people were aroused and a hue and a cry went up against the inhumanity and cruelty of a powerful government and a rich nation. But I have seen Indians within a few weeks, from whom rations have been withdrawn, at work in Oklahoma for $1.50 a day and they are beginning to say they like work and wages better than idleness and Uncle Sam's free lunch counter.

It has long been held that the reservation system ought to go and the Indian left as soon as possible to care for himself. But the Indian agent, when a civilian, has ordinarily been a politican [*sic*] and a political appointee. He is nominated by the President and confirmed by the Senate, and the politican and the agent have been loath to see a reservation go because that lets the agent out and the politician has lost an earnest supporter. But 23 agencies out of a total of 62 are now out of politics in charge of school superintendents, and in a decade or two the Indian agent, the reservation and the rations system, are destined to be as extinct as the dodo.

Another forward movement must be made before there will be the highest efficiency of service and the greatest economy in the use of funds, and I submit for your kindly consideration this my eighth proposition. The selection of a superintendent of an Indian school and his employees ought to be entirely independent of the United States civil service commission. I say this is not as an enemy, but as a friend of civil service and the present United States civil service commission. The present method, I believe, is the very best selection of employes [*sic*] for the post-office [*sic*], revenue, and all other departments of the United States service, the Indian school service alone excepted. President Harrison, in 1892, by executive order, placed in the classified list the position of superintendent, physician, matron and teacher, and the list has been gradually extended until practically all school employes are in the classified list. This condition is preferable to the spoils system—far in advance of it.

A careful consideration of the reason that led to an extension of the civil service to the school service and its present method of administration, will sustain my proposition. Under the spoils system instances of inefficiency were common and scandals and immorality disgraced the service. It was not infrequent that uneducated men were made superintendents solely as a reward for political service and that subordinates obtained their positions for similar reasons. When the late Commissioner Morgan wished to appoint as school superintendents educated men of successful experience in school work, an official high in position and authority at Washington said to him, "The Senators want Mr. Blank appointed, and, since it is no use to try to educate Indians, you had better let the Senators have their way or you will have a fight on your hands." On one occasion a senator presented himself before Commissioner Morgan as he was sitting at his desk. With out-stretched [*sic*] arms and clenched fists he angrily said, "I've got on my war paint, I'm going to fight you. I'll fight everything you do." And he very generously kept his word. On another occasion when a bill had been introduced into the Senate to make Commissioner Morgan's salary $5,000 instead of $4,000, that it might be the same as that of commissioners in other departments and the same as the salary of the present Indian Commissioner, a senator, out of spite, on account of the Commissioner's strong stand against the spoils system, went among his collegues [*sic*] and by personal effort succeeded in defeating the measure by a vote of 22 to 24.[130] His revenge cost Commissioner Morgan one thousand dollars a year, but President Harrison, upon his recommendation, placed the four most important positions in the school service under the civil service. Opposition on the part of politicians to civil service reform was so great that a member of the lower branch of Congress complained to his constituents that he had been shorn of his power and divested of his right to such an extent that he could not even get one of his constituents appointed to the position of farmer in the school located in his district.

I speak of these occurrences, not to rekindle animosities but by way of contrast with the present and to show that at that time the only road from the spoils system to better things led to the doors of the civil service commission, but the schools are on a different basis now. A decade or more has wrought a great change and most of the schools have superintendents of higher character and more trustworthiness and therefore better fitted for their work than was the case fifteen years ago. Now, few, if any, have any, political pull, or are effected [*sic*] by political pressure, as was the case with nearly all before the advent of President Harrison's administration. The superintendent should nominate all of his employees and be held responsible by the General Superintendent of Indian schools and the commissioner of Indian affairs for a wise selection. There are only two redeeming features about the present system. A superintendent or other employe can be transferred from one school to another and a subordinate promoted to a higher position. If a vacancy can not be filled by a transfer, the superintendent must ask the Commissioner of Indian Affairs to send him some one [*sic*]. The commissioner applies to the Civil Service Commission and a list of eligibles from the certified list is sent him. He selects, we will assume, Miss Smith, of Mansfield, Ohio, who is directed to report to the Superintendent of the school at Phoenix, Arizona. Superintendent Goodman has long been impatient on account of the delay in filling the vacancy, and anxiously awaits the coming of Miss Smith.[131] In due time Miss Smith receives the franked letter of the Honorable Commissioner and with high hopes she breaks the seal and reads, and her high hopes are dashed to the ground, for Arizona is a long way off and it will cost a month's salary to go to Phoenix, and her summer vacation at home will eat up the salary of two months. The salary is $50 a month, or possibly, as the climate of Phoenix is much like that of the place we all want to escape and the cost of living is so high, it may be $750 a year. After a family council has been held, the Smiths decide that their daughter shall not go to the far Southwest and then they indulge in some pleasant references to the businesslike methods of the U.S. Government. Miss Smith sends her declination to Commissioner Jones, who informs Superintendent Goodman that Miss Smith declines to come to him in his dire distress. The commissioner of Indian affairs again appeals to the Civil Service Commission for another eligible. In the meantime Superintendent Goodman is trying with anything but an equable mind to maintain his reputation as a Christian by suppressing a whole vocabulary of words that would not please his wife or look well in print, while up in Prescott at the very time of the vacancy was Miss White, an excellent teacher, just the person wanted and willing to come.

Every official of the Indian school service within the sound of my voice knows that the case I have stated is typical. The distance is not always as great, but frequently it is sufficient for an adverse decision on the part of an eligible. The present Indian school superintendent is not to be envied. He is in a position of great responsibility, with his hands practically tied in the selection of his co-workers [*sic*]. Self-respecting, broad-minded men of culture chafe under such restrictions, and will not long submit to them unless they are imbued with the missionary's love of the children of the forest and prairie, and even then the best service cannot be rendered. There should be the same common sense methods in selecting school workers that are followed by superintendents of public schools, school committees, regents and trustees of institutions of learning.

Some of these schools like Haskell, Carlisle, Chilocco, Phoenix, Harrison, Genoa and others, are as large or larger than some of the well-known colleges of national reputation, and require men of good education, wide experience and a high order of executive ability to preside over and manage them successfully. Men should be selected for such positions because of their natural endowment, their education, high character and recognized fitness through previous success in some important field of educational work. There must also be the missonary [*sic*] spirit, for the best work will not be done when the motive is merely to earn one's bread and butter. In selecting superintendents for the large industrial training schools the entire country should be looked over by the general superintendent of schools and the Commissioner of Indian affairs [*sic*], and consultation should be had with men prominent in education and in positions where a high order of executive ability is required, just as is done by the trustees of a college or the regents of a state University. And, when once chosen, he should have the selection of all his employees, subject, of course, to the approval of his superior officers. This would be as satisfactory to the general superintendent of schools and the Commissioner of Indian Affairs as to the superintendent himself, for at the present time it frequently happens that there is no one on the eligible list and the Commissioner is obliged to authorize a temporary appointment outside of the Civil Service from the locality of the school until an eligible can be found. There is another injustice done the superintendent. In every instance, except Carlisle, where a military officer is detailed as superintendent, he is under a heavy bond and can't even name his financial clerk.

It may be said that the superintendents can not be trusted, and have not asked for the change for which I plead. A superintendent is expected to obey orders and never complain, so I have made bold to speak for him for I was for some years superintendent of a large Indian school and I have kept myself conversant with details of administration since I left the service. It is folly to assert that superintendents with the ability and experience and high character of men like Peairs, and Seger, and Pratt and McCowan and Goodman and McKoin and Lemmon and Potter and Hall and others whom I know personally, cannot be trusted, as presidents of colleges and chancellors of State Universities are trusted, to do their work without being influenced in the selection of their co-workers by political or other unworthy motives.[132] Merit instead of spoils in the public service is now so strongly intrenched in public opinion that there would be no danger of a relapse to the system of Andrew Jackson. Such a reform as I plead for [is] necessary to complete academic freedom as well as the most efficient civil service. In fact, it would be the most fitting cap-stone [*sic*] to the monument of civil service reform.

JOHN T. DOYLE, *Secretary of the U.S. Civil*
*Service Commission, Washington* DC

Source: NEA *Proceedings*, 1903, 1057–63, contains a shortened version of his
paper. A complete version was published in *Good Government: Official Journal of
the National Civil Service Reform League* 20, no. 8 (August 1903): 125–28, titled
"Tenure in the Civil Service: Address by Dr. John T. Doyle, Secretary, U.S. Civil
Service Commission, before the Department of Indian Education at Boston, July
8, 1903." That version is reprinted here.

New Yorker John T. Doyle (1859–1941) began his federal service career
in 1878 as a copyist with the New York Post Office. He became the only
employee of the civil service commission upon its creation in 1883. Congress
established the commission over the outcry following the assassination in
1881 of President James A. Garfield by Charles Guiteau, a disappointed
office seeker. The position of secretary to the commission was created in
1886, and President Grover Cleveland appointed Doyle to it, a position he
held until his retirement in 1932. By then the commission employed seven
hundred federal workers. He was also instrumental in establishing similar
merit systems for employees in major cities such as Chicago and Kansas
City, as well as in several states. No one understood the requirements of a
merit system better than Doyle. He earned both a law degree and a doctor-
ate in civil law, credentials that come through in the paper that follows.[133]

That Doyle spoke to the Department of Indian Education in 1903 and
again in 1904 may be a direct result of Estelle Reel's "difficulties" with the
civil service commission in 1902. However, there was a long history of corruption in the Indian service, with attendant calls for reform, and the civil
service commission already controlled much of the hiring in the Indian
school service well before Reel's run-in with it. The root of the corruption
within the Indian service lay at the feet of the spoils system, where corrupt
individuals were placed in lucrative positions owing to their allegiance to

the victors in political elections. As Indian education was becoming more formalized in the 1880s, reformers sought to ensure political patronage would not tarnish the all-important educational processes.[134] President Cleveland appointed reformer John H. Oberly first to the civil service commission and then as commissioner of Indian affairs (1888–89).[135] An increasing number of positions within the Indian school service fell under civil service rules during the 1890s.[136]

Reel and other educational administrators had expressed dissatisfaction with those rules. Charles F. Meserve, president of Shaw University, told the gathered educators that he supported civil service rules for everyone except Indian schools. Doyle provided the same group of educators the historical background to the employee classification system and a dispassionate review of the need for the system to appoint and to remove employees, such as the Indian service workers. Because Doyle gave this defense of the civil service immediately after Meserve's attack, it "made the session a most interesting one."[137]

THE LAW RELATING TO THE exercise of the appointing power in the civil service is rapidly assuming great importance, with the development of administrative science, and the literature relating to it, though still partial and fragmentary, has become voluminous. A distinct body of law has arisen from the decisions of the courts and the practice under various statutes and regulations. This body of law and practice is important in securing honest and efficient administration of the Government, as upon that honesty and efficiency depend the integrity and maintenance of republican institutions.

More than two hundred thousand persons are employed in the Federal civil service, and perhaps as many more in the State and city governments. The conditions of appointment and removal as related to this great body of employees are vitally important, not merely to the personal welfare of the individuals concerned, but to the nation. If the principles of appointment and tenure are vicious or unsound, abuses will necessarily arise in the administration of government; the civil service will become extravagant and corrupt, threatening the whole fabric of government. It is essential, therefore, that there should be sound teaching on this subject.

The power to make a removal is allied to the power to appoint. In our early history, few restrictions were placed either upon the power of appointment or the power of removal, and these restrictions were not at all uniform. When the civil service of the country was small there was little need of regulations to govern appointments and removals; and administrative reform, along with many other great reforms, only began in the latter half of the century. The use of the patronage system in Great Britain to influence legislation, the giving of colonial positions as sinecures to the privileged classes and to personal favorites, was one of the causes which brought about the American Revolution. The debates on the Constitution show that our earliest statesmen had a clear appreciation of the evils of the patronage system and sought to avoid them in founding the new government. It was their intention that the administrative officers should hold office during good behavior and efficiency. During the first forty years of the Constitution this principle was given thorough and practical effect. Madison, the expounder of the Constitution, said that the wanton removal of a meritorious officer was an impeachable offense. It was not until nine years after the passage of the four-year tenure of office act in 1820 that any material departure arose from this traditional policy of the Government. This act was passed at the instance of an appointing officer for the purpose of using its power to secure his nomination as a Presidential candidate. The abuse of the power of removal which then had its inception, like that of the power of appointment, has been one of the most potent agencies by which the public service has been demoralized and degraded and the spoils system established.[138]

The theory regarding removals before the spoils system arose was laid down by Madison. It was this, that—"Whatever may be said of a technical legal *power*, no officer can have a right to remove a worthy public servant except for adequate public reasons, nor any right to forbear to remove an unworthy one, unless the removal would, for peculiar reasons, be at the moment a public detriment."[139]

The courts have said that where there is a tenure of good behavior it is plain there must be a good cause, arising from the bad conduct of the official, to justify removal. Removal in such a case must be preceded by such action as is equivalent to a conviction of misbehavior; and upon that charge there should be a trial and an opportunity for defense. It is clear that the exercise of the power of removal should be governed by the same moral obligation which would forbid the use of public money for private or party purposes. Whether or not there is abuse of public office in this respect largely depends upon the state of public opinion; and it is of the highest importance, for the purification of politics and the elevation of official life, that public opinion should be informed on this subject.

The subject of the term and tenure of the President, members of Congress, and the Federal judiciary was discussed in the early debates on the Constitution, but nothing was said about the term and tenure of subordinate officeholders. There is not a word on the subject in the Constitution. It is one of those matters which are left to mere inference and construction. The tenure of the great body of Federal officeholders, with an annual payroll of more than a hundred million dollars, is not governed by any statutory enactment. The power of removal of this large army is full of peril if left to be influenced by personal corruption and partisan despotism.

Certain of the Federal judges have a tenure of good behavior, and there is a statute forbidding the head of a Department from removing certain officers except for cause stated in writing, which shall be submitted to Congress at the session following such removal. But these are trifling exceptions to the great body of officials. There is also the greatest divergence in the terms and tenures of judges in the Federal and State services, school officers, commissioners, mayors, State senators and Governors. This divergence exists not merely in practice, but also in the views of public men. On the one hand, permanency in office is insisted upon by some as essential to efficiency, and on the other denounced as an aristocratic monopoly. Some regard a fixed term of years as a corrective of party despotism and corruption, while others regard such a term as increasing both those evils. Rotation in office is demanded to guard against bureaucracy, and Congress has been urged to fix a short term of office for all subordinate officials.

There is a wide divergence of opinion as to how long a term of office the law should provide, or whether removal should only be made for cause, trusting to sound principles and good administration. In European governments, down to within a century, offices were given as a matter of favor, and often sold outright or leased. This has been changed in all civilized states and the patronage lessened, so that offices are given only to those who are found to have the requisite education and experience. Short and precarious terms and tenure have given way to comparative stability of tenure. In our Army and Navy, offices are held during the pleasure of the President. This practice, Senator Benton said, was a departure from the principle of our public institutions, which requires tenure during good behavior and efficiency.[140]

Now, what are the reasons which require a stable and independent tenure rather than a short, fixed term? The reason[s] in the case of the great body of mere administrative positions which are filled by appointment, and not by election, are: First, that the duties are in objects and methods the same, to be performed in the same spirit and manner at all times and under all circumstances; and second, that officers of this class are not representative of either interests, opinions, times, classes, or sections. These reasons apply equally to the tenure of judges and to officials who, unlike Cabinet officers, heads of departments, and ambassadors, are not appointed to carry out a political policy.

The reasons for a stable tenure do not apply to elective officers. Such officers represent interests, opinions, and policies which are constantly changing. Representative government requires short terms for legislators in order that the changing phases of public opinion should be adequately represented in debate and in framing legislation. By frequent elections the people can instruct their officials and call them to account, and thus change the methods of government. The citizen is the judge of the fitness of the candidate for whom he votes. It is necessary that the terms of officials of towns and villages should be short, to make rotation in office for the diffusion of information concerning public affairs.

As we get away from these merely local offices which are filled by election by the people we find that the terms of office become longer. This is because the officers do not represent public opinion to the same extent, and that experience acquired in the service is more important than ideal representation. So manifest is the value of experience of certain members of Congress that they continue to be reelected notwithstanding great changes in party measures and opinions.

We come now to the great body of subordinate officials, who have nothing to do with the policies or principles of administration, whose duties are to be performed in the same way no matter which party is in power, and whose political opinions have no relation to their duties. There is very great harm when they become active partisans and use their offices to control political movements. This means, as President Roosevelt has said, that in consideration of fixity of tenure and of appointment in no way due to political considerations[,] the man in the classified service, while retaining his right to vote as he pleases and to express privately his opinions on all political subjects, should not take any active part in political management or in political campaigns, for precisely the same reasons that a judge, an army officer, a regular soldier, or a policeman is debarred from taking such active part.

The civil service act of 1883 was intended to cure in part the evils which grew out of that relic of feudalism, the four-year-tenure-of-office act. Our administrative system presents the contradiction of filling the great body of the civil service upon competitive tests of merit, free from removals for political reasons, and at the same time of subjecting the positions of postmasters, other than the fourth class, and collectors of customs and internal revenue to a term of four years. It is a marked advance that fourth class postmasters are now no longer changed every four years but only for some reason other than political. The positions subjected to this periodical change require the largest capacity and longest experience for their successful conduct. As it is, they are attained by partisan zeal and party service for a term of four years. Calhoun, Webster, Clay, Benton, and many other able and patriotic statesmen have declaimed against the evils of the four-year tenure law and advocated its repeal. It is becoming a physical impossibility for the President and Cabinet officers to examine the papers and to hear the arguments and complaints relating to the nearly ten thousand officers to be commissioned, and the repeal of the four-year tenure law would afford needed relief to permit more time to be given to the consideration of public business.

Briefly stated, the existing law respecting removals is that the power of appointment implies an absolute and unrestricted power of removal, except in so far as there are express restrictions imposed by statutes consistent with the Constitution. In the Federal service the tenure of office is at the will and discretion of the head of the department, who has the Constitutional power of appointment, provided he does not violate the civil service act, which is the only provision of Congress that curtails or abridges the right of removal. Legally speaking, the appointing power may make removals without any accountability, except that he is liable to impeachment or to removal by the President. The civil service act provides for procuring a body of employees whose appointment is made to depend upon fitness, and not upon political favor. Although the act does not limit the power of removal, the filling of a vacancy must not be controlled by political considerations, and the appointment must be made from among those who pass highest in the examinations. The temptation to make a removal for other than just cause is usually to make room for a favorite. By removing this temptation and relieving the appointing officers from the pressure to make appointments for political or personal reasons, removals are kept within proper limits and there is less need for statutory restrictions.

With a view of preventing removals upon secret charges and to diminish political intrigues for removals, the civil service rules require that within the classified service no one shall be removed from a competitive position except for such cause as will promote the efficiency of the public service, and for reasons given in writing; and the person whose removal is sought shall have notice and be furnished with a copy thereof, and be allowed a reasonable time for answering the same in writing. This rule does not create any legal interest and cannot be invoked before the courts, but merely has force as an administrative order of the Executive. It is further provided that no examination of witnesses or any trial or hearing shall be required, except in the discretion of the officer making the removal. This rule is an authoritative expression by the Executive of his desire and command to his subordinates, with respect to removals from office of those coming within the scope of the civil service act. The Executive has the Constitutional authority to regulate for himself the manner of appointment and removal. He may direct his subordinates who exercise under him, in certain cases, the power of appointment and removal, and may regulate the manner in which they may act for him; but this is an administrative order, not done in compliance with any law, but simply an instruction to those who hold positions by virtue of his appointment, as to the manner in which they shall discharge their duties in respect to the removal of their subordinates. The only authority or duty the Civil Service Commission has in a removal is to see that the procedure required by the rule is carried out. The appointing officer is the final judge of the qualifications of his subordinates, and the question whether such cause exists as requires a removal for the efficiency of the service is for him to determine. The Commission has no power to review his finding in this respect.

The civil service act did not, of course, intend that there should be a life tenure or that persons who became inefficient should be retained. The authority of removal and its exercise for proper reasons are necessary for the discipline and efficiency of the service. The results under the civil service act are infinitely more beneficial to the service and just to the employees than under the old system where removals were made for political or less worthy reasons. An investigation at the New York custom house showed that during the five years preceding its classification there were 1,678 removals. This was three times the number removed in the last five years, although the force is now much larger. In the four years from 1858 to 1862, one collector at that custom house removed 389 out of a force of 690; another, of the opposite party, in the three and a half years next following, removed 525 out of a force of 702. Nearly all of these removals were for political reasons.

In the Indian service only persons who can readily adapt themselves to the conditions which prevail remain in the service, but the separations have decreased from about one-fourth of the number of employees annually prior to classification, to about one-tenth at the present time. An average of but one removal to every eighty employees is made annually for cause.

Of the entire number of classified competitive employees, only about two per cent. [*sic*] are removed each year for cause, less than one per cent of such employees of the Departments at Washington being removed, and only a little more than than [*sic*] one-half of one per cent of the employees of the Railway Mail Service. The largest number of removals is from the services in which many positions are of a mechanical or trades character, as in the assistant custodian and janitor service, where the removals amount to about ten per cent, and the Quartermaster's Department at large, where they amount to a little more than four per cent.

The effect of the civil service act and rules has been to put an end to the political intrigues which were the chief cause of removals. They can no longer be made upon secret charges by unknown accusers, without opportunity for defense, explanation, or denial. The old system was inquisitorial, inconsistent with republican institutions and our civilization. It encouraged falsehood and slander which were protected by the veil of official secrecy, and the confiscation of the office for the benefit of the informer completed the injustice.

The amendment of the rules in 1897, requiring charges and a hearing before removal, supplemented by the amendment of 1899, requiring that the reasons for any change in rank or compensation shall be made a part of the records of the proper department or office, has given stability and permanence to the service, and based the tenure of employees upon efficiency and good behavior. The training received by employees in the Government service is of peculiar value, because of the radical differences between the methods of public and private business; and, as a rule, employees are far more efficient and useful after several years' experience than when they first enter the service. It is not good policy to exchange men trained in technical public work for untrained and inexperienced persons. Such changes often involve large losses to the Government, cause delays in doing the work, and require the employment of a larger force than would otherwise be necessary. The regulations requiring the keeping of records of efficiency, and promotion examinations, also afford protection indirectly against improper removals.

The act and rules require that entrance to the service shall be upon the basis of ascertained merit, and consistency, as well as the efficiency of the service, requires that tenure shall be upon that basis. Under the civil service act and the rules prior to 1897 there were no other restrictions upon removal than that it should not be made for refusal to contribute to a political fund or for a political purpose or to render political service, or for refusal to be coerced in political action. These prohibitions, together with the doing away with the temptation to make removals for the mere purpose of creating vacancies for favorites, of themselves greatly diminished the number of removals within the classified service, and lessened the outside pressure for such removals. The recent amendments to the rules, so far from impairing the exercise of the power of discipline in making removals, aid its exercise. It is the duty of appointing officers to remove from the service those who fail to show adequate qualifications and retain those who do possess them. No restriction has been or should be placed upon the exercise of that power, which would tend to keep the inefficient in the service.

Reluctance to dismiss inefficient subordinates usually arises where the head of an office is a politician who does not desire to make enemies needlessly. The most inefficient employees as a rule have the greatest influence. As vacancies caused by dismissal must be filled by selection from registers of eligibles, the mere politician has nothing to gain, personally, by a change, and there is the certainty of making enemies. So, unless the conduct of a subordinate threatens to create scandal or becomes a source of personal annoyance, the official remains

"To his virtues very kind,
To his faults a little blind."[141]

Removals are no longer made without cause, and political considerations do not now prevail in the competitive service.

BY THE TIME OF THE St. Louis meeting, held in conjunction with the 1904 World's Fair, the ideas of the old assimilationists had run their course.[1] The World's Fair demonstrated the fallacy in their notion that the American Indian would simply merge with equality into white society, indistinguishable from their white neighbors, save for the color of their skin. Consistent with this reality was the overt acknowledgment of the value in "Indianness" evidenced by the Department of Indian Education papers delivered during the meeting. The success of the traditional Indian business model at the fair and the positive reception by fairgoers to various Native exhibitions pointed to a future where American Indians, under limited and defined boundaries, would remain American Indians. There was also a contemporary refurbishing of the national view of Native Americans. However, this refurbishment was frequently driven by the very people—such as Estelle Reel and the Indian school educators—who were endeavoring to remake Natives into English-speaking, capitalistic-laboring, Christian-loving societies with endearing aboriginal characteristics, which the old assimilationists had wanted to "kill off."[2] Likewise, the era's scientific racism meant that, "refurbished" or not, Natives would remain on the periphery of white society rather than merge with it.[3] All of these ideas percolated in the 1904 meeting.

The St. Louis annual meeting of the NEA Department of Indian Education was an unusual one on many levels. First, when she notified Indian school administrators about the meeting, Reel called it a "Congress of Indian Educators."[4] The only other time she used that term with distinction was for the Pan-American Exposition of 1901 in Buffalo, New York, which was held immediately following the NEA meeting in Detroit that year.[5] A news release from Reel's office stated that it was held "with the special object of giving the Indian teachers opportunities of studying the literary and industrial educational methods of the world, as evidenced in the exhibits."[6] A World's Fair would offer the same opportunity, if not more, to the Indian school workers. Moreover, after the dismal attendance of Indian service employees at the Boston meeting in 1903, expectations were high that the St. Louis congress would prove far more attractive.[7] Reality met expectations when the St. Louis Congress of Indian Educators convened at the Hall of Congresses on the fairgrounds with "about 1,000 delegates" present at the opening on Saturday, June 25, an attendance that "far surpassed that of any similar gathering."[8] That number represented about one-third of all Indian school workers, many of whom reportedly belonged to the NEA.[9] That this gathering occurred simultaneous with a Congress of Indian Educators, that so many members attended the meeting, and that it was held in conjunction with a World's Fair ensured its uniqueness within the ten-year history of the Department of Indian Education.

Another distinctive feature of this meeting was that Reel was not focused on organizing a student display. Reel's enthusiasm about demonstrating the success of the work done by her educators with student exhibits garnered the most positive responses to the Department of Indian Education at the annual NEA meetings. Reel went to great lengths to improve on these exhibits each year and took much pride in the resulting accolades. The World's Fair proved decidedly different when Emily S. Cook, a longstanding Indian Office employee, and anthropologist Alice Fletcher organized a display. This exhibit appears to have been put up without much fanfare, unlike in previous years, and certainly to the chagrin of Samuel McCowan, Chilocco Indian School superintendent, who ran the "Government Indian Exhibit" for the exposition.[10] With a 1902 congressional appropriation of $65,000, he organized a reservation of "old Indians" demonstrating and selling tradition Native arts, and a model school of a hundred or so American Indian students showing the gains made by modern—that is, white—education.[11] "'Blanket Indians,' men and women who refused to relinquish their Native customs, attire, and attitudes," write Nancy Parezo and Don Fowler, "would demonstrate their artistry inside the school on one side of the hall, while on the other, children would display their achievements in writing, reading, and manual labor."[12]

The conspicuousness of American Indians at the fair represented the largest number of Native Americans anywhere in the vicinity of a meeting of the Department of Indian Education. As an Indian school newspaper observed about the first meeting of the department in 1900: "The Indian was made conspicuous by his absence at the Charleston Indian Institute."[13] Other conventions featured limited numbers of Native students, who entertained the educators or otherwise participated at meetings, and student work was on display at all of them.[14] Never, however, had the Indian school workers been at an annual meeting where hundreds of American Indians, "old" and white-educated, used their intellectual and artistic skills to demonstrate that they had learned to navigate in two worlds: the world of their ancestors, and the world being forced upon them by the dominant white, Christian society. Indian service workers witnessed fairgoers mostly interested in traditional Indian industries that resulted in robust sales of Native objects, to the point that some vendor booths had to limit orders in order to keep up with demand.[15] Historian Robert A. Trennert concludes about the briskness of the Native business at the World's Fair, "It was, perhaps, the greatest distribution of Indian goods in the general marketplace to that date."[16] The juxtaposing of old and new and the excitement generated by the robust traditional Native arts sales prompted a lady from Philadelphia to muse, "I bought a bracelet. I wanted something genuine. I do hope the Indians won't become too Americanized and lose their originality in design."[17] Yet Indian school workers were in St. Louis to learn how better to "Americanize" their Native students.

Another distinctive feature of this meeting in St. Louis was the lack of time spent in departmental meetings on the topic of Indian education. When the Congress of Indian Educators convened on the morning of June 25, Native students provided musical entertainment, and dignitaries and officials welcomed and heaped lavish praise on the Indian service workers. One such dignitary was Governor Alexander M. Dockery of Missouri, who told the gathering, "A grateful nation . . . looks on and applauds your efforts to augment still further the usefulness of the 'Red Man of the Forest.'"[18] He also complimented the idea of having a department within the NEA:

Miss Reel first came to the National Educational Association with a small department and a few Indian children, and I wish to say that within the past five or six years the growth and development of this department in the NEA has commanded the respect and admiration of all from an ethical standpoint, as well as having a distinctive value from a scientific standard for the educational work of this country. I take great pleasure, afforded by this opportunity, of publicly expressing our great satisfaction in this department.[19]

Responses to the many welcoming addresses came from Louisiana Purchase Exposition officials, such as Dr. William J. McGee, the exposition's chief of the Department of Anthropology, whom Reel had invited both in person and by letter to address the congress, and the department's own Superintendent McCowan.[20] Once all the speeches had been made, the congress adjourned, not to reconvene until Monday evening, allowing time for the members to see "the wonders of the World's Fair."[21]

Monday, June 27, was the first official day of the NEA annual meeting, and that evening the musical Native students again entertained "an audience whose admiration for the young performers was generously shown by their frequent applause."[22] On Tuesday, June 28, Indian school workers attended the NEA general sessions in the morning and a model school presentation early in the afternoon. Then the department held its first meeting at 2:30 p.m., Tuesday, where two papers were presented, a roundtable discussion was held, and a presenter showed various Indian baskets and explained their designs' meanings.[23] On Wednesday, June 29, the Department of Indian Education met, as it had the year before, with the Department of Manual Training, once again demonstrating the similar thrust of Indian schools and the nation's public schools.[24] Though few members participated, "owing to the extreme heat," those that did attend heard presentations on manual training in Sweden and analyses of various fair exhibits of manual training from around the country.[25]

The next day the Indian service employees and their colleague public school educators attended the meeting of the Department of Elementary Education.[26] At this session they learned that in the Philippines all instruction had been given in English since the war of 1898, when the Philippines became a territory of the United States. "Why not teach the Filipinos in their own language?" the Filipino speaker asked. "One reason is because we see in our country the necessity of a common language for all the Filipino people. . . . There are a very large number of . . . dialects spoken in the islands, and most Filipinos understand but one of these. . . . The second reason for teaching English," the speaker continued, "is that there is no literature in the dialects of the Philippines. . . . Without a literature we should be unable to enlarge the knowledge of this people."[27] Such arguments would have resonated with the Indian school workers and demonstrated to them that the issues inherent in "Americanizing" nonwhite, colonized peoples were similar, whether the people were Filipino, Cheyenne, or any other nonwhite, non-English-speaking group.

Finally, on Friday, July 1, the last day of the annual meeting of the NEA, the Department of Indian Education met again to hear two more papers and hold a roundtable discussion to review the educational "points acquired from the study of the various exhibits and model schools and from the joint sessions."[28] Among the points made were the realizations that manual training and English instruction were universal in the process of making "good" American citizens.[29] That is certainly what they heard in the joint and general sessions. They also heard about a growing emphasis on practical education. At a general session one speaker explained, "The second great movement in the education of the country child is to relate the school training more and more to the life of the country child. The course of study for the country child should be more practical."[30] Substitute "country" with "Indian" and the speaker could have been Estelle Reel.

While the general and joint sessions clearly signaled the growing similarity in the practical and vocational pedagogies among Indian school and public school educators, the Indian service educators' engagement with Natives, on reservations or at boarding schools, made their work distinctive. In that environment the educational exchange had been between the old assimilationists and the new progressive educators. As mentioned earlier, by 1904 those arguments had been settled and the old assimilationist view to "kill the Indian and save man" had run its course. Nothing demonstrated this reality more than Pratt's removal from the superintendency of the Carlisle Indian Industrial School just prior to this NEA annual meeting.

Pratt had been a growing source of irritation to the Office of Indian Affairs. His incorrigibility had been a well-known characteristic of his for a considerable time. Back in 1899 one journal posited about Reel, "If she should not win the hearty appreciation of that rugged and heroic leader, Captain Pratt of Carlisle, she will not be the first to meet with such a fate."[31] After that he made it clear in correspondence with Reel that he had no intention of introducing Native arts into Carlisle's curriculum, regardless of what the *Course of Study* required.[32] He also let her know that money spent on "segregating" Indians—that is, keeping them on reservations—was wasted money.[33] Moreover, he had been consistently and vocally opposed to any education on the reservations. One of his fellow superintendents noted about Pratt in 1901:

His attitude toward reservation schools has long been conspicuously and vigorously antagonistic. In the plainest possible language, with the utmost possible publicity, and without any qualifications or exceptions, he has, for years, asserted that all such schools are a detriment to the Indian, and an obstacle to his education and civilization. And, on at least one occasion, his arraignment of the schools in question was coupled with equally plain, sweeping, and unqualified denunciation of those employed in conducting them, as being interested in the perpetuation of the schools, instead of the civilization of the Indian.[34]

Pratt had more recently attacked organizers of the Indian exhibit at the World's Fair for plans to demonstrate traditional Indian ways.[35] Then, in May 1904, as Indian service workers were preparing for their trips to St. Louis, Pratt delivered a forty-minute talk to a Baptist convention in New York City in which he continued his attacks: "Better, far better, for the Indians, had there never been a[n] [Indian] Bureau. . . . Indian schools on the reservations are weak and inefficient, because lacking in the essential elements of practical experience, association and competition, and are calculated to educate the Indian to shrink from the competition necessary to enable him to reach his place as an independent man and citizen."[36]

News reports of his comments reached the secretary of the interior, who asked Pratt to explain himself. In response he simply sent the secretary a copy of his address. Later, an uncontrite Pratt wrote, "There were no statements in it I was not then, and am not now, ready to meet."[37] On June 11, one month after sending the copy of his address to the secretary, Pratt learned the consequences of his attacks on the Indian Office, his fellow superintendents, and reservation schools. The next issue of Carlisle's *Red Man and Helper* ran the simple headline "General Pratt Relieved."[38] Two weeks later nearly one thousand members of the Congress of Indian Educators convened at the Hall of Congresses on the St. Louis fairgrounds. Certainly, the topic of Pratt's dismissal must have buzzed through that audience of Indian school workers.

The Department of Indian Education adjourned its 1904 annual meeting one week later. After having had so few meetings, only a handful of papers delivered at those meetings, and having held two joint meetings at which Indian school workers did not present papers, Reel, as department secretary, had to decide what to submit to the NEA for printing in the 1904 journal. She devoted most of her allowed publication space to welcoming addresses and responses to those speeches, both of which are filled with platitudes, lavish praise, and self-congratulatory comments. Additionally, she included two papers and one roundtable discussion. Both papers included in the NEA journal are included here, as are two papers she also included in her annual report but did not include in the journal. What is most striking in her selection of papers delivered that year, and her inclusion of those papers in her annual report and the NEA journal, is that three of them provide an exclamation point to the end of the Prattian old assimilationist era. One of those papers is about preserving Indian music, and two are sympathetic toward Native languages and names. All three topics were anathema to the old assimilationists. These papers also represent the previously mentioned refurbishment of the Native image by those, like Reel and her educators, who were continuing their full assault on American Indian cultures while encouraging the preservation of selected "Indianness," such as their music and basketry and the making of blankets for the marketplace. At best these efforts and the following papers of the Department of Indian Education demonstrate a backhanded refurbishment.

JOHN T. DOYLE, *Secretary of the U.S. Civil Service Commission, Washington* DC

Source: NEA *Proceedings*, 1904, 977–79.

That Doyle addressed the Indian workers in the two years immediately following Reel's 1902 "difficulties" with the civil service commission is certainly not a coincidence. Reel implemented her version of damage control in 1902 to convince Commissioner James R. Garfield that she adhered to civil service rules. The next year she invited Doyle to address the Department of Indian Education, and she invited him again the year after that. Garfield became her boss in 1907, when he was appointed secretary of the interior, and she attributed her problems with the civil service commission in 1902 to difficulties between herself and Secretary Garfield.[39] Inviting Doyle to make civil service presentations to the Indian service employees apparently did nothing to calm the waters between herself and Garfield.

This second and last address by Doyle to the Department of Indian Education is important in that it breaks from his first, in which he lectured the Indian school workers on the history and rules of the civil service without showing much appreciation for their distinctive work. His tone in 1904 was decidedly different, as he acknowledged the difficulties in filling Indian school service positions. In rules adopted the year before, the wives of superintendents of Indian schools were exempted from competitive examinations for appointments as teachers or matrons.[40] This official softening of the regulations governing hiring for the Indian school service may be reflected in Doyle's more conciliatory address.

The Indian school educators also heard Doyle echo a theme to which they had repeatedly been exposed: that the "uplifting" of nonwhite races required similar work whether one were dealing with Indians, Puerto Ricans, Cubans, Hawai'ians, or any of the other colonized races America now placed under the umbrella of "Americanizing." This theme, which had been growing since the conclusion of the war of 1898, reflects how Indian service educators were increasingly viewed as participants in the global white man's burden. At the eighteenth Lake Mohonk Indian conference in October 1900, the Board of Indian Commissioners president said, "Whether we look eastward toward Cuba and Porto [*sic*] Rico, or westward toward Hawaii [*sic*] and the ten millions of Filipinos, we stand face to face with the question, 'As a nation, what are we able to do for the less-favored races with whom we are brought into close relation?'"[41] The idea of scientific racism had been fully integrated into the answer to that question and into the theories of education. Few were the speakers or theorists anymore who argued that Native Americans, or any people of color, were just like whites, only with a different color skin. McGee, chief of anthropology for the World's Fair, told the Indian school workers, "Let it not be imagined for a single moment that in dealing with the red race we Caucasians are dealing with an inferior type of mankind," although he argued elsewhere that, in mental development, whites had evolved to the top of the human hierarchy.[42] Regarding his second point, by the time of the St. Louis World's Fair, few educated white Americans disagreed.

SINCE THE METHODS EMPLOYED IN other schools need adaptation to fit them to the teaching of Indians, the subject of Indian education has problems which are peculiar to itself. Out of the deliberations of Indian educators in congresses such as this come improved methods of instruction, appropriate text-books [*sic*], unity of effort, and an organized system of education. As I have been identified with the cause of civil-service reform, I presume I shall be expected to speak to you upon the relations of that reform to Indian education, but I shall try to speak to you practically rather than professionally. The character of Indian teaching depends upon the character of the teaching force, and it is therefore fundamental that those appointed shall be capable and of good character. The method of their selection should be designed to this end. To obtain suitable employees, particularly at remote places, where the surroundings are not attractive, is very difficult, but vital. Then, too, the qualifications required are unusually varied. Work among the Indians reverts to earlier types, and there is little subdivision of labor attempted upon reservations. This makes it difficult sometimes to obtain persons who have all the qualifications required for the particular position. For instance, the clerk of an agency or of a school should have integrity, should be a good accountant, and should have sufficient executive ability to enable him to perform, in the absence of the agent, the duties of that position also. The physician of an agency or of a school should bring to his work, to even a larger degree than usual, the skill and self-denial which characterize the profession, because of the ignorance and helplessness to which he ministers and the need of winning the Indian away from the superstition of the medicine man. The farmer must be familiar with the different kinds of farming that the locality of the reservation requires, and be able to impart his knowledge to others, to induce the Indians to become interested in farm work, and to encourage the indolent to be industrious. The blacksmith should be acquainted with ironworking in general, ingenious enough to work in various allied lines of handicraft, even without a complete outfit of tools; as should also the carpenter, the miller, the sawyer, and other mechanics.

It will thus be seen that the inherent difficulties in the way of securing employees for the Indian service are much greater than in almost any other service. The law requires that the service shall be recruited thru free, open, competitive examination, and there is therefore the widest possible field for securing employees irrespective of party, creed, or personal influence. In view of the peculiar conditions existing in the Indian service, persons selected for all positions, with the possible exception of physician, should have teaching ability, as the purpose of their employment is essentially that of instruction. The examinations are designed, therefore, to test the knowledge of the competitor, and to determine as far as possible his ability to impart instruction to others. They are made as practical as possible, and are modified from time to time as experience requires. Previous experience is given consideration in some of these examinations, and in the non-educational [*sic*] examinations it constitutes 60 per cent. [*sic*], while the elements of age and physical condition constitute the remaining 40 per cent.

The progress that is being made in civilizing the Indian is largely due to the efficiency of the teaching force. Upon your individual efforts as teachers, and your missionary zeal, the Indian comes out of his isolation and savagery into assimilation with his white neighbors. From being a menace to social order he becomes a contributor to it and is absorbed into the civilization of the Republic.

It is your privilege and opportunity to aid in this civilizing work, and to bring your intelligence, skill, and zeal to the betterment of the condition of these fellow-beings [*sic*] of ours, leading them in a few generations into the wisdom and opportunities which it has taken long centuries of struggle for the white race to attain. We take by the hand the Cuban, the Hawaiian, the Porto [*sic*] Rican, the Filipino, and the Indian, and bid them be our brothers and share our blessings with us. In this benevolence we obey the injunction of John Locke, who said: "I think everyone, according to the way Providence has placed him in, is bound to labor for the public good as far as he is able."[43]

I have said that your work in civilizing the Indian is a privilege, a duty, and an opportunity. In this I do not wish to be understood as indulging in mere commonplace expressions, or as underrating the difficulties or self-sacrifice required in the task. Your task is a very difficult one, and only as it is inspired and directed by more than ordinary zeal and intelligence will it result in good to the Indians and to yourselves. There used to be many who refused to believe in the possibility of good resulting from governmental, religious, or humanitarian effort to redeem the Indian from his deplorable condition, just as there are many even now who refuse to believe that we can assist the Filipino, of untutored mind and body, to bear the hard burden of civilized life. The prophets to the contrary, we have helped the Indian, and we are helping the Filipino, and we shall keep on in our work until with sound bodies and disciplined minds, capable of systematic labor, they are living lives of contentment and happiness. We have but to witness the wise and good work that you are doing for the elevation of the Indian to see how ready has been his response to your appeal to his moral nature. That response has been greatest where your sympathies and labors have been strongest. Your work has proved that the Indian will advance in civilization by methods which will win his confidence.

One of the greatest forces in the betterment of the Indian has been the raising of the standard of the civil service and in retaining faithful employees in office. We now have a system enforced to the end that the persons appointed in the Indian work shall be possessed of integrity, the requisite degree of knowledge, of experience, and of administrative capacity, sympathy for the Indian, and enthusiasm in the work of teaching. Where the lives and welfare of human beings are at stake it is vital that those put in charge shall be honest and capable.

The teacher who enters the service thru a civil-service examination is appointed upon probation, and that probation is the most important part of his examination. The same laws which determine success or failure in the business world apply in much the same way in the public service. It is true that the motives are different and that personal favoritism, political influence, and prejudices of one sort or another incident to human nature, sometimes vitiate appointments, promotions, and removals, and operate to defeat the just claims of merit; but, taking the classified service in the main, the competent and deserving are advanced. It is no disparagement of the employee's faithfulness to find him after many years of service in either a private or a public institution still holding a distinctly subordinate position. He may be the best of employees, courteous, obliging, obedient, prompt; and yet, if he lacks force, he may spend all his life in the sphere in which he started and make no gain in rank or authority. It is hard for such an employee to realize that the trouble lies in a fault of his own. The employee who wants to go on must keep his interest and intellectual activity alive. He must not only obey orders, but obey them intelligently and with discretion, and in doing so he will learn to command and be fit for promotion.

The outlook in the Indian work is full of hope. The service has been largely taken out of politics, abuses are being remedied, and the Indians are making steady progress toward civilization and self-support. The noble missionary efforts of Christian men and women have prevented the entire destruction of the race, preserved its native arts and crafts, and directed the forces of civilization against nomadic and lawless tendencies. It rests with you to carry on this work.

NATALIE CURTIS, *New York, New York*

Source: *NEA Proceedings*, 1904, 979–81.

Natalie Curtis Burlin (1875–1921) was a classically trained pianist who took an interest in Native American music during a visit to Arizona in 1900. Fearing that such music would be lost forever, she personally and successfully appealed to President Theodore Roosevelt, a "hereditary" family friend, to lift a ban on Native music in federal schools.[44] Following her visit in 1904 to St. Louis, where she gave the following address, she and her brother, with letters of endorsement from Roosevelt, visited many Indian schools and reservations to continue her work of recording and preserving Native music.[45] "In a few years," writes biographer Michelle Wick Patterson, "Curtis had refashioned herself from a classically trained pianist and composer to an active collector of Native American music and a major voice calling for its appreciation and preservation."[46] Curtis amassed songs, stories, illustrations, and art by and about Native Americans that she published in *The Indians' Book* in 1907. President Roosevelt endorsed the book, writing, "These songs cast a wholly new light on the depth and dignity of Indian thought, the simple beauty and strange charm—the charm of a vanished elder world—of Indian poetry."[47] In the introduction Curtis wrote, "This book reflects the soul of one of the noblest types of primitive man—the North American Indian. It is the direct utterance of the Indians themselves. The red man dictated and the white friend has recorded. Songs, stories, and drawings, all have been purposely contributed by Indians as their separate offerings to a volume that should be their own."[48] Curtis also became interested in the preservation of African and African American music and accepted a music position at Virginia's Hampton Institute, where she continued her research.

She married the artist Paul Burlin in 1917. They traveled to Europe in 1921—he as an artist expatriate; she less of one—where she participated in recitals of the music she had collected.[49] A few days following a performance at the Sorbonne, after descending from a streetcar, she was struck and killed by an automobile on a Paris street.[50] One eulogist said about her work, "The most competent musical critics have pronounced that the work of Natalie Curtis in the field of native American folksong is the work of a masterly genius and will endure forever."[51]

What follows is undoubtedly a drab version of her presentation to the Indian school educators. The next month the *Indian's Friend* reported that "a very charming feature" of her address was "the rendering of several Indian songs."[52] The following April she gave a similar presentation at the 8th Conference for Education in the South in Columbia, South Carolina. Her published paper in the proceedings of that conference included comments such as "Here Miss Curtis, in a sweet and cultured voice, sang in the Indian dialect, a song, the theme of which she had just outlined."[53] The NEA version of her paper completely ignores that dimension to her address.

A month after the NEA meeting, she published an article titled "The Value of Indian Art" in which she directly expressed her philosophy about the preservation of the Native artistic contribution to the nation. She wrote:

> But if all that is best in the Indian—his aspiration toward the good, the true, and the beautiful—be developed along natural lines, instead of being suppressed; if, as at Hampton, native art and native industries be encouraged, not supplanted, then shall we have gained when the Indian becomes a citizen and the red man not have lost. And if the striking characteristics of Indian art be eventually absorbed into the art expression of our country, we shall have woven into the fabric of our national culture a strand of color, instead of adding to a monotone of grey. Therefore do I think that every Indian at Hampton who can help to save from extinction the art-life of his people, will do a service not only to his race but to the country.[54]

That Curtis addressed the Department of Indian Education in St. Louis may have been serendipity. She was not listed in the official program, but was visiting the World's Fair with her brother in preparation for a research trip into the West.[55] She was undoubtedly also working on her first major publication promoting American Indian music, *Songs of Ancient America: Three Pueblo Indian Corn-Grinding Songs from Laguna, New Mexico*, published in 1905.[56] She once again addressed the Indian school workers in 1905, but was not on the official program then either.[57] Her addresses, delivered two years in a row, which touted the value of Native artistry, certainly represented the growing desire to preserve some level of Indianness in educational programs, if not a growing anxiety about its impending loss. Historian Brian Dippie astutely observes that the American Indian was "legitimately a native, and no celebration of national progress could properly ignore 'the only people who can rightfully be called Americans.'" Thus, "Americans at the turn of the century were being invited to look with some tenderness on the few living remnants of their own beginnings."[58] Natalie Curtis represented some of that "tenderness" with her address to the Indian service workers.

IT IS A GREAT PLEASURE to me to confer with you today, for altho [sic] I am not a teacher in Indian schools, I share with you the love and interest in the Indians that must be felt by all who have lived among them.

You are all aware that at Hampton, Va., special effort is made to preserve among the negro students the old plantation melodies and typical negro songs. These songs are sung at the anniversaries and commencement exercises at Hampton. Overwhelming is the effect of this natural folk-music [sic] as it pours from hundreds of untutored throats. Great is the service rendered by Hampton to the world by the perpetuation of this music, not only for the intrinsic value of the music itself, but for its reactionary effect upon the students.

The problems of negro education and the problems of Indian education differ, yet what I believe to be the ideal of Hampton holds good for the education of all races to develop character and individuality as the basis of all self-respecting citizenship.

This year, at its annual exercises, Hampton had its Indian students sing their native melodies. The music of the Indians is beautiful, striking, and unique, and its effect was a revelation to the listeners.

On my return to New York last winter I sang for representative and famous musicians some of our Indian melodies. These musicians had gathered in New York for the season from all parts of Europe and America. One of them was a German court conductor who leads concerts in London, Paris, and all the great cities of the civilized world. He was thrilled with the beauty of the Indian songs. "But these things are wonderful," he cried; "they are unique. How rich your country is in artistic material! This is something truly remarkable. Would that Wagner could have heard these songs. You have a wealth of inspiration in your country."

In the Government Building here at the World's Fair you will see models of ancient Indian architecture. Among the great buildings of the world this architecture stands unexcelled in its simplicity and dignity of line, its harmony of detail, its grace and beauty of ornament.

It is for the Indian schools to help fulfill America's duty of preserving for the world the striking and beautiful features of Indian life, Indian character, and Indian arts. If you are already attempting to retain the arts of basketry, weaving, and pottery, extend your efforts to the other arts as well—the poetry and music of the Indians. Let the Indian student record in written form all that he can find of his native art and of his people's unwritten literature; for literature it is. Let this be done now—now before it is too late. Begin in the kindergarten. Draw out the Indian himself, the real child. Allow his creative instinct a chance to develop along natural lines. Where you have native teachers the task becomes an easier one. Confer with these native teachers as to the best means of gaining your aim.

In the Government Building you will see a mantelpiece designed by Angel de Cora, an educated, gifted, and noble young Indian woman.[59] On this mantel are carved the fire symbols and fire sticks of the Indian. Framed amid these symbols is a painting of a fire-lit [*sic*] Indian camp, full of suggestive poetry and charm. Such work shows what native talent developed along native lines can mean economically as well as artistically to our country; for who can say, from a purely commercial standpoint, if we must indeed have it so, that such work is not of far more worth than the sort of wood-carving that means nothing to anybody and can be turned out wholesale by any machine?

Why, then, do we want Indian art preserved? For our own sake as well as for the best development of the Indian. As the Indian is to become part of the nation, it behooves us to absorb, in absorbing him, that which will add to our own native strength.

If the Indian woman sings as she grinds her corn; if the Indian sees poetry and beauty, not dollars only, in his waving field of grain, let us thank God with reverent hearts.

In the cultured circles of our eastern coast we hear the cry: "There is no art in America; our children must go to Europe to be educated." Did we but open our eyes and unstop our ears, we should find in our own land a wider road for inspiration in artistic development than can be offered by the time-beaten pathways of the Old World.

The Indian has much to bring to us—rich gifts of poetry, of art; yea more—gifts of human character rare and noble; and these gifts, if absorbed into our national life, might flower into such a garden of national art, character, and culture as would make it as distinct among nations as any country on the globe. Our civilization is but an aftermath of European culture; it is but a conglomerate reflection of the thought of the Old World. Yet there is one poem in our literature known thruout [*sic*] Europe as distinctively American; one poem taught in all the public schools of our land. What is it? *Hiawatha.* My friends, there are unwritten *Hiawathas* by the hundreds and the thousands.

Mistake me not. In pleading the cause of Indian individuality I am not one of those who believe that the Indian should be kept in a glass case like an ethnological specimen. The Indian is a man, not a curiosity. As a man and a noble man will he develop, and there is no logical reason why good citizenship and self-supporting industry be not compatible with the true and rightful growth of individuality. In our schools in the East we believe in the development of the individuality of each and every scholar, knowing that this is the way to make citizens. Once then, and for all, the Indian is a factor and a worthy factor in our national life. And if he be led to feel this true, if he be taught that we are glad and eager for his gifts, if he be gathered close to the very heart of our country and made to feel that in his own pulses throb its life-impulse, who shall say that this will make him less loyal to his country, less industrious as a citizen?

Oh, Indian workers, think of your possibilities! Think what your schools may mean! You are history-makers. To conserve all the noblest gifts and qualities of the Indian nature is your task. No man can consecrate himself too wholly; no man can give himself too utterly to this national cause. It is a debt we owe not only to the Indian and to our country; it is a debt we owe to our own manhood and womanhood, to our own fatherhood and motherhood, to posterity our children, and our God.

EMILY S. COOK, *Office of Indian Affairs, Washington DC*

**Source:** ARCIA, 1904, 423–24.

Emily Smith Cook (1848–1927), originally from Connecticut, graduated from the second class of Ripon College, Wisconsin, in 1868.[60] She joined the Indian service in 1872, working in the field until 1873, when she transferred to Washington DC, to become a clerk in the office of her uncle Edward P. Smith, upon his appointment as commissioner of Indian affairs (1873–75).[61] She remained in the Indian Office until 1915.[62] During her tenure in that service, she became highly regarded. When introducing her at the 1900 Lake Mohonk conference of Friends of the Indians, the conference president said, "When we want information in Washington about the Indian service, and want facts promptly, and marshaled with common sense and accuracy, we send for Miss Emily S. Cook of the Indian Bureau." Event organizer Albert Smiley responded to that introduction: "Twenty years ago she was the oracle of the Indian Department."[63]

Sought after for her perceived expertise in Indian affairs, she and Alfred J. Standing, assistant superintendent of Carlisle Indian Industrial School, organized the Indian exhibit in 1897 for the Tennessee Centennial Exposition in Nashville, and she, along with famed anthropologist Alice C. Fletcher, organized the Indian Office's exhibit for St. Louis.[64] Cook and Fletcher were not strangers to each other; they both worked actively with the Women's National Indian Association and attended Lake Mohonk conferences, sometimes together.[65] Cook's involvement with the World's Fair went further than the Indian display they put together. The Fair's Board of Lady Managers appointed her an alternate judge for anthropology exhibits.[66]

Cook and Fletcher also both prepared papers for the Department of Indian Education under the topic "Indian Names." They were absent, however, from the closing session of the department on Friday, July 1, so Indian school service employees read their papers to the gathering.[67] Although

Cook was listed on the official program to give an address that Friday, her participation was not recorded in the secretary's minutes for that session, nor was her address published in the *NEA Proceedings*.[68] Reel did include Cook's presentation in her annual report.[69]

While expressing sympathies for Indian language and names, Cook also supported patrilineal surname protocols for legal requirements. She alluded to the legal difficulties created with the passage of the 1887 Dawes Act to allot Indian lands to individuals. Indian names and the protocols under which they were given then ran headlong into the American legal system. It became obvious by 1890 that land tenure and inheritance would require the renaming of American Indians, often with English cognomen. Commissioner Thomas Jefferson Morgan issued a circular that year to begin the process. It had achieved limited success by 1902 and was reinvigorated through conversations among Indian "friends" and President Roosevelt. Commissioner William A. Jones issued a circular in December, referred to by Cook, that injected new life into renaming Indians. Not surprisingly, as Daniel Littlefield and Lonnie Underhill write, "the Indians were not considered in the matter, and it becomes obvious that one motive in supplying them with new names was to make easier the processing of papers relating to Indian affairs."[70] Cook called such a reason "a short-sighted, lazy practice." One wonders how Cook's sympathies for Indian languages and names would have set with her uncle, who ordered Sitting Bull to return to the Great Sioux Reservation in 1875, putting into motion what ultimately became the Lakota and Cheyenne victory over George A. Custer in 1876.[71]

"I DON'T THINK INDIAN NAMES are hard to remember," said a newly arrived doctor on one of the Chippewa reservations over thirty years ago. "What do you call that Indian standing over there?" "Mo cúj e wénce," was the reply, "and the one who can not say it correctly by supper time shall bring the water for the mess." The doctor unhesitatingly agreed, but it was he who humbly carried the full water pail three hours later. Nevertheless, he persevered, until such names were readily memorized; for on that reservation Indian names, as a rule, have been retained, translations have not been in vogue, and the names of philanthropic patrons or of persons of wide fame have been only sparingly introduced.

I still remember how we used to speak of Mrs. Wah bón a quod, wife of the stalwart and shrewd chief of the tribe, Mrs. Moh cúj e wénce, Mrs.

Mesha ké gheshig, and others who were leading lights in the sewing society. I suppose those names had meanings, but we never knew them. Why should we? I can see now short-statured Kish kŭn i kŭt (his name meant "Stumps"), who used to kick the dogs out of church; or old wrinkled I áh by, whose name always seemed to me particularly musical; and I find on the allotment rolls to-day [*sic*] such attractive names as Ain dŭs o gwón, John Sang wáy way, Wah sáh yah, Min o ké shig, Mah je ké shig, E quáy saince. They strike me as quite as desirable cognomens and quite as easy to remember as Lemenager, Magruder, Rosenberger, Westermeyer, or Von Dachenhausen, which I find in the Washington directory.

To be sure a teacher would be at a disadvantage in trying to be either affectionate or disciplinary with an eight-syllabled girl like Sáh gah ge way gáh bów e quay; but the e quay, which is only a feminine terminal meaning woman, might be dropped and a competent interpreter could cut out more syllables and still leave enough of the "gist" of the name to make it recognizable by her parents. Or, better yet, the father's name might chance to be the euphonious one of 'Mon dá min, and Katherine Mon dá min, for instance, would be a dignified name heritage.

Not so with poor Mary Swollen Face, whose painful appellation appears on a pretty bit of sewing over in the Government building. Why should Nancy Kills a Hundred be doomed to go through life with such a bloodthirsty patronymic, or Eunice Shoot at hail with such an idiotic one? Louie Firetail is quite justified in writing as follows to the Indian Office: "My Indian name of Firetail as a family name is most unpleasant to me, especially the thought that my children must bear the name and hand it down in their turn. I therefore request you to assist me, through the proper channels, to change my name to Louie F. Finley, Finley being my wife's name."

If it is now too late for Peter Poor Elk or Sam Slow Fly or John Bad Gun or Ada Parts His Hair or Lizzie Looks Twice to escape their name inflictions, at least the misfortune can be lessened by having their names written as one word with no hyphenating or capitalizing of syllables. But how much less handicapped for entrance into white civilization are Richard Sitahpetah, a Kiowa; and Ruth Cheschesbega, a Navaho, whose names I ran across recently with great satisfaction.

The names given by Indian parents to their children are often as suitable (even from our standpoint) for given names as for surnames. Why should

Imogen be preferred to the Kiowa name Imguna, or Jack to Zapko? Why not have a few less Marys and Johns in the world and enrich our nomenclature by picking out gems from aboriginal matrices?

To saddle upon a child a name uncouth or silly or unknown to his relatives is bad enough, but to give to brothers and sisters varying surnames is a blunder hardly short of criminal. It has not been infrequent—more's the pity—for children of the same father and mother to be named, say Jane Moore, Harry Selden, and Christopher Columbus; wholly unnecessary embarrassment and confusion are likely to result in the future from such a short-sighted, lazy practice.

Of course reform should always have begun in the previous generation when it was much easier and there was much less of it needed. If thirty years ago schools and agencies had exercised the forethought and taken the trouble to enroll and address Indians by their own names, much of the present and more of future complications as to land titles and heirship rights would have been forestalled. But there is another generation on the threshold, and it was to give them a "fair show" that the circular of December 1, 1902, was issued by the Indian Office. The purpose of the circular was misunderstood and also, for the sake of smart paragraphing, was misrepresented in the newspapers.[72] Nevertheless, it remains true that if its principles are followed, particularly in the schools—if women and children are recorded with the names of their husbands and fathers as surnames—much loss, litigation, and fraud will be prevented in the days to come. Since we can not begin this work a generation behind us, let us begin it to-day [*sic*], a generation before.

Let the Indian keep both his personal and his race identity. Individuality is as highly prized by him as by us. For the sake of his property it is necessary that he adopt our system of family names, but that is no reason why we should ruthlessly thrust on him our English names when his own will answer just as well, even better. We want to educate the Indian—lead him on, not stamp him out.

# 34 | Indian Names

ALICE C. FLETCHER, *Ex-President of the Anthropological Society, Washington* DC

**Source:** Alice C. Fletcher, "Indian Names," *Southern Workman* 33, no. 9 (September 1904): 474–77.

Alice Cunningham Fletcher (1838–1923) was born in Cuba but raised in New Jersey and New York. After a formal education reaching only into her adolescence, Fletcher left home to become first a governess and later a teacher, in New York City and in Boston. She became active in women's clubs that drew in female intellectuals in the sciences and the arts—women that were excluded from similar men's clubs. The early discipline of anthropology attracted her to study by 1879 at the Peabody Museum of Harvard University, where she launched her lifetime interest and study in American Indian women's social roles and organizations. She served as president of the Anthropological Society of Washington in 1903, and as president of the American Folk-lore Society in 1905.

Fletcher was much influenced by the work of Lewis Henry Morgan, who established the theory of social evolution postulating that people passed through stages from savagery to civilization, and that private property ownership was vital to advancing through those stages. Despite holding some sympathies for the American Indians, as reflected in her paper, Fletcher was equally confirmed in the allotment of Indian lands and the end of reservations because of the evils she saw in them. Consequently, she actively supported the breaking up of tribal lands.[73]

Fletcher provided her listeners with an overview of her anthropological understanding of the origination of Anglo names and its similarity to the names among American Indian peoples. While this sounded compassionate to the Natives, she held steadfastly to the belief that the "career of [the American Indian] race, as such, is over." Fletcher was listed on the official program to make a presentation under the topic "Indian Names," but her participation was not listed in the secretary's minutes for that session, nor was it published in the *NEA Proceedings*.[74] She was absent from the session at which her paper was read to the Indian school workers, but Reel published it in her annual report, and it was reprinted in Hampton's *Southern Workman*.[75]

A FEW DAYS AGO IN one of our leading newspapers my eye caught the following: "They have strange names, these Omahas; the name of the father was Stomach Fat, while his boy's was Walking Forked Lightning."[76]

This sentence was in a fragmentary account of an old Omaha ceremony in which the child was consecrated to the Great Spirit or Mystery, its feet symbolically clothed and set in the path of life, the sign of his kinship group put upon him and he was enrolled as a member of the tribe. The ceremony was one of deep significance to the Indian and it is equally so to the student who is seeking to trace the development of religious thought and expression. Its acts were accompanied by rituals replete with reverent feeling and emphasized the dependence of man upon the Great Spirit and man's obligation to serve that power which gave him life. Yet the writer of the sentence quoted failed to catch the meaning of the ceremony and by his flippant use of strange sounding names turned a serious and interesting rite into burlesque.

The careless treatment of such rites and the misrepresentation of native ideas in the translation of Indian names deserves the attention of those interested in the welfare of the race. If we are to lift the Indian to our highest civilization in which he is to take his place and act his part, we must not strike a blow at his self respect [*sic*] by ignoring, on the one hand, the attainments of his ancestors, or, on the other, by giving him a name which conveys a repulsive or vulgar suggestion under the notion that it is the equivalent of his native name.

We have become accustomed to treat Indian names in an unfortunate manner. This treatment has several aspects, some have a moral significance, others an historical bearing. Let us look at the latter a moment.

In tracing the history of our own personal names we are led backward toward the time when our ancestors lived and thought along lines not unlike those which obtain among the aborigines of this country. As we work our way backward in our search we catch glimpses of days when the members of the Alfred or elk-council were designated by this society;

when the power of the spear in the warrior's hand gave the name Gerald; or as in the term daughter when not relationship but the avocation of the girls as milkers of the cows was indicated; or as in later times, when the office or avocation became the sur-name [sic] as Abbot, Marshal, Smith, Carpenter, Fletcher, (arrow maker) and the like. While we can thus catch glimpses of the history of our names we are not able to trace the connection between the clan and the family name, or the kinship name and the individual name. To find these connections we need a knowledge of lines of thinking that have long since been overlaid and lost. It is just at this point that aid is found by a study of peoples who are still living and thinking along more primitive lines of thought. It is a well-known fact that if we would understand the growth and development of law, of government, of social relations and of religious thought, we must follow the stream of human progress back toward its sources, to the laws, gov-ernment, social relations and religious thought of peoples whose forward march has been at a slower pace than our own. Among such peoples we are able to observe conditions that lie back of recorded history and to investigate some of the foundations upon which rest the social structure of our own environment. The native tribes of our country afford a rich field for research of this character, for owing to peculiar conditions of fauna and flora the American race had moved forward less rapidly than our own more favored race, therefore the past history of the human family has been here conserved so that social and other customs long since outgrown by us are found here in living force. This valuable ethnological research can be judiciously carried on without detriment to the Indians themselves by keeping it strictly confined to recording the past; a past that had its use but its function is forever gone, as far as the Indian youth of to-day [sic] are concerned, for it cannot survive under the conditions which now obtain save in cruel travesty. Every intelligent Indian will agree with me that while the ancient rites, customs and languages of his race should be carefully preserved in writing as a part of the human record, the sooner they are enclosed within books the sooner will the race become one in language, and be united in customs and religion and brought into close and friendly relations with their white neighbors, and so be best for all.

Turning to the specific subject, Indian names, we find that the tribes of our country are divided into kinship groups, similar to the clan or sept, or the Latin gens. Each one of these groups had its name which usually referred to some natural phenomena or object, as the earth, the water, the thunder and lightning, the animals, etc. From these names arose a system of heraldry, the sign or totem of the object from which the group took its name became the symbol of the group and belonged to it exclusively. The individuals of the clan had a common right in the name but could not use it as a personal designation. For instance, one of the gens of the Omaha tribe was called Tapa, but no man or woman could bear that name or add it as a sur-name to his individual name. Each person of this gens, however, was given one of a series of names all of which referred to the deer, the sign or totem of the gens, so when an Omaha heard a person spoken of by one of this series of names he knew at once that the man or woman was a member of the Tapa gens.

The clan name was always given with religious ceremonies. These took place at infancy, during childhood or later at maturity. In the latter instance the name taken replaced the baby-name. These are sometimes fanciful but many tribes have a series of six or seven names, one for boys and one for girls, denoting the order of their birth. Winona is the Dakota child name for the eldest or first born daughter; Konokaw is the Winnebago name for the eldest or first born son.

The custom for a man to take a new or added name to commemorate some individual experience or achievement is wide spread [*sic*] among the Indians. These names are generally taken, or announced, at some public gathering and in such manner as to tie the act to a religious thought or rite.

Briefly stated, we learn from the rites connected with the bestowal of clan names and the customs pertaining to their use that a man cannot live for himself alone, that he is bound to his kinship group by ties he may not break, must never forget or disregard. This obligation is kept in mind by certain usages, as the tabu, which forbids the man to touch, use, or eat of the object referred to by his clan totem or sign, the custom which prohibits speaking to a person by his or her personal name or mentioning it in the bearer's presence; and the exclusive use of terms of relationship as a mode of address. Instances could be cited of the survival of some of these customs among ourselves aside from those of the home circle, father, mother, etc., but time forbids dwelling upon the long schooling of the race to inculcate the idea of the interdependence of men.

Turning to the use of translated Indian names we are at once made aware of the wide difference between the structure of the English and the Indian languages. This difference is so great as to make a concise and truthful translation suitable for practical use all but impossible. In the Indian tongues the nouns are all qualified by descriptive suffixes or by some other device, so that it is impossible to speak of any object without describing it as, round, long, etc., or of any animal without indicating its position or action, as walking, running, sitting, lying, etc.; verbs are also qualified so that a few words in an Indian language will present a picture or describe an action that can only be set forth in a more or less complex sentence of English. To illustrate: there is a well known [*sic*] Dakota name generally translated as; "Young man afraid of horses." This translation gives an erroneous idea of the true meaning of the name, which is, "the young man whose valor is such that even the sight of his horses brings fear to his enemies." The impracticability of using such a sentence as a name is apparent, the Dakota is far better.

Again, all clan names refer to the heraldic sign or totem of the clan and deal with some detail of the object or animal. In the latter instance it may be with some physical part, or some peculiar trait of the creature. The Indian regards animals as endowed by the Great Spirit with life and what we may for convenience term character. They bring help to man as by food, or they strengthen him by their peculiar gifts, therefore no part of an animal is regarded with dishonor. All natural functions and conditions are accepted simply, so, in the instance given at the beginning of this paper, Stomach Fat, a translation which does not carry the meaning of the original, does not present a disagreeable thought. The word refers to the fat that envelops some of the internal organs, "suet" we say, fat that was serviceable to the people and was one of the gifts of the Great Spirit made to man through the animal; the name commemorates this gift.

The loss of original Indian names through the substitution of inadequate translation would be loss to the history of the human mind. Aside from this historic aspect such a substitution would be a grave injustice to the people who used these names. Adequate translation is impracticable, as we have seen, and any thing [*sic*] less will place the people in a false light, not by any fault of their own, but because of ignorance and carelessness on our part. Humanity, not to speak of the higher claims of Christianity, demands that we beware of such action.

To a body of teachers I need not hesitate to speak of the obligation we are under to do all that lies in our power to the race who called this country home before our fathers discovered the land we now love so well. We desire the Indian's education that he may be fitted to enter upon the duties of manhood and cultivate the gentle graces of Christianity, but we cannot successfully accomplish this desire if we disregard his rights as an individual, or if we fail to recognize what was noble and worthy in his past history. It is not an easy task to substitute a strange language for one's mother tongue, nor is it easy to accept the fact that the career of one's race, as such, is over, yet such is the task before the Indian youth. His language, his ancient avocations, his racial beliefs belong to a time that has gone never to return, but there remains to him many noble heritages from that past which it should be our pleasure, as it is our duty, to conserve, that he may feel the touch of Christian brotherhood as we help him to a place by our side, where he may be known by a name that was sacred to his fathers.

# Conclusion

THREE DISTINCT RESULTS CAME FROM the creation of the NEA Department of Indian Education. First, the annual meetings' general and department sessions provided Indian school educators with professional development opportunities unavailable to them prior to the department's establishment. Regrettably, some of that "professional development" involved prominent speakers sanctioning the era's scientific racism. Secondly, Indian school workers were folded into the national conversation about the educational trends that spanned America's burgeoning population, including the country's immigrants and colonized people in the far-flung corners of its empire. Conversely and thirdly, the department exposed the rest of the NEA to their work "uplifting" and "assimilating" a marginalized population through "practical" and vocational education. Other educators and participants in the NEA meetings were quick to draw the comparison of the work of the members of the Department of Indian Education to the educational endeavors in schools for the masses in the cities, in rural America, and on insular possessions. Commentators approvingly speculated that Indian schools had provided a model of education for an industrializing society. In 1904 Estelle Reel must have felt great satisfaction in these outcomes.

"There would be a great advantage to the Indian school workers," she told her fellow NEA directors at the 1899 annual meeting in Los Angeles, should they have their own Department of Indian Education and be integrated into the Brotherhood and Sisterhood of national educators.[1] She told a reporter with the *San Francisco Call* that being part of the NEA would allow her teachers "to study method" in education and to hear "eminent scholars discuss pedagogic questions" making her teachers "stronger and . . . imbued with a higher conception of their calling."[2] Reel, in short, desired to bring Indian school workers into the fold of the national education landscape, making Indian education a mainstream pedagogical endeavor while enhancing their professionalism through participation at the NEA annual meetings that brought together eminent scholars, school administrators, and classroom teachers. Her fellow NEA directors agreed and created the Department of Indian Education. Reel's assumption must have been that such an alignment with the national organization would further enhance the opportunities that were already offered through her predecessor's Indian school service summer institutes.

Dr. William Hailmann's summer institute agendas prior to 1900 looked very much like those of the NEA Department of Indian Education beginning in 1900. Both Hailmann's and Reel's sessions brought together Indian service educators to talk to each other. Often that meant superintendents addressing employees, and occasionally political or public figures speaking to Indian workers. Many of the same individuals or political figures who addressed the Indian school employees before 1900 spoke to them again at the meetings of the Department of Indian Education.[3] Thus, there was much overlap between the sort of institutes Hailmann organized for his educators and the resulting agendas for the department.

Hailmann and Reel also both worked to make summer institutes more accessible to Indian service workers. Superintendent Dorchester had complained in the early 1890s about the financial difficulties associated with putting together summer institutes, as well as Indian Office agents who did not "encourage such gatherings."[4] Hailmann oversaw the 1894 reorganization of Indian education that put the superintendent in charge of the educators. He noted that this change enabled him "to control more directly the various educational forces that enter into the work" of the Indian schools.[5] In that way obstructionist Indian Office agents were removed as roadblocks to attendance at summer institutes. Reel also alleviated some of the financial constraints by allowing educators to attend the NEA meetings while drawing their full salaries. Moreover, during this era, railroads competed for convention business by offering remarkably low rates for travel to and from those events. Through the creation of the Department of Indian Education, Indian school workers as NEA members now benefited from available lower transportation rates. Therefore, the confluence of eliminating obstructionist Indian Office agents from preventing such attendance, as well as available lower railroad rates and supporting the annual NEA meeting by paying Indian service employees to attend, created an environment more conducive to professionalizing the Indian school workers. These factors contributed to making attendance at summer institutes easier for these educators, and Hailmann and Reel both worked to make that happen.

The establishment of an NEA Department of Indian Education, however, added an entirely new level of national prominence for Indian service educators, both in their department sessions and in the general sessions of the annual meetings. This new national exposure was not a part of Hailmann's agenda but became an integral component of Reel's NEA department. For example, the Indian service workers heard addresses in 1900 at Charleston by such notable individuals as William Oxley Thompson, who served as president of Ohio State University for twenty-six years;[6] noted African American educator Booker T. Washington, president of Tuskegee Institute; and others of equal national education distinction.[7] They listened the next year to Reverend J. Lancaster Spalding, a preeminent educator and the first bishop of Peoria, Illinois, who said, "In scientific and technical education, in commercial, agricultural, and industrial education, we are making genuine and rapid progress."[8] His talk must have resonated with Reel's educators who conducted agricultural and mechanical training at their schools. The U.S. secretary of agriculture in 1902 pleaded with the nation's educators for more agricultural training and less "ornamental education" in what must also have sounded to Indian school educators like an endorsement of their *Course of Study*.[9]

Some speakers challenged their thinking. "The instinct for the useful," a 1903 speaker cautioned, "is being perverted and exalted above the love of knowledge as a chief end."[10] Other speakers undoubtedly perplexed the Indian service workers. In 1904 a professor addressing the St. Louis assemblage on "Education in the Philippines" wished to demonstrate the difference between "Christian Filipinos" and "wild, un-Christian tribes." He said, "There is no closer connection between these [wild] tribes and the Filipino people than there is between the American Indian and the audience that is assembled before me in this room."[11] The Indian school educators must have fumed at this man's ignorance regarding their work to "Americanize" the Indians; he had obviously not visited the fairground's model school, where their students displayed "their achievements in writing, reading, and manual labor," making them very much into the image of the audience he addressed.[12]

Eminent educators and public figures provided similar general session addresses and they would not have attended Hailmann's summer institutes. Once an NEA Department of Indian Education had been created, however, Indian school educators benefited from hearing the trends in the national education landscape from prominent speakers. At their department sessions as well, the Indian service workers heard from equally eminent presenters and on a much more intimate level. For example, they listened to William T. Harris, U.S. education commissioner, deliver the general session address, "How the School Strengthens the Individuality of the Pupils," and they also sat with him in department meetings, where he presented "Civilization and Higher Education" and "Newspapers in Indian Schools."[13] Likewise, they heard Calvin M. Woodward's address "The Opportunity and Function of the Secondary School" in a general session, and his "What Shall Be Taught in an Indian School?" at their department meeting.[14] Other speakers addressed the department meetings, but not the general sessions, such as John T. Doyle, secretary of the civil service commission, who had not addressed gatherings prior to the creation of the NEA Department of Indian Education.[15] Although it is impossible to quantify the result of this sort of intellectual pollination on the Indian service employees, it is safe to say that such presentations, both in the general assembly and in the department meetings, brought Indian school workers into the fold of the national education landscape and increased their professional development opportunities, just as Reel had hoped.[16] Such national exposure also certainly affected how they saw their students.

Indian school educators entered this national education milieu at a time of extraordinary change in their country. These changes added to or adjusted the lenses through which they saw their students and the "Americanization" processes they implemented at their schools. It was a time when scientific reasoning permeated all societal endeavors, a time when educational philosophers such as John Dewey argued "that content and methods of instruction should be governed by the best scientific knowledge available."[17] Such scientific thought, however, supported a major lens of educators: racism, the strongest lens used by Indian school workers in viewing their students.

Scientific racism, a notion that "claimed to offer empirical support for a hierarchy of 'superior' and 'inferior' peoples," writes cultural historian Alan Trachtenberg, "had become an article of faith among most Euro-Americans" by 1900. "Skin color," he concludes, "became a sign of innate and unchanging capabilities."[18] It is because of this article of faith that Hampton's Frissell could tell fellow educators in 1900, "As a race the Indians are people of the child races."[19] It is also provided the intellectual underpinning to the eminent educator G. Stanley Hall's 1903 address "The White Man's Burden versus Indigenous Development for the Lower Races."[20] It motivated Reel to tell a reporter that "the Indians cannot master mathematics or the higher branches of education, but are apt pupils in domestic and manual labor."[21] This "article of faith" in scientific racism dominated the papers of the NEA Department of Indian Education. Indian school educators believed they were helping their students move from savagery and barbarism to a higher stage of civilization, a belief they were now basing upon scientific "fact." Indian service workers may have come first to the NEA meetings possessing only a rudimentary understanding of "white superiority." Exposure to the ideas of scientific racism through their interaction with the NEA no doubt solidified that belief and sharpened the focus of that lens with which they viewed their Native students. After all, they were hearing about it from prominent national scholars and society's most respected thinkers.

The other lens brought into sharper focus with the NEA meetings was that of solving the "Indian problem." That Indian problem was the special category in the American system that American Indians occupied. When Claude Covey told his 1901 colleagues that the desired end of their work was to bring the "Indian to the point where he will be able to become a complete American citizen, be swallowed up, as it were, in the body politic and the vexing Indian problem be forever solved";[22] and when Hervey B. Peairs, Haskell Institute superintendent, told his 1903 audience, "Abolish all reservations and permit civilization to advance," the other educators knew they both meant to stop any programs that distinguished American Indians from American citizens.[23] In other words, eliminate tribal organizations, break up tribal lands, distribute tribal trust funds to individual Natives, teach American Indian children in state public schools, and, in the end, stop treating Native Americans as if they were anything but a laboring class in the United States. Charles F. Meserve told the Indian workers in 1903, "In a decade or two the Indian agent, the reservation and the rations system, are destined to be as extinct as the dodo." The Indian educators adopted a resolution in 1902 attesting to this very position: "*Resolved,* That we strongly indorse the firm stand on Indian matters taken by the President in his annual message, in which he stated that we should treat the Indian as an individual, not as a member of a tribe; that the reservation and ration systems are barriers to progress and should be abolished."[24] They knew what it meant to solve the Indian problem.

That view also came from the top of the Indian Office. Although he never attended a department meeting, Commissioner William Jones oversaw Indian policy for the entire time covered by the papers in this volume. He addressed the Lake Mohonk conference in 1904, his last year as commissioner, and said,

> What shall we do . . . with this whole Indian business? . . . I would wind up his affairs with the general government as soon as possible, and turn the Indian over to the States to which he belongs. I would do away with all class distinctions, which have hemmed him in like a wall and kept him from joining in the progress of the world, and put him on an equality with all men before the law. I would give him the same opportunity and afford him the same protection as others, and let him look out for himself.[25]

The lens to solve this "Indian problem" was also brought into sharper focus at the NEA meetings as a surge of new immigrants requiring Americanizing came to America's shores. When Frissell in 1900 invoked the words of George Bird Grinnell, he was saying exactly that: the Native Americans "exist as an element of our population; they are Americans, and they should be put in a position to develop into a constituent part of our new race, just as the immigrants from a dozen foreign lands have developed into good, useful citizens of these United States."[26] There was little difference between what Indian school educators believed they were doing in Indian schools, and what their urban counterparts were doing in schools serving immigrants. A guest speaker from England told a 1901 general session, "It is quite true that the American schools do literally help to transform the child of the newcomer into an American citizen, and it is indeed one of the chief glories of the American schools that they are able to effect such a conversion as deep and thoro [*sic*] as any other conversion, religious or otherwise."[27] While the American Indian students were not "newcomers," historian Kim Cary Warren reminds readers that "although born in the United States, Native American and African American children were nonetheless treated as immigrants, foreigners, or aliens because their cultural identities seemed incompatible with the dominant society."[28] The idea of Americanizing non-dominant-society peoples took on a mainstream hue with the arrival of millions of new immigrants. Urban teachers were "increasingly confronted by large classes of students whose fluency in English, past academic preparation and performance, interest in schooling, and intentions for the future varied enormously, making instruction far more difficult"—sentiments that would resonate with Indian school educators.[29] The creation of the Department of Indian Education and subsequent interaction at annual meetings made Indian service workers and their NEA colleagues who taught immigrants more closely aligned and likely empathetic to each other's challenges after 1900 than before it.

Finally, the nation's new imperialism, which brought other colonized people of color under the American flag, changed the lenses of the educators, further distorting the image of their own Native American students by uncritically grouping them together with other nonwhite people in America's new overseas possessions. The acquisition of overseas territories brought Kipling's global "white man's burden" to the doorstep of America. The nonwhite populations of Hawai'i, Puerto Rico, Cuba, and the Philippines became new fertile ground for reformers bent on propagating the American way of life.[30] It became commonplace to equate the educational endeavors among Native Americans with those involving other colonized populations. As John Doyle, civil service commission secretary, told the Indian workers in 1904, "We take by the hand the Cuban, the Hawaiian, the Porto Rican, the Filipino, and the Indian, and bid them be our brothers and share our blessings with us."[31]

One manifestation of the reformers' views of this overlap among American Indians and the people of the newly acquired territories is found in the proceedings of the Lake Mohonk annual conference, which was frequently attended by many of the same educators who attended the NEA meetings.[32] Former Indian commissioner Thomas J. Morgan delivered a paper in 1901 titled "The Relation of the Government to its Dependent Classes," in which he argued for the same governmental system under which American Indians were educated to be implemented in Puerto Rico and the Philippines.[33] The platform of the twentieth Lake Mohonk conference in 1902 read, "Other dependent races in our newly acquired possessions have demanded the attention of the Conference. We have been intensely interested in listening to statements in regard to the condition of those in Hawaii [*sic*], Porto [*sic*] Rico, the Philippines, and Alaska."[34] The next year, Reverend Lyman Abbott, a Lake Mohonk conference leader, stated that it was "the duty of the Federal Government to see to it that all its dependent peoples are adequately educated, whether they are Filipinos, or Hawaiians, or Porto Ricans, or North American Indians."[35] Finally, to punctuate that nonwhite people in acquired territories, contiguous or overseas, required the reformers' attention, the conference changed its name in 1904 to "Lake Mohonk Conference of Friends of the Indian and Other Dependent Peoples."[36]

Another demonstration of the perceived similarities in working with nonwhite people regardless of geographical location was the hiring of Indian service educators to work in these new lands, and, in some cases, to recruit aggressively those workers. Newspapers in 1904 reported that teachers serving in the Philippines could expect good salaries, "paid in gold," they were provided government funded transportation to and from the islands, and that "no distinction in pay or promotion is made between men and women."[37] It is not evident how many educators left the Indian school service to take advantage of such an appeal; however, some did.[38] The general superintendent of education in the Philippines reported in 1902 that one of his division superintendents "has had many years' experience in the Indian school work in the United States."[39] Michigander James W. Travis began with the Indian school service in New Mexico in 1898 at an annual salary of $840. He started teaching in the Philippines in January 1904 for what a local newspaper reported was "a much larger salary," at $3,000 a year.[40] In some of these cases, teachers began in the Indian school service, spent time in the overseas possessions, and then returned to the Indian schools. For example, Moses Friedman began his career in the Indian service as a teacher at Phoenix Indian School in Arizona, in 1901.[41] He left Arizona in 1903 to accept a government position as a teacher in the newly acquired Philippines and quickly became the supervisor of industrial training on the island of Cebu.[42] In 1906 he returned to the United States to become the assistant superintendent at Haskell Indian Institute.[43] In the spring of 1908 he became the superintendent of Carlisle Indian Industrial School.[44] These examples illustrate that America's overseas imperialism directly impacted Indian service educators who were now functionaries in the global Americanization processes that engulfed nonwhite, colonized peoples regardless of geographic location—a theme raised at NEA meetings.[45]

Reel believed that her influence in this global process loomed larger than it was. She told a local reporter for the *Cheyenne Daily Leader* during a 1902 visit to her Wyoming hometown that six thousand additional copies of her *Course of Study* had been printed for use "by the government in the Philippines and Porto Rico."[46] This is a doubtful claim. There was a reprint of her revised *Course of Study* in 1902, but there is no indication that it was for use in Puerto Rico or the Philippines.[47] When the Philippine Commission sent an agent to the American Indian reservations "to gain information as to the results obtained by the present administration of Indian affairs," he determined that "the whole system is exceedingly expensive and is nearly useless to the Indian."[48] It is unlikely that he would recommend embracing Reel's curriculum after having come to that conclusion. Furthermore, the October 1902 course of study adopted for use in Puerto Rico included "English and Spanish literary development," as well as reading Caesar and Virgil classics in Latin, all anathema to Reel's *Course of Study*.[49] Likewise, the new director of the educational bureau in the Philippines in 1903 "wanted to provide a predominantly 'literary' education for young Filipinos—to emphasize academic subjects, at the expense of manual training"—another contradiction to Reel's educational curriculum.[50] Finally, in Anne Paulet's study of "Indian education" in the Philippines, and in Elisabeth Eittreim's *Teaching Empire*, there are no references to the use of Reel's *Course of Study*, which would have been major arguments for the influence of Indian education in the colonial territories.[51]

Despite Reel's false claim, the reality is that Indian education did influence education in America's newly acquired territories. Reformers and educators grouped the American Indians with the other nonwhite, colonized people believing that for "dependent peoples" their educational needs were similar. In other words, "uplifting" colonized people looked the same regardless of where one stood on the globe. Such conclusions were discussed at NEA meetings and among Indian service educators. Therefore, this national trend affected how Indian school workers viewed their students.

In the final analysis, Reel's desire to bring Indian school educators into the mainstream of American education and to provide professional development opportunities for them did materialize with the creation of the NEA Department of Indian Education in 1899, and it did impact how

Indian service workers viewed their students. In the first five years of this alignment with the national organization, Indian school workers no doubt gained confidence in their scientific racism, in their drive to solve the Indian problem, in their Americanizing endeavors along with their colleagues "Americanizing" millions of immigrants, and in their understanding of their role in the global white man's burden.

The Department of Indian Education also brought Indian education into the national consciousness, something that would not have happened had Indian school educators remained segregated from mainstream educators. As we have seen, national speakers and major media outlets heaped praise on Reel and her educators for the "practical" and vocational education they were providing America's indigenous people, to include proposing that Indian education was setting a standard for the rest of the country. The second half of the life of the department witnessed an increase in that sentiment. One prominent journal summarized the tone of the 1908 meeting in Cleveland, pronouncing, "How often was heard the cry: 'Let us educate normal white boys and girls as well as we are educating Indians, negroes, and the atypical!'"[52] The creation of the NEA Department of Indian Education helped make such a pronouncement possible.

The second half of the life of the department also saw Indian service educators involved in what cultural historian Alan Trachtenberg calls the national effort to "refurbish the image of Indians."[53] This process was already evident in the papers of the department from the 1904 St. Louis meeting. The selected writings from the years 1905 through 1909 demonstrate the Indian school educators' role in that refurbishment while continuing their headlong rush into cultural genocide through education.

# Notes

INTRODUCTION

1. The association officially changed its name in 1907 to the National Education Association. After that the official name of its journal reflected that new name. Throughout this study I use the shortened version, *NEA Proceedings*, followed by the year of the annual meeting, to indicate either title.

2. Pratt to Reel, January 15, 1903, letter no. 4308/1903, RG 75, CISDRC.

3. Isaac Stein writes, "The Carlisle administration's professed ideas of what race meant were ground in its constant incentives to obtain maximum funding and political support for the school from both public and private sources." He persuasively argues that Pratt and his staff structured what they believed to be acceptable racial arguments for white public and private benefactors, and assimilation of American Indians was one of those arguments. See Stein, "Lift the Red," 69.

4. For an excellent discussion of Reel generally and her racist views, see Lomawaima, "Estelle Reel."

5. "Indian Schools," newspaper name illegible, H60–110, box 2, "Scrapbooks: Indian Affairs and Institutes," ERM-WSA.

6. Hoxie, *Final Promise*, 196.

7. For background on Jones, see W. David Baird, "William A. Jones," in Kvasnicka and Viola, *Commissioners of Indian Affairs*, 211–20; the quotation is from 211–12.

8. Leupp resigned in mid-June 1909, and the NEA Department of Indian Education met for the last time on July 3–9, 1909. The NEA board of directors invited the Indian school educators to have an affiliated relationship with the NEA, but there was no longer a department for them within the organization. Parman, "Francis Ellington Leupp," in Kvasnicka and Viola, *Commissioners of Indian Affairs*, 230; *NEA Proceedings*, 1909, 43.

9. *NEA Proceedings*, 1907, 1018–19.

10. For a summary of the differing views of Pratt and Leupp, which encapsulates these two approaches to "Indian education," see Pratt, "Indigenous Agencies and the Pluralism of Empire," 13–21.

11. Of the fifty-nine papers I selected for the years 1900–1909, thirty-nine were by educators who were then currently at, who had been at, or who were administrators overseeing boarding schools.

12. "'Canada's Responsibility': Trudeau Responds to Report of Unmarked Graves at Residential School Site," CBC, June 24, 2021, https://www.cbc.ca/news/politics/trudeau-responds-marieval-residential-school-discovery-1.6078601.

13. "Secretary Haaland Announces Federal Indian Boarding School Initiative," U.S. Department of the Interior, June 22, 2021, https://www.doi.gov/pressreleases/secretary-haaland-announces-federal-indian-boarding-school-initiative. The first report of this initiative was Newland, *Federal Indian Boarding School Initiative Investigative Report*, published in May 2022.

14. Keller, *Empty Beds*, 154.

15. Peairs, "Our Work," 435.

16. *NEA Proceedings*, 1909, 923, 921.

17. "Hayward Indian School," in "Indian Appropriation Bill," Senate Report 818, 62nd Cong., 2nd sess., 56; "Appropriations for Indian Affairs Office, 1913," *U.S. Cong. Serial Set* (1911): 56.

18. Treuer, *Heartbeat of Wounded Knee*, 140.

19. Irwin Shepard (1843–1916) served for the NEA first as a part-time secretary (1893–1898), then as the first full-time secretary (1898–1912). He maintained an office in his home in Winona, Minnesota, where he served as president of the State Normal School (1879–1898), a position he resigned upon being elected as the NEA's full-time secretary. During the Civil War, he served with the 17th Michigan Infantry, receiving the Congressional Medal of Honor for actions in 1863 and discharged for wounds received in 1864. "V.F. Copy of *Who Was Who In America*, 1897–1942," MS 2266, box 699, folder 20, NEA-Gelman; Wesley, NEA, 374–75.

20. "To Appointees on the Program for the Los Angeles Meeting of the NEA," June 13, 1899; "Program-Circular 1899," both in MS 2266, box 550, folder 6, NEA-Gelman.

21. *NEA Proceedings*, 1902, 861.

22. *NEA Proceedings*, 1901, 893.

23. *NEA Proceedings*, 1903, 1040.

24. I use the phrase "as Reel edited them" with the understanding that edits may have been done by her staff. But, since she served as department secretary and was the superintendent supervising the work of her staff, I believe that edits to papers reflected her intentions in conveying what she wanted published in the NEA journals. I thank Emily J. Will, D-BFDE, forensic document examiner, QDEwill.com, for examining a very limited sample of extant edited

documents from MS 120, box 1, folder 27, ERM-JEFRA, to determine if Reel had personally edited those documents. Will's conclusion, based on the sample, is that the evidence provides qualified support for the proposition that someone other than Reel may have made the pen-and-ink changes on those documents. However, I believe those edits reflect her editorial intentions as head of the agency.

25. For examples, see A. J. Standing's and Josephine E. Richards's papers in *NEA Proceedings*, 1900, 692, 701. A full version of Standing's paper was published in the Carlisle's publication, the *Red Man and Helper* 1, no. 2 (July 20, 1900): 1, 4. Richards's more complete paper is found in the *Southern Workman* 29 (September 1900): 507–10. Of the fifty-nine papers selected for 1900–1909, thirty-nine of them are complete versions found in archives, published in other journals or reports, or are versions supplemented by materials found in other publications. Twenty of the selections are annotated versions that were published in the *NEA Proceedings*.

26. *NEA Proceedings*, 1900, 11, 682; ARCIA, 1899, 621; *NEA Proceedings*, 1901, 893; NEA, *Fiftieth Anniversary Volume*, 918; *NEA Proceedings*, 1907, 15; *NEA Proceedings*, 1908, 1153; *NEA Proceedings*, 1909, 915.

27. This analysis of the editing process is based on the papers for the 1909 NEA annual meeting that are in MS 120, box 1, folder 27, ERM-JEFRA. Among these papers are the originals provided to Reel, and the copies she then provided to the NEA for publication. Comparing those papers to the published versions provides evidence of the editing done by the NEA editors.

28. For a complete discussion of the NEA's involvement in this movement, see Wesley, *NEA*, 218–29.

29. Roosevelt to Stillings, August 27, 1906, in Office of the Public Printer, *Simplified Spelling*, vi. Quotations are from "Changes in Spelling," *Daily Red Bluff* (California), May 8, 1900, 2, which also includes the twelve words NEA chose to simplify: "catalogue," "pedagogue," "demagogue," "prologue," "decalogue," "although," "though," "thorough," "thoroughfare," "through," "throughout," and "programme."

30. David Hackett Fischer writes, "The meaning of any empirical statement depends upon the context from which it is taken. No historical statement-in-evidence floats freely outside of time and space" (*Historians' Fallacies*, 63).

31. "Conference of Indian Workers," Southern Workman 30, no. 8 (August 1901): 425.

32. For example, see Doyle's address, in *NEA Proceedings*, 1904, 978.

33. There are many excellent examples of these works: Lomawaima (Creek Nation, not enrolled), *They Called It Prairie Light*; Child (Ojibwe), *Boarding Schools*

*Seasons*; Archuleta (Pueblo-Hispanic), Child (Ojibwe), and Lomawaima (Creek Nation, not enrolled), *Away from Home*; Lajimodiere (Turtle Mountain Band of Chippewa), *Stringing Rosaries*; Trafzer, Keller, and Sisquoc (Fort Sill Apache), *Boarding School Blues*.

34. *Illustrated London News*, July 5, 1924, 6.
35. Treuer, *Heartbeat of Wounded Knee*, 139. Pratt's path to and journey at the Carlisle Indian School is recounted in his memoir, *Battlefield and Classroom*. Pratt's quotation is taken from *National Conference of Charities and Correction* (1892), 46; quoted in Bishop, "I Pledge Compliance," 1.
36. Native American Rights Fund, *Legal Review*, 1. The Native American Rights Fund also published *Trigger Points*, an excellent bibliographical resource of available literature on Indian boarding schools. For seminal works on Indian education in general, see Adams, *Education for Extinction* (citations refer to the rev. ed.); Trennert, *Phoenix Indian School*; Lomawaima, *They Called It Prairie Light*; and Ellis, *To Change Them Forever*.
37. Lomawaima and McCarty, "When Tribal Sovereignty Challenges Democracy," 280.
38. For a discussion of these two schools of thought and the transformation of these ideas into government policies, see Hoxie, *Final Promise*, chapters 2 and 6.
39. "From Thomas Jefferson to Chastellux, 7 June 1785," Founders Online, National Archives, https://founders.archives.gov/documents/Jefferson/01-08-02-0145 (accessed January 11, 2023).
40. "The Indians could be saved from extinction only by destroying their culture," writes historian Noble Cunningham, "for [Jefferson] had no doubt that their culture must ultimately bend to the rule of reason" (*In Pursuit of Reason*, 276).
41. Bergh, *Writings of Thomas Jefferson*, 16:452; Brodie, *Thomas Jefferson*, 434.
42. Quoted in Prucha, "Thomas Jefferson Morgan, 1889–93," in Kvasnicka and Viola, *Commissioners of Indian Affairs*, 196.
43. See Fear-Segal's discussion of such Enlightenment thinking in *White Man's Club*, xiii.
44. Adams, *Education for Extinction*, 8–24. The quotation is from 23.
45. Fallace, *Race and the Origins of Progressive Education*, 3, 8.
46. Historian Fred Hoxie writes that the white leaders during this era believed that the "gulf between American Indian communities and their own Victorian society was deep and unbridgeable" (*Talking Back to Civilization*, 1).
47. Fear-Segal, *White Man's Club*, xiv.
48. Echo-Hawk, *In the Courts of the Conqueror*, 250.
49. Leupp, "Outlines of an Indian Policy," 946. Leupp included this entire article, with only slight modifications, in his first ARCIA, 1905, 1–7. In expressing this

view, Leupp was criticizing the opinion of Thomas Jefferson when it came to the nature of Native Americans. As one historian has noted, Jefferson believed that "the Indian was really a white man in moccasins and a breech-clout" (Jackson, *Thomas Jefferson and the Stony Mountains*, 34).

50. Leupp, "Improvement, Not Transformation," 369.

51. Child, *Boarding School Seasons*, v–vi; Greer, *Property and Dispossession*, 436. For his discussion on "commodification," see 220–27.

52. A 1969 congressional report on Indian education demonstrated as much when it concluded: "Federal policy toward the Indian was based on the desire to dispossess him of his land. Education policy was a function of our land policy" (quoted in Newland, *Federal Indian Boarding School*, 25).

53. For a synopsis of the arguments in this debate, see Adams, *Education for Extinction*, 33–35.

54. Adams, *Education for Extinction*, 33. For an analysis of these three institutions, see 33–64.

55. Quoted in Trennert, *Phoenix Indian School*, 7.

56. For a discussion of the controversy surrounding the boarding school students returning to their Native communities, see Adams, *Education for Extinction*, 299–334.

57. Carlos Montezuma (1866–1923), "The Indian Problem from an Indian's Standpoint," an address reprinted in RCE, 1896–97, 2:1520–22; the quotations are from 1522. See also Emery, *Recovering Native American Writings*, 180–88. Martinez argues against an overarching perception of Montezuma's support for assimilation. See his "Carlos Montezuma's Fight against 'Bureauism.'"

58. Prucha, *Americanizing the American Indians*, 1; Dr. E. E. White, quoted in "Indian Institute at Los Angeles," *Red Man* 15, no. 7 (July–August 1899), 2.

59. Prucha, *Americanizing the American Indians*, 1; Trennert, *Phoenix Indian School*, 3.

60. This summary of the history of the NEA is from two publications: Fenner, *NEA History*; and Wesley, *NEA*.

61. As mentioned previously, another renaming occurred in 1907 when the association dropped the "al" from "Education" and became the National Education Association, as it remains today (*NEA Proceedings*, 1907, 8).

62. Fenner, *NEA History*, 12.

63. Fenner, *NEA History*, 21–22. Membership numbers can be found in Fenner, *NEA History*, 155; and Wesley, *NEA*, 397.

64. Shepard, general secretary, NEA, "Historical Sketch of the National Education Association, July 8–14, 1911," 4–5, NEA 1007. RG, box 2964, file 7, misfiled in box 3003, NEA-Gelman; the quotation is from 5.

65. Quotation from "Constitution of the National Educational Association," Art. 3, Sec. 8, NEA *Proceedings*, 1899, 3. For a discussion of the implementation process and functions for NEA departments, see Wesley, NEA, 274–91.

66. Wesley, NEA, 289; NEA, *Fiftieth Anniversary Volume*, 565, 693.

67. NEA, *Fiftieth Anniversary Volume*, 693; *Official Program of the National Educational Association, July 5–12, 1895*, 22, 1008.RG, box 3958, folder 1, NEA-Gelman.

68. NEA *Proceedings*, 1895, 80–86.

69. "Resolutions," MS 2266, box 682, folder 7, NEA-Gelman.

70. "Resolutions," MS 2266, box 682, folder 7, NEA-Gelman.

71. NEA *Proceedings*, 1890, 39.

72. NEA *Proceedings*, 1895, 33.

73. Art. 4, Sec. 8, NEA Constitution, provided for the insertion of a new department's name in the constitution (NEA *Proceedings*, 1899, 3).

74. Child, *Boarding School Seasons*, v–vi.

75. For example, see NEA *Proceedings*, 1903, 1040.

76. In 1900, the first year the Department of Indian Education was listed in the NEA constitution, the only other category of students also having a distinctive department was "Education of the Deaf, Blind, and Feeble-Minded." By 1902 a name change occurred for that department making it the Department of Special Education (NEA *Proceedings*, 1900, 1; NEA *Proceedings*, 1902, 1).

77. For the year Reel became an NEA member and the two years she did not serve as secretary (1900 and 1901), see NEA, *Fiftieth Anniversary Volume*, 918, 650.

78. "Biography for Pan-American History," May 1901, H60–110, box 1, "Biographies," file 3, ERM-WSA; Bohl, "Man's Work in a Woman's Way," 3–23. Some writers claim Reel is the first woman in the United States elected to a statewide office (see Bohl, 23), however, that honor goes to Laura Eisenhuth, North Dakota superintendent of public instruction, who won her statewide election in 1892 (Wefald, "Breaking an 1889 Glass Ceiling"). Regarding claims that Reel was the first woman holding statewide office, see Bohl, "Wyoming's Estelle Reel."

79. Bohl, "Man's Work in a Woman's Way," 62–68; Lomawaima, "Estelle Reel," 8; Prucha, *Great Father*, 821; Morris, *Rise of Theodore Roosevelt*, 572.

80. "Biography for Pan-American History, May 1901," H60–110, box 1, "Biographies," file 3, ERM-WSA; Bohl, "Man's Work in a Woman's Way," 68–71.

81. "Gazette July 18, 98," page H+1, H60–110, box 2, "Scrapbooks: Indian Affairs and Institutes," ERM-WSA.

82. Bohl, "Man's Work in a Woman's Way," 68; Indian Rights Association, "Answers to Charges Made against Wm. N. Hailmann," 1.

83. For the kindergarten movement in the NEA, see Wesley, *NEA*, 156–64. For Hailmann's presidencies, see 161. Hailmann attended the annual meeting in 1863, but could have joined prior to that year (Barnard, *Proceedings*, 302).

84. Wesley, *NEA*, 161; NEA *Fiftieth Anniversary Volume*, 548, 626, 696; Ahern, "Experiment Aborted," 170.

85. "Hailmann's Removal," *Indianapolis News*, June 11, 1898, 10; Bohl, "Man's Work in a Woman's Way," 70–71; Ahern, "Experiment Aborted," 291; "Woman May Get the Place," *Alton Telegraphy* (Illinois), April 28, 1898, 1.

86. Bohl, "Man's Work in a Woman's Way," 72–81; "Biography for Pan-American History, May, 1901," H60–110, box 1, "Biographies," file 3, ERM-WSA. Historian Cathleen Cahill demonstrates that the later decades of the nineteenth century saw women appointed to senior positions in the Indian service. This trend undoubtedly worked to Reel's advantage as she actively pursued the superintendency. See Cahill, *Federal Fathers and Mothers*, 64–65. For a discussion on Senate confirmations of females in the nineteenth century, see Blevins, "Women and Federal Officeholding."

87. "Hailmann's Removal," *Indianapolis News*, June 11, 1898, 10.

88. Fred Nicklason, "Welsh, Herbert," in Washburn, *History of Indian-White Relations*, 4:694.

89. According to Durward Howes's *American Woman*, Reel was born November 26, 1862 (375). Moreover, when she died in August 1959, she was said to be ninety-six years old (Bohl, "Man's Work in a Woman's Way," 138). With a November birthday, she would have turned ninety-six in November 1958 had she been born in 1862. The 1920 U.S. Census also lists her as fifty-seven years old in January, again making her birthyear 1862 ("United States Census, 1920," Estelle Reel in entry for Court F. Meyer, familysearch.org, accessed April 10, 2023). However, there are some conflicting birthyears for her. According to the 1870 U.S. Census she was a six-year-old in June, putting her birthyear as 1863 if she had had a November birthday ("United States Census, 1870," Estelle Reel in entry for Michael A. Reel, familysearch.org, accessed April 10, 2023). Furthermore, her employment record when she joined the Indian Service in 1898 lists her as being born in 1864 (Estelle Reel service record card, RG146, Records of the U.S. Civil Service Commission, St. Louis, Missouri, NARA).

90. Welsh, "Murrain of Spoils," 13.

91. Estelle Reel service record card, RG 146, Records of the U.S. Civil Service Commission, St. Louis MO, NARA; Bohl, "Man's Work in a Woman's Way," 92; "Denver News, 7/18/98," page H+1, H60–110, box 2, "Scrapbooks: Indian Affairs and Institutes," ERM-WSA; RSIS, 1898, 6.

92. Wesley, *NEA*, 87, 17.

93. Adams, *Education for Extinction*, 74.

94. RSIS, 1898, 6; Cahill, *Federal Fathers and Mothers*, 212–13.

95. ARCIA, 1891, 482–83.

96. RSIS, 1894, 23.

97. "To Superintendents, Teachers, Matrons, Industrial Teachers, and All Others Interested in Indian Education," n.d., letter no. 24422/94, box 1206, RG 75, NARA; RSIS, 1894, 23.

98. ARCIA, 1895, 354.

99. RSIS, 1896, 19–20.

100. RSIS, 1897, 14.

101. Other Indian school educators had raised the issue of an association with the NEA prior to Reel becoming superintendent. At an 1896 summer Indian school institute at Haskell Institute, Kansas, Charles W. Goodman, superintendent of Pawnee School, Ponca, Oklahoma, delivered a paper in which he stated, "It is not enough that the Indian service claims prominent and active members of the National Educational Association. Is it not time for our association to demand recognition by the National Educational Association with the addition of the Indian school department, and representation on the general programme [*sic*]?" (ARCIA, 1896, 23, 71). The next year at the Indian service summer institute in Ogden, Utah, Indian service educators passed a resolution asking that the "next national institute be held in any city in which the Trans-Mississippi Exposition and the NEA shall be held" (ARCIA, 1897, 33).

102. *NEA Proceedings*, 1895, 10; *NEA Proceedings*, 1896, 7; *NEA Fiftieth Anniversary Volume*, 570; *NEA Proceedings*, 1898, 9.

103. Bohl, "Man's Work in a Woman's Way," 39–40.

104. Reel, June 7, 1899, H60–110, box 1, "Circular Letters, DOI, OSIS, Supt. 4," ERM-WSA. This development must have pleased that city's chamber of commerce, which invited the Indian school workers to hold a summer institute there in 1897 (RSIS, 1897, 34). The city thus hosted these educators and the NEA in 1899.

105. Reel, April 10, 1899, H60–110, box 1, "Circular Letters, DOI, OSIS, Supt. 3," ERM-WSA; *Official Program and Guide of the nea Thirty-Eighth Annual Meeting, Los Angeles, California, July 11 to 14, 1899*, cover, 1008.RG, box 3958, folder 1, NEA-Gelman; RSIS, 1899, 13–15.

106. Secretary, "Sent to 8 Inspectors and 5 Supervisors," MS 2266, box 550, folder 6, NEA-Gelman.

107. RSIS, 1899, 15; "Their Mission the Uplifting of the Indian," *San Francisco Call*, July 11, 1899, 3.

108. "Indian Education, a New NEA Department May Soon Be Organized," *Los Angeles Times*, July 10, 1899, 7.

109. "Their Mission the Uplifting of the Indian."

110. *Official Program and Guide of the nea Thirty-Eighth Annual Meeting, Los Angeles, California, July 11 to 14, 1899*, 17, 1008.RG, box 3958, folder 1, NEA-Gelman; NEA *Proceedings*, 1899, 35–36. The twenty-five "active members" who signed her petition included many Indian boarding school superintendents, the president of Columbia University, and the U.S. commissioner of education (NEA *Proceedings*, 1899, 35). For Commissioner William Jones's positive reaction to the creation of this department, see Cahill, *Federal Fathers and Mothers*, 214.

PART 1

1. NEA *Proceedings*, 1900, 114.

2. NEA *Proceedings*, 1900, 681–711.

3. Official Bulletin of the Executive Committee No. 1, February 5, 1900, MS 2266, box 550, folder 1, NEA-Gelman. As it turned out, low attendance marked the Charleston meeting. Newspapers reported that from 2,700 to 3,000 attendees sweltered in the southern July heat, despite the committee's guarantee that "Charleston in July, with its prevailing sea breezes, is essentially the same as the north Atlantic coast cities, and much more likely to be comfortable than in the interior cities of the north central states." At the next year's meeting, the treasurer reported with relief that despite "so small a meeting as the one at Charleston," the receipts of that meeting "met all of the expenses of the year." For the Executive Committee's quotation, see Official Bulletin of the Executive Committee No. 1, February 5, 1900, MS 2266, box 550, folder 1, NEA-Gelman. For examples of the news reports on attendance, see the *Times-Picayune* (New Orleans), July 12, 1900, 6; and the *Bystander* (Des Moines), July 13,1900, 6. For the treasurer's report of 1901, see NEA *Proceedings*, 1901, 24.

4. *Official Program of the National Educational Association, Thirty-Ninth Annual Meeting, Charleston sc, July 7–13, 1900*, 28, NEA 1008.RG, box 3958, folder 2, NEA-Gelman. Bakeless's attendance as "our Carlisle School representative," indicating the absence of Pratt, is found in the *Red Man and Helper* 1, no. 2 (July 20, 1900): 1. For information on Bakeless, see the introduction to his paper in part 2.

5. Chernow, *Alexander Hamilton*, 122.

6. Official Bulletin of the Executive Committee No. 1, February 5, 1900, NEA MS2266, box 550, folder 1, NEA-Gelman.

7. Shepard to managing editor of the *Independent*, August 4, 1900, NEA MS2266, box 550, folder 6, NEA-Gelman.

8. "Negroes at the Educational Association," *Independent* (New York), July 26, 1900, 1814.

9. Shepard to managing editor of the *Independent*, August 4, 1900, box 550, folder 6, NEA-Gelman.

10. "No Discrimination Intended," *Independent* (New York), August 23, 1900, 2063.

11. For Washington's varnishing of slavery, see *NEA Proceedings*, 1900, 114. About his NEA speech, one newspaper reported that Washington "speaks to the southern white man . . . [who] manifests a disposition to listen to his message" (*Des Moines Register*, July 15, 1900, 11). The same newspaper that accused the police of driving Blacks from their seats also said about Washington's speech that it was "one of the kind which he is obliged to make to secure the tolerance or support of the Southern whites" ("Negroes at the Educational Association").

12. *NEA Proceedings*, 1900, 683.

13. Tonner, acting commissioner, to agents and superintendents, May 3, 1900, H60–110, box 1, "Circular Letters, DOI, OIA, Supt. 7," ERM-WSA.

14. Reel, March 15, 1900, H60–110, box 1, "Circular Letters, DOI, OSIS, Supt. 6," ERM-WSA.

15. Reel, April 10, 1899, H60–110, box 1, "Circular Letters, DOI, OSIS, 3," ERM-WSA.

16. Reel, March 15, 1900, H60–110, box 1, "Circular Letters, DOI, OSIS, Supt. 6," ERM-WSA. For a complete discussion of Reel's educational exhibits, to include photographs, see Lentis, *Colonized through Art*, chapter 7.

17. *News and Courier* (Charleston), July 7, 1900, H60–110, box 2, "Scrapbooks: Indian Affairs and Institutes," 65, ERM-WSA.

18. *Evening Post* (Charleston), July 6, 1900, H60–110, box 2, "Scrapbooks: Indian Affairs and Institutes," 63, ERM-WSA.

19. Sloyd is a method of manual training instruction (Gustaf Larsson, *Sloyd*, 9). For a discussion of the history of sloyd, see Thorbjornsson, "Swedish Educational Sloyd," 11–34.

20. *News and Courier* (Charleston), July 8, 1900, H60–110, box 2, "Scrapbooks: Indian Affairs and Institutes," 67, ERM-WSA.

21. Quoted in the *News and Courier* (Charleston), July 7, 1900, H60–110, box 2, "Scrapbooks: Indian Affairs and Institutes," 65, ERM-WSA.

22. Hoxie, *Final Promise*, 196.

23. *Red Man and Helper* 1, no. 2 (July 20, 1900): 2. A student may have placed this comment in the paper, as the masthead reads, "Printed every Friday by apprentices." However, as Jacqueline Emery points out, such papers were "white-edited," and Pratt played a dominate role in editing the Carlisle paper, therefore this comment could be his indictment of the Department of Indian Education's first meeting (see Emery, *Recovering Native American Writings*, 19, 324n3). Lincoln Levering, born March 1899, was the infant

son of Levi Levering, Omaha, and his Bannock wife Vena Bartlett ("Indian Delegate to General Assembly," Levi Levering Student Record, RG 75, series 1327, box 133, folder 5245, CISDRC); Levi Levering in entry for Philip Lavatta, "United States Census, 1900," FamilySearch, https://www.familysearch.org /ark:/61903/1:1:MSR6-MDW (accessed December 2, 2021).

24. Ahern, "Experiment Aborted," 264.

25. Ahern, "Experiment Aborted," 264.

26. There could be many reasons for the lack of Native educators at the Charleston meeting, including financial limitations, long distances, and positions held within the Indian school service that may have seen fewer Native educators interested in attending. Regardless, the fact that few Natives did attend indicates, at least, the lack of concerted effort to have them attend.

27. "Dr. Hollis B. Frissell, Educator, Is Dead," *Times Dispatch* (Richmond VA), August 7, 1917, 2; *Southern Workman: Memorial Number Hollis Burke Frissell*, November 1917, 565; Reyhner and Eder, *American Indian Education*, 115–16; Molin, "Indian Education at Hampton Institute," 91–92, quotation about Washington from 91.

28. Cahill, *Federal Fathers and Mothers*, 26.

29. Reyhner and Eder, *American Indian Education*, 115–16; Molin, "Indian Education at Hampton Institute," 91–92. For a definitive discussion of Indian education at Hampton, see Lindsey, *Indians at Hampton Institute* (Folsom's quotation from 248). For a biographical sketch of Folsom, see her paper in part 2 of this volume.

30. NEA *Proceedings*, 1900, 482–89, contains this address; the quotation is from 483. Frissell retold the story in 1901 to the Indian service educators. See his paper "Learning by Doing" in part 2 of this volume.

31. Gould, *Mismeasure of Man*, 147.

32. NEA *Proceedings*, 1900, 681; *Official Program of the National Educational Association, Thirty-Ninth Annual Meeting, Charleston SC, July 7–13, 1900*, 29, NEA 1008.RG, box 3958, folder 2, NEA-Gelman.

33. The Exposition Universelle was held in Paris in 1900. Undoubtedly, Frissell is referring to providing exhibits for it. For an analysis of the work of one of the photographers whose pictures were part of that American exhibit, including pictures of students at Hampton Institute, Carlisle Indian Industrial School, and Tuskegee Institute, see Cooper, "Scenes of Seeing." For a discussion of the American exhibit and its depiction of American Indian, African-American, and colonized people in the United States' new overseas possessions, see Rydell, "Gateway to the 'American Century,'" 119–44. For a discussion of Indian educators' involvement in world fairs generally, see Trennert, "Selling Indian Education," 203–20.

34. General Eliphalet Whittlesey (1821–1909), born and raised in Connecticut, received his education at Yale University and Andover Seminary. He served in the Union Army during the Civil War. Following the war he began his philanthropic work as assistant commissioner of the Freedman's Bureau, a period of his life not without controversy. He later turned his attention to American Indians and served for twenty-five years as secretary of the board of Indian commissioners. "Gen. Whittlesey Dead," *York Daily* (Pennsylvania), October 2, 1909, 12; "Eliphalet Whittlesey (1821–1909)," North Carolina History, 2016 http://northcarolinahistory.org/encyclopedia/eliphalet-whittlesey -1821-1909/ (accessed September 20, 2021).

35. Edward Everett Hale (1822–1909) was a writer, clergyman, reformer, and Boston Brahmin who is most remembered for his short story "The Man without a Country." Although ordained a Congregationalist, he helped establish the Unitarian Church of America. As a young man, Hale had visited the home of President John Quincy Adams, and as an elder intellectual, had been befriended by presidents Theodore Roosevelt and Willian Howard Taft. In 1903 he was elected chaplain of the U.S. Senate. Upon his death a senator rose to panegyrize him: "Dr. Hale's death puts a period to the life of a history figure. It seems like the passing away of our own history for 100 years in visible form." Francis J. Bosha, "Hale, Edward Everett," American National Biography, February 2000, www.anb.org/articles/16/16-00682.html (accessed January 12, 2023); "Eminent Advocate of Peace is Dead," *Indianapolis Star*, June 11, 1909, 2.

36. The Lake Mohonk Conference of the Friends of the Indian was held annu ally near New Paltz, New York, from 1883 until 1917. "At the October meetings," Francis Paul Prucha writes, "in the beautiful surroundings of the resort more than a hundred persons gathered each year to hear reports on the past year's Indian affairs, to listen to prepared papers on a variety of topics related to Indian reform, to discuss the subjects formally and informally, and to draw up a platform of recommendations" (*Americanizing the American Indians*, 5).

37. Charles Sumner (1811–1874) served Massachusetts as its U.S. senator from 1851 until his death in 1874. An ardent abolitionist, Sumner was deeply hated by the Southern slaveholding society. In 1856 a South Carolinian congressman beat Sumner with a cane in the chambers of the U.S. Senate. It took Sumner three years to recover from his injuries. Charles F. Howlett, "Sumner, Charles," in Heidler and Heidler, *Encyclopedia of the American Civil War*, 4:1902–3.

38. Henry B. Whipple (1822–1901), a native New Yorker, entered the ministry when he was ordained in 1849. Ten years later he became the first Episcopalian bishop for the diocese of Minnesota. The deplorable conditions endured by

the Chippewa and Eastern Sioux (Dakota) tribes in his diocese convinced him of the threat of an uprising, a premonition he communicated to Washington in 1860. Two years later the Dakota uprising confirmed his worst fears. Following the uprising, when a 5-man military commission hastily condemned to death 303 Indian men, Whipple appealed to President Abraham Lincoln, "We cannot hang men by the hundreds" and thus "purchase the anger of God." Lincoln commuted the sentences of most of the condemned, leaving, however, 38 to die on the gallows in Mankato the day after Christmas, 1862. Following this episode reform of the Indian service and the civilization and Christianizing of Indians became Whipple's lifelong work. Robert W. Murdock, "Whipple, Henry B.," in Washburn, *History of Indian-White Relations*, 4:695–96; Prucha, *Great Father*, 443–45.

39. Michael E. Strieby (1815–1899) served as secretary of the American Missionary Association for thirty years. Prior to and during the Civil War, he was an ardent abolitionist and later turned his attention to Native Americans. One writer posited that "probably no man in the country was better informed concerning the work for the elevation of the colored people than Dr. Strieby" (*Outlook*, March 25, 1899, 696).

40. By 1900 federal funding was eliminated for contract schools, although Catholics managed to secure some funding from Indian treaty rights, a practice confirmed in 1907 by the U.S. Supreme Court in *Quick Bear v. Leupp*. Frissell, principal of a nonreservation boarding school, is undoubtedly here criticizing the work of religious leaders and their on or near reservation day schools. For discussions of the removal of federal funds to sectarian schools and the *Quick Bear* decision, see Prucha, *Great Father*, 707–11, 776–78; Prucha, *American Indian Policy in Crisis*, 318–19; Reyhner and Eder, *American Indian Education*, 128–29; and Markowitz, *Converting the Rosebud*, 30–31.

41. William H. Hare (1838–1909) became an Episcopal clergyman in 1859 and upon his request was transferred to the Minnesota diocese of Bishop Whipple (identified earlier) during the aftermath of the Sioux uprising of 1862. Two years later he was reassigned to the East but returned to present-day South Dakota in 1872, when he became bishop of the Missionary Jurisdiction of Niobrara. In 1883 he became bishop of South Dakota, where he remained most of the remainder of his life. In 1909 he died in Atlantic City, New Jersey, but was interred in South Dakota in accordance with his last wishes. His burial site remains beside Calvary Cathedral in Sioux Falls. Robert W. Murdock, "William Hobart Hare," in Washburn, *History of Indian-White Relations*, 4:648; Howe, *Life and Labors of Bishop Hare*, 400–401.

42. Stephen Return Riggs (1812–1883), Mary Ann Clark Longley Riggs (1813–1869), and their son Alfred Longley Riggs (1837–1916) were Congregation-

alist missionaries to the Sioux (Dakota and Lakota). The male Riggses were actively involved in translating English documents into the Siouan language. The elder Riggs developed a Siouan grammar and dictionary. Mrs. Riggs involved herself in the family interest in language by teaching English to Indian women. Raymond J. DeMallie, "Alfred Longley Riggs," and "Stephen Return Riggs," in Washburn, *History of Indian-White Relations*, 4:679–80; Renville, Zeman, and Derounian-Stodola, *Thrilling Narrative of Indian Captivity*, 289; "Mrs. Mary Ann C. Riggs," *Missionary Herald* 65, no. 5 (May 1869): 151. For the Riggses' missionary and educational work, see Fear-Segal, *White Man's Club*, 76–100.

43. Thomas Smith Williamson (1800–1879) began his professional life in medicine, which he studied at Yale Medical School and practiced in Ohio. When he and his wife, Margaret, lost their first three children, they both turned to religion for comfort. He studied in Cincinnati, and, following his ordination in 1834, he was appointed to begin missionary work among the Indians west and near the Mississippi River north of the state of Missouri. He spent the next forty-four years of his life in missionary work, collaborating with Stephen Return Riggs (see note 42) in translating the Bible into the Siouan language. Later in his paper, Frissell references "his sons," and Williamson had three sons who survived into adulthood, but only one joined his father in missionary work. "Obituary Record of Graduates of Yale College," June 30, 1880 (http://mssa.library.yale.edu/obituary_record/1859_1924/1879–80.pdf), 412.

44. Josiah White, a Philadelphia Quaker, left $40,000 in his 1850 will to establish schools in Indiana and Iowa "for poor children, white, colored, and Indian." In response to his wishes, schools were established near Salem, Iowa, and Wabash, Indiana, but neither thrived. In 1883 the focus turned to manual training for American Indians at the two schools. A fire destroyed the main building of the Iowa school in 1887, and the Native children were transferred to Haskell Indian School, Kansas. The Indiana school continued, but, after 1890, it increasingly suffered as the federal government withdrew funding of sectarian schools. This lack of funds resulted in sending students back to their homes following the 1894–95 school year. "So the work of White's Indiana Institute as a distinctive Indian school came to a close" (Kelsey, *Friends and the Indians*, 234–41; Jones, *Quakers of Iowa*, 215-216; quotation in Kelsey, 238).

45. The General Allotment Act or Dawes Act of February 8, 1887. For a discussion of the Dawes Act, see Prucha, *Great Father*, 666–71.

46. Of 303 Dakota men condemned to death, Abraham Lincoln commuted the sentences of all but 39 of them. However, at the last minute, one more man was reprieved, leaving 38 to die on the gallows. Prucha, *Great Father*, 443–45; see also note 38 this chapter.

47. Frissell is undoubtedly referring to Helen Hunt Jackson's *A Century of Dishonor*, her exposé of the government's mistreatment of Native Americans, and its duplicity in federal Indian policies. Jackson (1830–1885) went to her grave disappointed that her work had not inspired more reform for the treatment of the Indians, although it certainly inspired other reformers (see Josephine Richards's paper). Rosemary Whitaker, "Jackson, Helen Hunt," American National Biography, April 2014, http://www.anb.org/articles/16/16-00836.html (accessed January 12, 2023). For a full treatment of Jackson's Indian reform work, see Mathes, *Helen Hunt Jackson*.

48. William West Kirby (1827–1907) from Lincolnshire, England, was ordained an Anglican deacon in 1854 and a priest the next year. He was appointed to a parish in Winnipeg, Manitoba, but by 1858 entered missionary work in the Canadian Northwest Territories and, later, along the Hudson Bay. By the 1880s he was serving in New York State, and he served for a short time in Florida. He is credited by one writer with having "evangelized ten thousand Indians of British America." Veronica Malerby, "150 Years of Missionary Service by the Anglican Church in Yukon," Diocese of Yukon, 2011 (http://anglican.yukon.net/history.html); quotation is found in "Industrial Education in the United States: A Special Report Prepared by the U.S. Bureau of Education," Sen. Ex. Doc. 25, 47th Cong., 2nd sess., 242.

49. William Duncan (1832–1918) was a British lay missionary who initially worked among Natives in British Columbia, Canada, and then in Canada's Northwest Territories. Eventually conflict with Anglican officials drove him and eight hundred Native followers into Alaska, where the U.S. government provided him land to found New Metlakatla in 1887 on Annette Island. Marjorie M. Halpin, "William Duncan," in Washburn, *History of Indian-White Relations*, 4:641. For a full discussion of Duncan's role within the Metlakatla community, see Hosmer, *American Indians in the Marketplace*, 109–224.

50. George Bird Grinnell (1849–1938), scion of an upper-class New York City family, writer, and conservationist. John F. Reiger, "Grinnell, George Bird," American National Biography, February 2000, www.anb.org/articles/13/13-00661.html (accessed January 12, 2023).

51. "About a year and a half ago the Lower Brulé Sioux Indians submitted to the office, through their agent, a proposition to cede to the United States, at $1.25 per acre, two townships of land embraced in their reserve, the fund thereby obtained to be used in the purchase of young range cattle and in the construction of a substantial wire fence to inclose [*sic*] the two sides of the reserve not bounded by the Missouri River" (ARCIA, 1901, 61). The commissioner does not indicate whether the petitioners had asked to have rations eliminated. Regardless, in June 1900 his office ordered that agents to

the "six great Sioux agencies . . . erase from the ration rolls all Indians who had become self-supporting" (6). Also, in May and June 1900, newspapers reported that the treaty between the United States and the Sioux that provided "clothing" to the Native Americans would expire, and the Lower Brulé were not seeking a renewal of those arrangements, but rather were seeking to become self-sufficient through the purchase of cattle. See, for example, *Plain Speaker* (Hazleton PA), June 18, 1900, 2; and "Lower Brule Tribe of Sioux Nation Desires Independence," *InterOcean* (Chicago), May 1, 1900, 13.

52. Frissell got the reservation wrong but was undoubtedly talking about J. George Wright (1860–1941) who served as Rosebud's agent from 1889–1896. There was no contemporaneous Agent Wright at Pine Ridge. Rosebud's Agent Wright was proud of his work in establishing day schools at Rosebud. He bragged in his final report as Rosebud's agent: "In 1889, at the time of my assuming charge, the Indians were more scattered over the reservation and 13 day schools were in operation; since which time gradual improvements have been made and buildings erected until now there is a total of 21 day and 2 mission boarding shools [*sic*]" (ARCIA, 1895, 298). Wright's service at Rosebud and his work with the day school movement is also referenced in James J. Duncan's paper in part 3 of this volume. For a short biography on Wright, see Foreman, "J. George Wright," 120–23.

53. The outing system was Pratt's signature program for "Americanizing" Indian students. It was an apprenticeship program in which Carlisle students were totally immersed in white—thus American—culture (e.g., language, lifestyles, religion) by living with white families in and around Pennsylvania. Trennert writes, "Boys worked at farming, harvesting, gardening, and blacksmithing. Girls generally devoted their time to housework and domestic tasks" ("From Carlisle to Phoenix," 267). Students received wages and were encouraged to learn thriftiness by handling their own money. Carlisle's Outing System peaked in 1903, when 948 students were placed in white homes. This system was replicated, with questionable success that even Pratt criticized, in government boarding schools in the West. At the 1902 meeting, a Carlisle employee, Laura Jackson, presented a paper defending the outing system (see part 3 of this volume).

54. After Reel's trouble with the civil service commission in 1902, she would edit out most criticism of the civil service from future papers.

55. The article by Leupp referenced is found in *Southern Workman* 29, no. 6 (June 1900): 365–69. When he became commissioner of Indian affairs in 1905, the same article was published in the Carlisle Indian School's *Arrow*, May 4, 1905, 1, 4.

56. The information on Standing comes from "Captain Alfred J. Standing," *New York Tribune*, June 4, 1908, 7; and, Pratt, *Battlefield and Classroom*, 230–31, 274. That Bakeless read Standing's paper is found in H60–110, box 2, "Scrapbooks: Indian Affairs and Institutes," 67, ERM-WSA. For information on Bakeless, see the introduction to his paper in part 2 of this volume.

57. Norrgard, *Seasons of Change*, 2. In addition to Norrgard's work, there are other recent studies that evaluate the consequences upon Native communities of the commodification of their work because of its integration into white capitalistic society. For examples, see Whalen, *Native Students at Work*; O'Neill and Hosmer, *Native Pathways*; Bauer, *We Were All Like Migrant Workers Here*; and Hosmer, *American Indians in the Marketplace*.

58. A paraphrasing of Gen. 8:22 (KJV) reads, "While the earth remaineth, seedtime and harvest, and cold and heat, and summer and winter, and day and night shall not cease."

59. "Deaths," *Los Angeles Times*, April 27, 1945, 10; "Boulder Survey of Historic Places, 1990," State ID No. 5BL2813, Office of Archaeology and Historical Preservation, Colorado Historical Society, Denver CO.

60. The consolidated Kamehameha Schools included three separate schools (boys, girls, and preparatory) that were first brought together under one administrative head, who was Dyke. "1900 to 1914: The Schools Consolidate," Kamehameha Schools Museum Archive, ksbe.edu (accessed July 29, 2022). Dyke became principal of the Kamehameha Schools on February 1, 1901. "Semi-Annual Report of the Principal of the Kamehameha Schools for the Term Ending June 30, 1901, Manual Department," *Annual Reports of the Kamehameha Schools, 1897–1909*, KSA, 1.

61. "Hard Hit," *Friend* [publication of the Hawaiian Mission Children's Society] 61, no. 4 (April 1904): 4; "Annual Report of the Principal of the Kamehameha Schools for the Nine Months Ending March 31, 1904," *Annual Reports of the Kamehameha Schools, 1897–1909*, KSA, 1; "Faculty, Staff, and Administrators of the University of Colorado, 1877–1931," *Boulder [Colorado] Genealogical Society Quarterly* 43, no. 3 (2011): 68.

62. "Charles Barlett Dyke, Principal," *Voice of South High*, 7–8, Mahoning Valley Historical Society Collections, Mahoning Valley Historical Society, Youngstown OH.

63. "Investigate Conduct," *Democratic Banner* (Mount Vernon OH), May 23, 1913, 1.

64. "School Man Is Upheld," *Daily Times* (New Philadelphia OH), May 27, 1913, 4.

65. "Appointments," *Teachers College Record* 17, no. 1 (1916): 101–2; email to editor from Lynne Ranieri, archivist, Millburn-Short Hills Historical Society, November 7, 2016.

66. "New Principal at Kamehameha School," *Evening Bulletin* (Honolulu), February 13, 1901, 1; "Training at Kamehameha," *Daily Pacific Commercial Advertiser* (Honolulu), October 2, 1901, 12; "Annual Report of the Principal of the Kamehameha Schools for the Year Ending June 30, 1902," 7, *Annual Reports of the Kamehameha Schools, 1897–1909*, KSA; "Annual Report of the Principal of the Kamehameha Schools for the Term Ending June 30, 1903, Course of Study," 10, *Annual Reports of the Kamehameha Schools, 1897–1909*, KSA.

67. For a biographical sketch of Harris, see his paper in part 2 of this volume.

68. This is a quotation from an NEA committee report. Harris chaired the subcommittee that authored a portion of that report. See NEA, *Report of the Committee of Fifteen*, 47.

69. Hunter, "Coming of Age," 39. Such priorities were not unique to Hampton Institute. In a 1900 publication titled *The New Education Illustrated*, the author wrote, "The cry of the New Education is for the triple training of hand, head, and heart" (quoted in Margolis, "Looking at Discipline," 67).

70. Biographical information on Rogers comes from "Hampton's Treasurer Retires," *Southern Workman* 61, no. 3 (March 1932): 140; and "Frank K. Rogers, Former Hampton Treasurer, Dead," *New York Age*, July 16, 1938, 3.

71. The Kickapoo Indian Medicine Company, and others of its ilk, combined the elements of Buffalo Bill Cody's Wild West and traveling medicine shows to hawk cure-all concoctions promoted to be of American Indian origin. These traveling troupes employed Natives and often pseudo-Natives to entertain town folk with "traditional" dances and staged warfare while salesmen plied gullible crowds. For a discussion of these shows and their wares, see McNamara, "Indian Medicine Show."

72. The NEA-published version reads "in red, black, or white" (*NEA Proceedings*, 1900, 699).

73. For an analysis of the sort of training young Indian women received at boarding schools, such as Hampton, see Lomawaima, "Domesticity in the Federal Indian Schools," 227–40.

74. "Josephine E. Richards," *Southern Workman* 48 (January 1919): 5–6.

75. "Miss Josephine Richards, 1918," *Indian's Friend* 32, no. 2 (November 1919): 6–7.

76. "Hampton Incidents," *Southern Workman* 42 (February 1913): 123.

77. "Virginia, Death Certificates, 1912–1987," FamilySearch, https:// www .familysearch.org/ark:/61903/1:1:QVR7-WP3R (accessed August 20, 2018).

78. "Josephine E. Richards," *Southern Workman* 48 (January 1919): 6.

79. Hampton Institute, *Fifty-Second Annual Report of the Treasurer*, 18.

80. For a discussion of this idea, see Simonsen, *Making Home Work*, 71–109.

81. For a discussion of the role anthropologist Alice Fletcher and Native couples Stablers and La Flesches played in the creation of these cottages, see Simonsen, *Making Home Work*, 79–81.

82. Merial A. Whipple Dorchester (1842–1895) married Methodist clergyman Daniel Dorchester (1827–1907) in 1875. In 1889 her husband became superintendent of Indian schools, a position he held until 1893. During the years that he served as superintendent, Mrs. Dorchester was more than "wife of." She was appointed as special Indian agent, touring many schools and filing reports of her findings. Robert D. Cross, "Dorchester, Daniel," American National Biography, www.anb.org/articles/08/08-00393.html (accessed January 13, 2023); "Mrs. M. A. Dorchester," *Olean Democrat* (New York), May 7, 1895, 2; Adams, *Education for Extinction*, 121; Cahill, *Federal Fathers and Mothers*, 65.

83. Named after Abby Williams May (1829–1888), the building was constructed in 1894 and paid for by May's northern friends. She was secretary of the U.S. Sanitary Commission, and a member of the Boston School Committee and the Massachusetts State Board of Education. The *Southern Workman* noted, "She was especially interested in the education of young women." A necrologist stated, "She was associated with many public and private charities, with religious work and the advancement of those rights which she claimed for her sex." Puryear, *Hampton Institute*, 52; *Southern Workman* 29 (January 1900): 9–10; "Miss Abby May," *New York Tribune*, December 2, 1888, 4; "Miss Abby Williams May," *New York Times*, December 2, 1888, 2.

84. Perry Pictures were inexpensive reproductions of famous paintings, monuments, and portraits sold through the mail from Malden, Massachusetts (Martinez, "At Home with Mona Lisa," 165).

85. Sybil Carter (1842–1908), an Episcopal missionary, promoted and encouraged lace-making on reservations by Native women, and the sale of resulting lace articles to East Coast consumers. In 1904 her friends established the Sybil Carter Indian Lace Association through which Indian women purchased and sold lace materials. Her work was actively promoted by the Women's National Indian Association, of which Carter became president in 1907. Hampton Institute hired a woman teacher recommended by Carter to teach lace-making to its young women. Mathes, *Women's National Indian Association*, 131; "New Head of the National Indian Association," *Reading Times* (Pennsylvania), January 25, 1907, 7; *Southern Workman* 29 (December 1900): 730; "Sibyl Carter, the Indians' Friend," *Missionary Review of the World* 21, no. 11 (November 1908): 877; "Sybil Carter Indian Lace Association," Mnopedia, October 4, 2018, www.mnopedia.org/group/sybil-carter-indian-lace-association. For a

description of her work, see Carter's address at Lake Mohonk in *Proceedings of the Twenty-Fourth Annual Meeting* (1906): 35–37.

86. Biographical information on Seger comes from Rairdon, "John Homer Seger," 203–16.

87. Seger to Reel, May 29, 1900, H60-110, box 1, "Correspondence 1899–Mar 1909," 2, ERM-WSA.

88. Seger to Reel, May 29, 1900, H60-110, box 1, "Correspondence 1899–Mar 1909," 2, ERM-WSA.

89. Rairdon, "John Homer Seger," 213.

90. Seger to Reel, May 29, 1900, H60-110, box 1, "Correspondence 1899–Mar 1909," 4–5, ERM-WSA.

91. "The Indian Department, Discussions at the Session This Morning," H60-110, box 2, "Scrapbooks: Indian Affairs and Institutes," 67, ERM-WSA. For more information on Seger, see his autobiography, *Early Days*.

92. This resignation refers to his position at the Darlington Cheyenne-Arapaho Indian Agency school. He later resumed working for the Indian school service when he established Seger Colony School. See Reyhner and Eder, *American Indian Education*, 62–67.

93. Walter Roe (1859–1913) and his wife, Mary (1863–1941), were missionaries to the Arapaho and Cheyenne at Seger Colony, Oklahoma, among other stations, but are most remembered as having mentored and "informally adopted" Henry Roe Cloud, the first American Indian to graduate from Yale University and considered the "foremost Indian educator." Messer, *Henry Roe Cloud*, 44–51, 113, 116.

94. Edward Payson Roe (1837–1888) was a Presbyterian minister and author born and raised in New York. During the Civil War he served as a unit chaplain and on the side began his writing career as a war correspondent for a New York newspaper. In 1871 he used the Chicago Fire as a story line for his first novel *Barriers Burned Away* (1872). Within four months this first novel sold over thirteen thousand copies. Propelled by that success, Roe wrote eighteen more novels, selling over one million books before his death. He is credited with making "the American novel acceptable and respectable reading for millions of Americans, especially women." Glenn O. Carey, "Roe, Edward Payson," American National Biography, www.anb.org/articles/16/16-01399. html (accessed January 13, 2023).

PART 2

1. *NEA Proceedings*, 1899, 36.

2. "The Conference of Indian Workers," *Southern Workman* 30, no. 8 (August 1901): 426.

3. "Interesting Exhibition of Indian Children's Work," *Detroit Free Press*, July 9, 1901, 2.

4. RSIS, 1901, 7.

5. "Biographical Sketch in Connection with Institute at Detroit, 1901," 2-3, in "Biographies," file 3, box 1, H60-110, ERM-WSA.

6. No title, n.d., "Articles," box 1, H60-110, ERM-WSA.

7. Adams, *Education for Extinction*, 67-68.

8. SIS, COS, 1901, 3, 189.

9. Quoted in Adams, *Education for Extinction*, 180.

10. Whelan, *Native Students at Work*, 38. Whelan is comparing the motivations of Pratt and of Superintendent Hall of Sherman Institute, but clearly the "frontier" schools' and Reel's motivations were aligned about the use of the outing system.

11. SIS, COS, 1901, 275-76; Slivka, "Art, Craft, and Assimilation," 233-35; Bohl, "Man's Work in a Woman's Way," 109; Fear-Segal, *White Man's Club*, 122-23, 123.

12. SIS, COS, 6.

13. Reel, *Course of Study*, 4.

14. Reel to CIA, January 20, 1906, no. 54735/1906, entry 173, PI 163, RG 75, NARA.

15. Adams, *Education for Extinction*, 172; Lomawaima, "Estelle Reel," 17.

16. Reel to CIA, December 22, 1905, letter no. 102605/1905, entry 173, PI 163, RG 75, NARA.

17. Pratt, *Battlefield and Classroom*, 291.

18. Pratt, *Battlefield and Classroom*, 291.

19. "The Indian Institute," *Indian's Friend* 12, no. 1 (September 1899): 8; Pratt, *Battlefield and Classroom*, 292. For his memoir Pratt edited out the phrase "and whereas, the ignorant prejudice and whimsical nature of the parents also militate against such attendance." He also changed the phrase "Indian school" to "industrial schools" (*Battlefield and Classroom*, 292).

20. Pratt, *Battlefield and Classroom*, 293.

21. ARCIA, 1899, 9; recounted by Pratt in *Battlefield and Classroom*, 293.

22. SIS, COS, 54.

23. Slivka, "Art, Craft, and Assimilation," 241.

24. Cooper, "Scenes of Seeing," 528.

25. Grinnell to Reel, April 14, 1902, "Materials Concerning Estelle Reel," entry 173, PI 163, RG 75, NARA.

26. She scheduled one on the afternoon of the first day of the meeting, July 8, and two more on the subsequent mornings of July 9 and 10. *Official Program, National Educational Association, Fortieth Annual Meeting, Detroit, Mich., July 8-12, 1901*, 24-25, NEA 1008.RG, box 3958, folder 2, NEA-Gelman.

27. Reel, March 15, 1900, H60–110, box 1, "Circular Letters, DOI, OIA, Supt. 6," ERM-WSA; Reel, March 26, 1901, H60–110, box 1, "Circular Letters, DOI, OIA, Supt. 10," ERM-WSA. Marinella Lentis argues "that the sale of pupils' Native industries did not occur at NEA meetings" (*Colonized through Art*, 306). Reel's directions regarding sale prices, however, indicates to me that items were sold. If there were no sales at the NEA meetings, why would Reel issue such instructions? Moreover, that the instructions were provided so matter-of-factly indicates to me that sales at the NEA meetings were probably routine despite the absence of accounting evidence, as Lentis maintains. The most compelling evidence, however, comes from J. J. Duncan, day school inspector at the Pine Ridge Reservation. He reported that fifty dollars in beadwork made by Indian students was sold at the annual meeting at Boston in 1903 (ARCIA, 1903, 313). Furthermore, prior to the exhibit items being moved to Detroit for the NEA meeting in 1901, items were offered for sale then on display at the Interior Department. "The prices are very modest," a news story promised, "and the money obtained will be sent to the scholar who manufactured the article" ("Local Topics about Town," *Evening Times* [Washington DC], June 18, 1901, 4). Robust sales or orders for sales at the final department meeting in Denver prompted Reel to report in 1909 that "from the many written and oral requests received for Indian rugs, baskets, pottery, bead work, etc., it is evident that an active demand has been created for the products of Indian handicraft" (RSIS, 1909, 14). In the end, it is clear that robust sales of student-made Indian artwork occurred during and as a consequence of NEA annual meetings.

28. *Official Program of the National Educational Association, Thirty-Ninth Annual Meeting, Charleston, S.C., July 7–13, 1900*, 28–31, NEA 1008.RG, box 3958, folder 2, NEA-Gelman.

29. *Official Program, National Educational Association, Fortieth Annual Meeting, Detroit, Mich., July 9–12, 1901*, 23, 24, 26, NEA 1008. RG, box 3958, folder 2, NEA-Gelman.

30. Pratt is undoubtedly referring to the Natives who lived and worked in the area of Saratoga Springs, New York, entertaining and providing Native art to the tourists who flocked to the spa. For her discussion of Saratoga's three Indian encampments, see Otis, *Rural Indigenousness*, 180–81.

31. In his second annual address to Congress delivered December 2, 1902, six weeks before Pratt's letter to Reel, President Theodore Roosevelt said, "Every effort should be made to develop the Indian along the lines of natural aptitude, and to encourage the existing native industries peculiar to certain tribes, such as the various kinds of basket weaving, canoe building, smith work, and blanket work" (American Presidency Project, December 2, 1902, https://www.presidency.ucsb.edu/documents/second-annual-message-16).

32. Pratt to Reel, January 15, 1903, letter no. 4308/1903, RG 75, CISDRC.

33. Hoxie, *Final Promise*, 197.

34. Coffin, "Education of Backward Races," 33–48.

35. Coffin, "Education of Backward Races," 43, 58.

36. Lawrence, *Lessons from an Indian Day School*, 151–52, 168.

37. *Proceedings of the Thirty-Fourth Annual Meeting of the Lake Mohonk Conference of the Friends of the Indian and Other Dependent Peoples*, 1916, 15; ARCIA, 1916, 9–23.

38. A. C. Tonner to agents and superintendents, May 1, 1901, H60–110, box 1, "Circular Letters, DOI, OIA, Supt. 11," ERM-WSA.

39. Trennert, "Selling Indian Education," 213.

40. Hoxie, *Final Promise*, xiii.

41. "Training Sons of the Prairie," *Detroit Free Press*, July 9, 1901, 2.

42. "Miss Reel and the Indians," *Journal of Education* 54, no. 5 (July 25, 1901): 95.

43. "Indian Education," *Chilocco Beacon* 1, no. 10 (August 1901): 174.

44. "Interesting Exhibition of Indian Children's Work," Detroit Free Press, July 9, 1901, 2.

45. "The Conference of Indian Workers," *Southern Workman* 30, no. 8 (August 1901): 425.

46. Fear-Segal, "Nineteenth-Century Indian Education," 327.

47. For the full recounting of this 1744 episode in colonial American history, see Sheehan, *Seeds of Extinction*, 113–14.

48. John 10:10 (KJV).

49. Quick, *Essays on Educational Reformers*. Reverend Quick (1831–1891) was an English schoolmaster and writer on education.

50. French philosopher Michel de Montaigne (1533–1592) is most famously known for the publication of his three *Essays*. Frissell is using Montaigne's arguments for an active life rather than erudition for erudition's sake to support his "Learning by Doing" philosophy. He did the same with other philosophers he quoted. For Montaigne's life and work, see Marc Foglia and Emiliano Ferrari, "Michel de Montaigne," *Stanford Encyclopedia of Philosophy*, 2019, ed. Edward N. Zalta, https://plato.stanford.edu/archives/win2019/entries /montaigne/ (accessed January 18, 2023).

51. Frissell is quoting from Quick's *Essays on Educational Reformers*, 78–79, which he referenced earlier.

52. Frissell is quoting from Quick's *Essays on Educational Reformers*, 168.

53. Jean-Jacques Rousseau (1712–1778) was a French philosopher, writer, and musician. For Quick's purposes in his *Essays on Educational Reformers*, he was most influenced by and quoted from Rousseau's 1762 publication *Emile, or On Education*.

54. Frissell is quoting from Quick's *Essays on Educational Reformers*, 270–71, although the order in which Quick presented these quotations is reversed.

55. Frissell is quoting from Quick's *Essays on Educational Reformers*, 403–4, although he has rearranged the order of the sentences.

56. John Dewey (1859–1952) was an American philosopher and educator. His *School and Society* referenced by Frissell was published in 1899. As will be seen in NEA papers delivered over this first decade of the twentieth century, Dewey's philosophy that "a pedagogy [should] take into account America's growing industrialization and urbanization" will resonate with educators. For a brief description of his life and works, see Larry A. Hickman, "Dewey, John (1859–1952), Philosopher and Educator," American National Biography, February 1, 2000, https://doi.org/10.1093/anb/9780198606697.article .2000289.

57. Romans 8:21 (KJV) reads, "Because the creature itself also shall be delivered from the bondage of corruption into the glorious liberty of the children of God."

58. Frissell is undoubtedly referring to the Oneida Indians in Wisconsin. A creamery trade journal reported in May 1901 that "contracts have been let for the establishment of a modern creamery on the Oneida Indian reservation, near Green Bay. The apparatus is already being put in, and the plant will be in operation in a few weeks. The Oneida creamery is the first ever installed on a reservation, but it is understood that if it proves successful others will be located." "Indians to Have Creamery," *New York Produce Review and American Creamery*, May 1, 1901, 20. In his work Lindsey references educating Oneida students for the creamery; see Lindsey, *Indians at Hampton Institute*, 237n21.

59. Frissell is paraphrasing Matthew 7:21 (KJV): "Not every one that saith unto me, Lord, Lord, shall enter into the kingdom of heaven; but he that doeth the will of my Father which is in heaven."

60. Louisa McDermott, "Indian Pupils' Ambitions," *Southern Workman* 30, no. 7 (July 1901): 401–5. McDermott (1864–1952) began her career as a teacher in Nebraska and joined the Indian school service in January 1896. In 1904 she completed a master's degree from the University of California, Berkeley, and became highly active in education in the San Francisco area, teaching and editing a bulletin for teachers. Her publications included national journals and major contributions to San Francisco newspapers. *Chase County Tribune and Chase County Enterprise, Consolidated* (Imperial NE), April 4, 1902, 1; ARCIA, 1902, 678; *San Francisco Examiner*, December 12, 1920, 95; *San Francisco Examiner*, February 18, 1911, 14.

61. George Washington Andrew Luckey (1855–1933) was a well-respected authority and active member of the NEA regarding teacher preparation. In 1895 he became professor of pedagogy at the University of Nebraska and later its dean of the graduate school of education. In 1918 he and other faculty were targeted for disloyalty by the Nebraska State Council of Defense, which pressured the Board of Regents for their dismissal. The board dismissed one faculty member for disloyalty, and two, including Luckey, for "indiscreet" utterances. Ironically, he then secured a position with the federal bureau of education, a position he held until his retirement. "Former Professor Dies," *Daily Nebraskan* (official student newspaper of the University of Nebraska), March 31, 1933, 1; University of Nebraska Omaha, 2008–9, Faculty Senate Minutes, November 12, 2008, 12; "Dr. Luckey Dies at Lincoln Home," *Beatrice Daily Sun* (Nebraska), March 31, 1933, 2.

62. Grinnell, *Indians of To-Day*, 387–88.

63. Douglas R. Anderson, "Harris, William Torrey," American National Biography, February 2000, http://www.anb.org/articles/20/20-00447.html (accessed January 18, 2023); "William Torrey Harris," *Saint Louis Public School Journal* 2, no. 1 (September 1958), 6–7, box 744, folder 8, NEA-Gelman; Richard J. Kohlbrenner, "William Torrey Harris, Superintendent of Schools, St. Louis," *History of Education Journal* 2, no. 1 (Autumn 1950), 18–24, NEA MS2266, box 744, folder 8, NEA-Gelman.

64. "Their Mission the Uplifting of the Indian," *San Francisco Call*, July 11, 1899, 3; NEA *Proceedings*, 1902, 875–77.

65. Genesis 1:28 (KJV): "Be fruitful, and multiply, and replenish the earth, and subdue it: and have dominion over the fish of the sea, and over . . . every living thing that moveth upon the earth."

66. In the original paper, this phrase reads, "If we come in contact with those races other than through our government we are more likely to adopt the second method." The NEA editors found it confusing and rewrote it to read as it is in the brackets in this reprint: As they rewrote it is probably what Harris intended. See NEA *Proceedings*, 1901, 896.

67. "Covey Does Quick Work with Petition," *[Portland] Oregon Daily Journal*, March 10, 1912, 4; "Will Boost Mission," *Argus-Leader* (Sioux Falls SD), January 6, 1921, 3; Clanco Realty Company advertisement, *Argus-Leader* (Sioux Falls SD), June 4, 1920, 4; "First Annual Meeting of S. D. Development Ass'n," *Daily Deadwood Pioneer-Times*, January 14, 1920, 4; "Well-Known Dakota Man Dies at Parents' Home," *Argus-Leader* (Sioux Falls SD), April 9, 1923, 4.

68. Pratt, *Battlefield and Classroom*, 292.

69. ARCIA, 1901, 684.

70. Certificate no. 247, May 13, 1893, letter no. 18072/93, box 1064, RG 75, NARA; "Descriptive Statement of Changes in School Employees," letter no. 32848/1900, RG 75, CISDRC; "Prof. Bakeless to Resign," *Sentinel* (Carlisle PA), August 7, 1902, 2; "Prof. O. H. Bakeless Resigns Position in Bloomsburg Faculty," *Harrisburg Telegraph* (Pennsylvania), May 1, 1929, 11; "Drops Dead Leading Prayer Meeting," *Reading Times* (Pennsylvania), September 7, 1933, 7.

71. Bakeless to Pratt, August 16, 1902, letter no. 54539/1902, RG 75, entry 91, box 2156, CISDRC.

72. Pratt, *Battlefield and Classroom*, 293.

73. Bakeless to Pratt, August 16, 1902, letter no. 54539/1902, RG 75, Entry 91, box 2156, CISDRC; "Prof. O. H. Bakeless Resigns Position in Bloomsburg Faculty," *Harrisburg Telegraph* (Pennsylvania), May 1, 1929, 11; "Drops Dead Leading Prayer Meeting."

74. Bakeless is undoubtedly referring to Booker T. Washington's article "Chickens, Pigs, and People," in which he extolled the virtues of farming and a closeness to nature. "To me," Washington writes, "there is nothing more delightful and restful than to spend a portion of each Sabbath afternoon in the woods with my family, near some little stream where we can gather wild flowers [*sic*] and listen to the singing of the mocking-birds and the ripple of the water. This, after a good sermon in the morning, seems to take us very near to nature's God." *Outlook* 68, no. 5 (1 June 1901): 291–300, quotation from 299.

75. Ralph Waldo Emerson (1803–1882), "Fable," in Thomas Raynesford Loundsbury, *Yale Book of American Verse*, 40, www.bartleby.com/102/ (accessed January 19, 2023).

76. "Programme of Dedication Exercises of the Calvin Milton Woodward School," December 7–8, 1922, Washington University Building Information files, 1892–2009 WUA00001, box ST-WO, folder 20, Woodward Memorial, Julian Edison Department of Special Collections, Washington University Libraries; Woodward Elementary School, "School History / School History," https://www.slps.org (accessed June 13, 2021).

77. Coates, *History of the Manual Training School*, 11.

78. Coates, *History of the Manual Training School*, 16.

79. "From Mrs. Cook's Journal," *Red Man and Helper* 1, no. 51 (July 19, 1901): 2.

80. "Indian Education," *Chilocco Beacon* 1, no. 10 (August 1901): 171.

81. Consistent with this process, in 1904 the conferees at the Lake Mohonk Conference changed its name to "Lake Mohonk Conference of Friends of the Indian and Other Dependent Peoples" (*Proceedings of the Twenty-Second Annual Meeting*, 1).

82. Herbert Spencer (1820–1903) was an English philosopher who is best known for advocating a doctrine of "Social Darwinism" that proposed a social

natural selection said to "promote unfettered competition between individuals and the gradual improvement of society through 'survival of the fittest,' a term that Spencer himself introduced." *Britannica Academic*, s.v. "Herbert Spencer," https://academic-eb-com.lib.bismarckstate.edu/levels/collegiate/article/Herbert-Spencer/69066 (accessed January 19, 2023). Woodward is invoking Spencer's classic question in his unsigned article "What Knowledge Is of Most Worth," *Westminster Review* 72, no. 141 (July 1859): 1–41; Holmes, "Herbert Spencer," 533–54.

83. Pan-American Exposition of 1901. See part 2 introductory comments.

84. "The Hampton Institute," *New York Age*, November 23, 1905, 7.

85. Trennert, *Phoenix Indian School*, 7; Pratt, *Battlefield and Classroom*, 292.

86. *Official Program, National Educational Association, Fortieth Annual Meeting, Detroit, Mich., July 9–12, 1901*, 26, NEA 1008.RG, box 3958, folder 2, NEA-Gelman.

87. A perusal of the twenty-two volumes of records of the Bureau of Indian Affairs, "Rosters of School Employees, 1884–1909" (Entry 979, PI 163, RG 75, NARA) reveals that, often, teachers married housekeepers, superintendents married teachers or matrons, cooks married carpenters, and so forth; then, as is seen with Joseph and Adaline Evans, they transferred together within the Indian school service. For examples, see Joseph and Lucy Hart, 1900, 83; Matthew and Lutie Murphy, 1901, 59; Russell and Laura Ratliff, 1901, 84; Lindley and Elva Compton, 1902, 153; Horace and Tama Wilson, 1902, 15; and Eugene and Clara Nardin, 1902, 81. For an excellent discussion of married couples as employees in the Indian service, see Cahill, *Federal Fathers and Mothers*, 82–103.

88. Biographical information on Joseph and Adaline Evans comes from Joseph W. Evans in entry for Clarence F. Mogle, "United States Census, 1900," FamilySearch, https://www.familysearch.org/ark:/61903/1:1:MMGF-89T (accessed March 9, 2022); ARCIA, 1901, 732–33; *Chilocco Farmer and Stock-Grower* 3, no. 1 (November 1902): ii; *Indian School Journal* 7, no. 5 (March 1907): 70; *Indian School Journal* 8, no. 2 (December 1907): 69, 71; *Indian School Journal* 10, no. 8 (June 1910): 57; *Indian School Journal* 12, no. 1 (November 1911): 106; Washington State Board of Health, Bureau of Vital Statistics, Certificate of Death, Joseph W. Evans, Record 9128, https://www.digitalarchives.wa.gov/DigitalObject/Download/791e17c6-f9ca-42e2-bc0f-a3269e9f9d93 (accessed January 20, 2023); "Joseph Evans Dead," *Buffalo Evening News* (New York), December 10, 1909, 1. That Yainax Boarding School was converted to a day school is found in ARCIA, 1908, 40.

89. "Composition of the Indian School Service, 1899," in Ahern, "Experiment Aborted," 273.

90. Quoted in Fear-Segal, *White Man's Club*, 145.

91. As noted in the source note to this paper, it was not published in the *NEA Proceedings*. I included it in these selected papers because it demonstrates day-to-day activities from a classroom teacher's perspective.

92. Elaine Goodale Eastman, "Letter to the Editor," *Berkshire County Eagle* (Pittsfield MA), June 9, 1943, 10. Malval, *Guide to the Archives of Hampton Institute*, provided her middle name as Mae (100); in *Fire Light*, Waggoner provided Folsom's middle name as Malinda (29). Contemporary news stories simply listed her name as "Cora M. Folsom." See, for example, "Miss Folsom Aided Indians at Institute," *Berkshire County Eagle* (Pittsfield MA), March 3, 1943, 16. De Cora's 1907 presentation is found in *NEA Proceedings*, 1907, 1005–7.

93. "Cora Folsom, Teacher of Indians, Dies," *Berkshire County Eagle* (Pittsfield MA), June 2, 1943, 13.

94. Lindsey, *Indians at Hampton Institute*, 248.

95. That Frissell read Folsom's paper is in "From Detroit," *Indian Leader* 5, no. 19 (July 26, 1901): 2.

96. Other biographical information about Folsom comes from Malval, *Guide to the Archives of Hampton Institute*, 100; and Molin, "Indian Education at Hampton Institute," 92. For examples of the fundraising activities in New York City including performances by Hampton students, see "Singing for Hampton," *New York Age*, January 15, 1914, 6; "Fifty Years of Freedom," *New York Times*, March 3, 1913, 7; "Financial Campaign for Hampton Institute," *Daily Press* (Newport News VA), February 18, 1913, 7; and "News of the Day," *Alexandria Gazette* (Virginia), February 24, 1909, 2.

97. Waggoner, *Fire Light*, 29.

98. Folsom, "Guiding the Indian: 'What system will best promote character building among Indian children and the courage and ability to enter and contend in the opportunities of civilized life?'" *Southern Workman* 30, no. 11 (November 1901): 605.

99. Folsom is referencing Emerson's *Essays: Second Series*, chapter 3, "Character": "Character is nature in the highest form. It is of no use to ape it or to contend with it. Somewhat is possible of resistance, and of persistence, and of creation, to this power, which will foil all emulation." https://www.gutenberg.org/files/2945/2945-h/2945-h.htm#link2h_4_0003 (accessed January 20, 2023).

100. Prov. 22:6 (KJV): "Train up a child in the way he should go: and when he is old, he will not depart from it."

101. See Seger's paper in part 1 of this volume.

102. In 2021 the sisters began an engagement in assessing the school's role in the "assimilation process." For the sisters' campaign, see Truth and Healing, https://www.fspa.org/content/ministries/justice-peace/truth-and-healing

(accessed April 19, 2022). For a Native reporter's evaluation of the school's history and the sisters' campaign to assess the school's role in the assimilation process, see Mary Annette Pember, "Our Ancestors Risked Their Lives and Freedom," *Indian Country Today*, April 18, 2022, https://ictnews.org/news/our-ancestors-risked-their-lives-and-freedom.

103. Biographical information comes from "Certificate of Baptism," July 9, 1940; "Subjects Taught," Johanna Murphy, n.d.; handwritten obituary, n.d., annotated no. 435; "Franciscan Sisters of the Perpetual Adoration, La Crosse, Wisconsin," registration for Sister M. Macaria (Anna) Murphy, n.d.; and Ludwig, *Chapter of Franciscan History*, 234–47, all from Franciscan Sisters of the Perpetual Adoration Archives (FSPA), St. Rose Convent, La Crosse WA. Quotation is found in Ludwig, *Chapter of Franciscan History*, 246. Sister M. Macaria's actual dates of service at St. Mary's Indian School are 1895–1919, 1921–22, and 1926–36 ("Subjects Taught," Johanna Murphy, n.d., FSPA Archives).

104. Office of Indian Affairs, "Employees in School Service," ARCIA, 1898, 650; Ludwig, *Chapter of Franciscan History*, 244.

105. Geniusz, "Decolonizing Botanical Anishinaabe Knowledge," 46; email to editor, April 26, 2021, Amy Cooper Cary, head, Special Collections and University Archives, Raynor Memorial Libraries, Marquette University.

106. Pember, "Our Ancestors Risked Their Lives."

107. Sister was referring to the pamphlet from the Office of Indian Affairs titled *Rules for the Indian School Service*, originally published in 1894. The most recent version in 1901, when Sister presented her paper, was published in 1898. It contained sections 133–49 dealing specifically with the operation of day schools (OIA, *Rules for the Indian School Service*, 1898, 19–21).

108. Entry for Charles W. Goodman, 1932, "California, County Birth and Death Records, 1800–1994," FamilySearch, https://familysearch.org/ark:/61903/1:1:QLB2-T95L (accessed March 1, 2021); "Stevens County Normal Institute," *Stevens County Sentinel* (Woodsdale KS), June 20, 1890, 1; "Chas. W. Goodman," *Hutchinson News*, April 30, 1932, 10; ARCIA, 1901, 732; Trennert, *Phoenix Indian School*, 85; ARCIA, 1899, 413; *Carlisle Arrow* 11, no. 7 (October 16, 1914), 6; "C. W. Goodman Critically Ill In California," *Arizona Republic*, October 24, 1929, 6.

109. Lomawaima, *They Called It Prairie Light*, 17.

110. S. M. McCowan, "The Value of an Agricultural School to the Indian," *Southern Workman* 31, no. 9 (September 1902): 494–95. For biographical information on McCowan, see his paper in part 3 of this volume.

111. "Rules and Regulations of the Indian Service," in *Rules and Regulations Governing the Department of the Interior in Its Various Branches*, Sen. Doc 396, Prt 4, 59th Cong., 2nd sess., 1907, 39–40.

112. Lomawaima, *They Called It Prairie Light*, 18.
113. Miscellaneous Receipts, Class IV, were defined as "money not to be covered into the Treasury, but to be retained by the agent subject to expenditure when authorized by the Commissioner of Indian Affairs for the sole benefit of the Indians from whose labor it was derived, that they may receive the benefit of their personal industry." Relative to Indian schools, the regulations specifically addressed funds derived from "sales of articles fabricated by Indian pupils in manual and training schools," and "sale of stock, produce, etc., raised by Indians, and of hides obtained from the increase of cattle belonging to school herds." Secretary of the Interior, *Rules and Regulations*, 87–88.

PART 3

1. *NEA Proceedings*, 1902, 858–92.
2. Bakeless to Pratt, August 16, 1902, letter no. 54539/1902, RG 75, entry 91, box 2156, CISDRC.
3. A. C. Tonner to agents and superintendents, May 2, 1902, H60–110, box 1, "Circular Letters, DOI, OIA, Supt. 23," ERM-WSA.
4. A. C. Tonner to agents and superintendents, May 2, 1902, H60–110, box 1, "Circular Letters, DOI, OIA, Supt. 23," ERM-WSA.
5. A. C. Tonner to agents and superintendents, May 2, 1902, H60–110, box 1, "Circular Letters, DOI, OIA, Supt. 23," ERM-WSA.
6. Reel to agents and superintendents, February 1902, H60–110, box 1, "Circular Letters, DOI, OIA, Supt. Circular No. 16," ERM-WSA.
7. For historical sketches of civil service rules and the Indian service, see *Nineteenth Report of the United States Civil Service Commission*, 256–58; and Prucha, *Great Father*, 731–33.
8. The three questions were: "Is there anything to prevent your being strictly loyal in every respect to my interests and to the rules of the Department under which I serve?"; "Will it be disagreeable to you to take your instructions from the chief clerk (colored), who acts in my place when I am absent, and also frequently when I am here?"; and "Will you agree to resign at any time should your services not be satisfactory?" Reel to CIA, June 23, 1902, "Estelle Reel Press Copy," entry 173, PI 163, RG 75, NARA.
9. Reel to CIA, June 23, 1902, "Estelle Reel Press Copy," entry 173, PI 163, RG 75, NARA.
10. Acting CIA to secretary of the interior, June 23, 1902, "Estelle Reel Press Copy," entry 173, PI 163, RG 75, NARA.

11. Reel to CIA, June 23, 1902, "Estelle Reel Press Copy," entry 173, PI 163, RG 75, NARA.

12. George Benjamin in household of Edward Benjamin, Cheyenne, Laramie, Wyoming Territory, "United States Census, 1880," FamilySearch, https://www.familysearch.org/ark:/61903/1:1:MWM2-SS3 (accessed January 15, 2022); "An Old Timer Gone," *Cheyenne Daily Leader*, June 11, 1900, 4.

13. "In Life's Struggle," *Cheyenne Daily Sun*, June 15, 1888, 2; "Wyoming State Notes," (Casper) *Wyoming Derrick*, November 11, 1898, 4; "Short Stories," *Cheyenne Daily Sun-Leader*, November 21, 1898, 4.

14. *NEA Proceedings*, 1900, 682.

15. "An Old Timer Gone"; Howard University, "1899–1900: Catalog," 71.

16. Howard University, "1899–1900: Catalog," 23; "Qualified for the Bar," *Evening Times* (Washington DC), May 27, 1901, 2; "New Colored Attorneys," *Evening Times*, May 28, 1901, 10.

17. Reel to CIA, June 23, 1902, "Estelle Reel Press Copy," entry 173, PI 163, RG 75, NARA.

18. Acting CIA to secretary of the interior, June 23, 1902, "Estelle Reel Press Copy," entry 173, PI 163, RG 75, NARA.

19. R. La Forte, "Garfield, James Rudoph (1865–1950), Lawyer and Secretary of the Interior," American National Biography, February 2000, http://www.anb.org/articles/06/06-00209.html (accessed January 20, 2023).

20. Reel to James R. Garfield, June 27, 1902, "Estelle Reel Press Copy," entry 173, PI 163, RG 75, NARA; RSIS, 1901, 74.

21. *Twentieth Annual Report of the Civil Service Commission*, 207; Prucha, *Great Father*, 732. Ironically, two years later, school superintendents' wives could be hired as matrons or teachers also without taking competitive examinations (Cahill, *Federal Fathers and Mothers*, 89).

22. "Special Schools," *Los Angeles Daily Times*, July 25, 1899, 5 (article also in H60–110, box 2, "Scrapbooks: Indian Affairs and Institutes," ERM-WSA); Woman's National Indian Association, "Indian Institute," 8.

23. Reel's infraction appears to have garnered no more attention. It is not listed in the investigation of the commission. The report acknowledged that "minor investigations have been omitted as of no permanent or important interest" ("Investigations," *Twentieth Annual Report of the Civil Service Commission*, 127).

24. Bohl, "Man's Work in a Woman's Way," 126.

25. "G. H. Benjamin Transferred," *Cheyenne Daily Leader*, April 6, 1903, 4; Entry for Edward A. Benjamin and George H. Benjamin, 1920, "United States Census, 1920," FamilySearch, https://www.familysearch.org/ark:/61903/1:

1: M48J-3X5 (accessed February 8, 2023); Indiana State Board of Health, Certificate of Death, Local #188, Registered #20010, June 12, 1937, ancestry .com.

26. I judge her actions with Benjamin contradictory because, while demonstrating her embrace of scientific racism regarding her Native students, racial hierarchy theories at the time would have placed American Indians on a higher evolutionary level than African Americans (Hoxie, *Final Promise*, 127; Parezo and Fowler, *Anthropology Goes to the Fair*, 388).

27. "Army of Teachers," *Appleton Crescent* (Wisconsin), July 12, 1902, 8; "Indian Dep't Pres't," *Minneapolis Journal*, July 5, 1902, 7.

28. "From Indian Hands," *Minneapolis Journal*, July 9, 1902, 8.

29. "From Indian Hands"; "The Indian Exhibit," *Minneapolis Tribune*, July 8, 1902, 6.

30. "The Department of Indian Education," *Southern Workman* 31, no. 8 (August 1902): 422.

31. The attacks on boarding schools did not appreciably reduce the number of American Indian students being educated at them. The commissioner of Indian affairs reported in 1909 that 20,940 students were enrolled in boarding schools while 4,678 were attending day schools. In 1902 those numbers were 20,576 and 3,544, respectively (ARCIA, 1909, 87). The location of boarding schools did not change, either. In 1902 there were 25 nonreservation boarding schools and 90 reservation boarding schools. In 1909 those numbers were 27 and 82, respectively (ARCIA, 1902, 628; ARCIA, 1909, 153).

32. ARCIA, 1895, 17.

33. NEA *Proceedings*, 1902, 859. In his first annual message of December 3, 1901, the president said, "In my judgment the time has arrived when we should definitely make up our minds to recognize the Indian as an individual and not as a member of a tribe." He referred to the General Allotment Act and its breaking up of tribal lands. He said, "The ration system, which is merely the corral and the reservation system, is highly detrimental to the Indians. It promotes beggary, perpetuates pauperism, and stifles industry. It is an effectual barrier to progress." About spirits, he said, "in dealing with the aboriginal races few things are more important than to preserve them from the terrible physical and moral degradation resulting from the liquor traffic." "First Annual Message," American Presidency Project, https://www.presidency.ucsb.edu /documents/first-annual-message-16 (accessed February 26, 2023).

34. "National Educational Association at Minneapolis," *Journal of Education* 56, no. 5 (July 24, 1902): 87.

35. "Department of Indian Education."

36. "The Indian Institute at Minneapolis," *Chilocco Farmer and Stock Grower* 2, no. 10 (August 1902): 280–81.

37. "Minneapolis Convention," *Red Man and Helper* 18, no. 1 (July 18, 1902): 2.

38. RSIS, 1902, 35.

39. "Prof. Samuel M. McCowan," Genealogy Trails, https://genealogytrails.com /ariz/mohave/bios.html (accessed March 29, 2023); "S. M. McCowan—Former Superintendent of Chilocco Is Dead," *Indian School Journal* 25, no. 13 (December 1925): 105; "Employees in Indian School Service," ARCIA, 1902, 674; Parezo and Fowler, *Anthropology Goes to the Fair*, 59; Trennert, *Phoenix Indian School*, 57; "Col. S. M. M'Cowan," *Weekly Republican-Traveler* (Arkansas City KS), January 16, 1902, 7.

40. Trennert, "Resurrection of Native Arts and Crafts," 275–76; Trennert, "Selling Indian Education," 212; Parezo and Fowler, *Anthropology Goes to the Fair*, 59.

41. "Col. S. M. M'Cowan."

42. "Noted Indian Authority Arrested," *Albuquerque Morning Journal*, February 9, 1909, 1.

43. "Two Face Charges of Fraud," *Wichita Daily Eagle*, January 5, 1913, 17; "Case May Not Come to Trial," *Boynton Index* (Oklahoma), April 14, 1911, 4; "Former Chilocco Superintendent Said to Be Critically Ill," *Arkansas City Daily Traveler* (Kansas), March 1, 1913, 1; "Government Awarded $8,000," *Baltimore Sun*, March 15, 1913, 3.

44. "S. M. McCowan—Former Superintendent of Chilocco Is Dead."

45. "Col. S. M. McCowan, One of the Star Attractions at the National Education Association at Minneapolis, Minnesota," *Arkansas City Daily Traveler* (Kansas), July 10, 1902, 1.

46. "The Indian Problem," *Minneapolis Journal*, July 8, 1902, 6.

47. ARCIA, 1891, 550.

48. McCowan is paraphrasing Joshua 9:21 (KJV): "And the princes said unto them, Let them live; but let them be hewers of wood and drawers of water unto all the congregation; as the princes had promised them."

49. "Poor Lo" is a corruption of English poet Alexander Pope's 1732 *Essay on Man*. Pope (1688–1744) wrote: "Lo! the poor Indian," but it became "the idiom 'Poor Lo,' which was used to refer condescendingly to Native Americans during the nineteenth century" (Behrens, "In Defense of 'Poor Lo,'" 4).

50. Edgar A. Allen, assistant superintendent of Carlisle Indian School.

51. Hervey B. Peairs, who followed Allen as department president. See biographical information on Peairs in part 4 of this volume.

52. Lomawaima, *They Called It Prairie Light*, 17; *Chilocco Beacon* 1, no. 10 (August 1901): 156–59; *Southern Workman* 31, no. 9 (September 1902): 494–95.

53. Metzger Academy began in Carlisle in 1881 and lasted until it was absorbed by Dickinson College in 1913. "Metzger College Focused on the Education of Women," *Sentinel* (Carlisle PA), September 2, 2016.

54. *NEA Proceedings*, 1902, 864, listed her old title, used here. "Descriptive Statement of Changes in School Employees," September 26, 1900, letter no. 47491/1900, RG 75, CISDRC; "Man=on=the=band=stand," *Red Man and Helper* 17, no. 52 (July 11, 1902): 3; Allen to CIA, April 7, 1902, letter no. 20335/1902, RG 75, CISDRC; Allen to CIA, April 15, 1902, letter no. 22412/1902, RG 75, CISDRC.

55. "Laura Jackson California Death Certificate," and "California Death Index, 1905–1939," FamilySearch, https://familysearch.org/ark:/61903/1:1:qks9-qxqb (accessed February 23, 2021), citing 46242, Department of Health Services, Vital Statistics Department, Sacramento, FHL microfilm 1,686,049; "Former Carlisle Teacher Dies at Berkeley, Calif.," *Sentinel* (Carlisle PA), December 29, 1936, 6.

56. In 1902, of the large schools, Carlisle was indeed the largest, with 1,086 students and 90 employees. Second and third places were Haskell with 871 students and 61 employees, and Phoenix with 763 students and 57 employees ("Statistics as to Indian Schools," ARCIA, 1902, 616–28).

57. For Carlisle's attendees, see "Man=on=the=band=stand."

58. "Edgar A. Allen," Certificate of Death, file no. 1937, registered no. 2, Missouri State Board of Health Bureau of Vital Statistics; "$100 to Alumni Fund," *Manhattan Republic* (Kansas), June 3, 1937, 6; "Report of Herbert Welsh Institute, Fort Mojave, Ariz.," ARCIA, 1891, 549–51; Fred Nicklason, "Welsh, Herbert," in Washburn, *History of Indian-White Relations*, 4:694.

59. E. A. Allen to CIA, February 21, 1893, letter no. 7594/93, box 1034, RG 75, CISDRC.

60. For examples, see the ARCIA from 1894 through 1915 that list Allen's varied schools and positions: 1894, 518, Chilocco OK principal teacher; 1895, 529 and 1896, 596, Perris CA superintendent; 1897, 535, 1898, 632, and 1899, 621, Albuquerque NM superintendent; 1901, 754, Seneca OK superintendent; 1902, 671 and 1903, 656, Carlisle PA assistant superintendent; 1905, 539, special agent; 1915, 59, Chilocco OK superintendent; "Wed A Former Pupil," *Los Angeles Herald*, January 13, 1895, 3.

61. "Descriptive Statement of Changes in School Employees," October 29, 1901, letter no. 60896/1901, RG 75, CISDRC; Allen to CIA, August 10, 1904, letter no. 58997/1904, RG 75, CISDRC; "Descriptive Statement of Changes in School Employees," October 7, 1904, letter no. 69925/1904, RG 75, CISDRC.

62. "Name New Superintendent," *St. Joseph News-Press* (Missouri), March 23, 1911, 1.

63. "$100 to Alumni Fund," *Manhattan Republic* (Kansas), June 3, 1937, 6; "Edgar A. Allen," Certificate of Death, file no. 1937, registered no. 2, Missouri State Board of Health Bureau of Vital Statistics.

64. Allen may be referring to William J. McConnell, who leveraged sensational charges against certain Indian Office employees, including those in the Indian school service. See "Bad Mess Stirred Up," *Tacoma Daily Ledger* (Washington), March 13, 1902, 1, and "Schools Are Dens of Vice," *Spokesman-Review* (Spokane WA), March 13, 1902, 1.

65. The U S. Supreme Court decision *Barker v. Harvey*, 181 U.S. 481 (1901), evicted the Californian Agua Caliente Indians from an area known as Warner's Ranch. That area had been a recognized reservation from 1875 to 1880, but the Agua Caliente continued living there after 1880. Because of the eviction, in May 1902 Congress provided funding to purchase and relocate the Indians to a new reservation. For background information, see U.S. Court of Appeals for the Ninth Circuit Case 17–16838, 01/17/2018, ID:10727932, docket entry: 8, 3–6. See also, ARCIA, 1903, 75–76.

66. Johnston Lykins (1800–1876) served as a teacher for missionary Isaac McCoy, first in Indiana and Michigan, then in present-day Kansas. McCoy, whom Allen will mention later, also became Lykins's father-in-law. Lykins translated portions of the Bible and other religious work into Native languages and served as a controversial physician due to his lack of medical training. For information on Lykins and McCoy, see Early, "Johnston Lykins," 82–96; and Murphy, "Potawatomi Indians of the West."

67. John B. Richardville, reported to be "about eighty years of age" in 1840, "born at Fort Wayne, Indiana" (ARCIA, 1840, 352).

68. Isaac McCoy, father-in-law of Johnston Lykins (identified earlier), detailed his missionary work in an 1840 publication titled *History of Baptist Indian Missions*.

69. Thomas F. Richardville (ARCIA, 1890, 395).

70. ARCIA, 1850, 39.

71. For a discussion of Allen's "Sequoyia Leagues" allusion, see Watkins, "Charles F. Lummis and the Sequoya League," 99–114.

72. The American Society for Promoting the Civilization and General Improvement of the Indian Tribes in the United States held its first meeting on February 6, 1824, and boasted among its members the list Allen recited, although most of them were statutorily included through its constitution. Among the "special objects of this Society," according to article 2 of that constitution, was "to secure for these tribes instruction in all branches of knowledge, suited to their capacities and conditions" and "suggest whatever means may be employed

for their improvement." For complete lists of objectives and of membership, see Converse, *First Annual Report 1824*, 3–4, 7–9.

73. From Titus Livius (Livy), *History of Rome*, book 44, chapter 22.

74. On February 20, 1902, Marcus A. Smith, Arizona delegate to the House of Representatives, sought unsuccessfully to remove funding for Carlisle Indian Industrial School "for transportation of pupils to and from said school," arguing, "I have always been opposed to this policy of educating an Indian at a distance from his native place, removing him from his regular environment, and bringing him up within an atmosphere that can never possibly aid him in his future struggle for bread" (*Congressional Record*, 57th Cong., 1st sess. v. 35, 2003).

75. For a discussion of Garland's sympathies for the Indians, see Underhill, "Hamlin Garland and the Indian," 103–13.

76. "A. O. Wright Passes Away," *Wisconsin State Journal* (Madison), June 20, 1905, 1.

77. *Fifteenth Report of the United States Civil Service Commission*, 420–21; *Sixteenth Report of the United States Civil Service Commission*, 411.

78. For example, see RSIS, 1901, 106–8.

79. "Supervisor Wright Dead," *Arrow* 1, no. 46 (July 20, 1905): 4.

80. For a discussion of Father Schell's allegations and subsequent events surrounding them, see Kennedy, "Some Day a Great Harvest," 140–86.

81. "Supervisor Wright Dead"; "A. O. Wright Passes Away."

82. The Baron de Hirsch Fund was established for the benefit of Russian and Romanian Jewish immigrants, and provided English, mechanical, agricultural, and industrial training ("Baron de Hirsch Fund," 42–49).

83. Knoxville College, *Catalogue*, 4–5; *Year Ending June, 1893*, 5; *Year Ending June, 1894*, 5.

84. "Certificate No. 567, United States Civil-Service Commission," November 3, 1894, letter no. 43269/94, box 1250, RG 75, NARA; "Employees in Indian School Service," ARCIA, 1895, 518.

85. "Report of the Superintendent of Pottawatomie School," ARCIA, 1898, 179.

86. "Report of the Superintendent of Cheyenne School," ARCIA, 1899, 286–87; "Report of the Superintendent of Arapaho School," ARCIA, 1900, 328–29.

87. McKellips, "Educational Practices," 13.

88. "Report of the Day-School Inspector, Pine Ridge Reservation," ARCIA, 1901, 368–70.

89. "J. J. Duncan, Native of Junction, to Be Buried Wednesday," *Muscatine Journal and News Tribune* (Iowa), December 8, 1924, 8.

90. NEA *Proceedings*, 1905, 954–55.

91. For more information on Wright, see part 1.

92. Reel to CIA, October 29, 1906, 5, letter no. 66415/1907, entry 173, PI 163, RG 75, NARA.

93. Andrews, "Turning the Tables on Assimilation," 408.

94. This is an obvious reference to the Ghost Dance episode on the reservations. During this time Wright was temporarily suspended from his agency job, certainly making it a most "trying" time for him. See Utley, *Last Days of the Sioux Nation*, 95, 133.

95. Quotation from "Accompanying Papers," ARCIA, 1890, 54.

96. RCE, 1907, 1:69 lists this NEA publication as one of the "Writings of William Torrey Harris" with no reference to it being published anywhere but in the *NEA Proceedings*, 1902.

97. ARCIA, 1903, 382. For a general overview of Indian school newspapers, see the section "The Indian School Press" in Littlefield and Parins, *American Indian and Alaska Native Newspapers*, xxviii–xxx.

98. Emery, *Recovering Native American Writings*, 18.

PART 4

1. Colleagueship with other educators is represented by the joint meetings that the Indian school educators held with the Manual Training and Elementary Departments during the Boston meeting (*National Educational Association Official Program Forty-Second Annual Convention*, 33, 1008.RG, box 3958, folder 2, NEA-Gelman. The schedule for that session is found at 18). That practical education had become a "national trend" is evidenced, for example, in a talk given to the Physical Education Department (*NEA Proceedings*, 1903, 839). The talk about "uplifting" people became routine whether one were talking about Native Americans or immigrants. For example, in a Kindergarten Department session in Boston, a speaker presented a paper titled "The Kindergarten: An Uplifting Social Influence in the Home and the District." He said about immigrants, "We are trying to Americanize this great mass in the best sense of the word." The examples he provided included Jewish and Italian immigrants (*NEA Proceedings*, 1903, 388–89). Admiration for the work of the Indian school educators continued to grow while they were a part of the NEA. Reel's emphasis on practical education, her *Course of Study*, and her displays of students' work drew adoring praise culminating with an observer in 1908 asking why "normal white boys and girls" cannot be educated "as well as we are educating Indians." "Jottings from the Convention," *Journal of Education* 68, no. 4 (July 16, 1908): 121.

2. *NEA Proceedings*, 1903, 1039–63.

3. Wesley, *NEA*, 391; "National Educational Association," *Pedagogical Seminary* 10 (1903): 270.

4. Shepard and Eliot, "Notes," *Elementary School Teacher* 3, no. 10 (June 1903): 740.

5. Stewart, "NEA Convention in Boston," 88.

6. Coburn, "Impressions of the Boston Convention," 116.

7. Meserve to McKee, July 13, 1903, Charles F. Meserve Collection, Office of the President, Correspondence 1903, Shaw University Library Archives.

8. Stewart, "NEA Convention in Boston," 88. The guidebook referred to by the newspaper was especially published for the NEA 1903 convention (Bacon, *Boston*).

9. "Indian Educators Coming to Boston In July," n.d., 1, H60–110, box 1, "Biographies," file 3, ERM-WSA.

10. Reel, October 27, 1902, H60–110, box 1, "Circular Letters, DOI, OIA, Supt. 54," ERM-WSA; Pratt to Reel, November 10, 1902, letter no. 67376/1902, RG 75, CISDRC.

11. Shepard and Eliot, "Notes," *Elementary School Teacher* 3, no. 10 (June 1903): 740. I credit Reel for instigating these changes. She was department secretary, and, with the extant letters of instruction about the operation of these meetings and invitations from her to superintendents and speakers, it is apparent that she made the decisions about programs and other details of the NEA convention.

12. Pratt to CIA, February 17, 1903, letter no. 11358/1903, RG 75, CISDRC; Pratt to CIA, March 2, 1903, letter no. 14390/1903, RG 75, CISDRC; Adams, *Alternative to Extinction*, 426n37.

13. "Teachers Preparing for Teachers," *Boston Globe*, July 2, 1903, 7.

14. In 1902 some departments used the "topics" format. See Department of Manual Training, *National Educational Association Official Program Forty-First Annual Convention*, 16–17. For an example of a letter to speakers, see Reel to Jackson, May 12, 1903, Sheldon Jackson Papers, RG 239, box 7, folder 8, PHS.

15. *National Educational Association Official Program Forty-Second Annual Convention*, 28, 33, 1008.RG, box 3958, folder 2, NEA-Gelman.

16. Bohl, "Wyoming's Estelle Reel," 33. She wrote from Arizona to the commissioner in 1904: "I have strained my eyes and will be compelled to stay in a dark room for a few days" (Reel to CIA, February 16, 1904, letter no. 12655/1904, entry 173, PI 163, RG 75, NARA).

17. "The NEA Meeting at Boston," *Chilocco Farmer and Stock Grower* 3, no. 9 (July 1903): 442.

18. *National Educational Association Official Program Forty-Second Annual Convention* 33, 1008.RG, box 3958, folder 2, NEA-Gelman. The schedule for that session is found at 18.

19. *NEA Proceedings*, 1903, 597.

20. During a 1901 summer institute, a superintendent captured what he believed to be the work of Indian schools: "The education the Indian children, as a class, should have is a broad, thorough training in the elementary branches. . . . Ours is above all else industrial training—training for the industrial world" (ARCIA, 1901, 463). In 1902 Reel complained about off-reservation boarding schools including kindergarten students (ARCIA, 1902, 397). Regarding the focus of Indian schools, the school supplies purchased during the 1902 school year demonstrates the preponderance of textbooks for elementary-level instruction and manual training (ARCIA, 1902, 580–82).

21. *Manual Training Magazine* 5, no. 1 (October 1903): 19.

22. Higgins, "Education for the Trades: From the Standpoint of the Manufacturer," *NEA Proceedings*, 1903, 597, 601.

23. "Effective Skills Can Be Taught Only in Real, Productive Shops," *Red Man and Helper* 18, no. 51 (July 17, 1903): 2.

24. Krohn to Shepard, December 14, 1903, MS2266, box 0551, folder 1, NEA-Gelman; *NEA Proceedings*, 1903, 817–18, 1040.

25. "Indian Educators Coming to Boston in July," n.d., 1, H60–110, box 1, "Biographies," file 3, ERM-WSA.

26. Reel to Smiley, August 11, 1902, HC.MC-1113, Smiley Family Papers, series 1, Lake Mohonk Conferences, box 5, folder 169, HCQSP. Albert K. Smiley (1828–1912), with his brother, purchased property and constructed a hotel near Poughkeepsie, New York, where the annual Lake Mohonk conferences were held. "His role in Indian work was chiefly as a catalyst for other groups and individuals interested in the Indian," although he also served on various federal boards, commissions, and committees dealing with Native issues (E. Arthur Gilcreast, "Smiley, Albert K.," in Washburn, *History of Indian-White Relations*, 4:685).

27. Reel to Smiley, October 6, 1902, HC.MC-1113, Smiley Family Papers, series 1, Lake Mohonk Conferences, box 5, folder 169, HCQSP.

28. Reel to Agents and Superintendents, April 1, 1903, H60–110, box 1, "Circular Letters, DOI, OIA, Supt. Circular No. 57," ERM-WSA.

29. ARCIA, 1903, 552.

30. "The NEA Meeting at Boston," *Chilocco Farmer and Stock Grower* 3, no. 16 (July 15, 1903): 442.

31. "Boston May See What Indians Can Do," *Boston Globe*, July 5, 1903, 42.

32. "National Educational Association," *Pedagogical Seminary* 10 (1903): 271.

33. Quotation from "National Educational Association," *Pedagogical Seminary* 10 (1903): 271. See also *Manual Training Magazine* 5, no. 1 (October 1903): 58.

34. "The National Educational Association," *Southern Workman* 32, no. 8 (August 1903): 357; "Longfellow House Washington's Headquarters," National Park

Service, https://www.nps.gov/long/learn/historyculture/alice-longfellow
.htm (accessed October 22, 2021).

35. "Superintendent Peairs Interviewed," *Indian Leader*, July 24, 1903, 2.

36. "Superintendent Peairs Interviewed."

37. *NEA Proceedings*, 1903, 1040.

38. Stewart, "NEA Convention at Boston," 89.

39. "H. B. Peairs, Former Superintendent of Haskell, Dies," *Indians at Work* 8, no. 3 (November 1940): 30; Connelley, *Collections*, 744–45.

40. Gough, "Way Out," 19; Adams, *Education for Extinction*, 145–46.

41. ARCIA, 1901, 540; Gough, "Way Out," 70.

42. "New Offices Created and Offices Omitted," in "Appropriations Made during 61st Cong., 2d sess.," *U.S. Cong. Serial Set* (1909), 749; ARCIA, 1910, 14; *Proceedings of the Twenty-Ninth Lake Mohonk Conference*, 38; "H. B. Peairs, Former Superintendent of Haskell, Dies" (this obituary incorrectly stated he became supervisor of Indian education in 1919 when it should read 1910).

43. For background to this report, see Prucha, *Great Father*, 808–13. Regarding Peairs's removal from his position as director of Indian education, see Trennert, *Phoenix Indian School*, 195.

44. "H. B. Peairs Will Become Superintendent at Haskell," *Lawrence Daily Journal World* (Kansas), June 30, 1930, 1; "Haskell Indians Head Will Retire in June," *Los Angeles Times*, May 5, 1931, 9.

45. "H. B. Peairs, Former Superintendent of Haskell, Dies."

46. Child, *Boarding School Seasons*, 33.

47. For a discussion of John Eliot (1604–1690) and the Indians, see Morison, *Builders of the Bay Colony*, 289–319.

48. For information on Gookins, see Morison, *Builders of the Bay Colony*, 304–5.

49. Hailmann, *Education of the Indian*, 4–5.

50. For a brief biographical sketch of Cotton (1639–1698) and one of his intriguing annotated journals, see Travers and Cotton, "Missionary Journal of John Cotton," 52–101.

51. For brief treatments of Bourne (1610?–1682) and his missionary work, see Ayer, *Richard Bourne*; and Gowen, "White Sachem."

52. Hailmann, *Education of the Indian*, 7.

53. This sentence and Peairs's following points were deleted from the published version of the *NEA Proceedings* and started again with the sentence that begins, "Encourage the building of railroads" (*NEA Proceedings*, 1903, 1047).

54. Commissioner Jones issued directives in 1901 to remove from ration rolls those Indians whom agents believed were capable of working. By 1903 this policy was regarded as "labor in lieu of issuing rations" and Native Americans received pay for their labor. In his final report as commissioner, Jones lauded

the results of "his order that forced the Indians to work for their living rather than languish in the 'devil's workshop'" (W. David Baird, "William A. Jones, 1897–1904," in *Commissioners of Indian Affairs, 1824–1977*, Kvasnicka and Viola, 215; ARCIA, 1903, 255).

55. Reel substantially sanitized his "Things We Need to Do" list for the NEA *Proceedings*. She excluded his first five points and edited his sixth point to state only, "Use the intelligence and judgment of a good guardian and see to it that the child's educational opportunities are not interfered with." She then included his final four points but reworded his comment about the civil service to state only, "Endeavor to secure competent industrial instructors" and eliminated criticism of civil service regulations. See NEA *Proceedings*, 1903, 1049.

56. *National Educational Association Official Program Forty-Second Annual Convention*, 28, 1008.RG, box 3958, folder 2, NEA-Gelman; NEA *Proceeding*, 1903, 1039.

57. Sheldon Jackson, "An Alaskan Start towards Citizenship," RG 239, box 8, folder 1D, Sheldon Jackson Papers, PHS. This is the only full version I found of Jackson's paper. It is, however, a typed copy dated in 1922. Comparing this paper to the 1903 NEA-published version and his official 1902 report "Education in Alaska," RCE, 1902, 2:1243–45, convinces me it is an accurate representation of the paper he delivered to the Indian school educators.

58. Bender, *Winning the West for Christ*.

59. Bender, *Winning the West for Christ*, 15.

60. Bender, *Winning the West for Christ*, 184.

61. Bender, *Winning the West for Christ*, 188–89. The funding for education without regard to race in Alaska went to the secretary of the interior, who chose to give that responsibility to the Bureau of Education. Consequently, "Indian education" in Alaska did not fall under Reel's office (see also Hinckley, "Sheldon Jackson and Benjamin Harrison," 69–70).

62. Reel to Jackson, May 12, 1903, Sheldon Jackson Papers, RG 239, box 7, folder 8, PHS.

63. Bender, *Winning the West for Christ*, 190.

64. Resolutions, "Indian and Alaskan Education," MS2266, box 0682, folder 7, NEA-Gelman; NEA *Proceedings*, 1895, 33.

65. Bender, *Winning the West for Christ*, 190–92.

66. Newman, "Infanticide"; Brogden, *Geronticide*, chapter 3, quotations from Brogden, 63, 61.

67. Diamond, *World until Yesterday*, 177. See 177–79 for his discussion of infanticide.

68. Diamond, *World until Yesterday*, 214–17, quotation from 214.

69. Lee, Kleinbach, Hu, Peng, and Chen, "Cross-Cultural Research," 132; Freeman, "Social and Ecologic Analysis," 1011–17.

70. For overview of the establishment of this and subsequent schools and the individuals Jackson named, see Jackson, *Presbyterian Church in Alaska*; Hinckley, "Early Alaskan Ministry," 175–96; and Hinckley, "We Are More Truly Heathen," 37–55.

71. Shumagin Islands.

72. Methodists.

73. Kuskokwim River.

74. The educational provision and appropriation were included in the organic act that provided a civil government for Alaska. See 23 Stat. L., 24, c 53, Sec. 13 (May 17, 1884).

75. From this sentence forward, Jackson presented his official 1902 report "Education in Alaska." See RCE, 1902, 2:1243–45.

76. The bracketed section is missing from the PHS copy but is in his 1902 report "Education in Alaska." See RCE, 1902, 2:1243. American Revivalist Dwight Moody (1837–1899) established the Mt. Hermon School for boys in 1881 in his hometown of Northfield, Massachusetts. In 1879 he had established in the same town the Northfield Seminary for girls. In 1971 they combined into a single coeducational institution that continues today. https://christianhistoryinstitute.org/magazine/article/the-northfield-schools, 1990; https://www.nmhschool.org/about/history (accessed October 22, 2021).

77. The bracketed words are missing from the PHS copy but are in his 1902 report "Education in Alaska." See RCE, 1902, 2:1244.

78. In his annual report, Jackson named the capitalist as Mr. Portus B. Weare and the young girl as Parsha (RCE, 1902, 2:1244). Jackson may not have named him in the NEA address because, in March 1903, just months before the Boston meeting, Weare was suspended from the Chicago Board of Trade for defrauding customers, then expelled the next year. He died in 1909 while living in California. "Defrauded His Country Patrons," *Rock Island Argus* (Illinois), July 6, 1904, 1; "P. B. Weare Dies Suddenly," *Chicago Tribune*, February 26, 1909, 6. According to news reports about Parsha, her last name was Block, and she arrived in Chicago in 1897 at the age of eleven. Her father was Russian, her mother "Siberian and Aleut." While Weare was her benefactor, she became the ward of a Mr. and Mrs. Charles H. Barber. "From Faroff Attu," *Owensboro Messenger* (Kentucky), September 12, 1897, 7; "Miss M. Elizabeth Mellor and Her Aleut Pupils Now in Chicago," *Chicago Tribune*, October 24, 1898, 10.

79. In his annual report, Jackson identifies her as Frances Willard (RCE, 1902, 2:1244). She was first raised as a small child by McFarland—the missionary Jackson discussed—and was called Fanny McFarland. Coming to the East Coast for education, her name was changed to Frances H. Willard, after

a woman in Auburn, New York, who was paying for her education. Upon becoming ill she returned to Sitka, Alaska, where she died in 1904. "At Rest— Frances H. Willard," *Fairmont West Virginian*, December 24, 1904, 2 (the page is misprinted with the date December 23). Her namesake, Frances H. Willard, should not be confused with famous temperance crusader Frances E. Willard. "Frances Willard," Encyclopedia Britannica, February 14, 2022, https://www.britannica.com/biography/Frances-Willard.

80. Kelly and Willard, *Grammar and Vocabulary of the Tlingit Language*.

81. Marsden arrived at Carlisle in September 1892 and departed for Marietta College the next month. Although he has a student record, in a 1910 letter to Superintendent Moses Friedman he wrote, "Very much as I would like to, I am sorry to say that I have not been a student of the Carlisle School." His "Report after Leaving Carlisle" indicates that he served as a missionary in Alaska. See his student record RG 75, Series 1327, box 1, folder 28, CISDRC.

82. Here ended Jackson's quoting of his 1902 annual report.

83. Jackson here referred to the congressional language of a bill during the 57th Congress to provide a delegate from Alaska to the House of Representatives that had a provision "as to the Indians, allowing them to become citizens, and therefore to vote, if they are living in a civilized state and have resided in Alaska for the period of five years." The final law, passed in 1906, deleted any reference to Natives and instead provided voting privileges to "all male citizens of the United States twenty-one years of age and over who are actual and bona fide residents of Alaska." "Delegate from Alaska," H Rpt 434, 57th Cong., 1st sess., *U.S. Cong. Serial Set* (1901); "Public Law 59–147 / Chapter 2083," 59th Cong., sess. 1; "An Act: Providing for the Election of a Delegate to the House of Representatives from the Territory of Alaska.," U.S. Statutes at Large 34 (1906), 170.

84. Goodchild, "G. Stanley Hall and an American Social Darwin Pedagogy," 71.

85. Goodchild, "G. Stanley Hall and an American Social Darwin Pedagogy," 63–65, 95. His *Journal of Race Development* was later renamed *Journal of International Relations* and in 1922 became *Journal of Foreign Affairs*, as it remains today (95).

86. Goodchild, "G. Stanley Hall," 95; Ryan, *John Dewey*, 37, 61.

87. Goodchild, "G. Stanley Hall," 98.

88. Goodchild, "G. Stanley Hall," 91.

89. "Superintendent Peairs Interviewed," *Indian Leader*, July 24, 1903, 2.

90. Diehl, "Paradox of G. Stanley Hall," 872.

91. Diehl, "Paradox of G. Stanley Hall," 876.

92. "Coeducation in the High School," and "Psychic Arrest in Adolescence," *NEA Proceedings*, 1903, 446–51 and 811–13, respectively.

93. Pruette, "Masters of Social Science," 551.

94. Should read "Beothuk."

95. Calle Shasta is reputed to be the illegitimate daughter of American writer and poet Joaquin Miller (1837–1913) and a Modoc woman named Paquita. For a brief discussion of Miller, see Herny, Rideout, and Wadell, *Berkeley Bohemia*, 22–25.

96. Should read "Samoyeds."

97. British biologist Thomas Huxley (1825–1895) wrote, "I have seen the Polynesian savage, in his primitive condition, before the missionary or the blackbirder [slavetrader] or the beach-comber got at him. With all his savagery, he was not half so savage, so unclean, so irreclaimable, as the tenant of a tenement in an East London slum" (quoted in McIlhiney, *Gentleman in Every Slum*, 9).

98. German historian Leopold von Ranke (1795–1886) was considered the father of historical science. For a discussion of his philosophy, see Barker, *Super-Historians*, 145–75.

99. In Islamic eschatology the messianic deliverer who will usher in the beginning of the end of the world by restoring the religious purity of Islam. "Mahdī," Encyclopedia Britannica, March 15, 2019, https://www.britannica.com/topic/mahdi.

100. American anthropologist Lewis Henry Morgan (1818–1881) is best known for his study of kinships and his theory of social evolution. "Lewis Henry Morgan," Encyclopedia Britannica, December 13, 2020, https://www.britannica.com/biography/Lewis-Henry-Morgan.

101. Hall is likely referring to H. Hesketh Prichard (1876–1922), a British adventurer who documented his Patagonian exploration in *Through the Heart of Patagonia*. In a chapter titled "Manners and Customs of the Tehuelches," he wrote, "The influence of the white who goes to live among the Indians as one of themselves, almost without exception, makes for evil" (94). For a discussion of the white settlements in Patagonia, see Williams, "Welsh Settlers and Native Americans in Patagonia," 41–66.

102. A German naturalist and explorer Alexander Humboldt (1767–1835) spent the years 1799–1804 traveling in Latin and South America. He compiled his travelogue into *Personal Narrative of Travels to the Equinoctial Regions of the New Continent During the Years 1799–1804*, 7 vols., 1814–29 (*Britannica Academic*, s.v. "Alexander von Humboldt," accessed June 21, 2021, https://academic-eb-com.lib.bismarckstate.edu/levels/collegiate/article/Alexander-von-Humboldt/41488). About Humboldt, professor of philosophy Millan-Zaibert writes, "Part of what made Humboldt such a beloved figure in Spanish America was his appreciation of the cultures he observed there: rather than judging all that he found in America with a European lens, as most of

his contemporaries did, Humboldt attempted to understand the people and cultures he encountered during his voyages on their own terms" ("Legacy of Humboldt, Krause, and Nietzsche," 10).

103. Hall undoubtedly means Thomas Belt (1832–1878), a British geologist and naturalist who spent the years 1868–1872 in Nicaragua and wrote about his adventures. See https://www.britishmuseum.org/collection/term/biog12115 (accessed January 24, 2023). In his book Belt described the evidence of higher civilizations that had existed in Nicaragua that, in his view, were laid to waste by the Spaniards. He wrote, "To me the conquest of Mexico, Central America, and Peru appears one of the darkest pages in modern history" (*Naturalist in Nicaragua*, 275). See his descriptions of prior civilizations on 128–32 and 275–78.

104. German geographer and explorer Adolf Bastian (1826–1905) published a two-volume set titled *The Cultivated Countries of Old America* (1878). See a review of his work in "Literary Notices," *Magazine of American History with Notes and Queries* 3 (1879): 212.

105. Augustus Le Plongeon (1826–1908) along with his wife Alice Dixon Le Plongeon (1851–1910) cleared, excavated, and documented Mayan sites at Chichen Itza and Uxmal (1873–1886). In 1881 Augustus published *Vestiges of the Mayas*. This is likely the source for Hall's reference to connections of the Maya people with Greece and Egypt. For studies of both the Le Plongeons, see Desmond and Messenger, *Dream of Maya*; and Desmond, *Yucatan through Her Eyes*.

106. Thucydides identified the Pelasgian among the early tribes of Greece. See Thucydides, *Peloponnesian War*, book 1, 3.

107. For a biographical sketch of Fletcher, see her paper in part 5 of this volume. Frank Hamilton Cushing (1857–1900) was a member of the Smithsonian's Bureau of Ethnology who traveled in 1879 with an expedition to study the Zunis. He remained for four and a half years, learned the language, received sacred rites, and lived as a Zuni before returning to work with the Smithsonian. For his time with the Zunis, see Cushing, *Zuni*.

108. Hall is no doubt referring to the Tsimshian of Canada's British Columbia, who migrated to Alaska with the Anglican missionary William Duncan (1832–1918) in 1887 and established Metlakatla Indian Community. See Dickason, *Canada's First Nations*, 244–46. For a full discussion of the Tsimshian peoples before and after this migration, the economic, social, and cultural ramifications of it, and Duncan's role within the Metlakatla community, see Hosmer, *American Indians in the Marketplace*, 109–224.

109. Anilco was most certainly a place, not a person. It named a river, province, or chiefdom, or all of these, during the time Hernando De Soto journeyed through what is now southern United States (1539–43). See Swanton, "Her-

nando De Soto's Route," 156–62; and Du Val, *Native Ground*, 26. In an 1835 publication, writer Theodore Irving, nephew of American author Washington Irving, referenced "the Chieftain Anilco," although his narrative defined various locations as "Anilco." It is possible that Hall meant the chieftain of Anilco in his usage. See Irving, *Conquest of Florida*, 2:146–236 for various references to Anilco, and particularly pages 152 and 155, where Irving references Chieftain Anilco and Cacique Anilco.

110. Arnold von Winkelried is a legendary fourteenth century folk hero of Switzerland (Hocker, *Arnold von Winkelried*).

111. This is a historically based fabrication. Hall made the same point to the Massachusetts Historical Society in January 1903. To that group he said, "In 1703 the Rev. Samuel Hopkins said God willed their [the Indians'] extermination, and with his approval Popham's men hunted them with dogs, and we are still proud of Indian hunters in our pedigree" (Hunnewell, Hall, and Green, "January Meeting, 1903," *Proceedings of the Massachusetts Historical Society*, 7–8). While inspired by a real incident, undoubtedly Hall's story is not true. In a 1937 article, historian Lewis Hanke, who found no collaborating evidence for the story, could only say about this alleged event, "G. Stanley Hall makes this assertion," then referenced Hall's Massachusetts Historical Society presentation (Hanke, "Pope Paul III and the American Indians," 69). The actual event occurred nearly one hundred years earlier at Popham Colony, founded in 1607 by George Popham and Raleigh Gilbert, and had nothing to do with Rev. Samuel Hopkins, who was born in 1693, nor his namesake theologian nephew, born in 1721. Historian Francis Parkman wrote that at the location of the Popham and Gilbert colony along the Kennebec River in Maine in 1611, Frenchmen encountered Indians "greatly enraged at the conduct of certain English adventurers, who, three or four years before, had, as they said, set dogs upon them and otherwise maltreated them." These culprits were certainly the "Popham's men . . . in Maine" Hall talked about in both his presentations. For unknown reasons, he misstated the date and attributed it to a clergyman who could not have been involved. For a history of Popham Colony, see Bilodeau, "Paradox of Sagadahoc," 1–35. For the Parkman quotation, see Parkman, *France and England In North America*, 1:217. For the Hopkinses' birth dates, see https://collections.dartmouth.edu/occom/html /ctx/personography/pers0261.ocp.html (accessed October 21, 2021).

112. Hall is quoting American novelist Hamlin Garland, who, in 1902, after an "unofficial inspection" of Indians of the Rocky Mountain states, wrote, "I count it a virtue in that Northern chief who said: 'I will not clean the spittoons of the white man's civilization'" ("Red Man's Present Needs," 91).

113. This is a consistent position for Hall. In 1902 while addressing the Harvard Teacher's Union, he said, "We teach the Indian to make butter, harnesses, carpentry, and blacksmithing despite the fact that a better curriculum for him could be devised in making bows and arrows, pottery, bead and basket work, canoes, moccasins, and other indigenous arts, which are being lost" ("Some Social Aspects of Education," 85).

114. Jesse Walters Fewkes (1850–1930) worked at the Smithsonian Institution and became chief of the Bureau of American Ethnology in 1918 (https://siarchives .si.edu/history/featured-topics/latin-american-research/jesse-walter-fewkes, accessed October 21, 2021); Walter Hough (1859–1935) was a curator of ethnology at the U.S. National Museum, Smithsonian Institution (https:// siarchives.si.edu/collections/siris_arc_393788, accessed October 21, 2021); Cyrus Thomas (1825–1910) worked at the Smithsonian's Bureau of American Ethnology, where he became director of the Division of Mound Exploration (http://collections.si.edu/search/detail/ead_collection:sova-naa-photolot-169, accessed October 21, 2021). A search of *List of Publications of the Bureau of American Ethnology with Index to Authors and Titles* fails to identify either Miller or Catchet as ethnologists to whom Hall referred.

115. General Valeriano Weyler (1838–1930) implemented the "reconcentration policy" in Cuba in 1897 to defeat the insurgency thereby confining them to concentration camps. He was unsuccessful, and propaganda surrounding his policy ignited war fever in the United States (https://loc.gov/rr/hispanic /1898/weyler.html, accessed October 22, 2021).

116. For Cushing's description of that trip, see Cushing, *Zuni*, 407–25.

117. Grady L. E. Carroll, "Meserve, Charles Francis," *Dictionary of North Carolina Biography*, ed. William S. Powell, 1991, https://www.ncpedia.org/biography /meserve-charles-francis (accessed January 24, 2023); *Lawrence Daily Journal* (Kansas), August 13, 1889, 2.

118. "Interesting and Prosperous," *Lawrence Daily Gazette* (Kansas), September 22, 1890, 4.

119. "The Indian School," *Kansas News and People's Advocate* (Topeka), October 5, 1889, 1.

120. *Lawrence Daily Journal* (Kansas), August 13, 1889, 2.

121. "The New Superintendent," *Capper's Weekly* (Topeka KS), March 20, 1890, 6.

122. "The Indian Boys Protest," *Chase Record* (Kansas), June 26, 1890, 2.

123. "A Big Little Row," *Concordia Blade* (Kansas), July 25, 1890, 1.

124. Grady L. E. Carroll, "Meserve, Charles Francis," *Dictionary of North Carolina Biography*, ed. William S. Powell, 1991, https://www.ncpedia.org/biography /meserve-charles-francis (accessed January 24, 2023); "Dr. Meserve Better,"

*News and Observer* (Raleigh NC), April 18, 1936, 3; "Dr. Charles F. Meserve," *News and Observer*, April 23, 1936, 11.

125. "Superintendent Peairs Interviewed," *Indian Leader*, July 24, 1903, 2.

126. "An act of March 3, 1893, authorized the commissioner [of Indian affairs], with the approval of the secretary of the interior, to assign the agent's duties to the superintendent at any agency where he felt the superintendent was qualified for the job" (Prucha, *Great Father*, 734).

127. In 1896 the Indian Rights Association commissioned Meserve to travel to the areas where the Dawes Act of 1887 had broken up reservations. In his subsequent report he "found allotment to be a good policy and argued the evils that it sought to address were much greater than any possible negative consequences of the policy itself" (Rosenberg, "Library of Professor Meserve," 96). See also Prucha, *Great Father*, 751–52.

128. "The Curtis Act of June 28, 1898, abolished tribal laws and tribal courts and brought all persons in the Indian Territory, regardless of race, under United States authority" (Prucha, *Great Father*, 748).

129. Meserve is referring to the defeat of Republican Benjamin Harrison in the 1892 election by Democrat Grover Cleveland, who was supported by pro-Catholics believing that the attacks on Catholic involvement in reservation contract schools would subside with Cleveland in the White House. That did not happen. And Meserve, a lifelong, committed Baptist, "preached the gospel of an Indian Service divorced from both politics and religious sectarianism" (Prucha, *Great Father*, 711; quotation is from Rosenberg, "Library of Professor Meserve," 94).

130. That the failure of this attempt to raise the salary of the commissioner of Indian affairs is tied to Morgan's opposition to the spoils system is suspect. During the debate Massachusetts Senator Henry L. Dawes rose in the chamber and told his fellow senators, "For the last ten years and more every Secretary of the Interior has recommended and urged upon Congress that his salary be raised to $5,000." Thus, the commissioner's salary had been a contentious issue for some time prior to 1890. For the Senate debate and final vote noted by Meserve see *Congressional Record*, 51st Cong., 1st sess., v. 21, pt. 7, 6299–300. Dawes's quotation is on page 6299.

131. Charles W. Goodman, superintendent of the Phoenix Indian School from 1902 until 1915 (Trennert, *Phoenix Indian School*, 85, 111).

132. Peairs, Seger, Pratt, McCowan, and Goodman have all been previously identified. John J. McKoin began his Indian school service in 1892 at the Quapaw Boarding School in Oklahoma (ARCIA, 1893, 584). At the time of Meserve's presentation, McKoin oversaw the Siletz Agency and Boarding School, Oregon (ARCIA, 1903, 292). Theodore G. Lemmon began his Indian

school service in 1890 at the San Carlos Agency's Apache Indian Boarding School (ARCIA, 1890, iii, 12; ARCIA, 1891, Pt 2, 28). By the time of Meserve's presentation, he served as superintendent at Grand Junction Boarding School in Colorado (ARCIA, 1903, 563). Thomas W. Potter began work as a teacher in the Indian school service in 1886 and in 1903 was superintendent at the Chemawa Indian Training School in Oregon (ARCIA, 1887, 328; ARCIA, 1903, 427–29). In 1903 there were two Halls as superintendents: J. Thomas Hall oversaw the Crow Creek School in South Dakota, and Harwood Hall superintended the Riverside and Perris schools in California (ARCIA, 1903, 302–3, 415). Meserve is probably referring to the latter, given the prominence of that institution.

133. "Odyssey of the Civil Service Commission," *Evening Star* (Washington DC), September 14, 1958, 9; "Civil Service Secretaryship Relinquished by J. T. Doyle," *Sunday Star* (Washington DC), July 3, 1932, 1; "John T. Doyle Dead; Former Civil Service Commission Official," *Evening Star* (Washington DC), September 8, 1941, A-2.

134. Adams, *Alternative to Extinction*, 74.

135. ARCIA, 1885, 75; Floyd A. O'Neil, "John H. Oberly," in Kvasnicka and Viola, *Commissioners of Indian Affairs*, 189.

136. *Nineteenth Report of the United States Civil Service Commission*, 256; Prucha, *Great Father*, 731–32.

137. "Superintendent Peairs Interviewed."

138. The Tenure of Office Act of 1820, in effect, created the spoils system by legitimizing the rotation of office with each president's ascension to office. Each president could withdraw appointments made by the preceding administration and make new appointments to fill those offices (Brubaker, "Spoils Appointments of American Writers," 556).

139. Doyle is quoting from Lalor, "Removals from Office," in *Cyclopaedia of Political Science*, 3:567.

140. Thomas Hart Benton (1782–1858) spent thirty years as Missouri's U.S. senator, followed by two years in the House of Representatives. "Thomas Hart Benton," *Britannica Academic*, https://academic-eb-com.lib.bismarckstate.edu/levels/collegiate/article/Thomas-Hart-Benton/78671 (accessed June 10, 2021).

141. From the poem "An English Padlock" (1707) by English Poet Matthew Prior (1664–1721). The actual stanza reads, "Be to her virtues very kind; / Be to her faults a little blind." Carpenter et al., *British Poets*, vol. 31, *Poems of Matthew Prior*, 159–62. The quoted stanza is on 162. For a biography of Prior, see Bickley, *Life of Matthew Prior*. Prior's birth and death dates are found on

33. The publication date of Prior's poem is found in Klepp and Wulf, *Diary of Hannah Callender Sansom*, 97n136.

PART 5

1. *NEA Proceedings*, 1904, 963–985.
2. Cultural historian Alan Trachtenberg writes, "Much of the effort to refurbish the image of Indians was sponsored and endorsed by the same ruling groups whose policies were responsible for disrupting native societies and attempting to destroy their cultures" (*Shades of Hiawatha*, xxiv).
3. Hoxie, *Final Promise*, 197.
4. Tonner, acting commissioner, to agents and superintendents, April 25, 1904, H60–110, box 1, "Circular Letters, DOI, OIA, Supt. Circular Letter No. 73," ERM-WSA. This term "congress" should not be confused with contemporary Indian congresses that brought together Indians at various fairs and expositions. See Parezo and Fowler, *Anthropology Goes to the Fair*, 7, 59, 237, 239–46.
5. Tonner to agents and superintendents, May 1, 1901, H60–110, box 1, "Circular Letters, DOI, OIA, Supt. 11," ERM-WSA. Reel did at times use the term "congress" in simply describing the gathering of Indian service workers. In her 1909 annual report she wrote that the NEA meeting in Denver was "the first congress of Indian workers" under a new commissioner. However, in her invitation letters to the NEA meetings, she used the title "Congress of Indian Educators" only in 1901 and 1904. The use of the word "congress" in the title of gatherings of special interest groups at expositions was common during the era. There was also a Congress of Indian Educators held in Seattle in 1909 in conjunction with the 1909 Alaska-Yukon-Pacific Exposition ("Program of the Congress of Indian Educators, Seattle, Washington, August 23 to 27, 1909," H60–110, box 1, ERM-WSA), but by then the NEA Department of Indian Education had already been disbanded. In a 1905 publication about the St. Louis World's Fair, Mark Bennitt, manager of the General Press Bureau of the Exposition, wrote that "international congresses have gradually come to be an important part of International Expositions." For his discussion of the various types of congresses at the St. Louis World's Fair, see his *History of the Louisiana Purchase Exposition*, 687–701, 687. Thus, Reel's use of "Congress of Indian Educators" in association with the Pan-American Exposition of 1901 and the St. Louis World's Fair of 1904 is consistent with that era's terminology.
6. "Congress of Indian Educators, Revised," n.d., labeled with handwritten "Article A" in "Articles," H60–110, box 1, ERM-WSA.
7. "Congress of Indian Educators," *Worthington Advance* (Minnesota), July 1, 1904, 6.

8. "Indian Educators Meet," *Pineville Herald* (Missouri), July 1, 1904, 7; "Congress of Indian Educators," *Anadarko Democrat* (Oklahoma), June 30, 1904, 2; "The Congress of Indian Educators," *Native American* 5, no. 28 (August 27, 1904): 224; ARCIA, 1904, 50.

9. General reports about the Department of Indian Education pegged a membership of 3,000, although that seems more likely the number of actual employees in the Indian school service, and not all of them would be NEA members. For examples, see "Congress of Indian Educators," in "Articles," H60–110, box 1, ERM-WSA; "Indian Summer Schools," *Indian Leader*, June 13, 1902, 2; and "Indian Dep't Pres't," *Minneapolis Journal*, July 5, 1902, 7. There may have been some confusion over NEA membership and those individuals in the employment of the Indian schools. NEA's official membership number for 1902 was 3,215; 3,000 of them would not have been in one department. Nevertheless, repeatedly, as indicated in the citations noted, the Department of Indian Education was judged to be the largest of the NEA departments. For official NEA membership numbers, see Wesley, *NEA*, 397.

10. Parezo and Fowler, *Anthropology Goes to the Fair*, 65; Lentis, *Colonized through Art*, 242. Lentis identifies Cook as a "teacher," but she worked for the commissioner as a clerk, not for Reel. See introduction to Cook's paper in this part.

11. For thorough examinations of the St. Louis Indian exhibit, see Trennert, "Resurrection of Native Arts and Crafts"; and Parezo and Fowler, *Anthropology Goes to the Fair*.

12. Parezo and Fowler, *Anthropology Goes to the Fair*, 136.

13. *Red Man and Helper* 1, no. 2 (July 20, 1900): 2.

14. For example, see the secretary's minutes for the 1902 meeting, *NEA Proceedings*, 1902, 858–59, that show performances by an Indian school band and a girls' mandolin club, both from Chamberlain, South Dakota.

15. Parezo and Fowler, *Anthropology Goes to the Fair*, 140–43; Trennert, "Resurrection of Native Arts and Crafts," 289–92.

16. Trennert, "Resurrection of Native Arts and Crafts," 290.

17. "Exhibit News Notes," *Indian School Journal: St. Louis World's Fair Daily Issue* 4, no. 28 (June 28, 1904): 1.

18. RSIS, 1904, 38.

19. "The 1904 Indian Teachers' Congress," *Indian School Journal* 4, no. 10[?] (August 1904): 25.

20. Parezo and Fowler, *Anthropology Goes to the Fair*, 35; McGee to Reel, April 1, 1904, letter no. 25000/1904, entry 173, PI 163, RG 75, NARA; "1904 Indian Teachers' Congress."

21. "1904 Indian Teachers' Congress," Indian School Journal 4, no. 10 [?], 27-28.

22. *NEA Proceedings*, 1904, i; "1904 Indian Teachers' Congress."

23. "1904 Indian Teachers' Congress," 28; *NEA Proceedings*, 1904, 963; ARCIA, 1904, 418.

24. The joint meeting of the Department of Manual Training and the Department of Indian Education was only reflected in the latter's secretary minutes, not the former's (*NEA Proceedings*, 1904, 593, 963), although that meeting was listed in the official program (*National Educational Association Official Program*, 43rd Annual Convention, Saint Louis, Missouri, 1904, 31, NEA 1008.RG, box 3958, folder 2, NEA-Gelman).

25. *NEA Proceedings*, 1904, 593–613; "1904 Indian Teachers' Congress," 28–29.

26. The Elementary Department held a joint meeting with the Kindergarten Department on Tuesday, June 28, and both departments reflected that meeting in their secretary minutes (*NEA Proceedings*, 1904, 379). However, the joint meeting of the departments was only reflected in the latter's secretary minutes, not the former's (*NEA Proceedings*, 1904, 380–81, 964), although that meeting was listed in the official program (*National Educational Association Official Program*, 43rd Annual Convention, Saint Louis MO, 1904, 31, NEA 1008.RG, box 3958, folder 2, NEA-Gelman).

27. *NEA Proceedings*, 1904, 470–71.

28. RSIS, 1904, 37.

29. For a summary of the roundtable discussion, see *NEA Proceedings*, 1904, 982–85.

30. *NEA Proceedings*, 1904, 92.

31. "Largest and Best Meeting of the NEA," *Journal of Education* 50, no. 6 (August 17, 1899): 107.

32. Pratt to Reel, January 15, 1903, letter no. 4308/1903, RG 75, CISDRC.

33. Pratt to Reel, November 10, 1902, letter no. 67376/1902, RG 75, CISDRC.

34. F. F. Avery, "Indian Reservation Schools," *Southern Workman* 30, no. 5 (May 1901): 246–47.

35. Parezo and Fowler, *Anthropology Goes to the Fair*, 69.

36. Pratt, *Battlefield and Classroom*, 336.

37. Pratt, *Battlefield and Classroom*, 335–36.

38. Pratt, *Battlefield and Classroom*, 337; "General Pratt Relieved," *Red Man and Helper* 5, no. 42 (June 17, 1904): 1. Pratt remained an unrepentant critic of the Indian Office. In 1914 he addressed the Ladies Missionary Societies of the Calvary M.E. Church in Washington DC. Among his numerous attacks on the Indian Office and particular commissioners, he said, "Slave holding thrived on limiting intelligence and could see no virtue in individual freedom and citizen chances for the negro. Indian holding has the same infirmity and therefore

contends for the meager education and the continuance of the environment which will not disturb the Indian System" (Pratt, *Indian Schools*, 19). Thus, as he had always contended, the "fight to keep the Indians intact as tribes means preeminently [Indian] Bureau perpetuation which can only be successfully maintained through keeping the Indians carefully laid away in the dark drawers of their tribal reservations" (Pratt, *Battlefield and Classroom*, 293).

39. Bohl, "Man's Work in a Woman's Way," 126.

40. Cahill, *Federal Fathers and Mothers*, 89; *Regulations of the Indian Office, 1904*, 15.

41. ARCIA, 1900, Pt. 2, 657.

42. *NEA Proceedings*, 1904, 973; Parezo and Fowler, *Anthropology Goes to the Fair*, 331.

43. John Locke wrote, "*Everyone*, according to what way providence has placed him in, *is bound to labor for the public good*, as far as he is able, or else he has no right to eat" (quoted in Marguerat, "The Origins of Property Rights," 103; emphasis in original).

44. Patterson, *Natalie Curtis Burlin*, 97–99.

45. Patterson, *Natalie Curtis Burlin*, 109–17.

46. Patterson, *Natalie Curtis Burlin*, 117.

47. Theodore Roosevelt, May 17, 1906, in Curtis [Burlin], *Indians' Book*, xix.

48. Curtis [Burlin], *Indians' Book.*, xxi.

49. Patterson, *Natalie Curtis Burlin*, 314.

50. Biographical information on Curtis comes from Patterson, *Natalie Curtis Burlin*; and James Deutsch, "Curtis, Natalie (1875–1921), ethnomusicologist," American National Biography, February 1, 2000, https://www.anb.org/view /10.1093/anb/9780198606697.001.0001/anb-9780198606697-e-1800166.

51. Patterson, *Natalie Curtis Burlin*, 4.

52. "The Indian Institute," *Indian's Friend* 17, no. 12 (August 1905): 6.

53. Curtis [Burlin], "Indian Character Revealed in Music," 83–86, 84.

54. Curtis [Burlin], "Value of Indian Art," 450.

55. *National Educational Association Official Program*, 43rd Annual Convention, Saint Louis MO, 1904, 30–32, NEA 1008.RG, box 3958, folder 2, NEA-Gelman.

56. Curtis [Burlin], *Songs of Ancient America*. For a bibliography of works by and about Curtis, see Rahkonen, "Special Bibliography," 511–22.

57. *NEA Proceedings*, 1905, 925; NEA, *Official Program-Bulletin*, July 3–7, 1905, 30–31.

58. Dippie, *Vanishing American*, 207.

59. Angel De Cora did the lettering on the title pages and some of the artwork for Curtis's 1907 publication *The Indians' Book* (Patterson, *Natalie Curtis*

*Burlin*, 139). See also Curtis, *Indians' Book*, 29, 35, 91, and other title pages for examples of De Cora's work.

60. "United States Census, 1900," FamilySearch, https://www.familysearch .org/ark:/61903/1:1:MMFS-3SG (accessed August 5, 2014); "Rites for Miss Cook," *Evening Star* (Washington DC), April 27, 1927, 9; Ripon College, "About History," https://ripon.edu/about/history/ (accessed October 23, 2021).

61. "Rites for Miss Cook"; Richard C. Crawford, "Edward Parmelle Smith, 1873–75," in Kvasnicka and Viola, *Commissioners of Indian Affairs*, 141–47; "Testimony in Regard to Management of Affairs in Indian Department," *U.S. Cong. Serial Set* (1875), 286.

62. "House Journal, 64th Cong., 1st Sess.," *U.S. Cong. Serial Set* (1915), 294.

63. ARCIA, 1900, 715.

64. "Government Exhibit at Tennessee Centennial Exposition, 1897," *U.S. Cong. Serial Set* (1900), 63–65.

65. Mathes, *Women's National Indian Association*, 229; ARCIA, 1900, 694, 715; Burgess, *Lake Mohonk Conference*, 39, 43.

66. "Final Report of Louisiana Purchase Exposition Commission, 1906," *U.S. Cong. Serial Set* (1905), 511–13.

67. "1904 Indian Teachers' Congress," 29.

68. *National Educational Association Official Program, Forty-Third Annual Convention, Saint Louis, Missouri*, 1904, 32, NEA 1008.RG, box 3958, folder 2, NEA-Gelman; *NEA Proceedings*, 1904, 963–64.

69. ARCIA, 1904, 418, 423–24.

70. For a full discussion of this policy, see Littlefield and Underhill, "Renaming the American Indian," 33–45, 36. See also Prucha, *Great Father*, 673–76.

71. Richard C. Crawford, "Edward Parmelle Smith, 1873–75," in Kvasnicka and Viola, *Commissioners of Indian Affairs*, 145.

72. For contemporary accounts of the commissioner's circular and attending news stories, see "New Names for Indians," *Kansas City Star*, March 29, 1903, 4; and "Indian Patronymics Billed for a Change," *Washington Times* (DC), April 6, 1903, 4.

73. Raymond J. DeMallie, "Alice Cunningham Fletcher," in Washburn, *History of Indian-White Relations*, 4:643–44; Fletcher, *Life among the Indians*, 17–24.

74. *National Educational Association Official Program, Forty-Third Annual Convention, Saint Louis, Missouri*, 1904, 32, NEA 1008.RG, box 3958, folder 2, NEA-Gelman; *NEA Proceedings*, 1904, 963–64.

75. ARCIA, 1904, 418, 424–26; "1904 Indian Teachers' Congress," 29; Fletcher, "Indian Names," *Southern Workman* 33, no. 9 (September 1904): 474–77.

76. The story was carried in a few national and regional newspapers. For the story

with the quotation, see "An Ictasanda Hair Cut," *Democrat and Chronicle* (Rochester NY), June 19, 1904, 11.

CONCLUSION

1. *NEA Proceedings*, 1899, 35–36.
2. "Their Mission the Uplifting of the Indian," *San Francisco Call*, July 11, 1899, 3.
3. For example, Haskell's Hervey B. Peairs addressed the Indian school workers at a summer institute in 1894 at Chilocco about "The Scope of Work of the Nonreservation School," and in 1903 he served as the NEA department president and delivered "Our Work: Its Progress and Needs" (ARCIA, 1894, 361; *NEA Proceedings*, 1903, 1039). At the same 1894 summer institute, Seger Colony Superintendent John Seger delivered "The Indian Home and the Indian School" to his fellow Indian service workers, and at the inaugural meeting of the new NEA department in 1900 he presented "Practical Methods in Indian Education" (ARCIA, 1894, 361; *NEA Proceedings*, 1900, 681). Alfred J. Standing, Charles W. Goodman, and Peairs all delivered papers at the 1896 institutes and subsequently addressed Indian school workers at the NEA annual meetings of 1900, 1901, and 1903, respectively. Hampton's Cora M. Folsom presented a paper to three separate institutes during the summer of 1897, then prepared a paper that was delivered at the 1901 NEA meeting (RSIS, 1897, 14; *NEA Proceedings*, 1901, 891; "From Detroit," *Indian Leader* 5, no. 19 [July 26, 1901]: 2). Archbishop John Ireland addressed the 1894 summer institute at St. Paul, Minnesota, and in 1902 he welcomed the NEA Indian school educators to Minneapolis (ARCIA, 1894, 362; *NEA Proceedings*, 1902, 858). The Indian service workers heard addresses by state public school superintendents from Kansas, California, Oregon, Colorado, New Mexico, and Nebraska, before there was an NEA department ("To Superintendents, Teachers, Matrons, Industrial Teachers, and All Others Interested in Indian Education," n.d., Letters Received, Letter #24422/94, box 1206, RG 75, NARA; RSIS, 1894, 25; RSIS, 1896, 22, 118; RSIS, 1897, 31; RSIS, 1898, 21). They likewise heard from public figures at NEA annual meetings after 1900, such as mayors, city and state superintendents, presidents of school boards, a lieutenant-governor, and governors (*NEA Proceedings*, 1900, 681; 1901, 890; 1902, 858; 1903, 1039; 1904, 963).
4. ARCIA, 1891, 482–83.
5. ARCIA, 1894, 340.
6. "William O. Thompson," Ohio History Central, https://ohiohistorycentral.org /w/William_O._Thompson (accessed October 15, 2021); *NEA Proceedings*, 1900, 61.

7. *NEA Proceedings*, 1900, 21–23, 114.

8. *NEA Proceedings*, 1901, 78.

9. *NEA Proceedings*, 1902, 95–96.

10. *NEA Proceedings*, 1903, 56.

11. *NEA Proceedings*, 1904, 100.

12. Parezo and Fowler, *Anthropology Goes to the Fair*, 136.

13. *NEA Proceedings*, 1902, iii; *NEA Proceedings*, 1901, vii; *NEA Proceedings*, 1902, viii.

14. *NEA Proceedings*, 1903, iii; *NEA Proceedings*, 1901, vii.

15. *NEA Proceedings*, 1904, ix. Doyle's name is not listed in any of Hailmann's nor Reel's reports regarding summer institutes, 1894–1899.

16. For example, believing interaction with the NEA at the 1904 St. Louis meeting was a professional development opportunity for him, Pine Ridge Day School teacher Edward Truman reported, "At all the meetings of the National Educational Association and of our own branch that I was able to attend, and in all of the exercises I witnessed, as well as in all the exhibits that I had the pleasure of inspecting, I found something on every hand to make lasting impressions that will, I trust, enable me in the future greatly to improve in my work as teacher in the Indian Service" (ARCIA, 1905, 404).

17. Frankel, "John Dewey's Legacy," 519–20.

18. Trachtenberg, *Shades of Hiawatha*, xiv.

19. News clipping from *News and Courier* (Charleston SC), July 7, 1900, "Indian Affairs and Institutes," H60–110, box 2, Scrapbooks, 63, ERM-WSA.

20. *NEA Proceedings*, 1903, 1053–56.

21. "Indian Schools," newspaper name illegible, H60–110, box 2, Scrapbooks, "Indian Affairs and Institutes," pg Y, ERM-WSA.

22. ARCIA, 1901, 467.

23. Peairs, "Our Work," 440.

24. RSIS, 1902, 58.

25. *Proceedings of the Twenty-Second Annual Meeting of the Lake Mohonk Conference of the Friends of the Indian and Other Dependent Peoples*, 1904, 29.

26. *NEA Proceedings*, 1900, 692.

27. *NEA Proceedings*, 1901, 153.

28. Warren, *Quest for Citizenship*, 35.

29. Olneck, "American Public Schooling and European Immigrants," 109.

30. Having replaced the Spaniards at three of those locations, commenters found that the one saving grace in educating the masses at these island locations is that they were already Christians—Catholics, maybe, but Christians none the less. *Proceedings of the Twenty-Second Annual Meeting of the Lake Mohonk Conference of the Friends of the Indian and Other Dependent Peoples*,

1904, 67; *Proceedings of the Twentieth Annual Meeting of the Lake Mohonk Conference of Friends of the Indian*, 1902, 163; NEA *Proceedings*, 1902, 110, 112.

31. NEA *Proceedings*, 1904, 978.

32. Using only the selected papers 1900–1904, speakers (who may have spoken only briefly) at the Lake Mohonk conference who also provided NEA addresses are: Frissell, who spoke at both in 1900 and 1901, and at Lake Mohonk in 1902; Fletcher, who spoke at Lake Mohonk in 1900 and 1903, and at the NEA in 1904; Jackson, who spoke at Lake Mohonk in 1900, 1901, and 1903, and at the NEA in 1903; Meserve, who spoke at Lake Mohonk in all the years 1900–1904, and at the NEA in 1903; Cook, who spoke at Lake Mohonk in 1901 and at the NEA in 1904; Reel, who spoke at every NEA meeting and the Lake Mohonk meetings in 1901, 1902, and 1904; Seger, who spoke at the NEA meeting in 1900, and the Lake Mohonk meeting of 1902; Peairs, who spoke at both meetings in 1903; and Standing, who spoke at the NEA meeting in 1900, and at Lake Mohonk in 1904 (Mohonk addresses found in Burgess, *Lake Mohonk Conference*, 66, 70, 74, 77, 79). There were others whose papers are not included in this study who also attended and addressed the Lake Mohonk conference—for example, Alice Robertson, who addressed the 1902 NEA department meeting and the 1904 Lake Mohonk conference (NEA *Proceedings*, 1902, 859; Burgess, *Lake Mohonk Conference*, 79).

33. *Proceedings of the Nineteenth Annual Meeting of the Lake Mohonk Conference of Friends of the Indian*, 1901, 19–24. Quotation is on 21–22.

34. *Proceedings of the Twentieth Annual Meeting of the Lake Mohonk Conference of Friends of the Indian*, 1902, 8.

35. Hazel Whitman Hertzberg, "Abbott, Lyman," in Washburn, *History of Indian-White Relations*, 4:617; *Proceedings of the Twenty-First Annual Meeting of the Lake Mohonk Conference of Friends of the Indian*, 1903, 40.

36. *Proceedings of the Twenty-Second Annual Meeting of the Lake Mohonk Conference of Friends of the Indian and Other Dependent Peoples*, 1904, 1.

37. "In Need of Teachers," *Oklahoma State Capital*, July 9, 1904, 6.

38. In addition to the examples I give, historian Elisabeth Eittreim provides appendices in her book showing teachers moving from Carlisle Indian Industrial School to overseas colonial jobs, and teachers from the Philippines transferring into the Indian service (*Teaching Empire*, 221–25). See also her discussions of what she calls "crossover" teachers: those who spent time in both Indian service and in colonial possessions (62–67, 174–81).

39. *Third Annual Report of the Philippine Commission*, 1902, part 2, 941.

40. ARCIA, 1899, 621; *Official Roster of Officers and Employees*, 1908, 62; "Interesting Items of News From All Over New Mexico," *Deming Headlight* (NM),

December 19, 1903, 3. The $3,000 salary seems high, but it is listed in the *Official Roster of Officers and Employees in the Civil Service of the Philippine Islands*, 1908, 62. A news story about teacher salaries in the Philippines lists them ranging from $800 to $2,000 ("In Need of Teachers," *Oklahoma State Capital*, July 9, 1904, 6).

41. *Official Register of the United States, 1907, Vol. 1, Directory*, 295; ARCIA, 1901, 749; "United States World War I Draft Registration Cards, 1917–1918", database with images, FamilySearch (https://www.familysearch.org/ark:/61903/1:1:KXTC-NDL, December 24, 2021), Moses Friedman, 1917–1918; "Thorpe's Carlisle School Superintendent Works Here," *Dayton Daily News* (OH), April 21, 1946, 2.

42. *Official Register of the Officers and Employees*, 68; Friedman, "Teaching Farming in the Philippines," *Southern Workman* 34, no. 1 (January 1905), 17.

43. *Indian Leader*, July 13, 1906, 2.

44. "The Carlisle Indian School," *Carlisle Arrow* 5, no. 20 (January 22, 1909): 3.

45. Woodward, "What Shall Be Taught in an Indian School," *Southern Workman* 30, no. 8 (August 1901): 431; NEA *Proceedings*, 1904, 978.

46. "Miss Reel Here," *Cheyenne Daily Leader*, September 19, 1902, 4.

47. The original request was for twelve thousand copies, but six thousand were printed. See "Indian Schools," Cong. Record 35 (1902): 3539; "Course of Study for Indian Schools," Cong. Record 35 (1902), 5270; *Concurrent Resolutions of Congress*, U.S. Stat. at Large 32 (1903), 1768; *Index and Review* 2, no. 3, May 1902, 55.

48. *Third Annual Report of the Philippine Commission*, 1902, part 1, 684–85.

49. RCE, 1902, 1222–27, 1225, 1227.

50. May, "Social Engineering in the Philippines," 156.

51. Paulet, "To Change the World," 173–202; Eittreim, *Teaching Empire*. While Reel may have had some DC conversations about use of her *Course of Study* in the Philippines, turmoil in the educational administration there in 1902 and 1903, contemporaneous to when her pamphlet was reprinted, may have scuttled any such plans (see May, "Social Engineering in the Philippines," 154–55).

52. "Jottings from the Convention," *Journal of Education* 68, no. 4 (July 16, 1908): 121.

53. Trachtenberg, *Shades of Hiawatha*, xxiv.

# Bibliography

ARCHIVES AND MANUSCRIPT MATERIALS

*Annual Report of the Superintendent of Indian Schools, 1894, 1896–1905. https://www.hathitrust.org/.*

Carlisle Indian Industrial School Collection. Cumberland County Historical Society, Carlisle PA.

Charles F. Meserve Collection. Shaw University Library Archives, Shaw University, Raleigh NC.

Department of Special Collections and University Archives. McFarlin Library, University of Tulsa, Tulsa OK.

East Tennessee Historical Society, Knoxville TN.

Emmett D. Chisum Special Collections. University of Wyoming Libraries, Laramie WY.

Estelle Reel Meyer Collection. Joel E. Ferris Research Archives, Northwest Museum of Arts and Culture, Spokane WA.

Estelle Reel Meyer Collection. Wyoming State Archives, Cheyenne WY.

Franciscan Sisters of the Perpetual Adoration Archives. St. Rose Convent, La Crosse WI.

Godfrey Memorial Library, Middletown CT.

Secretary of the Interior. "Rules and Regulations of the Indian Service." *Rules and Regulations Governing the Department of the Interior in Its Various Branches.* Sen. Doc. 396, part 4, 59th Cong., 2nd sess., 1907.

Historical Center and Research Library Milwaukee County Historical Society, Milwaukee WI.

Julian Edison Department of Special Collections. Washington University Libraries, St. Louis MO.

Kamehameha Schools Archives. Kamehameha Schools, Honolulu HI.

Mahoning Valley Historical Society, Youngstown OH.

"Charles Bartlett Dyke, Principal." *Voice of South High* (South High School, Youngstown OH) 1, no. 1 (December 1911): 7–8.

Malden Public Library, Malden MA.

Manuscript Division. Library of Congress, Washington DC.

Millburn-Short Hills Historical Society, Short Hills NJ.

Minneapolis History and James K. Hosmer Special Collections Library. Minneapolis Central Library, Hennepin County Library, Minneapolis MN.

National Archives and Records Administration, Washington DC, Kansas City and St. Louis MO.

Newspaper Archives. Oklahoma Historical Society, Oklahoma City OK.

Office of Archaeology and Historical Preservation, Colorado Historical Society, Denver CO.

Pasadena Museum of History, Pasadena CA.

Records of the National Education Association. Special Collections Research Center, Gelman Library, George Washington University, Washington DC.

Sandwich Historical Commission.

> Gowen, Garrett. "The White Sachem: The Conversion of the Cape Cod Indians, and the Founding of Mashpee." https://sandwichhistory.org/the-white-sachem-the-conversion-of-the-cape-cod-indians-and-the-founding-of-mashpee/ (accessed June 22, 2021).

Sheldon Jackson Papers. Presbyterian Historical Society, Philadelphia PA.

Smiley Family Papers. Haverford College Quaker & Special Collections, Haverford College, Haverford PA.

Special Collections and University Archives. Raynor Memorial Libraries, Marquette University, Milwaukee, WI.

Stephen H. Hart Research Center at History Colorado, Denver CO.

University Archives. Hampton University, Hampton VA.

> Howard University. "1899–1900: Catalog of the Officers and Students of Howard University" (1899). Howard University Catalogs. https://dh.howard.edu/hucatalogs/8 (accessed March 27, 2023), 8.

University of Illinois Archives. University of Illinois at Urbana-Champaign, Urbana IL.

William A. Wise Law Library. University of Colorado Law School, Boulder CO.

Yale Collection of Western Americana. Beinecke Rare Book and Manuscript Library, Yale University, New Haven CT.

> Pratt, R. H. *Indian Schools: An Exposure.* "Address before the Ladies Missionary Societies of the Calvary M. E. Church, Washington DC, April 6 [1914?]." Series 3, Addresses, Diaries, Writing, and Notes, box 19, folder 662.

PUBLISHED WORKS

Adams, David Wallace. *Education for Extinction: American Indians and the Boarding School Experience, 1875–1928.* 2nd ed. Lawrence: University Press of Kansas, 2020.

Ahern, Wilbert H. "An Experiment Aborted: Returned Indian Students in the Indian School Service, 1881–1908." *Ethnohistory* 44, no. 2 (Spring 1997): 263–303.

Andrews, Thomas G. "Turning the Tables on Assimilation: Oglala Lakotas and the Pine Ridge Day Schools, 1889–1920s." *Western Historical Quarterly* 33, no. 4 (Winter 2002): 407–30.

*Annual Report of the Civil Service Commission,* 1897–1903.

*Annual Report of the Commissioner of Education,* 1896–97, 1902–5, 1907.

*Annual Report of the Commissioner of Indian Affairs,* 1840, 1850, 1885, 1887, 1890, 1891, 1893–1915. https://search.library.wisc.edu/digital/A3YVW4ZRARQT7J8S.

*Annual Report of the Philippine Commission,* 1902.

*Annual Report of the Superintendent of Indian Schools, 1894, 1896–1905.*

*Congressional Record.*

*Congressional Serial Set.* "Appointments." *Teachers College Record* 17, no. 1 (1916): 101–2.

Archuleta, Margaret L., Brenda J. Child, and K. Tsianina Lomawaima, eds. *Away from Home: American Indian Boarding School Experiences.* Phoenix AZ: Heard Museum, 2000.

Avery, F. F. "Indian Reservation Schools." *Southern Workman* 30, no. 5 (May 1901): 246–47.

Ayer, Mary Farwell. *Richard Bourne, Missionary to the Mashpee Indians.* Boston: David Clapp & Son, 1908.

Bacon, Edwin M. *Boston, A Guide Book: Prepared for the Convention of the National Educational Association, July 6–10, 1903, under the Direction of Edwin D. Mead, Frank Foxcroft, and George P. Morris, the Committee on Guide Books Appointed by the Local Executive Committee.* Boston: Ginn, 1903.

Barker, John. *The Super-Historians: Makers of Our Past.* New York: Charles Scribner's Sons, 1982.

Barnard, Henry. *Proceedings of the National Teachers' Association afterward the National Education Association from its Foundation in 1857 to the Close of the Session of 1870.* Syracuse NY: C. W. Bardeen, 1909.

"Baron de Hirsch Fund: 45 Broadway, New York City." *American Jewish Year Book* 1 (1899): 42–49.

Bastian, Adolf. *The Cultivated Countries of Old America.* New York: B. Westermann, 1878.

Bauer, William J., Jr. *We Were All Like Migrant Workers Here: Work, Community, and Memory on California's Round Valley Reservation, 1850–1941.* Chapel Hill: University of North Carolina Press, 2009.

Behrens, Jo Lea Wetherilt. "In Defense of 'Poor Lo': The Council Fire's Advocacy of Native American Civil Rights, 1878–1889." Master's thesis, University of Nebraska Omaha, 1992.

Belt, Thomas. *The Naturalist in Nicaragua: A Narrative of a Residence at the Gold Mines of Chontales; Journeys in the Savannahs and Forests*. New York: E. P. Dutton, [1874] 1911.

Bender, Norman J. *Winning the West for Christ: Sheldon Jackson and Presbyterianism on the Rocky Mountain Frontier, 1869–1880*. Albuquerque: University of New Mexico Press, 1996.

Bennitt, Mark, and Frank Parker Stockbridge, eds. *History of the Louisiana Purchase Exposition*. St. Louis MO: Universal Exposition, 1905.

Bergh, Albert E., ed. *Writings of Thomas Jefferson*. Vol. 16. Washington DC: Issued under the Auspices of the Thomas Jefferson Memorial Association of the United States, 1907.

Bickley, Francis. *The Life of Matthew Prior*. London: Sir Isaac Pitman & Sons, 1914.

Bilodeau, Christopher J. "The Paradox of Sagadahoc: The Popham Colony, 1607–1608." *Early American Studies* 12, no. 1 (2014): 1–35.

Bishop, Sara. "I Pledge Compliance: Nineteenth-Century Indigenous Residential Schools as Indicators of Multigenerational Trauma." Master's thesis, California State University, Chico, 2018.

Blevins, Cameron. "Women and Federal Officeholding in the Late Nineteenth Century U.S." *Current Research in Digital History* 2 (2019). https://doi.org/10.31835/crdh.2019.08 (accessed January 10, 2023).

Bohl, Sarah Ruth. "'A Man's Work in a Woman's Way': The Career of Estelle Reel, Progressive Educator." Master's thesis, University of Wyoming, 2004.

———. "Wyoming's Estelle Reel: The First Woman Elected to a Statewide Office in America." *Annals of Wyoming* 75, no. 1 (Winter 2003): 22–36.

Brodie, Fawn M. *Thomas Jefferson: An Intimate History*. New York: W. W. Norton, 1974.

Brogden, Mike. *Geronticide: Killing the Elderly*. London: Jessica Kingsley, 2001.

Brubaker, B. R. "Spoils Appointments of American Writers." *New England Quarterly* 48, no. 4 (December 1975): 556–64.

Burgess, Larry E. *The Lake Mohonk Conference of Friends of the Indians: Guide to the Annual Reports*. New York: Clearwater, 1975.

Burlin, Natalie Curtis. "The Indian Character Revealed in Music." *Proceedings of the Eighth Conference for Education in the South*, April 26–28, 1905, 83–86. Atlanta GA: Massey Reporting, 1905.

———. *The Indians' Book: An Offering by the American Indians of Indian Lore, Musical and Narrative, to Form a Record of the Songs and Legends of Their Race*. New York: Harper & Brothers, 1907.

———. *Songs of Ancient America: Three Pueblo Indian Corn-Grinding Songs From Laguna, New Mexico*. New York: G. Schirmer, 1905.

——. "The Value of Indian Art." *Southern Workman* 33, no. 8 (August 1904): 448–50.

Butler, Nicholas Murray, ed. *Education in the United States: A Series of Monographs Prepared for the United States Exhibit at the Paris Exposition.* Albany NY: J. B. Lyon, 1900.

Cahill, Cathleen D. *Federal Fathers & Mothers: A Social History of the United States Indian Service, 1869–1933.* Chapel Hill: University of North Carolina Press, 2011.

Carpenter, J., J. Booker, Roswell and Martin, G. and W. B. Whittaker, R. Triphook, J. Ebers, Taylor and Hessey, R. Jennings, G. Cowie and Co., N. Mailers, J. Porter, B. E. Lloyd and Son, C. Smith, and C. Whittingham, et al., eds. *The British Poets, Including Translations, In One Hundred Volumes. Vol. 31, The Poems of Matthew Prior.* Chiswick: C. Whittingham, 1822.

*Catalogue of Colby University 1886–87.* archive.org.

Chernow, Ron. *Alexander Hamilton.* New York: Penguin, 2004.

Child, Brenda J. *Boarding School Seasons: American Indian Families, 1900–1940.* Lincoln: University of Nebraska Press, 2000.

Coates, Charles Penney. *History of the Manual Training School of Washington University: St. Louis Manual Training School.* Department of the Interior, Bureau of Education, Bulletin no. 3, 1923.

Coburn, Frederick W. "Impressions of the Boston Convention." *School Journal* 67, no. 5 (August 15, 1903): 116–20.

Coffin, Ernest W. "On the Education of Backward Races: A Preliminary Study." *Pedagogical Seminary* 15, no. 1 (March 1908): 1–62.

Connelley, William S., ed. *Collections of the Kansas State Historical Society, 1923–1925.* Topeka: Kansas State Printing, 1925.

Converse, S., ed. *American Society for Promoting the Civilization and General Improvement of the Indian Tribes within the United States: First Annual Report, 1824.* New Haven CT: S. Converse, 1824.

Cooper, Tova. "The Scenes of Seeing: Frances Benjamin Johnston and Visualizations of the 'Indian' in Black, White, and Native Educational Context." *American Literature* 83, no. 3 (September 2011): 509–45.

Cunningham, Noble E., Jr. *In Pursuit of Reason: The Life of Thomas Jefferson.* Baton Rouge: Louisiana State University Press, 1987.

Cushing, Frank Hamilton. *Zuni: Selected Writings of Frank Hamilton Cushing.* Edited and introduced by Jesse Green. Lincoln: University of Nebraska Press, 1979.

Desmond, Lawrence G. *Yucatan through Her Eyes: Alice Dixon Le Plongeon, Writer and Expeditionary Photographer.* Albuquerque: University of New Mexico Press, 2009.

Desmond, Lawrence G., and Phyllis Messenger. *A Dream of Maya: Augustus and Alice Le Plongeon in Nineteenth-Century Yucatan.* Albuquerque: University of New Mexico Press, 1988.

Diamond, Jared. *The World until Yesterday: What Can We Learn from Traditional Societies?* New York: Penguin, 2012.

Dickason, Olive Patricia. *Canada's First Nations: A History of Founding Peoples from Earliest Times.* Toronto: McClelland & Stewart, 1992.

Diehl, Lesley A. "The Paradox of G. Stanley Hall: Foe of Coeducation and Educator of Women." *American Psychologist* 41, no. 8 (August 1986): 868–78.

Dippie, Brian W. *The Vanishing American: White Attitudes and U.S. Indian Policy.* Lawrence: University of Kansas Press, 1982.

Doyle, John T. "Tenure in the Civil Service: Address by Dr. John T. Doyle, Secretary, U.S. Civil Service Commission, before the Department of Indian Education at Boston, July 8, 1903." *Good Government: Official Journal of the National Civil Service Reform League* 20, no. 8 (August 1903): 125–28.

Duncan, J. J. "Indian Day Schools." *Southern Workman* 31, no. 10 (October 1902): 541–45.

Du Val, Kathleen. *The Native Ground: Indians and Colonists in the Heart of the Continent.* Philadelphia: University of Pennsylvania Press, 2006.

Early, Joseph Everett. "Johnston Lykins: Missionary and Mayor of Kansas City." *American Baptist Quarterly* 25, no. 1 (2006): 82–96.

Echo-Hawk, Walter R. *In the Courts of the Conqueror: The 10 Worst Indian Law Cases Ever Decided.* Golden CO: Fulcrum, 2010.

Eittreim, Elisabeth M. *Teaching Empire: Native Americans, Filipinos, and U.S. Imperial Education, 1879–1918.* Lawrence: University Press of Kansas, 2019.

Ellis, Clyde. *To Change Them Forever: Indian Education at the Rainy Mountain Boarding School, 1893–1920.* Norman: University of Oklahoma Press, 1996.

Emerson, Ralph Waldo, III. "Character." *Essays, Second Series.* https://www.gutenberg.org/files/2945/2945-h/2945-h.htm#link2h_4_0003 (accessed January 10, 2023).

Emery, Jacqueline, ed. *Recovering Native American Writings in the Boarding School Press.* Lincoln: University of Nebraska Press, 2017.

Evans, J. W. "Practical Methods of Indian Education." *Chilocco Beacon* 1, no. 10 (August 1901): 160–63.

"Faculty, Staff, and Administrators of the University of Colorado, 1877–1931." *Boulder (Colorado) Genealogical Society Quarterly* 43, no. 3 (2011): 66–72.

Fallace, Thomas D. *Race and the Origins of Progressive Education, 1880–1929.* New York: Teachers College Press, 2015.

Fear-Segal, Jacqueline. "Nineteenth-Century Indian Education: Universalism versus Evolutionism." *Journal of American Studies* 33, no. 2 (1999): 323–41.

———. *White Man's Club: Schools, Race, and the Struggle of Indian Acculturation.* Lincoln: University of Nebraska Press, 2007.

Fenner, Mildred Sandison. *NEA History: The National Education Association, Its Development and Program.* Washington DC: National Education Association, 1945.

Fischer, David Hackett. *Historians' Fallacies: Toward a Logic of Historical Thought.* New York: Harper Perennial, 1970.

Fletcher, Alice C. "Indian Names." *Southern Workman* 33, no. 9 (September 1904): 474–77.

———. *Life among the Indians: First Fieldwork among the Sioux and Omahas.* Edited and introduced by Joanna C. Scherer and Raymond J. DeMallie. Lincoln: University of Nebraska Press, 2013.

Folsom, Cora M. "Guiding the Indian: 'What System Will Best Promote Character Building among Indian Children and the Courage and Ability to Enter and Contend in the Opportunities of Civilized Life?'" *Southern Workman* 30, no. 11 (November 1901): 605–10.

Foreman, Grant. "J. George Wright." *Chronicles of Oklahoma* 20 (June 1942): 120–23.

Frankel, Charles. "John Dewey's Legacy." In *The American Scholar Readers*, edited by Hiram Haydn and Betsy Saunders, 506–22. New York: Atheneum, 1960.

Freeman, Milton M. R. "A Social and Ecologic Analysis of Systematic Female Infanticide among the Netsilik Eskimo." *American Anthropologist* 73, no. 5 (1971): 1011–18.

Friedman, Moses. "Teaching Farming in the Philippines." *Southern Workman* 34, no. 1 (January 1905): 17–22.

Frissell, H. B. "Learning by Doing." *School Journal* 63, no. 3 (July 20, 1901): 73–77.

Garland, Hamlin. "The Red Man's Present Needs (April 1902)." *North American Review* 258, no. 4 (1973): 90–95.

Geniusz, Wendy Djinn. "Decolonizing Botanical Anishinaabe Knowledge: A Biskaabiiyang Approach." PhD diss., University of Minnesota, 2006.

Goodchild, Lester F. "G. Stanley Hall and an American Social Darwin Pedagogy: His Progressive Educational Ideas on Gender and Race." *History of Education Quarterly* 52, no. 1 (February 2012): 62–98.

Goodman, C. W. "The Necessity for a Large Agricultural School in the Indian Service." *Chilocco Beacon* 1, no. 10 (August 1901): 156–59.

Gough, Alexandria L. "A Way Out: The History of the Outing Program from the Haskell Institute to the Phoenix Indian School." Master's thesis, University of Arkansas, 2012.

Gould, Stephen Jay. *The Mismeasure of Man.* Rev. ed. New York: W. W. Norton, 1996.

Greer, Allen. *Property and Dispossession: Natives, Empires, and Land in Early Modern North America.* New York: Cambridge University Press, 2018.

Grinnell, George Bird. *The Indians of To-Day*. New York: Duffield, 1915.

Hailmann, William N. *Education of the Indian*. Vol. 19 of *Monographs on Education in the United States*, edited by Nicholas Murray Butler. Albany NY: J. B. Lyon, 1899.

Hall, G. Stanley. "Some Social Aspects of Education." *Pedagogical Seminary: A Quarterly International Record of Educational Literature, Institutions, and Progress* 9 (1902): 81–91.

Hampton Institute. *Fifty-Second Annual Report of the Treasurer, the Hampton Normal and Agricultural Institute*. Hampton VA: Hampton Normal & Agricultural Institute, 1920.

Hanke, Lewis. "Pope Paul III and the American Indians." *Harvard Theological Review* 30, no. 2 (1937): 65–102.

Heidler, David S., and Jeanne T. Heidler, eds. *Encyclopedia of the American Civil War: A Political, Social, and Military History*. 5 vols. Santa Barbara CA: ABC-CLIO, 2000.

Herny, Ed, Shelley Rideout, and Katie Wadell. *Berkeley Bohemia: Artists and Visionaries of the Early 20th Century*. Salt Lake City UT: Gibbs Smith, 2008.

Hinckley, Ted C. "The Early Alaskan Ministry of S. Hall Young, 1878–1888." *Journal of Presbyterian History (1962–1985)* 46, no. 3 (1968): 175–96.

——— . "Sheldon Jackson and Benjamin Harrison: Presbyterians and the Administration of Alaska." *Pacific Northwest Quarterly* 54, no. 2 (April 1963): 66–74.

——— . "'We Are More Truly Heathen than the Natives': John G. Brady and the Assimilation of Alaska's Tlingit Indians." *Western Historical Quarterly* 11, no. 1 (1980): 37–55.

Hocker, Gustav. *Arnold von Winkelried: The Hero of Sempach*. Translated by George P. Upton. Chicago: A. C. McClurg, 1908.

Holmes, Brian. "Herbert Spencer." *Prospects: The Quarterly Review of Comparative Education* 24, nos. 3–4 (1994): 533–54.

Hosmer, Brian C. *American Indians in the Marketplace: Persistence and Innovation among the Menominees and Metlakatlans, 1870–1920*. Lawrence: University Press of Kansas, 1999.

Howe, Mark Anthony DeWolfe. *The Life and Labors of Bishop Hare: Apostle to the Sioux*. New York: Sturgis & Walton, 1914.

Howes, Durward. *American Women: The Official Who's Who Among the Women of the Nation, 1935–36*. Los Angeles: Richard Blank, 1935.

Hoxie, Frederick E. *A Final Promise: The Campaign to Assimilate the Indians, 1880–1920*. Lincoln: University of Nebraska Press, 1984.

——— . *Talking Back to Civilization: Indian Voices from the Progressive Era*. Boston: Bedford/St. Martin's, 2001.

Hunnewell, James F., G. Stanley Hall, and Samuel A. Green. "January Meeting, 1903. Prehistoric Bunker's Hill; Civilization and Savagery; Early American Imprints." *Proceedings of the Massachusetts Historical Society* 17 (1903): 1–75.

Hunter, Wilma King. "Coming of Age: Hollis B. Frissell and the Emergence of Hampton Institute, 1893–1917." PhD diss., Indiana University, 1982.

Indian Rights Association. "Answers To Charges Made against Wm. N. Hailmann, Superintendent of Indian Schools, Submitting Quotations from His Writings, etc." June 1, 1898. Philadelphia, Pennsylvania. https://babel.hathitrust.org/cgi/pt?id=bc.ark:/13960/t6rz7286w&view=1up&seq=1 (accessed March 27, 2023).

Irving, Theodore. *The Conquest of Florida by Hernando De Soto.* 2 vols. Philadelphia: Cary, Lean & Blanchard, 1835.

Jackson, Donald. *Thomas Jefferson and the Stony Mountains: Exploring the West from Monticello.* Foreword by James P. Ronda. Norman: University of Oklahoma Press, 1993.

Jackson, Helen Hunt. *A Century of Dishonor: A Sketch of the United States Government's Dealings with Some of the Indian Tribes.* Boston: Roberts Brothers, 1888.

Jackson, Sheldon. *The Presbyterian Church in Alaska: An Official Sketch of Its Rise and Progress, 1877–1884.* Washington DC: Thomas McGill, 1886.

Jones, Louis Thomas. *The Quakers of Iowa.* Iowa City: State Historical Society of Iowa, 1914.

Keller, Jean A. *Empty Beds: Indian Student Health at Sherman Institute, 1902–1922.* East Lansing: Michigan State University Press, 2002.

Kelly, William A., and Francis H. Willard. *Grammar and Vocabulary of the Tlingit Language of Southeast Alaska.* Washington DC: GPO, 1905.

Kelsey, Rayner Wickersham. *Friends and the Indians, 1655–1917.* Philadelphia: Associated Executive Committee of Friends on Indian Affairs, 1917.

Kennedy, Patrick M., "Some Day a Great Harvest: A History of the Foundation of St. Augustine's Indian Mission, Winnebago, Nebraska, 1888 to 1945." Master's thesis, University of Nebraska, 2004.

Klepp, Susan E., and Karen Wulf, eds. *The Diary of Hannah Callender Sansom.* Ithaca NY: Cornell University Press, 2010.

Knoxville College. *Catalogue of the Officers and Students of Knoxville College for the Year Ending June, 1892–1894.* Knoxville TN: Ogden Brothers, 1892–94.

Kvasnicka, Robert M., and Herman J. Viola, eds. *The Commissioners of Indian Affairs, 1824–1977.* Lincoln: University of Nebraska Press, 1979.

Lajimodiere, Denise K. *Stringing Rosaries: The History, the Unforgivable, and the Healing of Northern Plains American Indian Boarding School Survivors.* Fargo: North Dakota State University Press, 2019.

Lake Mohonk Conference. *Proceedings of the Annual Meeting of the Lake Mohonk Conference of Friends of the Indian* (1900–1903).

——— . *Proceedings of the Annual Meeting of the Lake Mohonk Conference of Friends of the Indian and Other Dependent Peoples* (1904–6, 1908, 1911, 1916).

Lalor, John J., ed. *Cyclopaedia of Political Science, Political Economy, and of the Political History of the United States.* Chicago: Melert B. Cary, 1884.

Larsson, Gustaf. *Sloyd.* Boston: Principal Sloyde Training School, 1902.

Lawrence, Adrea. *Lessons from an Indian Day School: Negotiating Colonization in Northern New Mexico, 1902–1907.* Lawrence: University Press of Kansas, 2011.

Lee, Yueh-Ting, Russ Kleinbach, Pei-Cheng Hu, Zu-Zhi Peng, and Xiang-Yang Chen. "Cross-Cultural Research on Euthanasia and Abortion." *Journal of Social Issues* 52, no. 2 (Summer 1996): 131–48.

Lentis, Marinella. *Colonized through Art: American Indian Schools and Art Education, 1889–1915.* Lincoln: University of Nebraska Press, 2017.

Le Plongeon, Augustus. *Vestiges of the Mayas, or, Facts Tending to Prove That Communications and Intimate Relations Must Have Existed, in Very Remote Times, between the Inhabitants of Mayab and Those of Asia and Africa.* New York: J. Polhemus, 1881.

Leupp, Francis E. "Improvement, not Transformation." *Southern Workman* 29, no. 6 (June 1900): 365–69.

——— . "Improvement, not Transformation." *Arrow* 1, no. 36 (May 4, 1905): 1, 4.

——— . "Outlines of an Indian Policy." *Outlook* 79 (April 15, 1905): 946–50.

Lindsey, Donal F. *Indians at Hampton Institute, 1877–1923.* Urbana: University of Illinois Press, 1995.

*List of Publications of the Bureau of American Ethnology with Index to Authors and Titles.* Washington DC: GPO, 1962.

Littlefield, Daniel F., Jr., and James W. Parins. *American Indian and Alaska Native Newspapers and Periodicals, 1826–1924.* Westport CT: Greenwood, 1984.

Littlefield, Daniel F., Jr., and Lonnie E. Underhill. "Renaming the American Indian: 1890–1913." *American Studies* 12, no. 2 (1971): 33–45.

Livy, Titus. *The History of Rome.* http://www.perseus.tufts.edu/hopper/text?doc= Perseus%3atext%3a1999.02.0149%3abook%3d44%3achapter%3d22 (accessed March 27, 2023).

Lomawaima, K. Tsianina. "Domesticity in the Federal Indian Schools: The Power of Authority over Mind and Body." *American Ethnologist* 20, no. 2 (May 1993): 227–40.

——— . "Estelle Reel, Superintendent of Indian Schools, 1898–1910: Politics, Curriculum, and Land." *Journal of American Indian Education* 35, no. 3 (Spring 1996): 5–31.

——— . *They Called It Prairie Light: The Story of Chilocco Indian School.* Lincoln: University of Nebraska Press, 1994.

Lomawaima, K. Tsianina, and Teresa L. McCarty. "When Tribal Sovereignty Challenges Democracy: American Indian Education and the Democratic Ideal." *American Educational Research Journal* 39, no. 2 (Summer 2002): 279–305.

Lounsbury, Thomas R., ed. *Yale Book of American Verse*. New Haven CT: Yale University Press, 1912.

Ludwig, M. Mileta. *A Chapter of Franciscan History: The Sisters of the Third Order of St. Francis of Perpetual Adoration, 1849–1949*. New York: Bookman, 1950.

Malval, Fritz J., comp. *A Guide to the Archives of Hampton Institute*. Westport CT: Greenwood, 1985.

Margolis, Eric. "Looking at Discipline, Looking at Labour: Photographic Representations of Indian Boarding Schools." *Visual Studies* 19, no. 1 (2004): 54–78.

Marguerat, Shelly Hiller. "The Origins of Property Rights: A Comparison on the Basis of John Locke's Concept of Property and His Natural Law Limits Based on Reason." PhD diss., University of Geneva, 2014.

Markowitz, Harvey. *Converting the Rosebud: Catholic Mission and the Lakotas, 1886–1916*. Norman: University of Oklahoma Press, 2018.

Martinez, David. "Carlos Montezuma's Fight against 'Bureauism': An Unexpected Pima Hero." *American Indian Quarterly* 37, no. 3 (Summer 2013): 311–30.

Martinez, Katherine. "At Home with Mona Lisa: Consumers and Commercial Visual Culture, 1880–1920." In *Seeing High and Low: Representing Social Conflict in American Visual Culture*, edited by Patricia Johnston, 160–76. Berkeley: University of California Press, 2006.

Mathes, Valerie Sherer. *Helen Hunt Jackson and Her Indian Reform Legacy*. Austin: University of Texas Press, 1990.

——. *The Women's National Indian Association: A History*. Albuquerque: University of New Mexico Press, 2015.

May, Glenn A. "Social Engineering in the Philippines: the Aims and Execution of American Educational Policy, 1900–1913." *Philippine Studies* 24, no. 2 (1976): 135–83.

McCowan, S. M. "The President's Address." *Chilocco Farmer and Stock Grower* 2, no. 9 (July 1902): 259–64.

——. "The Value of an Agricultural School to the Indian." *Southern Workman* 31, no. 9 (September 1902): 494–95.

McCoy, Isaac. *History of Baptist Indian Missions: Embracing Remarks on the Former and Present Condition of the Aboriginal Tribes; Their Settlement within the Indian Territory, and Their Future Prospects*. Washington DC: William M. Morrison, 1840.

McDermott, Louisa. "Indian Pupils' Ambitions." *Southern Workman* 30, no. 7 (July 1901): 401–5.

McIlhiney, David B. *A Gentleman in Every Slum: Church of England Missions in East London, 1837–1914*. Eugene OR: Pickwick, 1988.

McKellips, Karen K. "Educational Practices in Two Nineteenth-Century American Indian Mission Schools." *Journal of American Indian Education* 32, no. 1 (October 1992): 12–20.

McNamara, Brooks. "The Indian Medicine Show." *Educational Theatre Journal* 23, no. 4 (1971): 431–45.

Meserve, Charles F. "A Survey of the Field and Another Step Forward." *Chilocco Farmer and Stock Grower* 3, no. 11 (September 15, 1903): 553–57.

Messer, David W. *Henry Roe Cloud: A Biography*. Lanham MD: Hamilton, 2010.

Millan-Zaibert, Elizabeth. "The Legacy of Humboldt, Krause, and Nietzsche in Latin America: Three Brief Accounts." *APA Newsletter on Hispanic/Latino Issues in Philosophy* 8, no. 1 (Fall 2008): 10–14.

"Miss Reel and the Indians." *Journal of Education* 54, no. 5 (July 25, 1901): 95.

Molin, Paulette Fairbanks. "Indian Education at Hampton Institute." *Minnesota History* (Fall 1988): 82–98.

Morison, Samuel Eliot. *Builders of the Bay Colony: A Gallery of Our Intellectual Ancestors*. 2nd ed. Boston: Houghton Mifflin, 1958.

Morris, Edmund. *The Rise of Theodore Roosevelt*. New York: Modern Library, 1979.

Murphy, Joseph Francis. "Potawatomi Indians of the West: Origins of the Citizen Band." PhD diss., University of Oklahoma, 1961.

National Education Association. *Fiftieth Anniversary Yearbook and List of Active Members of the National Educational Association for the Year Beginning July 1, 1906, and Ending June 30, 1907*. Chicago: University of Chicago Press, 1907.

——. *Journal of Proceedings and Addresses of the National Educational Association*. Winona MN: National Educational Association, 1895, 1896, 1898–1906.

——. *Journal of Proceedings and Addresses of the National Education Association*. Winona MN: National Education Association, 1907–9.

——. *Report of the Committee of Fifteen on Elementary Education*. New York: American, 1895.

Native American Rights Fund. *Legal Review* 38, no. 2 (Summer–Fall 2013). https://www.narf.org/news/legal-review/ (accessed March 27, 2023).

——. *Trigger Points: Current State of Research on History, Impacts, and Healing Related to the United States' Indian Industrial/Boarding School Policy* (2019). Boulder CO. www.narf.org (accessed March 27, 2023).

Newland, Bryan, Assistant Secretary, Indian Affairs. *Federal Indian Boarding School Initiative Investigative Report*. May 2022. www.bia.gov/sites/default/files/dup/inline-files/bsi_investigative_report_may_2022_508.pdf (accessed March 27, 2023).

Newman, Sandra. "Infanticide." November 27, 2017. https://aeon.co/essays/the
-roots-of-infanticide-run-deep-and-begin-with-poverty.

Norrgard, Chantal. *Seasons of Change: Labor, Treaty Rights, and Ojibwe Nation-
hood.* Chapel Hill: University of North Carolina Press, 2014.

Office of Indian Affairs. *Rules for the Indian School Service.* Washington DC:
GPO, 1898.

Office of the Public Printer. *Simplified Spelling.* Washington DC: GPO, 1906.

*Official Register of the United States.* Washington DC: GPO, July 1, 1905, & July 1, 1907.

*Official Roster of the Officers and Employees in the Civil Service of the Philippine
Islands.* Manila: Bureau of Public Printing, [1904] 1908.

Olneck, Michael R. "American Public Schooling and European Immigrants in
the Early Twentieth Century: A Post-Revisionist Synthesis." In *Rethinking the
History of American Education,* edited by William J. Reese and John L. Rury,
103–41. New York: Palgrave Macmillan, 2008.

O'Neill, Colleen M., and Brian C. Hosmer. *Native Pathways: American Indian
Culture and Economic Development in the Twentieth Century.* Boulder: University Press of Colorado, 2004.

Otis, Melissa. *Rural Indigenousness: A History of Iroquoian and Algonquian
Peoples of the Adirondacks.* Syracuse NY: Syracuse University Press, 2018.

Parezo, Nancy J., and Don D. Fowler. *Anthropology Goes to the Fair: The 1904
Louisiana Purchase Exposition.* Lincoln: University of Nebraska Press, 2007.

Parkman, Francis. *France and England in North America.* New York: Literary
Classics of the United States, 1983.

Patterson, Michelle Wick. *Natalie Curtis Burlin: A Life in Native and African
American Music.* Lincoln: University of Nebraska Press, 2010.

Paulet, Anne. "To Change the World: The Use of American Indian Education in the
Philippines." *History of Education Quarterly* 47, no. 2 (May 2007): 173–202.

Peairs, H. B. "Our Work, Its Progress and Needs." *Chilocco Farmer and Stock
Grower* 3, no. 16 (July 15, 1903): 433–40.

Pratt, Richard Henry. *Battlefield and Classroom: Four Decades with the American Indian, 1867–1904.* Edited and with an introduction by Robert M. Utley.
Lincoln: University of Nebraska Press, 1964.

Pratt, Scott L. "Indigenous Agencies and the Pluralism of Empire." *Philosophical
Topics* 41, no. 2 (2013): 13–30.

Prichard, H. Hesketh. *Through the Heart of Patagonia.* New York: D. Appleton, 1902.

Prucha, Francis Paul. *American Indian Policy in Crisis: Christian Reformers and
the Indian, 1865–1900.* Norman: University of Oklahoma Press, 1976.

——— . *Americanizing the American Indians: Writings of the "Friends of the
Indian," 1880–1900.* Lincoln: University of Nebraska Press, 1978.

——. *The Great Father: The United States Government and the American Indians*. 2 vols. Lincoln: University of Nebraska Press, 1984.

Pruette, Lorinne. "Masters of Social Science: G. Stanley Hall." *Social Forces* 5, no. 4 (June 1927): 549–60.

Puryear, Byron N. *Hampton Institute: A Pictorial Review of Its First Century, 1868–1968*. Hampton VA: Prestige, 1962.

Quick, Robert Hebert. *Essays on Educational Reformers*. Edited by William T. Harris. New York: D. Appleton, 1901.

Rahkonen, Carl. "Special Bibliography: Natalie Curtis (1875–1921)." *Ethnomusicology* 42, no. 3 (1998): 511–22.

Rairdon, Jack T. "John Homer Seger: The Practical Indian Educator." *Chronicle of Oklahoma* 34 (Summer 1956): 203–16.

Reel, Estelle. Outline Course of Study for Wyoming Public Schools. Laramie WY: Republican Book & Job Print, 1897.

Renville, Mary Butler. eds. Carrie Reber Zeman and Kathryn Zabelle Derounian-Stodola. *A Thrilling Narrative of Indian Captivity: Dispatches from the Dakota War*. Lincoln: University of Nebraska Press, [1863] 2012.

Reyhner, Jon, and Jeanne Eder. *American Indian Education: A History*. Norman: University of Oklahoma Press, 2004.

Rogers, Frank K. "An All-round Mechanical Training for Indians." *Chilocco Beacon* 1, no. 11 (September 1901): 176–79.

Rosenberg, Daniel. "The Library of Professor Meserve." *Maine History* 46, no. 1 (2011): 90–106.

Rousseau, Jean-Jacques. *Emile, or On Education*. New York: Basic Books, [1762] 2019.

Ryan, Alan. *John Dewey and the High Tide of American Liberalism*. New York: W. W. Norton, 1995.

Rydell, Robert W. "Gateway to the 'American Century': The American Representation at the Paris Universal Exposition of 1900." In *Paris 1900: The "American School" at the Universal Exposition*, edited by Diane P. Fischer, 119–44. New Brunswick NJ: Rutgers University Press, 1999.

Secretary of the Interior. *Regulations of the Indian Office, Effective April 1, 1904*. Washington DC: GPO, 1904.

——. *Regulations of the Indian Office, with an Appendix Containing the Forms Used*. Washington DC: GPO, 1894.

——. "Rules and Regulations of the Indian Service." *Rules and Regulations Governing the Department of the Interior in Its Various Branches*. Sen. Doc. 396, part 4, 59th Cong., 2nd Sess., 1907.

Seger, John H. *Early Days among the Cheyenne and Arapahoe Indians*. Edited by Stanley Vestal. Norman: University of Oklahoma Press, 1956.

Sheehan, Bernard W. *Seeds of Extinction: Jeffersonian Philanthropy and the American Indian*. Chapel Hill: University of North Carolina Press, 1973.

Shepard, Irwin, and Charles W. Eliot. "Notes: The National Education Association. Boston, July 6 to 10, 1903." *Elementary School Teacher* 3, no. 10 (1903): 729–40.

Simonsen, Jane E. *Making Home Work: Domesticity and Native American Assimilation in the American West, 1860–1919*. Chapel Hill: University of North Carolina Press, 2006.

Slivka, Kevin. "Art, Craft, and Assimilation: Curriculum for Native Students during the Boarding School Era." *Studies in Art Education* 52, no. 3 (2011): 225–42.

Stein, Isaac. "Lifting the Red, Stay in the Black: The Public and Private Economics of Race Ideas at the Carlisle Indian School, 1879–1904." *Chicago Journal of History* 7 (Autumn 2016): 69–89.

Stewart, Jane A. "The NEA Convention at Boston." *School Journal* 67, no. 4 (July 25, 1903): 87–90.

Superintendent of Indian Schools. *Course of Study for the Indian Schools of the United States, Industrial and Literary*. Washington DC: GPO, 1901.

Swanton, John R. "Hernando De Soto's Route through Arkansas." *American Antiquity* 18, no. 2 (1952): 156–62.

Thorbjornsson, Hans. "Swedish Educational Sloyd—An International Success." *Journal of Research in Teacher Education*, nos. 2–3 (2006): 11–34.

Thucydides. *The Peloponnesian War*. Revised and with an introduction by T. E. Wick. New York: Modern Library, 1982.

Trachtenberg, Alan. *Shades of Hiawatha: Staging Indians, Making Americans, 1880–1930*. New York: Hill & Wang, 2004.

Trafzer, Clifford E., Jean A. Keller, and Lorene Sisquoc, eds. *Boarding School Blues: Revisiting American Indian Educational Experiences*. Lincoln: University of Nebraska Press, 2006.

Travers, Len, and John Cotton. "The Missionary Journal of John Cotton Jr., 1666–1678." *Proceedings of the Massachusetts Historical Society* 109 (1997): 52–101.

Trennert, Robert A., Jr. "From Carlisle to Phoenix: The Rise and Fall of the Indian Outing System, 1878–1930." *Pacific Historical Review* 52, no. 3 (August 1983): 267–91.

——. *The Phoenix Indian School*. Norman: University of Oklahoma Press, 1988.

——. "A Resurrection of Native Arts and Crafts: The St. Louis World's Fair, 1904." *Missouri Historical Review* 87, no. 3 (April 1993): 274–92.

——. "Selling Indian Education at World's Fairs and Expositions, 1893–1904." *American Indian Quarterly* 11, no. 3 (Summer 1987): 203–20.

Treuer, David. *The Heartbeat of Wounded Knee: Native America from 1890 to the Present*. New York: Riverhead, 2019.

Underhill, Lonnie E. "Hamlin Garland and the Indian." *American Indian Quarterly* 1, no. 2 (Summer 1974): 103–13.

U.S. Bureau of Education. "Industrial Education in the United States: A Special Report." Sen. Ex. Doc. 25, 47th Cong., 2d sess. (1883).

U.S. Department of the Interior. "Final Report of Louisiana Purchase Exposition Commission, 1906." U.S. Cong. Serial Set (1905).

U.S. Supreme Court. *U.S. Reports*, 181 U.S. 481, 1901. FindLaw. Accessed March 30, 2023. https://caselaw.findlaw.com.

Utley, Robert M. *The Last Days of the Sioux Nation*. 2nd ed. New Haven CT: Yale University, [1963] 2004.

Waggoner, Linda M. *Fire Light: The Life of Angel De Cora, Winnebago Artist*. Norman: University of Oklahoma Press, 2008.

Warren, Kim Cary. *The Quest for Citizenship: African American and Native American Education in Kansas, 1880–1935*. Chapel Hill: University of North Carolina Press, 2010.

Washburn, Wilcomb E., ed. *History of Indian-White Relations*. Vol. 4 in *Handbook of North American Indians*, edited by William C. Sturtevant. Washington DC: Smithsonian Institution, 1988.

Washington, Booker T. "Chickens, Pigs, and People." *Outlook* 68, no. 5 (June 1, 1901): 291–300.

Watkins, Frances E. "Charles F. Lummis and the Sequoya League." *Quarterly: Historical Society of Southern California* 26, nos. 2–3 (1944): 99–114.

Wefald, Susan E. "Breaking an 1889 Glass Ceiling: Laura J. Eisenhuth, First Woman Elected to Statewide Office in the United States." *North Dakota History* 79, no. 1 (December 2014): 13–25.

Welsh, Herbert. "The Murrain of Spoils in the Indian Service, a Paper Read at the Annual Meeting of the National Civil-Service Reform League at Baltimore MD, December 16, 1898." New York: Published for the National Civil-Service Reform League.

Wesley, Edgar B. *NEA, The First Hundred Years: The Building of the Teaching Profession*. New York: Harper & Brothers, 1957.

Whalen, Kevin. *Native Students at Work: American Indian Labor and Sherman Institute's Outing Program, 1900–1945*. Seattle: University of Washington Press, 2016.

Williams, Glyn. "Welsh Settlers and Native Americans in Patagonia." *Journal of Latin American Studies* 11, no. 1 (May 1979): 41–66.

Woman's National Indian Association. "The Indian Institute." *Indian's Friend* 12, no. 1 (September 1899): 7–8.

Woodward, Calvin M. "What Shall be Taught in an Indian School." *Southern Workman* 30, no. 8 (August 1901): 429–35.

Wright, A. O. "Some Criticisms and Some Hints." *Chilocco Farmer and Stock Grower* 2, no. 10 (August 1902): 288–93.

# Index

Abbott, Lyman, 281–82

Abby May Home, 42, 303n83

abolitionists, 296n37, 297n39

Adams, John Quincy, 165, 296n35

African Americans. *See* Blacks

agriculture, as educational subject, 28–30, 46–50, 65–66, 102, 119, 128–32, 151–53, 313n113

Agua Caliente Indians, 162, 318n65

Ahern, Wilbert, 6

Alaska and Alaskans: about, 212–14; and citizenship, 217–22, 327n83; customs and character of, 215–17; educational work with, 217–22, 325n61

Alaska-Yukon-Pacific Exposition (Seattle, 1909), 334n5

Aleuts, 215, 221, 326n78

Allen, Edgar A., xxiv, 139, 154, 161–68, 318n64

Allen, Ida Johnson, 161

allotment system: education affecting, 152, 210–11; land quality in, 130; misuse of, 201–2; need for, 117; recommendations for, 99; results of, 18–19, 21, 269, 299n51, 316n33, 331n127; as solution to Indian problem, 230–31

Americanization, 249, 250, 255–56, 277, 278, 280–81, 282, 284

*American Journal of Psychology*, 223

American Society for Promoting the Civilization, 164–65, 319n72

Andrews, Thomas G., 179

Anilco (place and imaginary chieftain), 226, 329n109

*Annual Report of the Commissioner of Indian Affairs* (1899), 54

Apache Indians, 21

Arapaho Boarding School, 178

arithmetic and mathematics, 70–71, 79, 99–100, 112, 113–15

Armstrong, Samuel Chapman, xxxii, 7, 9, 35, 116

artisans, 87–88, 91

arts and crafts: income from, 248–49, 303n85, 305n27; opposition to, 56; preservation of, xxvi, 43, 330n113; support for, 43, 51–52, 54–55, 227, 303n85, 330n113

assimilation, of Indians: approaches to, xxi, xxvii–xxix, 57, 58, 133, 196, 247, 251; assessment of, 312n102; children targeted in, xiii; complexity of, xxix–xxx, 211; in decline, 54; Department of Indian Education affecting, 275; education affecting, 25, 81, 162, 257; exceptions allowed in, xiv, xxvi, 51, 253; extermination contrasted with, 14; funding affected by, 285n3; goals of, xxx–xxxi; Indian employees in, 6; land issues affecting, xxix; resistance to, 183

assimilation, of minority groups, 211, 341n38

Associated Press Dispatches, 216

Athabaskan Indians, 214

attention, types of, 184–85

Bakeless, Oscar H.: about, 85–86; on academic education, 88, 90–91; at association meetings, 1, 25, 154; and Indianness, 133; on practical education, 87–91, 92–95, 310n74; on school-related activities, 91–92

Baptists, 217

Barber, Charles H. and Mrs., 326n78

*Barker v. Harvey* (1901), 318n65

Baron Hirsch Trades School, 173, 320n82

*Barriers Burned Away* (Roe), 304n94

Bartlett, Vena, 294n23

basket-making, 54–55, 227

Bastian, Adolf, 226; *The Cultivated Countries of Old America*, 329n104

*Battlefield and Classroom* (Pratt), 86, 288n35, 305n19

Belt (Bolt), Thomas, 226, 328n103

Bender, Norman J., 212

Benjamin, Edward, 135

Benjamin, George H., 3, 135–38, 315n26

Bennitt, Mark, 334n5

Benton, Thomas Hart, 240–41, 331n140

Bible, 14, 205, 298n43, 319n66

Blacks: education for, 7, 35, 73, 105, 123, 178, 230; as employees, 136–38; enslavement as boon for, 12–13, 155; music of, 260, 262; press on, 294n11; racial theories on, 9–10, 315n26; as students, 135–36; as teachers, 1, 166–67, 277; treatment of, 1–3, 280

Block, Parsha, 221, 326n78

Board of Lady Managers (World's Fair), 265

Boas, Franz, 223

books: experience broadened by, 79, 114; historical role of, 271; importance of, 184; specialization needed in, 100, 101; as symbol, 87; as tools, 10, 62; usefulness of limited, 69–70, 172–73

Boston MA, 187–88, 189

Bourne, Richard, 197

boys: as apprentices, 172–73; character-building for, 121–22; and citizenship, 211; in day schools, 208–9; education for, 172; home influence on, 202, 203; in hypothetical invasion, 144; and outing system, 156, 300n53; religious training for, 149, 205, 206; work desired, 72–73. *See also* men

boys, practical education for: agricultural, 46–48, 65–66, 102, 129–30; in Alaska, 216–17, 219–20; arithmetic in, 113–14; chores in, 180; importance of, 37–38; variety in, 106–8, 205, 206

Brady, John G., 217

Brogden, Mike, 213

Buchanan, James, xxxi–xxxii

Bureau of Education. *See* U.S. Bureau of Education

Bureau of American Ethnology of the Smithsonian, 86, 329n107

Bureau of Indian Affairs. *See* U.S. Bureau of Indian Affairs

Burlin, Natalie Curtis. *See* Curtis, Natalie

Burlin, Paul, 260

Cahill, Cathleen, 291n86

Canada, xxii, 227

Carlisle Indian Industrial School: comparisons with, 105; conference participation of, 1; criticism of, 142; curriculum of limited, 251; defense of methods of, 140, 166; enrollment of, 318n56; establishment of, 7, 25; funding for, 285n3, 297n40, 319n74; on goals for Indians, xxx; opinions on, 98; outing system of, 30, 52–53, 154–60, 300n53; policies of, 29–30;

as representative school, 27; students of, 96–97, 216, 327n81

Carnegie, Andrew, 50

Carter, Sybil, 43, 303n85

Catholics, 17, 72, 210, 218, 281, 297n40, 332n129, 340n30

cattle, 46–49, 299n51

Central Woman's Christian Temperance Union, xl

*Century of Dishonor* (Jackson), 39, 298n47

character, in Indians: education improving, 38, 82, 118–20, 121–24; natural, 117–18, 120–21

Charleston SC, 1–3, 293n3

Chesterton, Gilbert K., xxvii

*Cheyenne Daily Leader*, 283

*Cheyenne Sun*, 135–36

Child, Brenda J., xxix, xxxiii

*Chilocco Beacon* (newspaper), 97

*Chilocco Farmer and Stock Grower* (newspaper), 139–40, 189–90, 192

Chilocco Indian School, 97, 109, 128–32, 141–42, 151

Chinese invasion, in dream, 142, 143–48

Chippewa (Ojibwe) Indians, 125–26, 296n38

Christian Endeavor societies, 159

Christianity: and Alaska Natives, 220, 222; in assimilation, xxix–xxx; in character building, 122; conversion to recommended, 49; in education, xxviii, 5, 7, 27, 35, 62, 196–97, 205; and evolutionary beliefs, 149; importance of, 16–18, 71–72; and Indian names, 273–74; in outing system, 159

citizenship: among Alaskan Natives, 208, 210–11, 217–22, 327n83; and assimilation, 86; as conference theme, 187, 188–89, 194; as educational goal, xxviii, xxxiii, 7, 22, 67–68, 82, 110, 251, 279–80; and individuality, 262, 264; laws about, 230–31; and reservation system, 21; self-support in, 97

civilization, for Indians: assimilation helping, xxx–xxxi; background for, 225–26, 328n103; education helping, 76–80, 82–83, 97–99, 162–65; as government policy, xxvii–xxviii; and money issues, 72; NEA role in, xxxiii; reservations holding back, 12–13; as slow process, 149–50; teachers helping, 32–33, 34

civil service: appointments by, 233–36, 238–39, 242–46; hiring procedures of, 258–59, 315n21; and Indian school service, 237–38, 243–44; opinions on, 230; and racial issues, 134–35, 136–38, 255, 300n54, 324n55; reform by, 16, 23, 231; removals by, 238–39, 242–46; suggestions for, 204–5; tenure in, 238, 239–42, 244–45; and unauthorized hiring, 169

civil service act. *See* Pendleton Civil Service Reform Act

Civil War, 1–2, 212, 286n19, 304n94

cleanliness, 41, 43, 173

Cleveland, Grover, 237, 238, 332n129

Cloud, Henry Roe, 304n93

clubhouses, for Indians, 49–50

Cody, "Buffalo Bill," and Wild West Show, 302n71

Coffin, Ernest W., 57

colonization, 45–46, 106, 283

commissioners, of Indian Affairs: and conference resolutions, 139; and hiring procedures, 234–36, 331n126; and pay issues, 233–34, 313n113, 332n130; and racial issues, 135,

136–37; and ration system, 299n51; reports of, 198–99, 201; role of, xxii

concentration camps, comparisons with, 227, 331n115

Congress of Indian Educators, 247–48, 249, 252, 334n5

Cook, Emily S., 248, 265–68, 335n10, 340n32

correlation, in Indian education, 69–70, 89, 134, 192, 209

courage, in Indians, 117, 119

*Course of Study* (Reel), xxi, 5, 51–59, 133, 154, 187, 277, 283, 321n1, 342n47, 342n51

Covey, Claude C., 81–84, 279

creameries, in Indian education, 67, 102, 119, 308n58

Creoles, Alaskan, 215

Crook, George, 227

Cuba, 331n115

Cubans, 255–56, 258, 281, 340n30

*The Cultivated Countries of Old America* (Bastian), 329n104

Curtis, Natalie (later Burlin), 260–64; *The Indians' Book*, 260, 337n59; *Songs of Ancient America*, 261

Curtis Act (1898), 332n128

Cushing, Frank Hamilton, 226, 227–28, 329n107

Custer, George A., 266

Dakota Indians. *See* Sioux Indians

Dakota Uprising (1862), 296n38, 297n41

Darlington Cheyenne-Arapaho Indian Agency, 45, 178, 304n92

Darwin, Charles, 223, 310n82

Dawes, Henry L., 231, 332n130

Dawes Act (1887), 230, 266, 331n127. *See also* land-in-severalty bill

Dawes Commission, 230–31

De Cora, Angel, 116–17, 263, 337n59

Department of Education of the Deaf, Blind, and Feeble-Minded, 290n76

Department of Elementary Education, xxxii, xxxiii–xxxiv, 190, 250, 321n1

Department of Higher Education, xxxii

Department of Indian Education: Blacks involved in, 3; and companion organizations, 247–53, 335n24, 336n26; controversy within, 190–91, 237–38; duration of, xxi–xxii, 285n8; formation of, xiii, xxxii, xxxiii–xxxiv, xxxix–xl, 1, 275–77; goals of, 194; and Indianness, 247; and Indian Problem, 279–81; influences on, 97; meeting attendance encouraged for, 133–34; membership size of, 334n9; papers of, xxiv–xxvii, xxxi; recognition of, 138, 139; references to, 294n23; results of, 275, 278, 281–84; role of, 51; and scientific racism, 278–79

Department of Kindergarten Education, xxxv, 321n1

Department of Manual Training, 190–91, 250, 321n1, 335n24

Department of Normal Schools, xxxii

Department of Physical Education, 191, 321n1

Department of School Superintendence, xxxii

Department of Special Education, 290n76

Department of the Interior, xxxv, 57, 169

De Soto, Hernando, 329n109

*Detroit Free Press*, 51

Dewey, John, 223, 278, 308n56; *School and Society*, 64, 308n56

Diamond, Jared, *The World Until Yesterday*, 213–14

Diehl, Lesley, 224

dignity, teaching of, 66–67

Dippie, Brian, 262

displays. *See* exhibits, of NEA

Dockery, Alexander M., 249

dogs, in hunting humans, 227, 330n111

Dorchester, Daniel, xxxvii, 276, 302n82

Dorchester, Merial A. Whipple, 42, 302n82

Doyle, John T.: about, 237–38, 255–56; on civil service history, 238–40, 242; conference participation of, 278; on contemporary civil service, 230, 240–46; on Indian education, 256–59

Duncan, James J., 178–82, 305n27

Duncan, William, 18, 226, 299n49, 329n108

Dyke, Charles Bartlett, 31–34, 301n60

Echo-Hawk, Walter R., xxix

education, academic, 76, 88, 90–91, 92–95, 100–101, 171, 184–86

education, general: assimilation policy in, xxvii–xxxi; balance in, 68–71, 126–27; character building in, 38; and Christianity, 27, 71–72; civilization in, 76–80; and civil service, 230–36; compulsory, 22; contemporary views on, xiii–xiv; description of, 117–20; development of, xxvi; for girls, 40–44; goals of, 163–68; minority groups compared in, 97–98; music in, 260–64; nature study in, 93–94; organizational involvement in, xxxii–xxxiv, xxxvi–xl, 3–6; outing system in, 52–53; progress in, 73–74; progressivism affecting, 8, 86; racism affecting, xxvi–xxvii; school types in, 82–84, 162–65, 316n31; societies promoting, 319n72; for special needs, 26;

statistics about, 196–201, 198–99t; suggestions for, 120–24; universal questions about, 143–44, 148–50

education, practical: and academic training, 87–91; acceptance of, by Indians, 99–100; agriculture in, 28–30, 46–50, 119, 128–32, 151–53; assimilation policy in, 25, 275; and citizenship, 67–68, 209–11, 251; community-based, 101–2; construction and repair in, 102–6; at elementary school level, 190, 322n20; free labor provided by, 61–62, 128–29, 195; goals of, 27–28; importance of, 10, 35–38; inadequacies of, 170–73; mechanical, 105–8; money matters in, 72; outing system in, 154–60; by Quakers, 298n44; results of, 72–73, 231; school types in, 164, 175–76; support for, 58–59; teaching methods for, 110–15, 176–77; work encouraged by, 63–67

Eisenhuth, Laura, 290n78

Eittreim, Elisabeth, 341n38; *Teaching Empire*, 283

Eliot, Charles W., 187

Eliot, John, 196–97, 208, 209, 211

Emerson, Ralph Waldo, 94, 117, 223

Emery, Jacqueline, 294n23

English language, 27, 76, 99, 111–12, 113, 158, 201, 250–51, 272–73, 297n42

Episcopalians, 217–18

Eskimos, 213–17, 219–20

*Essay on Man* (Pope), 317n49

*Essays* (Montaigne), 307n50

*Essays on Educational Reformers* (Quick), 63

ethnology and ethnologists, 225, 227, 271, 330n114

Evans, Adaline O'Brien, 109, 311n87

Evans, Joseph W.: about, 109–10, 311n87; on practical education, 110–15

evolution, social, xxviii–xxix, 148–49, 223–24, 269, 328

executive branch, 243

exhibits, of NEA, 4–5, 55, 58–59, 133, 134, 138, 191–93, 247–49, 258

Exposition Universelle (Paris, 1900), 295n33

extermination, of Indians, 14, 76, 197

Fallace, Thomas, xxviii

Fear-Segal, Jacqueline, xxviii–xxix, 61–62

Fewkes, Jesse Walters, 227, 330n114

Filipinos. *See* Philippines and Filipinos

Five Civilized Tribes, 201, 230–31

Fletcher, Alice, xxvi, 40, 226, 227, 248, 265, 269–74, 340n32

Folsom, Cora M.: about, 116–17, 311n92; educational philosophy of, 123–24; on Indians, 117, 118–23; presentations by, 338n3; on school principal, 8; on teachers, 117–18, 120

Fort Mojave, 161

Fort Sill, 25

Fowler, Dan, 248

Franciscan Sisters of Perpetual Adoration, 126

Friedman, Moses, 282, 327n81

Friends (Quakers), 17, 298n44

Friends of the Indian, 97, 117, 265, 296n36. *See also* Lake Mohonk Conference of the Friends of the Indian

Frissell, Hollis B.: about, 7–8, 61–62, 208; on academic education, 70–71; addresses by, 179, 340n32; on citizenship for Indians, 67–68; on general education, 68–70, 72–73; on Indian problem, goals for, 20–24; on Indian problem, progress in, 15–20, 297n40, 300n52; on Indians, 8–11, 210–11; influence of, 35, 52; influences on, 208; opinions on, 116; on practical education, 62–67, 72–73; on racial differences, 13–15, 278–79, 280; on religious education, 71–72; on school types, 208–10; on slavery, 3, 12–13; on Williamson family, 298n43

Froebel, Friedrich, 63–64

fundraising schemes, xxi, 285n3

gardening, in education, 22, 64, 110–11, 122

Garfield, James A., 136, 237

Garfield, James R., 136–37, 255

Garland, Hamlin, 166, 167, 227, 330n112

General Allotment Act (1887), 21, 316n33

genocide, cultural, xxvii–xxviii, 284

geography, teaching of, 70, 79–80, 100

geronticide, 213–14, 215–16

Ghost Dance, 320n94

Gilbert, Raleigh, 330n111

girls: and citizenship, 211; in day schools, 208–9; health care by, 50; as helpers, 171–72; home influence on, 202, 203; in hypothetical invasion, 144, 145, 146; and outing system, 156–60, 300n53; practical education for, 66, 106–7, 120–21, 122, 180, 205, 206; religious training for, 205, 206; role of, 40–44, 103–4, 164; work desired, 73. *See also* women

God: in fabricated stories, 330n111; human lives revealing, 71; in human work, 63, 65; and hypothetical invasion, 147; and Indian education, 140; in literature, 76; in nature, 11, 310n74; work of, 15, 62, 149, 205, 216, 222

Goodman, Charles K., 128–32, 234–35, 236, 292n101, 338n3

Gookins, Daniel, 197

Gould, Stephen Jay, 8

Greater American Exposition (Omaha, 1898), 141

Greer, Allen, xxix

Grinnell, George Bird, 23, 55, 280; *The Indians of Today*, 21, 73–74

Guiteau, Charles, 237

Haaland, Deb, xxii

Hailmann, Eudora, xxxv

Hailmann, William, xxxii–xxxiii, xxxv–xxxviii, 196–97, 276–77

Hale, Edward Everett, 15–16, 193, 296n35

Hall, G. Stanley, 223–28, 279, 328n101, 328n103, 329nn108–109, 330nn111–113

Hall, Harwood, 236, 305n10, 332n132

Hall, J. Thomas, 332n132

Hampton Institute: educational focus of, 36–37, 53, 105, 106–7, 108, 123; Indian art at, 261; influence of, 52; music at, 262; outing system of, 121; practical education at, 177; professional staff of, 8–9, 35, 39, 116

Hanke, Lewis, 330n111

Hare, William H., 17, 41, 297n41

Harris, William T., 33, 75–80, 183–86, 278, 302n68, 309n66

Harrison, Benjamin, 232, 233–34, 332n129

Haskell Institute, 177, 195, 229–30, 298n44, 318n56

Hawai'i and Hawai'ians, 31–32, 225, 255–56, 258, 281–82

Herbert Welsh Institute, 161

*Hiawatha*. See *The Song of Hiawatha* (Longfellow)

history, teaching of, 70

*History of Indian Baptist Missions* (McCoy), 319n68

Hopkins, Samuel, 227, 330n111

hospitals, in Indian schools, 50

Hough, Walter, 227, 330n114

Hoxie, Fred, 5, 57, 288n46

humans, as exterminators, 224–25

Humboldt, Alexander, 226; *Personal Narrative of Travels*, 328n102

Huxley, Thomas, 225, 328n97

Hydah Indians, 214–15

immigrants, 280–81, 284, 320n82, 321n1

the *Independent* (newspaper), 2–3

Indian agents, xxxvii, 16, 19, 182, 227, 232, 276, 299n51, 302n82, 331n126

Indian Bureau. *See* U.S. Indian Bureau

Indianness, xxvi, xxvii, xxix, xxx, 133, 139–40, 247, 253, 261–62

Indian Office. *See* U.S. Indian Office

Indian Problem: about, xiii–xiv, 279–80; Blacks' circumstances compared to, 12–13; challenges to solution for, 23; and education, 82, 197; Indian viewpoint in, 13–14; and NEA, xxxii–xxxiii; perceived improvements in, 15–19, 24; solution to, 20–23, 230–31; time affecting, 142–43; and universalism, xxviii; white ignorance about, 14–15

Indian Research Project, 125–26

Indian Rights Association, xxxvi, 164, 331n127

Indians: attitudes toward, xxi–xxii, 8–9, 21, 25, 117–18, 264, 288n49, 317n49, 333n2; boarding conditions for, xxii–xxiii, 199–200; comparisons with, 12–13, 224–28; employment of, 109–10; music of, 260–64; names of explained, 265–74; natural state of, 13–14; and NEA meetings, 5–6, 294n23, 295n26; perceived needs of, 88; president's views on, 316n33; and religion, 227–28, 296n38, 299n48; statistics on, 210–11

Indians, Alaskan: description of, 214–17; recommendations for, 217–22

*The Indians' Book* (Curtis), 260, 337n59

Indian school service: agriculture taught in, 128–32, 151–53; and civil service, 255–56, 258–59; conference participation of, xxxi–xl, xxxix, 338n3, 339n16; day schools in, 127; focus of changing, 5, 52–53; goal of, 139; hiring difficulties of, 255, 256–57; imperialism affecting, 282; Indians employed by, 6, 109–10; marriages in, 109, 311n87; and minority groups, 282–84; organizational position of, xxi; practical emphasis of, 61–62, 187; in professional organizations, 187, 193–94, 249–51, 276–79, 281, 292n101; and slavery, 3; teacher qualifications for, 255–59

Indian service: and civil service, 136–37, 169, 204–5, 223–24, 230–35, 236, 237–38, 243–44; focus of changing, 16; women in, xxxvi, 291n86

*The Indian's Friend* (magazine), 39, 261

*The Indians of Today* (Grinnell), 21, 73–74

Indian Territory, 45, 231, 332n128

industrial education. *See* education, practical

infanticide, 213–14, 215

intermarriage, xxviii, 227

Ireland, John, 338n3

Irving, Theodore, 329n109

Islam, 328n99

Jackson, Andrew, 236

Jackson, Helen Hunt, *Century of Dishonor*, 39, 298n47

Jackson, Laura: about, 154; addresses by, 155–60, 300n53

Jackson, Sheldon: about, 212–14; addresses by, 340n32; description of Alaskans by, 214–17; recommendations for Alaskans by, 217–22, 326n78, 327n83

Jefferson, Thomas, xxvii–xxviii, 165, 288n49

Jim Crow, 2, 3

Jones, William A., xxii, 53, 189, 211, 235, 266, 280, 324n54

Josephine E. Richards Memorial Book Fund, 39

*Journal of Education*, 58, 139, 193

*Journal of Proceedings of the NEA. See NEA Proceedings*

*Journal of Race Development*, 223

*Journal of Speculative Philosophy*, 75

Kamehameha Schools, 31–32, 301n60

Keller, Jean A., xxii

Kellogg, Fanny, 217

Kickapoo Indian Medicine Company, 35–36, 302n71

kindergarten, xxxv, 10, 63–64, 190, 321n1, 322n20

Kirby, William West, 18, 299n48

lace-making, 43, 303n85

Ladies Missionary Societies of the Calvary M.E. Church, 336n38

Lake Mohonk Conference of the Friends of the Indian: focus of, 97, 256, 310n81; and Indian reform, 15–16, 191–92, 280, 296n36; location of, 323n26; lodge funded by, 49; and nonwhite races, 281–82; participants in, 265, 340n32

land, in agricultural education, 46, 47, 48–49, 130

land grabs, xxix, 225, 289n52

land-in-severalty bill, 17, 18–19, 20. *See also* Dawes Act (1887)

land ownership: allotment system in, 18–19, 99, 201–2, 204, 210–11, 230–31, 269, 299n51; in character building, 117, 118–19; encouraged, xxxiii, 45–46

Lawrence, Adrea, 58

*Lawrence Daily Journal*, 229

Lemmon, Theodore G., 236, 332n132

Lentis, Marinella, 305n27

Le Plongeon, Alice Dixon, 329n105

Le Plongeon, Augustus, 226; *Vestiges of the Maya*, 329n105

Leupp, Francis E., xxii, xxix, 23, 285n8, 288n49, 297n40

Levering, Levi, 46, 294n23

Levering, Lincoln, 6, 294n23

Levy (Roman historian), 165–66

Lincoln, Abraham, 296n38, 298n46

liquor consumption, 139, 169–70, 202, 316n33

Littlefield, Daniel, 266

Locke, John, 258, 337n43

"The Lodge" clubhouse, 49–50

Lomawaima, K. Tsianina, xxvii, 128

Longfellow, Alice, 193

Longfellow, Henry Wadsworth, *Hiawatha*, 193, 264

Los Angeles CA, xxxix, 292n104

*Los Angeles Times*, xxxix

Louisiana Purchase Exposition. *See* World's Fair (St. Louis, 1904)

Luckey, George Washington Andrew, 73, 308n61

Lutherans, 218

Lykins, Johnston, 163, 319n66

Madison, James, 165, 239

Mahdi (Islamic leader), 225, 328n99

*Manual Training Magazine*, 190

marriage, 43–44, 109, 146, 227, 311n87

Marsden, Edward, 222, 327n81

Martinez, David, 289n57

Massachusetts Historical Society, 330n111

mathematics. *See* arithmetic and mathematics

May, Abby Williams, 303n83

Maya Indians, 226, 329n105

McCarty, Teresa L., xxvii

McConnell, William J., 318n64

McCowan, Samuel M.: about, 141–43; on agricultural education, 128–29, 151–53; and conferences, 248, 250; dream of, interpreted, 148–50; dream of, revealed, 143–48; as superintendent, 161, 236

McCoy, Isaac, 163, 319n66; *History of Indian Baptist Missions*, 319n68

McCoy, Lillie S., 192

McDermott, Louisa, 72–73, 308n60

McFarland, A. R., Mrs., 217, 326n79

McFarland, Fanny. *See* Willard, Frances (Aleut girl)

McGee, William J., 249–50, 256

McKinley, William, xxxiv–xxxv, xxxv–xxxvi

McKoin, John J., 236, 332n132

mechanics, teaching of, 105–8

medicine shows, 35–36, 302n71

men: education for, 163–64, 219–21; in hypothetical invasion, 145, 146; role of, 20; skills of, 40, 105–6; voting rights for, 327n83. *See also* boys

Meriam Report (1928), xxiii, 195

Meserve, Charles F.: about, 229–30; on civil service, 238; on conference meetings, 188; on general education, 230–36; on government policies, 279, 331n127; on Indian Service, 332n129

Methodists, 217

Metlakatla (Metacathlah) Indian Community, 226, 299n49, 329n108

Millan-Zaibert, Elizabeth, 328n102

Miller, Joaquin, 327n95

*Minneapolis Journal*, 138

Minnesota massacre (1862), 17

Miscellaneous Receipts, Class IV, 132, 313n113

missionary work, 24, 39, 162–63, 197–98, 213–18, 259, 298n43, 299nn48–49, 303n85, 304n93

Mohonk Lodge, 49–50, 123

money, of Indians, 72–73, 77–78, 121, 159–60, 220, 300n53, 305n27, 313n113

Monroe, James, 164–65

Montaigne, Michel de, 63; *Essays*, 307n50

Montezuma, Carlos, xxx, 289n57

Moody, Dwight, 220, 326n76

morals, teaching of, 71–72, 110, 164

Moravian Church, 217

Morgan, Lewis Henry, 226, 269, 328n100

Morgan, Thomas Jefferson: as assimilationist, xxviii, xxxi, 57; as Commissioner of Indian Affairs, xxxiii, 51–52, 229–30, 233–34, 266, 332n130; educational theories of, 281

Moses (Biblical character), 166

Mt. Hermon School for Boys, 220, 326n76

Murphy, M. Macaria, 125–27, 313n107

music, of Indians, 260–64

names, of Indians, 265–74

National Educational Association. *See* NEA (National Educational Association)

National Education Association. *See* NEA (National Education Association)

National Teachers' Association. *See* NTA (National Teachers' Association)

Native American Rights Fund, xxvii

nature study, 93–94

NEA (National Educational Association): constitution of, xxxiii; Department of Indian Education within, xiii, xxi–xxii, xxxviii–xl, 138, 249–50, 275–78, 292n101; Indian education as focus of, xxxii–xxxiii, 279–84; Indian participation in, 295n26, 305n27, 334n5; leadership, xxxiv, 134–35; meetings, 1–6, 51–59, 133–40, 187–94, 247–53, 293n3, 321n1, 335n24, 336n26; membership, 335n9; organizational structure, xxxii; praise for, 339n16; racism in, xxvi–xxvii, xxxi, 1–3; records of, edited, xxiii–xxv, 137, 193–94, 261, 287n27; reindeer project endorsed by, 213; renaming of, 289n61; speakers at meetings of, 338n3, 340n32; teachers highlighted by, 247–48

NEA (National Education Association), xxi, 285n1

*NEA Proceedings*: about, xxi, xxxii; contents of, xxxiv, 8, 224, 252–53; editing of, xxiii–xxv, 8, 196, 230, 266, 270; ethnocentrism in, xxxi; guidelines for, xxiii–xxiv; historical context of, xxv–xxvi; on reservations, 56

Negroes. *See* Blacks

Newman, Sandra, 213

newspapers, in education, 183–86

nonwhites, 250, 255, 281–83

Northfield Seminary, 326n76

novels, 304n94

NTA (National Teachers' Association), xxxi–xxxii, xxxv, xxxvii

Oberly, John H., 238

Odanah Day School (St. Mary's Indian School), 125–26

Office of Indian Affairs. *See* U.S. Office of Indian Affairs

Ojibwe (Chippewa) Indians, 125–26, 296n38

Omaha Indians, 19, 270, 272

Oneida Indians, 21, 67, 308n58

outing system, xiv, 30, 52–53, 121, 154–60, 300n53, 305n10

Pan-American Exposition (New York, 1901), 58, 247

Paquita (Modoc woman), 327n95

Parezo, Nancy, 248

Parkman, Francis, 330n111

Patterson, Michelle Wick, 260

Paulet, Anne, 283

payment, at Indian schools, 132, 313n113

Peairs, Hervey B.: about, 195–96; addresses by, 338n3, 340n32; observations of, 196–203, 205–6; praise for, 236; recommendations of, 203–5, 206–7, 279, 324n55

*Pedagogical Seminary* (journal), 223

Pelasgian tribe, 226, 329n106

Pember, Mary Annette, 126

Pendleton Civil Service Reform Act (1883), 242–45

Perry Pictures, 43, 303n84

*Personal Narrative of Travels to the Equinoctial Regions* (Humboldt), 328n102

petitions, for department formation, xl, 292n110

Philippines and Filipinos: attitudes toward, 256, 258; comparisons with, 97–98, 277; education for, 281–83, 342n51; language of, 250; misconceptions about, 228; religion of, 340n30; and teachers, 341n38, 341n40

philosophers, 63–64, 307n50

*Phoenix Gazette* (newspaper), 142

Pine Ridge Reservation, and Pine Ridge Day School, 22, 174–75, 178–81

Pope, Alexander, *Essay on Man*, 317n49

Popham, George, 227, 330n111

Popham Colony, 330n111

Potter, Thomas W., 236, 332n132

Pratt, Richard H.: as assimilationist, xxi, 285n3; *Battlefield and Classroom*, 86, 288n35, 305n19; colleagues of, 25, 86; as conference nonparticipant, 1, 53, 55–56, 61; as conference participant, xxxii, xxxviii, 53; disagreements with, 8, 53–54, 251–52; early career of, 7; educational philosophy of, xxvii, 53–54, 55–57, 306n30, 336n38; influence of, 294n23; and outing system, 52, 154–55, 156, 300n53, 305n10; praise for, 18, 23, 236; professional decline of, 54, 188–89

Presbyterians, 178, 212, 213, 217–18, 222

Pritchard, H. Hesketh, 226; *Through the Heart of Patagonia*, 328n101
*The Problem of Indian Administration* (Meriam Report), xxiii, 195
progressivism, xxi, xxviii–xxix, 8, 61, 86, 223, 251
Protestants, 17, 72, 210
Prucha, Francis Paul, xxxi, 296n36
Puerto Rico and Puerto Ricans, 97–98, 255–56, 258, 281–82, 283, 340n30

Quakers (Friends), 17, 298n44
Quick, Robert Herbert, *Essays on Educational Reformers*, 63
*Quick Bear v. Leupp*, 297n40

racism, scientific. *See* scientific racism
Rairdon, Jack, 45
Ranke (Rancke), Leopold von, 225, 328n98
ration system: abolition of, 211, 231, 232, 324n54; as bad influence, 10, 67–68, 201–3, 206, 279–80, 316n33; Indians rejecting, 21–22, 299n51; starting point of, 197
*Red Man and Helper* (newspaper), 5–6, 140, 190, 252, 294n23
Reel, Alexander Hector "Heck," xxxiv
Reel, Estelle: age of, 291n89; arts and crafts supported by, 51–52, 54–55, 102, 305n27; attitudes toward, 55–59, 139, 224, 249, 251; beliefs of, 183, 315n26, 322n20; as conference speaker, 340n32; as confidante, 45; contemporary trends helping, xxxvi, 291n86; controversy caused by, 135–38, 237–38, 255, 314n8, 315n23; *Course of Study*, xxi, 5, 51–59, 133, 154, 187, 277, 283, 321n1, 342n47, 342n51; editing by, xxiii–xxv, 196,

230, 252–53, 266, 270, 286n24, 287n27, 300n54, 324n55; goals of, 275–76; health of, 189–90, 322n16; influences on, 52; legacy of, 283–84; misunderstandings about, 290n78; organizational roles of, xxxiv–xl, 1, 3–6, 133–38, 188–94, 212–13, 247–48, 276–77, 322n11, 334n5; and outing programs, 154, 305n10; practical emphasis of, 52–53; as progressive, xxi, 86; self-image of, 283; on subordinates, 179
reindeer project, 212–13, 219
religion, 49, 71–72, 122, 147, 226, 227–28, 232, 319n66, 332n129
Republican Party, xxxiv–xxxv
reservations and reservation system: abolition of recommended, 204, 206, 232; court decisions about, 318n65; criticism of, 156, 162, 167, 202–3, 227, 251–52, 269, 316n33, 336n38; in dream, 144–45; education affecting, 66–68; plantation system compared with, 12–13; progress shown by, 126; as temporary situation, 20, 21–22, 197, 279–80, 331n127; whites taking over land of, 19
responsibility, teaching of, 10–11, 68, 120–21
Richards, Josephine E., 39–44
Richardville family (Miami chiefs), 163
Riggs, Alfred Longley, 297n42
Riggs, Mary Ann Clark Longley, 297n42
Riggs, Stephen Return, 297–98nn42–43
Riggs family, 17, 18
Robertson, Alice, 340n32
Roe, Edward Payson, 49, 304n94; *Barriers Burned Away*, 304n94
Roe, Mary, 304n93
Roe, Walter, 49–50, 304n93

Rogers, Frank Knight, 35–38, 105–8

Roosevelt, Theodore, xxv, 139, 170, 232, 241–42, 260, 266, 296n35, 306n31, 316n33

Rosebud Reservation and Rosebud Day School, 141, 174–75, 179, 300n52

Rousseau, Jean-Jacques, 63, 307n53

*Rules and Regulations of the Department of Interior*, 129

*Rules for the Indian School Service*, 127, 313n107

*San Francisco Call* (newspaper), xxxix, 275

Santee Indians, 18

Schell, Joseph, 169–70

*School and Society* (Dewey), 64, 308n56

schools, off-reservation boarding: about, xiii, xiv, xxii–xxiii, xxx; and day schools, 182; failures of, 116–17; justification for, 170; kindergarteners in, 190, 322n20; opposition to, 81–82, 83–84, 139, 300n53, 319n74; practical education in, 209; results of, 203; role of, 22–23, 68, 206; statistics on, 198–99, 316n31, 318n56; support for, 139, 162–68, 188–89, 204, 230; usefulness of limited, 173–76

schools, public, 53–54, 73, 75, 157, 167, 171, 172–75, 218–19, 250–51

schools, reservation boarding: about, xiii, xiv, xxii–xxiii, xxx; and day schools, 182; failures of, 116–17; individual study in, 120; justification for, 170; non-reservation schools compared with, 204; opposition to, 81–82, 83–84, 162–68, 173–74, 188; practical education in, 209; role of, 22, 68; statistics on, 198–99, 316n31; usefulness of limited, 175–76

schools, reservation day: about, xiii, xiv, xxx, 170, 179–80; far-reaching influence of, 81–84, 125–27, 180–82, 208–9; opposition to, 17, 162–68, 188, 204, 297n40; role of, 22; rules for, 127, 313n107; statistics on, 198–99, 316n31; support for, 26, 56, 174–76, 179, 230, 300n52

scientific racism: acceptance of, xxii, 275; and Americanization, 284; as conference topic, 189, 247; education affected by, xxvi–xxvii; as global theme, 256; inconsistency in, 138, 315n26; and progressivism, xxviii–xxix, 8, 61; of teachers, 32, 117, 278–79

secretary of the interior, 218–19, 331n126, 332n130

Seger, John, 45–46, 236, 304n92, 338n3, 340n32

Seger Colony and Seger Colony School, 45–50, 304nn92–93

segregation, xxix, xxxiii–xxxiv, 2, 188–89, 251

Seneca (philosopher), 63

Sequoya League, 164

Shasta, Calle, 224–25, 327n95

Shaw University, 230

Shepard, Irwin, xxiii–xxiv, xxxix, 2, 191, 286n19

Simplified Spelling movement, xxv, 287n29

Sioux Indians, 13–14, 17–18, 19, 20, 21–22, 156, 296n38, 297n42, 298n46, 299n51

Sioux Uprising (1862), 296n38, 297n41

Sitka Training School, 219

Sitting Bull (Sioux chief), 40, 266

slavery, 1–2, 3, 7, 12–13, 15–16, 155, 166–67, 225, 294n11, 336n38

Slivka, Kevin, 54
Smiley, Albert K., 191–92, 265, 323n26
Smith, Edward P., 265, 266
Smith, Marcus A., 319n74
Smithsonian Institution, 329n107, 330n114
Social Darwinism, 223, 310n82
*The Song of Hiawatha* (Longfellow), 193, 264
*Songs of Ancient America* (Curtis), 261
South Carolina, 1
*Southern Workman* (magazine), 23, 51, 59, 72, 116, 138–39, 193, 270, 303n83
Spalding, J. Lancaster, 277
Spanish conquest, 328n103, 340n30
spelling, simplified, xxv, 287n29
Spencer, Herbert, 97, 223, 310n82
spittoons, cleaning of, 227, 330n112
spoils system, 134–35, 233–34, 237–38, 239, 332n130, 333n138
Standing, Alfred John, 25–30, 265, 338n3, 340n32
Stein, Isaac, 285n3
St. Louis Philosophical Society, 75
St. Mary's Indian School (Odanah Day School), 125–26
Strieby, Michael E., 17, 297n39
Sumner, Charles, 15–16, 296n37
superintendents, school, 23, 181–82, 205, 231, 232–33, 234–36, 276, 331n126, 338n3
Sybil Carter Indian Lace Association, 303n85

Taft, William Howard, 296n35
teachers: beliefs of, 76–77; Black, 1; conferences for, xxxvi–xxxviii, 187–88, 193, 247–48, 277–78, 321n1, 339n16; employment of, 234–36; expertise of overlapping, 90–95; expertise of separated, 87–90; importance of, 255–59; Indians as, 5–6, 117, 295n26; job mobility of, 282, 341n38; marriages of, 109, 311n87; organizations for, xxxi–xxxii, xxxix–xl, 275–76, 292n101, 292n104; pay for, 282, 341n40; practice, 33–34; priorities of, 78; racism of, 138, 278–79, 315n26; on reservation schools, 180–82, 208–9; training for, 32–34
*Teaching Empire* (Eittreim), 283
Tehuelche Indians, 226, 328n101
Tennessee Centennial Exposition (1897), 265
Tenure of Office Act (1820), 333n138
Thlinget (Tlingit) Indians, 214–15, 221–22
Thomas, Cyrus, 227, 330n114
Thompson, William Oxley, 277
*Through the Heart of Patagonia* (Pritchard), 328n101
Thucydides, 329n106
Tonner, A. C., 133
Trachtenberg, Alan, 278, 284, 333n2
Travis, James W., 282
treaties, 179, 197–98, 231–32, 297n40, 299n51
Trennert, Robert A., xxxi, 58, 249, 300n53
Treuer, David, xxvii
tribal system, xxii, 18–19, 67, 76–78, 279
Truman, Edward, 339n16
Tsimshian Indians, 226, 329n108
tuberculosis, xxiii

Underhill, Lonnie, 266
Unitarians, 17, 296n35
universalism, xxvii–xxix

uplifting, of minorities: for citizenship, 7; by community members, xxx; by day schools, 125–27; as educational goal, xxvi, 275, 321n1; of females, 39–40, 44; as global endeavor, 255, 283; for practical work, 187

U.S. Bureau of Education, 212, 218–19, 325n61

U.S. Bureau of Indian Affairs, 86, 311n87. *See also* U.S. Indian Bureau; U.S. Indian Office; U.S. Office of Indian Affairs

U.S. Census (1920), 291n89

U.S. Congress: civil service commission established by, 237; funding by, 197–98, 212–13, 218, 231, 318n65; inspections authorized by, xxxvii; and religious liberty, 232; on student transfers, 176; and term and tenure limits, 240; and voting rights, 222, 327n83

U.S. Constitution, 232, 239, 240, 242, 243

U.S. Indian Bureau, 223–24, 252, 336n38. *See also* U.S. Bureau of Indian Affairs; U.S. Indian Office; U.S. Office of Indian Affairs

U.S. Indian Office, xxi, xxxvii, 47, 57, 172, 268, 276, 280, 336n38. *See also* U.S. Bureau of Indian Affairs; U.S. Indian Bureau; U.S. Office of Indian Affairs

U.S. Office of Indian Affairs, 251, 313n107. *See also* U.S. Bureau of Indian Affairs; U.S. Indian Bureau; U.S. Indian Office

U.S. Senate, 296n35, 296n37

U.S. Supreme Court, 297n40, 318n65

Valentine, Robert G., 195

*Vestiges of the Maya* (Le Plongeon), 329n105

Waggoner, Linda, 117, 311n92

Warner's Ranch, 318n65

Warren, Kim Cary, 280

Washington, Booker T., 1, 7, 277, 294n11, 310n74

Weare, Portus B., 221, 326n78

Welsh, Herbert, xxxvi, 161

Weyler, Valeriano, 227, 331n115

Whelan, Kevin, 52, 305n10

Whipple, Henry B., 17, 24, 296n38

White, Josiah, 298n44

White Institute, 17

white man's burden, 97, 193, 197, 224–28, 255–56, 281, 284

whites: among Indians, 163, 328n101; and Blacks, 13, 155, 294n11; civilizing work by, 257–58; and educational theories, xxvii–xxxi; employment advantage of, 109–10; Indian girls influenced by, 157–58; Indian perception of, 13–15; land takeover by, 19, 45; in outing system, 300n53; as superior humans, 32, 256, 279

Whittlesey, Eliphalet, 14, 295n34

Will, Emily J., 286n24

Willard, Frances (Aleut girl), 221–22, 326n78

Willard, Frances E., 326n79

Willard, Frances H. (New York woman), 326n79

Williamson, Margaret, 298n43

Williamson, Thomas Smith, 18, 298n43

Williamson family, 17, 18, 298n43

Winkelried, Arnold von, 227, 330n110

Winnebago Indians, 19, 169–70

*Winning the West for Christ* (Bender), 212

Winship, Alfred E., 193

witches, in Alaskan belief, 216

women: Alaskan Native, 215–16; arts and crafts of, 303n85; employment for, xxxvi, 255, 282, 291n86; in hypothetical marriage, 146; as men's equal, xxxiv–xxxv, 58; and men's misconduct, 31; organizations of, 269; role of, 20, 39–40; single, 224; skills of, 106

Women's National Indian Association, 265

Woodward, Calvin M.: about, 96–97; addresses by, 278; on educational goals, 97–98, 99–101; influences on, 310n82; on practical education, 101–5; on school types, 98–99

work, manual, 9–10, 13, 22–24, 25–26, 29–30, 63–67, 95, 101–3, 131–32

Works Progress Administration, 125–26

World's Fair (St. Louis, 1904), 141, 247–50, 252, 263, 265, 334n5

*The World Until Yesterday* (Diamond), 213–14

wpa (Works Progress Administration), 125–26

Wright, Albert Orville: about, 169–70; on education system, 170–75; improvements suggested by, 175–77

Wright, J. George, 22, 179, 300n52, 320n94

Young, S. Hall, 217

Zuni Indians, 228, 329n107

IN THE INDIGENOUS EDUCATION SERIES

*Urban Indians in Phoenix
Schools, 1940–2000*
Stephen Kent Amerman

*American Indians, the Irish,
and Government Schooling:
A Comparative Study*
Michael C. Coleman

*White Man's Club: Schools, Race, and
the Struggle of Indian Acculturation*
Jacqueline Fear-Segal

*Carlisle Indian Industrial
School: Indigenous Histories,
Memories, and Reclamations*
Edited by Jacqueline Fear-
Segal and Susan D. Rose

*Without Destroying Ourselves:
A Century of Native Intellectual
Activism for Higher Education*
John A. Goodwin

*The Bearer of This Letter: Language
Ideologies, Literacy Practices, and the
Fort Belknap Indian Community*
Mindy J. Morgan

*Education beyond the Mesas:
Hopi Students at Sherman
Institute, 1902–1929*
Matthew Sakiestewa Gilbert

*To Educate American Indians:
Selected Writings from the National
Educational Association's Department
of Indian Education, 1900–1904*
Edited and with an introduction
by Larry C. Skogen
Foreword by David Wallace Adams

*Indian Education in the
American Colonies, 1607–1783*
Margaret Connell Szasz

*Assimilation, Resilience, and
Survival: A History of the Stewart
Indian School, 1890–2020*
Samantha M. Williams

*This Benevolent Experiment:
Indigenous Boarding Schools,
Genocide, and Redress in Canada
and the United States*
Andrew Woolford

To order or obtain more information on these or other University
of Nebraska Press titles, visit nebraskapress.unl.edu.

Printed in the USA
CPSIA information can be obtained
at www.ICGtesting.com
LVHW090808261123
764578LV00021B/2